Norwegians and Swedes in the United States

NORWEGIANS
AND SWEDES
IN THE
UNITED STATES

Friends and Neighbors

Edited by
PHILIP J. ANDERSON *and*
DAG BLANCK

MINNESOTA HISTORICAL SOCIETY PRESS

The publication of this book was supported though a generous grant from the Dale Hanson: Swedes in Minnesota Fund.

www.mhspress.org
The Minnesota Historical Society Press is a member of the Association of American University Presses.
Manufactured in [the United States of America/Canada]

10 9 8 7 6 5 4 3 2 1

♾ The paper used in this publication meets the minimum requirements of the American National Standard for Information Sciences—Permanence for Printed Library Materials, ANSI Z39.48–1984.

International Standard Book Number
ISBN: 978-0-87351-816-1 (paper)
ISBN: 978-0-87351-841-3 (e-book)

Library of Congress Cataloging-in-Publication Data

Norwegians and Swedes in the United States : friends and neighbors / edited by Philip J. Anderson and Dag Blanck.
   p.   cm.
   Includes bibliographical references and index.
   ISBN 978-0-87351-816-1 (pbk. : alk. paper) — ISBN 978-0-87351-841-3 (e-book)
   1. Norwegian Americans—Social conditions. 2. Swedish Americans—Social conditions. 3. Immigrants—United States—History. I. Anderson, Philip J. II. Blanck, Dag.
E184.S2N864   2011
305.9'06912073—dc23

                                                            2011035287

Contents

Foreword

Donna R. Gabaccia

Twenty years ago, Rudolph J. Vecoli made a powerful appeal to scholars to begin writing from "an inter-ethnic perspective on American immigration history." And as he did so, Swedes, at least, were very much on his mind. Vecoli discussed this "inter-ethnic perspective" and its development as a new direction for scholars at the 1991 Symposium on Swedes in America. The event was held in Sweden, in Växjö, and sponsored by the Swedish Emigrant Institute (SEI). Vecoli's paper subsequently was published in 1993 both in *MidAmerica,* the journal of Michigan State University's Center for the Study of Midwestern Literature and Culture, and as part of a volume of conference proceedings published by the SEI.[1]

Much has changed in the scholarly field of immigration and ethnic studies since 1991, but Vecoli's plea is still relevant. The field of immigration and ethnic studies has become even more international in its personnel and in its perspectives. It has also become less U.S.-centered. In Växjö in 1991, a single scholar from Norway and four from Denmark joined an international group which also included two from Germany and twenty-eight from Sweden. But the largest group of participants was made up of thirty-one scholars, including Vecoli, who lived and taught in the United States. Clearly the American paradigm of scholarship, with its emphasis on immigration and on the life of immigrants in North America, still predominated in 1991 in a way that it no longer does.

Americans also led this field of study. Both scholars delivering introductory keynote lectures in Växjö taught in North America (Vecoli at the University of Minnesota and Werner Sollors at Harvard). Both the keynoters emphasized, in differing ways, the importance of finding analytical frameworks that include immigrants from multiple backgrounds. Sollors, for example, talked about researching the literature produced by what he called "undistinguished" immigrants of diverse origins. In publishing the proceedings from the meeting, Ulf Beijbom nodded more vigorously toward the new North American directions that Vecoli had introduced, using the words "interethnic" and "intercultural" in subtitling the book.

I am quite sure that both Vecoli and Sollors anticipated making their respective pleas to an audience—no matter how international—that was still overwhelmingly engaged in writing the histories of single immigrant groups and mainly, also, of course, to an audience interested in studies of Swedes. Indeed, most of the papers at the conference focused on Swedish emigration and the lives of Swedish immigrants in America. Still, the 1991 SEI symposium was nevertheless pioneering in bringing together those interested in encouraging not only a "multiethnic per-spective" on Swedish emigration and immigrant life but by doing so with input from scholars in several affiliated disciplines (from literature and art history to bibliography, ethnology, geography, linguistics, and theater). A beginning had been made.[2]

Twenty years later, we can assess the results: the beginning did not become a dead end. Nevertheless, much remains to be done to answer Vecoli's charge, for the power of the single-group paradigm of study remains quite strong. Few individual researchers even today master more than two or three immigrant languages; while multilingual collaborations are more common than they were thirty years ago, they too remain the exception, as are comparative studies of multiple groups or studies of interactions of one or more immigrant groups. Transnational and diasporic studies have widened the spatial purview of immi-gration studies without undermining the power of national languages to confine studies of how immigrants from a single origin remained connected to friends and relatives in several countries or how they organized lives they experienced and lived in more than one place. The study of single ethnic, linguistic, and reli-gious groups continues to hold the center of the field of immigration and ethnic studies, whether in history or in other disciplines.

Even in this collection of essays, quite explicitly focused on comparing and connecting the histories of two groups—Swedes and Norwegians—the knowl-edgeable reader will quickly see the lasting power of professional networks that continue to form around the study of single groups. Contributors to this volume who have a Swedish education, who have completed early studies of Swedish migrations and of Swedes in America, or who work at institutions either in Sweden or historically associated with Swedes in America significantly out-number their Norwegian and Danish counterparts, although perhaps not to the extreme degree as in Växjö in 1991. The balance of contributing scholars working and living in North America versus those in Norway or Sweden also still favors the former group—although this is perhaps less a reflection of the composition of Norwegian American and Swedish American studies as it is of the fact that this volume is an English-language publishing project, undertaken by a North American press.

Certainly the biographies of many of the contributors to this volume also reflect the increasing globalization of scholarly life that has occurred over the past two decades. One might even say that Vecoli and Sollors pioneered in developing the kind of scholarly border crossing that recent advances in com-munications technology have facilitated in the 1990s and 2000s. Both led (and, in the case of Sollors, continues to lead) transnational lives in which interna-tional collaborations played a prominent role. Most of the contributors to this volume, too, are bilingual; most have done research in more than one country;

several have also developed what can only be called bi- or multinational careers, having received education and training or having worked in both North America and Sweden or Norway.

While a network of Swedish-centered scholars may still be visible at the heart of the list of contributors to this volume, it is quite decidedly not a Swedish-centered collection. It is not about Swedes' interactions with Norwegians (as were the 1991 conference proceedings) but rather about the two groups' interactions with each other. The collection's editors have succeeded admirably in encouraging even those scholars whose earlier work may have been limited to the study of Swedes to expand their research into Swedish-Norwegian (and less frequently -Finnish or -Danish) relations. The smaller number of specialists on Norwegian migration and Norwegian American life represented here have, also admirably, done the same thing. The meeting ground of the two groups is very clearly the focus here. Rudolph Vecoli would be pleased, I am sure; one of the reasons I decided, as director of the Immigration History Research Center (which Vecoli nurtured for over forty years), to prepare this foreword was to acknowledge Vecoli's work. The beginning he made in Växjö has not, in the intervening twenty years, been derailed; the train he set in motion continues to move along the track.

That track, however, now travels through transformed intellectual territory. The transformation of the field of immigration and ethnic studies since 1991 is not just obvious in professional practices. The field's methods have changed and expanded, as has its geographical reach. So have the questions that most captivate its scholars.

In 1991, Vecoli, as a social historian, was interested primarily in encouraging studies of group and individual interaction; he assumed that this focus on social interaction would reveal new insights into assimilation, ethnic group formation, and the persistence of ethnicity in American life—a theme to which he also devoted considerable attention over the course of his long scholarly career. Over two decades, however, the so-called cultural turn in the humanities and the ensuing interest among almost all scholars in the social construction of groups and of individual identities has altered how researchers in this scholarly field understand both the group and the individual. Studies of the construction of groups, the construction of ethnicity itself, and even the construction of individual selves or identities have become more common themes of scholarship, while comparisons of two or more groups remain a minority and they now also coexist with comparisons being made of past and present immigrants. Already in 1991 in Växjö, social scientists and humanities scholars from outside history were adding their voices to a field of study still dominated by historians; today, by some reckonings, including my own, historians are a significant but no longer predominant cluster in an interdisciplinary field. Already in 1991, if not yet in Växjö, scholars focused on the lives of Asian and Latin American immigrants were also growing in number; more influenced by the cultural turn than older scholars studying Europe's migrants, they introduced new questions and modes of analysis that would gradually push the field beyond the approaches that had dominated empirical studies in history and the social sciences and away from social historical methods.[3]

The complex evolution of the field of migration studies could itself be traced by an interested reader through the many chapters of this volume. The long legacy of social historical methods is alive and well here, although an interest in the construction of groups and of individual identities is also very much on display. Not surprisingly, perhaps, only a few chapters in this volume approach the relations of Norwegians and Swedes as an exercise in comparative history. Although such comparisons can be useful in understanding interactions between groups, it is around the metaphor of "friends and neighbors" that the editors have chosen to organize this volume. Friends and neighbors can be compared, of course, but it is their relationships and interactions with each other that make them friends and that make them neighbors. Apparently reluctant to dispense with structuralist notions of "groups"—or, one might say, to venture too far along the cultural "turn" in the road—most of the contributors to this volume are, at least most of the time, comfortable to write of Norwegians and of Swedes as bordered groups and to ground their interpretations of their interactions or comparisons through attention to two clearly identifiable groups that speak differing languages. Norwegian and Swedish, at least as presented here, do not constitute a linguistic continuum but rather a dichotomy; and while change and flux along the linguistic borders of the two languages can certainly be identified (as can many examples of bilingual speakers), those individual speakers of one or both languages are generally understood in this volume to be identified with one language or the other, even in those cases where they embraced Scandinavian identities.

Careful readers will want to keep in mind that most of the authors of both the comparative studies of the two groups and the studies of interactions of the two share this assumption about groups as units of analysis. But they will also want to observe the methodological differences between comparison and interaction as they plunge into the fascinating historical detail on display in the chapters that follow. What do comparisons of Norwegian and Swedish speakers, when offered, show? What do studies of interaction reveal? My own conclusion, after reading these essays, is that both point in the same direction. Even those contributors who focus on moments of conflict between the two groups (for example, the 1905 independence of Norway) conclude by downplaying the importance of contention between them. Those who focus on interactions between the two groups around issues related to language and religion manage to acknowledge how these aspects differentiated between the two without ignoring how religion and language also differentiated between Norwegians in America and Norway and between Swedes in Sweden and America, thus highlighting the Americanization that brought both groups of immigrants closer to each other.

It is hard to read this book without being impressed by how much Norwegians and Swedes had in common and how their interactions—through marriage, neighborliness, shared education, and religious faith—strengthened those commonalities without ever erasing completely the lines of difference that most, on either side of the linguistic dividing lines, continued to recognize. Even in the early twenty-first century, long after the languages and lived connections to family or friends in modern Norway or Sweden have been lost, Americans tell census takers of their Norwegian or Swedish roots. (And one wonders if more are willing to embrace their Norwegian than Swedish roots, since the number of Norwegian Americans—unlike the number of immigrants arriving in the nineteenth century—exceeds the number of Swedish Americans.) In such identities, one senses that modern nations retain a great deal of their symbolic power while the major challengers of national identities—notably regional and local loyalties and identities or ethnic and panethnic racial American identities—have enjoyed at most intermittent and minor successes. While immigrants at times did identify themselves as or express solidarities as "Hovlanders" or "Willmarians" (i.e., residents of Hovland or Willmar, Minnesota), these are not the group categories they evoke when labeling their ethnicity for census takers in the late twentieth or early twenty-first centuries. Neither, apparently, do many today identify as Scandinavians.

Interest in the histories and flux of identity, as evidenced in this volume, are as much a product of the cultural turn as they are of social history. Those attending the 1991 conference in Växjö were surely aware of how post-structuralist philosophers and the so-called "cultural turn" were pushing scholarship toward greater attention to the malleability of groups and of group and individual identity. Certainly it was the case that both Vecoli, the historian, and Sollors, the literary scholar, were struggling with the implications of this malleability for the methods and questions of their shared field of study. By the time Sollors arrived in Växjö to mount the keynoters' podium, he had (in 1989) published his influential book, *The Invention of Ethnicity* (Oxford University Press), adding a new paperback edition earlier that year. The following year, in 1992, Vecoli's own thoughts on the malleability of ethnicity would appear as part of a coauthored (together with other leading scholars on European migration to the United States Kathleen Neils Conzen, David A. Gerber, Ewa Morawska, and George E. Pozzetta) article, "The Invention of Ethnicity," published in the *Journal of American Ethnic History*. The common titles of these two much-cited works are an indicator of how deeply scholars of many disciplines were engaged with the challenges of culture and postmodernism.[4]

While it would certainly be a useful exercise for all readers of this volume to revisit both of these now-classic works and to ponder their influence on the scholarly field, I will simply note here how studies of panethnicity and of whiteness—which built on one or both of these publications—have found their way into the essays collected in this volume. Sollors's and the historians' similarly titled works were by no means the only influences, however. Beginning at almost the same time, scholars in the growing interdisciplinary fields of ethnic studies and American studies became fascinated with the construction of ethnic and panethnic identities. Much of their work focused on Asian Americans and Latino or Hispanic immigrants. Aware that there were no Asians in Asia (where people were instead Japanese, Korean, or Chinese) and no Latinos or Hispanics in immigrants' home countries, scholars in these fields focused on the invention of panethnicity and also participated in the creation of another panethnic group, the "whites" or "Euro Americans."

While only a few of the contributors to this collection have embraced the study of the invention of whiteness or panethnicity, situating their own studies of Norwegians and Swedes in relationship to studies of Latinos or Asian Americans, this volume nevertheless should provoke readers to consider such historiographical connections. A number of panethnic formulations can be discerned in the chapters that follow. Several contributors are explicitly interested in the use of the term *Scandinavian* as a mechanism for creating common ground among Norwegians and Swedes. Several others note the employment of other panethnic terms, such as *Nordic*. Which people were understood to fall within such categories? In the eyes of Americans? In the eyes of those being labeled? Did Finns number among the Nordics? Among the Scandinavians? Did Danes? The essays collected here suggest that the answer to that question depended very much on the time, the context, and the local dynamics of social interaction—a clue that cultural and historical methods might better be viewed as complementary rather than mutually exclusive. Whether in 1905 or in 2005, however, it seems—at least from the studies collected here—that *Euro Americans,* the preferred invention of many ethnic studies scholars in the 1990s, has never been widely used either by scholars studying Swedes and Norwegians or by the people they study.

This raises interesting questions—only partially addressed here—about the dynamics of invention of ethnic groups and individual identities and of panethnic groups and identities, on the one hand, and the invention of racial groups and racial identities, on the other. The two, of course, are not always as easy to separate as I have done in writing the previous sentence. At least in a North American context, and in the years before 1924, the label *Nordic,* for example, resonated more strongly with the terminologies and debates over scientific racism and immigration restriction than did the label of *Scandinavian*. But whether or not, over the long course of the twentieth century, as other and newer immigrant groups from Europe engaged in the cultural project that David Roediger has called "working toward whiteness," both the term *Scandinavian* and the terms *Norwegian* or *Swedish American* may have begun to carry with them the valences of race or of whiteness. This is a possibility that still cannot be confirmed or rejected—indeed, it is not really posed in most of the essays in this collection. But the questions remain: were any ethnic and panethnic markers alternatives, or even rejections, of whiteness and the white racial identities for migrants from the northern fringes of Europe? Or were they a way of claiming and signaling whiteness and its privileges without embracing a racial identity— something that has been theoretically possible for Europeans in a society where only non-whites are understood to be marked by race? This last option has been the one theorizers about Euro Americans in a multicultural society have generally assumed to have been the case.[5]

One additional dimension of the "invention of ethnicity" (or panethnicity or race) should be abundantly clear to the careful reader of this volume: scholars who ignore religion in the construction of any category or identity—whether local, national, panethnic, or racial—will miss key dimensions of the social and cultural dynamics involved. Whether studied as discourse or as social practice, the "invention" of the Norwegian, Swede, Scandinavian, or Nordic in America is never neatly extractable from the lesser-known, but equally important, transformation and evolution of religious labels, groups, and identities. The evidence on religion in this volume is rich, complex, and—for the moment at least— unclear in its implications. Nevertheless, here is a lesson from the study of Euro Americans that scholars of Asian American and Latino panethnicities might want to borrow.

Notes

1. Rudolph J. Vecoli, "An Inter-Ethnic Perspective on American Immigration History," *MidAmerica* 75 (1993): 223–35; an article of the same title is printed in *Swedes in America: Intercultural and Interethnic Perspectives on Contemporary Research: A Report of the Symposium Swedes in America: New Perspectives,* ed. Ulf Beijbom (Växjö: Swedish Emigrant Institute, 1993).

2. Raymond Jarvi, " 'Report: Swedes in America: New Perspectives,' A Conference at the House of Emigrants, Växjö, 31 May–3 June 1991," *Swedish-American Historical Quarterly.* Jarvi's report includes a photograph of Dag Blanck, one of the editors of this volume, at an earlier moment in his scholarly career. Blanck and co-editor Philip Anderson presented papers at the Växjö conference. A digital version of

Jarvi's report is available: http://collections-test.carli.illinois.edu/cdm4/item_viewer. php?CISOROOT=/npu_sahq&CISOPTR=4467&CISOBOX=1&REC=5

3. See, for example, the work of Nancy Foner, *In a New Land: A Comparative View of Immigration* (New York: New York University Press, 2005).

4. "The Invention of Ethnicity," *Journal of Ethnic History* 12 (1992): 3–41.

5. David R. Roediger, *Working toward Whiteness: How America's Immigrants Became White: The Strange Journey from Ellis Island to the Suburbs* (New York: Basic Books, 2005).

Preface and Acknowledgments

This book, which explores in a fresh and unprecedented way facets of the relationship between the two largest immigrant groups from Scandinavia to the United States, has come about through the work of many persons and the institutions they represent. It originated as a conference held at Augustana College in Rock Island, Illinois, in October 2007 called "Friends and Neighbors? Swedes and Norwegians in the United States." The well-attended event was arranged by the Swenson Swedish Immigration Research Center at Augustana College and the Swedish-American Historical Society in Chicago, marking yet another joint venture over the decades by these two institutions. The topic met with such interest that we decided to invite additional scholars to submit essays for a book on the theme of Norwegian-Swedish relations in the United States. We thank all contributors for their willingness to work with us on this project and for the insightful expertise brought to bear from their respective areas of research, writing, and teaching.

We also wish to recognize the Minnesota Historical Society Press and its staff, in particular managing editor Shannon M. Pennefeather, who wisely guided us from beginning to end, and director Pamela J. McClanahan, who supported the idea and scholarly contribution of this book since the days following the conference. It has once again been a delight to work with the press and all its personnel. Others who provided encouragement and support of different kinds include Christina Johansson, Jill Seaholm, and Susanne Titus of the Swenson Center; Michael Nolan, Larry Scott, and Thomas Tredway of Augustana College; Terje Leiren of the University of Washington; and Harald Runblom of Uppsala University. Special gratitude is extended to Donna Gabaccia for writing the foreword, which sets the tone of the chapters that follow in the larger context of current studies in immigration and ethnic history.

Finally, we wish to acknowledge the Dale Hanson: Swedes in Minnesota Fund, the Swedish Council of America, the Swenson Center, Augustana College, the Swedish-American Historical Society, and North Park University for their generous financial and material support.

Chicago and Uppsala
Philip J. Anderson and Dag Blanck

Norwegians and Swedes in the United States

Context

CHAPTER 1

Friends and Neighbors?

Patterns of Norwegian-Swedish Interaction in the United States

DAG BLANCK

In 1980 the Norwegian American professor Sverre Arestad of the University of Washington recalled his childhood in a small settlement known locally as "Snus Hill," near Bellingham, Washington, consisting of ten Swedish and twenty-four Norwegian households. Reflecting on the relationship between the two groups, he noted that the larger number of Norwegians on Snus Hill might have given them an advantage over their Swedish neighbors. Still, Arestad remembered, this did not seem to be the case. The real divide was not between the two national groups but rather was seen in religious terms, between a pietistic majority and those who belonged to the local Norwegian Synod congregation. Nationality was, according to Arestad, of little concern. He rarely heard some private complaint against Swedes in general on political grounds, and he noted that in school, "We always spoke our respective languages on the playground and got along just fine. Norwegian or Swede, who cared? Just leave this problem to the children."[1]

A second vignette comes from the Midwest, where a retired Norwegian American professor of English at Illinois's Augustana College, established in 1860 by Swedish immigrants, reflected on his childhood. In talking about ethnic relations in his hometown—a compact Norwegian American rural settlement in southeastern Minnesota—he noted that he was ten years old before he realized that there was a group of people called Swedes.[2]

These observations by two Norwegian American academics raise questions about the nature of Norwegian and Swedish American identity in the United States and of the relationships between the two groups. How did these groups see and interact with each other? Did they cooperate or was there hostility? What role did ethnic background play in relationship to other modes of identification? And what have the labels *Norwegian* and *Swedish* meant over time? Is it also possible to speak of Scandinavians?

In a 1976 article comparing Swedish and Norwegian ethnicities in America, the noted Norwegian American linguist Einar Haugen observed that so far no history of the Scandinavians in America has been written. Thirty-five years have passed, but Haugen's comment is still correct. This book is not a comprehensive history of Scandinavian Americans, but it seeks to examine the relationships between the two largest Scandinavian immigrant groups in the United States, the Swedes and the Norwegians. It casts a wide net, attempting to capture the dynamics of inter-Scandinavian contacts in the United States in a variety of social spheres. It covers topics such as politics, religion, folklore, literature, language, and identity formation among Norwegians and Swedes, as well as offering several community and regional studies.[3]

Norwegians and Swedes were, by far, the two largest Scandinavian immigrant groups in the United States. A total of about 2.9 million Danes, Finns, Icelanders, Norwegians, and Swedes came to the United States over the course of roughly a century, between 1825 and 1930. Of these, close to three-fourths, or 2.1 million, were Norwegians and Swedes. The Swedes were more numerous than the Norwegians, sending some 1.3 million persons to America, while the Norwegian immigrants numbered about 800,000. They settled in many parts of the United States, with a concentration in the Midwest, the Pacific Northwest, and parts of the East Coast. In some areas, such as the Upper Midwest, they have left long-lasting imprints on local and regional cultures and identities.

In 1910 there were one million first- and second-generation Norwegian Americans and close to 1.4 million first- and second-generation Swedish Americans. The groups came out of similar yet distinctive social, cultural, and linguistic circumstances in Europe. Once in the United States they developed their own, often thriving, ethnic communities along separate trajectories. Still, their commonalities were also visible, partly because the American host society tended to group them together, partly because they settled in proximity of each other. In many ways, they were the groups with which both interacted the earliest and most extensively once Norwegians and Swedes began reaching beyond their own ethnic boundaries. They were often neighbors, had similar occupations, married each other, cooperated, and developed comparable—but not identical—religious, cultural, and ethnic traditions. The relationship was not always harmonious; there was also friction and competition, and H. Arnold Barton, the well-known historian of Swedish America, speaks of a "sibling relationship."[4]

The book covers many aspects of Norwegian-Swedish relations in the United States. This chapter will first give a basic chronology of the patterns of relations, followed by a discussion of one of the fundamental aspects of Norwegian-Swedish interaction: intermarriage.

A Chronology of Norwegian-Swedish Relations

Similar to other European immigrants in the United States during the nineteenth and early twentieth centuries, Norwegians and Swedes began creating new Norwegian and Swedish American identities. These processes were often complex and involved an intricate interplay between local, regional, and national affiliations, and they are well expressed by the Swedish American author and journalist Johan Person, who claimed that the loyalties of Swedish immigrants rested within provinces rather than in the Swedish nation and that the identifications of the surrounding American society made it important to address the question of what it meant to be Swedish American. Whether the Norwegians and Swedes related to the larger concept of Scandinavia or a possible sense of Scandinavian identity created an added and important dimension in the identity formation processes. As John Jenswold and Jørn Brøndal have pointed out, to many Americans the distinction between the Norwegians and Swedes was small, and they were seen as one group, as "Scandinavians." In Minneapolis in the 1850s and 1860s, Norwegians were sometimes called "Swedes" by their Yankee neighbors, and in 1878 a Norwegian pastor visiting Salina, Kansas, learned from a Yankee hotelkeeper that there were several Scandinavians in the town. When the pastor asked if he knew of any Danes, Norwegians, or Swedes among them, the hotelkeeper answered, "No. There don't seem to be representatives of those nationalities, most are Scandinavians."[5]

It seems possible to isolate three periods during which the relationship between and significance of the national and the regional modes of identifications changed. The *first period,* from approximately 1840 to 1890, was characterized by attempts to create a sense of pan-Scandinavianism in the United States. It can be argued that conditions for nurturing a sense of Scandinavianhood were never as favorable as during those early years of mass migration. First, because of the relatively small numbers of Scandinavian immigrants, especially prior to the Civil War, there was a natural tendency among Danes, Norwegians, and Swedes to seek out each other. As the prominent Norwegian immigrant, author, and academic Hjalmar Boyesen noted in an article in the *North American Review* in 1892, Scandinavian immigrants were at times accused of "clannishness"; Boyesen further states that at the time, their size meant that they "were completely lost in the ocean of American life, which beat upon them on all sides." As several contributors to this book also point out, the existence of a pan-Scandinavian cultural and political movement in Scandinavia may also have played a role for the immigrants in the United States.[6]

A number of pan-Scandinavian institutions were established during the decades surrounding the Civil War. Ulf Beijbom records "forty-odd associations" established by Swedes between 1855 and 1880, of which half were Scandinavian. Eventually, however, many of these groups split along ethnic lines. As John Jenswold has argued, the situation was similar elsewhere. The central ethnic institution built during the formative years of Scandinavian immigration was, however, the church, where a number of primarily Lutheran denominations were organized. One example will illustrate this point. In 1860

Descendants of Norwegian immigrants posed by the replica sloop Restauration *at the Minnesota State Fairgrounds in 1925 during the centennial celebration of Norwegian emigration*

the Scandinavian Evangelical Lutheran Augustana Synod—best known as the Augustana Synod—was organized in Jefferson Prairie, Wisconsin. Its membership was both Swedish and Norwegian, consisting of thirty-six Swedish and thirteen Norwegian congregations. To the early leaders of the synod, ethnicity—Swedish or Norwegian—seems to have played only a small role, and historian George Stephenson has pointed out that the leadership had no intention of building up a church on the basis of nationality.[7]

Still, ten years later the Norwegians decided to leave the synod, and it divided into two nationally based groups. Why did the Augustana Synod split along national lines in 1870? Clearly theological differences were at play—these had also been among the prime reasons for establishing the church in the first place, when the Swedes and Norwegians left a larger Lutheran community dominated by German Americans. For example, in 1870 there was a fear among the Norwegians that the synod was approaching other Lutheran denominations before confessional issues had been clarified and that the study of secular subjects had become too prominent at the synod's college.

On the other hand, August Wenaas, the Norwegian professor at the college, also argued in national terms. "Norwegians and Swedes are brothers and in many respects kinsmen," he wrote in *Den norske lutheraner* in 1869. Still, he continued, the Swedes could not fully understand "our peculiar Norwegian character and our ecclesiastical and national traditions," which led him to the conclusion that both groups would "be happier" and "cooperate best" when "each one works in his house, with his household and his own farm to care for, although in the same community."[8]

The breakup of the Augustana Synod can thus be partly interpreted in ethnic terms. To the early leadership, religion was obviously more important than ethnicity, and it is even possible to argue that religion defined ethnicity: that is, in their view, to be Swedish (or Norwegian) was to be Lutheran—of the correct dogmatic variety, of course. By the end of the nineteenth century this balance between religion and ethnicity had changed, as the ethnic dimension assumed greater independence. It is thus possible to see the beginnings of a national ethnic awareness working against the pan-Scandinavian tendencies within the Scandinavian Augustana Synod already in 1870.

The quarter century following 1890 marks a *second period* in Norwegian-Swedish relations, characterized by clear national lines of demarcation. In the decades around the turn of the century, the Norwegian and Swedish American communities stood at their peaks, both in terms of numbers and of ethnic awareness. In 1910, the top year for foreign-born Scandinavians, the census bureau recorded 665,000 Swedes and 400,000 Norwegians and the ethnic communities were well on their way toward institutional completeness. The earlier pan-Scandinavianness had broken down in many social spheres, and churches and organizations were now developing along national lines. This process was, however, not uniform, and in some areas a sense of continued pan-Scandinavian identity or cooperation can be observed. The best such example was, as Jørn Brøndal, Sten Carlsson, and Bruce Larson have shown, probably politics. Here, much more so than in the private or the religious spheres, Scandinavian Americans had to come to terms with rules defined strictly by the new environment. In the political arena, where frequent communication with Americans of other ethnic backgrounds was required, of course, the Scandinavian label was commonly employed.[9]

Much of Scandinavian American politics has played out in Minnesota. As Sten Carlsson has observed, Scandinavians entered Minnesota politics relatively late. The breakthrough seems to have come in the 1880s and was closely associated with Knute Nelson, who during his very successful career represented Minnesota in both houses of the U.S. Congress and also served as governor of the state. Nelson's initial success in Minnesota politics can be attributed to what Carlsson labels "the ethnic factor," as he received strong support from both

Norwegian and Swedish voters in his 1882 campaign in Minnesota's fifth congressional district. Nelson's foreignness was clearly an element in the campaign—his opponents referred to him as "the little Norwegian"—and a majority of the non-Scandinavian voters in the Republican primary opposed him. Once in office, however, he was twice reelected to the House of Representatives, with both Scandinavian and non-Scandinavian support.[10]

Nelson was followed by a large number of Scandinavian American politicians in Minnesota, on both the state and national levels. Bruce Larson has observed that among Minnesota governors, Scandinavian Americans have been over-represented in relationship to the size of their groups, regardless of their political affiliations, and to the strong support given agrarian populist politics, the Nonpartisan League, and the Farmer-Labor Party from Scandinavian immigrants in Minnesota. Scandinavian Americans in Minnesota in the late nineteenth and early twentieth centuries thus became quite successful in state politics. In fact, Sten Carlsson observes that they performed better than the Germans, the other large immigrant group in the state, and partly attributes this success to the fact that "good relations predominated" between the Swedes and Norwegians, making it possible for them to unite as Scandinavians to support each other's political candidates.[11]

The half century or so following World War I marked a definite turning point in Scandinavian American history and can be considered a *third period* in Norwegian-Swedish relations. As was the case for many other European groups, Scandinavian mass immigration to the United States dwindled during the 1920s, ending almost a century of transatlantic migration. As immigration ceased, Scandinavian American communities were gradually becoming dominated by American-born individuals. By 1940, for example, two-thirds of Swedish Americans were American born, and the tendency was similar among the other groups.[12]

In many ways, the national differences among Scandinavian Americans still prevailed, and Scandinavian American organizations, for example, continued to be largely Danish, Norwegian, or Swedish American in character. However, as the differences between the two "homeland Scandinavians" (to paraphrase H. Arnold Barton's designation) and the Scandinavian Americans grew stronger, the ethnic identities which developed among the three groups were also increasingly shaped by their gradual removal from the mother countries and their interaction with American society. The experience of World War I, with its strong emphasis on loyalty to the United States, and its aftermath also meant that the "American" element in the Scandinavian American identities became increasingly emphasized.[13]

The decades after 1965 witnessed an increased interest in ethnicity in the United States. This "ethnic revival" was initially associated with European-origin

Americans with roots in eastern and southern Europe—the so-called new immigrants of the final decade of the nineteenth century and the early decades of the twentieth—and with African Americans. In the 1980s and 1990s, issues of ethnic diversity and pluralism were largely focused around the discussions of multiculturalism, a debate which, although it seems to have subsided some, is still ongoing. Although ethnic revival and multiculturalism have not primarily focused on Scandinavian Americans—indeed, some would probably question their inclusion under a multicultural umbrella—these groups have at least indirectly been affected by the past decades' renewed emphasis on ethnicity and cultural diversity in America. Affirming one's ethnic or racial background has become an integrated and accepted part of American life. In the 2000 Census, for example, over 90 percent of the ancestry identifications given indicated a national or ethnic origin from outside the United States and only some 7 percent chose to identify their ancestry as "United States" or "American." When asked, most Americans are thus able to specify one or several ethnic origins.[14]

Few systematic studies of contemporary ethnic patterns among Scandinavian Americans exist, but much of the evidence suggests that the tendency to continue to identify along national ethnic lines, rather than pan-Scandinavian ones, continues. The most recent data come from the 2000 Census and the 2008 American Community Survey, with very similar numbers. During the first decade of the twenty-first century, the great majority of Scandinavian Americans identified themselves with a particular Scandinavian nationality—1.5 million persons of Danish ancestry, 4.5 million of Norwegian background in 2000 and 4.7 in 2008, and 4 million claiming Swedish ancestry in 2000 and 4.4 million in 2008. The number of persons who identified themselves as "Scandinavian" was some 400,000 in 2000 and 500,000 in 2008.[15]

Moreover, the vitality of organizations among Danish, Norwegian, and Swedish Americans attests to a continued ethnic life along national lines. Among the Swedes, for example, over 375 organizations, groups, or institutions with a Swedish American focus in the United States were noted in 1997. Many of these have been founded in the last several decades, suggesting the enduring significance of organized Swedish American life. The Sons of Norway is an example of a continually active Scandinavian American fraternal organization. In 1995, its centennial year, it reported 360 lodges in the United States with some 67,000 members, compared with 153 lodges and 11,000 members just before World War I.[16]

Still, as before, it is also possible to observe a sense of pan-Scandinavian identities in some social spheres. Although the many ethnic festivals among Scandinavian Americans are mostly arranged along national lines—such as the Syttende Mai (May 17) festivities all over Norwegian America or Svenskarnas Dag (Swedish Day) in Minneapolis—there are also examples of some Scandinavian

Norwegian Americans gathered around Ole Bull statue at Syttende Mai celebration, Loring Park, Minneapolis, 1936

American events. In the late 1980s, for example, a group in Turlock, California, put on a Scandinavian American festival, clearly inspired by contemporary ethnic celebrations among other groups in California. In September 1991 the first "Skandi-Fest" was held in Turlock, emphasizing the community's Scandinavian heritage; it lasted for three days and attracted several thousand visitors.[17]

Other areas where the national Scandinavian lines seem to have become more blurred include religion and politics. American Lutheranism in the twentieth century was characterized by a series of mergers through which ethnically based Lutheran denominations successively formed a number of larger entities. Among the Swedish Americans the discussion began in the 1920s, as the Augustana Synod was undergoing both a generational and a linguistic transformation. At this time, however, there was no discussion about re-creating a pan-Scandinavian church body; rather, the focus was on the role ethnic background could and should play in relationship to the larger forces of American Lutheranism. When criticized that it was abandoning a national or ethnic heritage, leading representative Conrad Bergendoff defended the church's move away from ethnicity, saying that the synod's position on the language question should be judged "from a religious, not a cultural stand-point" and maintaining that "the preservation of the Swedish language has never been, is not, and can never be the Synod's objective." The church, he concluded "exists for the sake of religion and not culture."[18]

One phase of this merger movement ended in 1962 when Swedish, some Norwegian, and Danish Lutherans came together in the Lutheran Church of America (LCA). In 1988 another merger created the Evangelical Lutheran Church in America (ELCA), which brought in the remaining Norwegian Americans who had belonged to the American Lutheran Church (ALC), organized in 1960. These mergers have resulted in an inter-mixing of religious, cultural, and ethnic traditions within the new church bodies: the older ethnic boundaries and loyalties are dis-appearing in many cases, and new configurations indicate a larger and ethnically quite diverse ELCA.[19]

Swedish poet Gunnar Wennerberg is honored with a statue at Minnehaha Park, Minneapolis.

The question of whether ethnicity plays a political role among contemporary Scandinavian Americans is difficult to answer. Impressionistic evidence comes from the traditional Scandinavian areas in the Midwest, especially in Minnesota, where we can see continuity in Scandinavian American political influence. In an analysis of 1970s gubernatorial politics in Minnesota, Bruce Larson suggested that Governor Wendell Anderson's Swedish background was a factor which helped him win elections and gain a positive image between 1970 and 1976. Larson also points out that "name recognition" can play an important role in Minnesota politics: a Scandinavian-sounding name might be a political advantage. In 2000, *St. Paul Pioneer Press* columnist Nick Coleman commented that "the best name for politics in Minnesota might still be . . . Sven Patrick Solberg Klinkenhammer," reflecting the state's four largest ethnic groups (Swedes, Irish, Norwegians, and Germans), "with a Nguyen, Muhammad or

Garcia maybe tossed in somewhere," mirroring more recent immigration to the state.[20]

Food, and its traditional practices, is a final area where it seems possible to observe a sense of pan-Scandinavian affinity. Although contents of the *smörgås-bord* can vary greatly between the Scandinavian groups, one dish in particular seems to have achieved a pan-Scandinavian status, namely *lutfisk* or, in its more common Norwegian form, *lutefisk*. Lutefisk occupies a special position in the Scandinavian American mind today. In the words of folklorist Barbro Klein, it has become "surrounded" by a great deal of "commotion" as people travel great distances to certain food stores to procure the item for at least the Norwegian and Swedish American Christmas table, especially in the Midwest. Moreover, "lutefisk dinners" served by Lutheran churches of Scandinavian origin attract large numbers of people in November and December each year.

Lutefisk is also the "center of countless jokes" among Scandinavian Americans, alluding to its "shaky consistency . . . tastelessness and the odor that it exudes when overcooked." Klein reports on bumper stickers, buttons, and signs in the Upper Midwest using the food item in contexts such as "Legalize Lutefisk" or "No Lutefisk Served Here." The centrality of the dish for Scandinavian Americans is further illustrated by the fact that it merits its own section in the book *Scandinavian Humor and Other Myths*—a jocular account of contemporary Scandinavian American life published in 1986. The author speaks of the "lutefisk mystique" among Scandinavian Americans, suggesting that the "Pan-Nordic Lutefisk Lobby" has ensured its survival in America by, among other things, manipulating the lyrics of popular songs so that they now read *Kan Du Glemma Gamla Lutefisk* (a parody on the Norwegian American song *Kan du glemme gamla Norge*—"Can you forget old Norway?") or *Your Old Mother is Waiting by Her Lutefisk Pot (in Stavanger)*.[21]

Intermarriage as a Factor in Norwegian-Swedish Relations

In the fourth and final volume of Vilhelm Moberg's classic literary account of Swedish emigration to Minnesota, *The Last Letter Home*, the main protagonist, Karl Oskar Nilsson (who by now has become Charles O. Nelson), hearing his grandchildren playing on his farm in central Minnesota, begins to reflect on how his family has changed. The grandchildren can trace their backgrounds to four different countries—Sweden, Norway, Ireland, and Germany. Karl Oskar's son Johan (or by now, John) has married an Irish American, a union which is a source of wonder to Karl Oskar: "Who would have imagined that he, the farmer from Småland, would become related to Stephen Bolle, the Irish miller in Taylors Falls?" His son Harald, who had gone into business in Minneapolis, married a German woman and had two children. Ulrika married a Norwegian farmer in Franconia and had three children: "This Norwegian son-in-law was bull-headed and difficult. He was stubborn as hell as most Norwegians tended to be." Daughter Märta (or Mary), finally, had married a Swedish-born storekeeper, and their three children "begotten by Swedish parents, [were] Swedish brats all through." Karl Oskar marveled at the "mixed group" they were, also recognizing that "through Charles O. Nelson, the old one in the old house, these human plants were linked together . . . And the Lord only knew what might come of all this mixture of people with different roots from different lands. Would they form a race of their own?"[22]

The changing nature of the Nilsson family reflects a fundamental aspect of American immigration history—the ways in which immigrants met and interacted with other groups in the new land, in particular with other immigrants or minority groups in American society. The meetings between immigrants from different countries in their new American settings constitute a dimension of U.S. immigration history that remains relatively understudied (although there are some notable exceptions). This is also true in Scandinavian American historiography, where the focus most often has been on different and varied aspects of the history of the individual immigrant groups in America, their relationships with the host society, or their contacts with their homeland.

Writing in the late 1950s and with a largely positive view of American society and its capacity to assimilate immigrants, Moberg works within a prevailing assimilatory paradigm, giving his readers an illustration of the American melting pot through the family history of Karl Oskar and Kristina. Clearly he and his protagonist are proud of the fact that the immigrants from Småland have played a small but important role in creating a new American "race." The marriage patterns of the Nilsson children are not statistically representative, which was true in general about the way Moberg depicted the migration in his novels. But the books do not make any claims to be scholarly accounts of Swedish immigrant life in Minnesota. Instead, they use fiction to capture much of the essence of the immigrant experience, based on readings of different sources. The centrality of intermarriage has certainly been emphasized by many scholars, and it provides an important way of examining relationships between different immigrant groups.[23]

As with many other European immigrants, both Norwegians and Swedes showed a tendency to marry within their own group. The rates of endogamy were quite high until well into the twentieth century, and according to Gunnar Thorvaldsen's calculations for Minnesota they started declining by the 1930s. There were large regional differences as well as divergences between urban and rural areas. As Jon Gjerde, Robert C. Ostergren, and John Rice have demonstrated, many of the Scandinavian (and other) immigrants settling in the rural Midwest showed strong endogamy, sometimes even on local and parish levels,

and also brought traditions in which marriages to a large degree were determined by the attachment to land.[24]

Several studies suggest that when Norwegians and Swedes started marry-
ing outside their own groups, they became each other's favorite partners.
Harald Runblom's analysis of the 1900 Census shows that the Norwegians were
by far the most common partner group for the Swedes, followed by Danes,
Germans, English, Irish, English Canadians, and Scots. He concludes that other
Scandinavians, Germans, and Anglo-Saxons ranked highest among the Swedish
preferences. Similarly, Sture Lindmark has computed intermarriage patterns for
Swedes based on the 1910 and 1920 U.S. censuses. His conclusion, based on an
analysis of children of one Swedish-born parent and another foreign-born parent, shows a strong preference for Norwegians. The non-Swedish parent was
Norwegian in 40 percent of cases, closely followed by a Danish and German
parent (14 percent), with the Finns and English in fourth and fifth places.[25]

Local studies in Minnesota provide similar results. Thorvaldsen's 1920 analysis shows the beginnings of out marriage for both groups. For Norwegians the
most popular partners were Swedes and Germans, whereas the Swedes preferred Norwegians and Danes. In Rice's study from Kandiyohi County in rural
south-central Minnesota based on the 1905 state census, only twelve instances
of Swedish marriages outside the group are noted, ten of which were with
Norwegians.[26]

Larger ethno-religious trends in the United States also affected Scandinavian
Americans. In the 1940s and 1950s, sociologist Ruby Jo Kennedy introduced
the concept of a triple melting pot in her studies of intermarriage patterns
among ethnic groups in Connecticut. American ethnic groups were indeed
intermarrying, argued Kennedy, but mostly along religious lines. A " 'triple-
melting-pot' assimilation is occurring through intermarriage, with Catholicism,
Protestantism, and Judaism serving as the three fundamental bulwarks,"
Kennedy concluded. This thesis and the inclusion of Danish, Norwegian, and
Swedish Americans in a larger Protestant ethno-cultural grouping was further
emphasized by sociologist Will Herberg in his influential study of American
religion, *Catholic, Protestant, Jew,* from 1955. These trends suggest that the ethnic
bonds among the Scandinavian American groups were changing in nature, with
a gradual expansion of identification taking place. As a result, a sense of pan-
Scandinavian identity was no doubt emphasized within the larger Protestant
cultural group, co-existing with the earlier national ethnic sentiments.[27]

Data from the late twentieth and early twenty-first centuries suggest that the
lines of ethnic demarcation in America have altered during the past decades.
Sociologist Richard Alba argues that only one in four marriages among
native-born white Americans includes persons of the same ethnic ancestry.

Intermarriage among European-origin groups has thus become the rule, rather than the exception. Today, the descendants of the European mass immigration of the nineteenth and early twentieth centuries are crossing both national and religious lines, and it is possible to see the emergence of a category of "European Americans," in addition to African Americans, Asian Americans, and Hispanic Americans. Such a reading of contemporary ethnic patterns among these two groups also emphasizes the racial aspect of contemporary Scandinavian American ethnic identities and the role "whiteness" plays for them and other European American ethnic groups.[28]

Friends and Neighbors?

Norwegian and Swedish immigrants and their descendants in the United States have experienced a close relationship, yet they have by and large also developed along different lines and maintained a noticeable degree of separateness. The early attempts toward cooperation in joint Scandinavian churches and secular organizations were short lived; during the heydays of the Norwegian and Swedish American communities between 1890 and 1920, the two groups developed markedly different ethnic trajectories.

Once in the New World, the immigrants settled in roughly the same areas of their adopted country, although the geographic concentrations do differ. In the classic Scandinavian destinations in the Midwest, for example, the Norwegians have been more apparent in the Upper Midwest, whereas the Swedes have been more widely dispersed. Still, Minnesota occupies a special position on both the mental and actual maps of both groups. Also, both groups made their livelihoods in the same sectors of the American economy, although the Norwegians were more tied to the land and remained one of the most agricultural and rural of all European immigrant groups in the nineteenth and early twentieth centuries.

Politics and intermarriage are areas where the two groups eventually found common ground and did grow quite close. Joint Norwegian and Swedish support for common candidates was clearly an important explanation for the relative success of Scandinavian American politics in at least Minnesota. And when Norwegian and Swedish immigrants began looking for spouses outside their own groups, a fellow Scandinavian was by far the most common choice. Finally, as American society seems to develop toward more inclusive ethnic groupings, national ethnicities exist both side by side and as a part of broader ethnic categories. Thus, to be Norwegian American or Swedish American today does not need to preclude a sense of being Scandinavian American. On the contrary, it seems possible to be both.

Notes

1. Sverre Arestad, "What Was Snus Hill?" in *Makers of an Immigrant Legacy: Essays in Honor of Kenneth O. Bjork* (Northfield, MN: Norwegian-American Historical Association, 1980), 172.

2. Interview with Roald Tweet, Rock Island, IL, October 2002.

3. Einar Haugen, "Svensker og nordmenn i Amerika. En studie i nordisk etnisitet," in *Saga och Sed. Kungl. Gustav Adolfs Akademiens Årsbok 1976* (Uppsala, 1976).

4. H. Arnold Barton, "Partners and Rivals: Norwegian and Swedish Emigration and Immigrants," *Swedish-American Historical Quarterly* 54 (April 2003): 104.

5. Johan Person, *Svensk-amerikanska studier* (Rock Island, IL: Augustana Book Concern, 1912), 114–17; John R. Jenswold, "The Rise and Fall of Pan-Scandinavianism in Urban America," in *Scandinavians and Other Immigrants in Urban America: The Proceedings of a Research Conference, October 26–27, 1984*, ed. Odd S. Lovoll (Northfield, MN: St. Olaf College Press, 1985), 160; Jørn Brøndal and Dag Blanck, "The Concept of Being Scandinavian-American," *American Studies in Scandinavia* 34 (Autumn 2002,) 1, 5–6. The latter article is an early version of my thinking about these issues, and I thank Jørn Brøndal for prompting me in this direction.

6. H. H. Boyesen, "The Scandinavian in the United States," *The North American Review* 155.432 (November 1892): 529, 533.

7. Ulf Beijbom, *Swedes in Chicago: A Demographic and Social Study of the 1846–1880 Immigration* (Stockholm: Läromedelsförlagen, 1971), 266–87; Jenswold, "The Rise and Fall of Pan-Scandinavianism," 159–70. George Stephenson, *The Religious Aspects of Swedish Immigration* (Minneapolis: University of Minnesota Press, 1932), 311.

8. *Den Norske Lutheraner*, February 10, 1869. See also Hugo Söderström, *Confession and Cooperation* (Lund: Gleerup, 1973), 99, and Dag Blanck, *Becoming Swedish-American: The Construction of an Ethnic Identity in the Augustana Synod, 1860–1917* (Uppsala: Acta Universitatis Upsaliensis, 1997), 40.

9. For two synthetic overviews that cover this phase in both Norwegian and Swedish American history, see Odd S. Lovoll, *The Promise of America: A History of the Norwegian-American People* (Minneapolis: University of Minnesota Press, 1984), and Ulf Beijbom, *Mot löftets land. Den svenska utvandringen* (Stockholm: LTs förlag, 1995).

10. Sten Carlsson, "Scandinavian Politicians in Minnesota at the Turn of the Century: A Study of the Role of the Ethnic Factor in an Immigrant State," in Harald Naess and Sigmund Skard, eds., *Americana Norvegica, vol. III: Studies in Scandinavian-American Interrelations Dedicated to Einar Haugen* (Oslo: Universitetsforlaget, 1917), 242–43.

11. Bruce L. Larson, "Scandinavian-Americans and the American Liberal Political Heritage," *Scandinavian Review* 86–87 (Winter 1998/1999): 11; Bruce L. Larson, "Swedish Americans and Farmer Labor Politics in Minnesota," in *Perspectives on Swedish Immigration*, ed. Nils Hasselmo (Chicago: Swedish Pioneer Historical Society, 1978). Carlsson, "Scandinavian Politicians in Minnesota," 266.

12. Sture Lindmark, *Swedish America, 1914–1932: Studies in Ethnicity with Emphasis on Illinois and Minnesota* (Uppsala: Studia Historica Upsaliensis, 1971), 28.

13. H. Arnold Barton, *A Folk Divided: Homeland Swedes and Swedish Americans, 1840–1940* (Carbondale: Southern Illinois University Press, 1994).

14. http://www.census.gov/prod/2004pubs/c2kbr-35.pdf.

15. Odd Lovoll, *The Promise Fulfilled: A Portrait of Norwegian Americans Today* (Minneapolis: University of Minnesota Press, 1998); Henrik Tallgren, *Svensk-amerikaner i Kalifornien. En studie av lågaktiv etnicitet* (Göteborg: Göteborgs universitet, 2000); Barbro Klein, "More Swedish Than in Sweden, More Iranian Than in Iran," in *Upholders of Culture: Past and Present,* ed. Bo Sundin (Stockholm: Royal Swedish Academy of Engineering Sciences, 2001), 71. The ancestry data from 2010 were not yet available for Scandinavian Americans as this book went to press. Data for 2000 can be found at http://factfinder.census.gov/servlet/QTTable?_bm=y&-geo_id=01000US&-qr_name=DEC_2000_SF3_U_QTP13&-ds_name=DEC_2000_SF3_U and for 2008 at http://www.census.gov/compendia/statab/2011/tables/11s0052.pdf.

16. *American-Swedish Handbook* (Minneapolis, MN: Swedish Council of America, 1997); Lovoll, *The Promise Fulfilled,* 198.

17. Tallgren, *Svenskamerikaner i Kalifornien,* 143, 151–60.

18. Quoted in H. Arnold Barton, "Conrad Bergendoff and the Swedish-American Church Language Controversy of the 1920's," *Swedish-American Historical Quarterly* 46 (July 1995): 211.

19. E. Clifford Nelson, *Lutheranism in North America, 1914–1970* (Minneapolis, MN: Augsburg Publishing House, 1972). See also Mark Granquist, "Conrad Bergendoff and the LCA Merger of 1962," *Swedish-American Historical Quarterly* 46 (July 1995).

20. Bruce L. Larson, "Gubernatorial Politics and Swedish Americans in Minnesota: The 1970s and Beyond," in Philip J. Anderson and Dag Blanck, eds., *Swedes in the Twin Cities: Immigrant Life and Minnesota's Urban Frontier* (St. Paul: Minnesota Historical Society Press, 2001), 333–39, 341. Nick Coleman, "How Swede It Is to Get the Perfect Name on Ballot," *St. Paul Pioneer Press,* July 31, 2000.

21. Klein, "More Swedish Than in Sweden," 71. See also Anne R. Kaplan, Marjorie A. Hoover, and Willard B. Moore, eds., *The Minnesota Ethnic Food Book* (St. Paul: Minnesota Historical Society Press, 1986), 103. John Louis Anderson, *Scandinavian Humor and Others Myths* (Minneapolis, MN: Nordbook, 1986), 80–83.

22. Vilhelm Moberg, *The Last Letter Home,* trans. Gustaf Lannerstock (St. Paul: Minnesota Historical Society Press, 1995) 209–11. The translator chose *race* for the Swedish *släkt.* A contemporary translation would be *family.*

23. Jens Liljestrand, *Mobergland. Personligt och politiskt i Vilhelm Mobergs utvandrarserie* (Stockholm: Ordfront 2009), 118–20. Gunnar Eidevall, *Vilhelm Mobergs emigrantepos. Studier i verkets tillkomsthistoria, dokumentära bakgrund och konstnärliga gestaltning* (Stockholm: Norstedts, 1974), 130–31. Paul Spickard, *Mixed Blood: Intermarriage and Ethnic Identity in Twentieth-Century America* (Madison: University of Wisconsin Press, 1989), 6–16.

24. Gunnar Thorvaldsen, "Marriage and Names Among Immigrants to Minnesota," *Journal of the Association for History and Computing* 1 (November 1998): 9, 12, available: http://quod.lib.umich.edu/cgi/p/pod/dod-idx?c=jahc;idno=3310410.0001.205. Jon

Gjerde, "Conflict and Community: A Case Study of the Immigrant Church in the United States," *Journal of Social History* 19 (1986): 683–84; John Rice, "Marriage Behavior and the Persistence of Swedish Communities in Rural Minnesota," in Hasselmo, ed., *Perspectives on Swedish Immigration*. See also Robert C. Ostergren, *A Community Transplanted: The Transatlantic Experience of a Swedish Immigrant Settlement in the Upper Middle West, 1835–1915* (Madison: University of Wisconsin Press, 1988), 318.

25. Harald Runblom, "Chicago Compared: Swedes and Other Ethnic Groups in American Cities," in Philip J. Anderson and Dag Blanck, eds., *Swedish-American Life in Chicago: Cultural and Urban Aspects of an Immigrant People, 1850–1930* (Urbana: University of Illinois Press, 1992), 81–82. Lindmark, *Swedish America 1914–1932*, 61.

26. Thorvaldsen, "Marriage and Names Among Immigrants to Minnesota," 9.

27. Ruby Jo Kennedy, "Single or Triple Melting-Pot? Intermarriage in New Haven, 1870–1950," *American Journal of Sociology* 58 (July 1952): 56. Will Herberg, *Protestant, Catholic, Jew: An Essay in American Religious Sociology* (Garden City, NY: Doubleday, 1955). See also Philip Gleason, "Hansen, Herberg, and American Religion," in Peter Kivisto and Dag Blanck, eds., *American Immigrants and Their Generations: Studies and Commentaries on the Hansen Thesis After Fifty Years* (Urbana: University of Illinois Press, 1990) for a discussion of the impact of the Herberg thesis.

28. Richard Alba, *Ethnic Identity: The Transformation of White America* (New Haven, CT: Yale University Press 1990), 291, 304–5, 312–18.

CHAPTER 2

Norwegians and Swedes in America

Some Comparisons

H. ARNOLD BARTON

Norwegians and Swedes were by far the largest Nordic immigrant groups in the United States. They are also particularly well suited for a comparative study, having since time immemorial shared the long Scandinavian Peninsula, and being closely related by blood, culture, language, and religion. Yet notable differences between the two peoples are due in part to geography but even more to their differing histories. These differences were carried over by emigrants from the two lands to America, where they interacted with other factors.[1]

My findings are necessarily tentative and speculative, based mainly upon my own reading on the two groups and personal impressions over the years, since their respective historians have tended to shy away from direct comparisons. For every generalization I make, exceptions come to mind. The differences I perceive are almost all matters of degree. Most of what one might say about the one group could—with some modification—also apply to the other. Altogether, the similarities between Swedes and Norwegians in North America were always greater than the differences, especially when compared with other, non-Scandinavian immigrant groups.

Both Norwegians and Swedes liked to consider themselves to be upright, staunchly Protestant, honest, hard-working, home-loving, and cleanly rural folk, and they were generally valued for these qualities by the dominant Anglo-Americans. Despite their rivalries, Swedish and Norwegian immigrants in the United States felt closer to each other than either felt for other, non-Nordic ethnic groups. When occasionally they married outside their own group, they most often married each other.

By 1930, an estimated 1.3 million Swedes and nearly 800,000 Norwegians had arrived in the United States, of whom around three quarters remained there. Although Sweden had established its short-lived and thinly populated "New Sweden" colony along the lower Delaware River in 1638, it was the Norwegians who first set in motion the great nineteenth-century Scandinavian migration. It began with a group of fifty-two persons from Stavanger that arrived in New York aboard the sloop *Restauration* in 1825. From 1836 on, sizable numbers of Norwegians emigrated to the United States each year.[2]

The Swedish emigration picked up speed nearly a decade thereafter with seventeen peasants from Kisa parish in Östergötland, led by Peter Cassel, who in 1845 established New Sweden in Iowa, the first lasting Swedish settlement in the Midwest. Swedish emigration remained modest during the first decades and only began on a large scale in the later 1860s. The timing for large-scale emigration from the two homelands was thus different, and timing—as will be seen—became an important factor in determining other distinctive differences between Norwegians and Swedes in the United States. These differences are the focus of this chapter.[3]

The Norwegian immigrants from the start were notably more nationalistic than their Swedish brothers and sisters. In 1873 the Swedish visitor to Norway Peter August Gödecke was greatly impressed by "the proudly independent spirit displayed by the whole people" and that the "feeling for the free citizen's patriotic duties is far stronger and more willingly active than among us." This difference elicited the sour comment from the Swedish visitor Paul Peter Waldenström, in his widely read account of the United States from 1902, that "the Norwegians there are more Norwegian than the Swedes are Swedish!" Ironically, because they came from the Swedish-Norwegian Dual Monarchy, Norwegians were sometimes taken to be Swedes. Knut Hamsun, during his time in America, found this doubly offensive, since he was Norwegian and Swedes were typically stereotyped as "dumb"! (Many Americans, however, very likely regarded both groups, as did a character in Stephen Crane's short story "The Blue Hotel." He described a Swedish stranger as probably "some kind of Dutchman.")[4]

The Norwegian Americans' stronger ethnic identification down to the present is verified by the U.S. Census, which since 1980 has permitted—but not required—persons receiving the long form to specify their ethnic background or that part with which they most strongly identify. Although total Swedish immigration was nearly one-third larger than Norwegian, in the 2000 Census, 4,641,254 Americans claimed Norwegian ethnicity—a number larger than Norway's total population—significantly more than the 4,339,357 who declared Swedish origins. While the Norwegian total grew, the Swedish, like most of the European ancestry groups, declined, in their case by over 340,000 since the 1990 Census. Meanwhile, some 500,000 respondents declared themselves to be "Scandinavian," most presumably of mixed Nordic descent.[5]

Historic reasons contributed to the Norwegian immigrants' proud nationalism. After a great medieval past, Norway was absorbed for over four hundred years into the Danish monarchy. During the Napoleonic Wars, Norway was at last revived as an autonomous nation in 1814, although until 1905 in a dynastic union with the more powerful Sweden. The nineteenth century was thus a period of an intense national revival in Norway, both politically and culturally, and Norwegian emigrants were strongly imbued with national pride. Although

Syttende Mai gathering, c. 1890

Norway was self-governing under its own remarkably democratic constitution after 1814, its union with Sweden often gave rise to frictions in the homelands that carried over to the United States as well. The more concentrated settlement of Norwegians in the new land was surely also a factor in reinforcing Norwegian pride and assertiveness.

Sweden, meanwhile, was an old nation with an entrenched aristocracy, archaic institutions, and lingering traditions of a grandiose military and imperial past only some two centuries back in time. Whereas Norwegian nationalism was democratic, progressive, and forward looking, Swedish patriotism was characteristically royalist, aristocratic, strongly conservative, and backward looking, and therefore held little appeal for the common folk who were most likely to emigrate. Numerous Swedish commentators lamented their compatriots' lack of national feeling both at home and in the United States, pointing out with regret this contrast with the Norwegians.[6]

Both Norwegians and Swedes were the most rural of American immigrant groups, but the Norwegians more so than the Swedes. In 1900, 63 percent of the Norwegian born and 74 percent of their children were rural, as compared with 46 percent of the Swedish born and 54 percent of their children. The Swedes were in general no less eager to become farmers, but timing seems largely responsible for the difference. Norwegian immigration on a sizable scale began earlier than Swedish. Up to 1870, Norwegians in America outnumbered Swedes by a wide margin. Norwegians therefore had the chance to acquire much of the good farmland, especially where water and wood were readily available. Norwegian immigrants were also able to benefit in greater numbers from the Homestead Act of 1862, before the Swedish immigration began to surpass the Norwegian. By then, second-generation Norwegian immigrants were already acquiring farms of their own. The second generation in both groups was more rural than the first.[7]

Another factor that likely kept the Norwegians on the land was a remarkably segregated pattern of Norwegian rural settlement, based on the *bygd*, or place of origin in Norway. Entire country townships were settled mainly by people from a particular fjord or mountain valley at home, and if some of them moved away to take land farther west, it was often to establish a "daughter colony" of people originally from the same place. Because of Norway's mountainous and rugged terrain, the different *bygder* were often highly isolated, with strongly differing dialects and traditions; thus immigrants from these *bygder* felt especially strong ties to the new settlements.[8]

Local isolation was less pronounced and there was greater mobility in the more heavily populated parts of Sweden from which most of the emigrants came. It would appear that Swedish rural settlers in America more often came from wider areas of the homeland. While both Norwegians and Swedes in time established societies based on old country places of origin, the Norwegian American *bygdelag*, characteristically for people from a small local area back home, were more active and long lived than the less numerous Swedish American *hembygds-föreningar*, more broadly based on home province.[9]

By the later nineteenth century, as good farmland in America became scarcer, Sweden, with its greater natural resources, was industrializing and urbanizing more rapidly than Norway. Thus more Swedes than Norwegians emigrated directly from urban and industrial areas, with corresponding skills, and gravitated toward similar places and occupations in America. As a result, the Swedes were seemingly more numerous in the American labor union and socialist movements than the Norwegians. Joe Hill, the legendary Industrial Workers of the World (IWW) leader and songwriter, was for instance, born Joel Hägglund in Sweden.[10]

Swedes and Norwegians often settled close to each other, as they did especially in Minnesota, Iowa, and the Pacific Northwest and eventually in Alaska and western Canada. There were large concentrations of both in Chicago, the Twin Cities, and Seattle. Norwegians were more prominent in Wisconsin, the Dakotas, Montana, and in Brooklyn, New York, however. Swedes predominated in Illinois (including Chicago), Michigan, Kansas, Nebraska, Colorado, Texas, and California, as well as in the New England states.[11]

Nevertheless, minorities—often quite small—of the one group generally lived in the other's areas of settlement, which raises interesting questions of accommodation. The evidence suggests that immigrants of either nationality adapted without great difficulty to the majority's ways. Where the only available church was Norwegian, the local Swedes would attend, and vice versa. Recalling his childhood in the small mixed settlement of "Snus Hill" in Washington State, Professor Sverre Arestad wrote that while the majority was Norwegian, like his family, the real divide was not between nationalities but between Haugean pietists and high-church Lutherans, who attended one or the other of the two local Norwegian churches. The Norwegians there did not celebrate May 17, Norway's Constitution Day, clearly out of consideration for their Swedish neighbors. Speaking of a rural township in western Minnesota settled by people from Gudbrandsdalen in Norway, an old-timer recalled that "even the local Swedes up there spoke *gudbrandsdaling*"![12]

A greater tendency to engage in political life is apparent earlier among the Norwegians than among the Swedes—although again this is a matter of degree. From the time of the Civil War, both were long-standing staunch Republicans, but from the 1880s onward Norwegians in particular were strongly represented in the agrarian-based Populist, Progressive, and Farmer-Labor movements in the upper Middle West, especially in the wheat-raising region of western Minnesota and the Dakotas.[13]

There were historical reasons for this in the homeland. Norway's four-hundred-year-long subservience under Denmark has been noted already. After 1660, the Danish monarch was endowed with absolute authority. Then, with the end of Danish rule in 1814, Norway suddenly became a self-governing state with its own constitution. To assure the greatest backing for the country's new status, the drafters of the constitution made it by far the most democratic of its time, second only to the U.S. Constitution. After 1830, and especially from the 1870s on, as emigration was reaching its height, peasant politicians played an increasingly active role in the basically unicameral Storting, or legislature. Moreover, once they gained a majority there, one of their first acts, in 1836, was to pass a local government bill that democratized the parish councils, which previously had been controlled by the local pastors and government officials. Thus Norwegian immigrants already had a good deal of practical political experience when they arrived in the United States.

But we must go further back than that. The Norwegian old nobility gradually died out or merged into the more prosperous landowning peasantry during the late medieval era, while the Danish kings had generally ruled over Norway with a light hand. The peasants preserved a proudly independent attitude. Although loyal to their kings in Copenhagen, they did not hesitate to send their own deputations to him with their grievances; at times they rebelled. Even before 1814, Norwegians practiced a healthy tradition of direct political activism.[14]

If the Swedes played a lesser role in politics—at least to begin with—this too has its historic reasons. On the whole, they brought less political experience with them to the United States. Although the Swedish Riksdag included an Estate of the Peasantry, it was elected by a small number of more prosperous peasant landholders. It was, moreover, held in check by the three other Estates of the Nobility, the Clergy, and the Burghers, as well as by the Crown, which held an absolute veto on all legislation. Local government was cautiously reformed on the Norwegian model only by degrees in 1843 and 1862.

The representation reform of the Riksdag in 1866 finally replaced the medieval four estates with a two-chamber legislature, but voting requirements were set so high that only a small minority was enfranchised; indeed, some eleven thousand peasants lost the vote as a result of the new requirements. While Norway enacted universal manhood suffrage in 1898, in Sweden this only followed in 1907, going into effect in 1909. Perhaps, too, owing to their relative lack of political experience and strong traditional loyalty to their kings, the Swedes were more inclined to accept authority from above.

As, on the whole, later arrivals in the United States than the Norwegians, most Swedes had less time to work themselves into the political process. Nonetheless, despite occasional frictions, Swedes and Norwegians generally tended to support each other's candidates in elections—especially if they were running against, say, a Catholic Irishman.[15]

Meanwhile the Swedes, it appears, excelled as engineers, architects, technicians, and skilled craftsmen in the United States, areas in which they were traditionally adept. Sweden also had a more highly developed system of technical training than Norway. Some Swedish immigrants made a name for themselves as scientists, and there were a surprising number of inventors among them, Captain John Ericsson being only the best known. They also were often very successful business entrepreneurs, perhaps especially in the building trades and contracting, reflecting among other things their rather higher degree of urbanization. A number of Swedish-born artists meanwhile achieved distinction in the United States, perhaps most notably Birger Sandzén in Kansas and Carl Oscar Borg in the Southwest.

A French wit once said that the French had only one religion but a hundred sauces; the English a hundred religions but only once sauce. This seems in its way to apply to the Scandinavians in the United States. The great majority of the Norwegians held fast to the Lutheran faith. Although they were divided into several competing synods, at least until 1917, Lutheranism remained a more powerful ethnic marker for Norwegians than for Swedes. From the start, the Swedes showed a greater tendency to join other denominations outside the Lutheran fold. The Eric-Janssonist sect that in 1846 established its utopian colony at Bishop Hill in Illinois was in direct revolt against the Lutheran state church in Sweden. Many Swedes became Methodists, Baptists, Pentecostals, Episcopalians, or Mormons. The Mission Covenant included many congrega-

Svenskarnas Dag window display, Dayton's Department Store, Minneapolis, 1957

tions that before the mid-1870s had been part of the Swedish American Lutheran Augustana Synod.

This difference is not easy to account for. In both Norway and Sweden there were strong pietist movements and much outspoken criticism of the state Lutheran churches. In both, freethinking and commitment to democratic principles gained ground. Still, on closer examination, the differences seem more a matter of form than of substance. The majority of both groups remained Lutherans. Among the Norwegians, theological and not least social differences gave rise to separate synods; among the Swedes it was to affiliation with other Protestant traditions. The essential conflict, in both cases, was between high-church and low-church varieties of religious life. Meanwhile, for most immigrants the local church was as much a social center as a temple of worship—although they would probably not have described it as such—especially in rural areas. Churches were a powerful bonding force within their communities.

Both Swedes and Norwegians were among the most culturally ambitious European immigrants in America. But it is unclear whether either was the more active in that regard. One indicator would be the colleges they established, many of them originally as preparatory academies for various theological seminaries. Considering the number of competing Norwegian Lutheran synods, it is not surprising that this gave rise to several colleges. Yet the Swedes established about the same number. In both cases many have disappeared. At present there are six Norwegian American and five Swedish American colleges and universities. The most recent is the basically Norwegian American California Lutheran University in Thousand Oaks, California, established as late as 1959.[16]

Both groups carried on a lively literary life. The Swedish American ethnic press is reputed to have been in its time second only to the German American in the number of newspapers and other periodicals in the native language it brought out, and the Norwegian American was close behind. The newspapers included a good deal of literary content. Ethnic presses (many of them attached to newspapers) published numerous books. Authors of both groups wrote under the same conditions and for similar publics. Yet there was a qualitative difference: the work of Swedish American writers consisted mainly of lyric verse and anecdotal short stories, both sentimental and humorous, but very few novels, whereas their Norwegian American (and Danish American) counterparts wrote a remarkable number of novels, many of them quite good. Indeed, Ole Rølvaag's *Giants in the Earth,* translated into English, became an immediate American bestseller in 1927 and is still regarded as the classic American immigrant novel. It would take the non-emigrant Swede Vilhelm Moberg to produce a Swedish epic of comparable stature, *The Emigrants* in 1949—a generation later than *Giants in the Earth.* It has been considered the most widely read Swedish novel of all time.[17]

Why Norwegian American authors have written so many novels and Swedish American so few is an intriguing question. The greater role of the Norwegian peasantry in public life during the nineteenth century and a highly creative national romanticism in Norway already by the mid-nineteenth century—decades earlier than the Swedish national romantic breakthrough by the 1890s—must have stimulated broader cultural interests earlier there than in Sweden.

Dorothy Skårdal, who in 1974 published her indispensable comparative study of Scandinavian American literature, *The Divided Heart,* believed that the powerful influence of the Danish antiquarian and bishop N. F. S. Grundtvig in Norway, as well as in Denmark—but not in Sweden—during the nineteenth century had much to do with this. Grundtvig combined a passionate fascination with Nordic antiquity with a belief that the peasants were both the true heirs of its heritage and the vanguard of national regeneration. Skårdal described as basic Grundtvigian traditions "joy in life on earth, peoplehood surviving the upheaval of immigration, and broad and activist definition of national culture." Grundtvig inspired the establishment of *folkehøjskoler,* or folk high schools, through which these values were widely disseminated among the Danish and Norwegian peasantry, in Norway from the later 1860s on. Grundtvig's ideas were strongly reinforced in Norway by the immensely popular *fortællinger,* or peasant novels, of Bjørnstjerne Bjørnson, which appeared between 1859 and 1868. In the early 1870s, the Swede Gödecke warmly admired the Norwegian peasants' "poetic vein." He even praised the more recent pietism in Norway for the way it encouraged lively interest in political and social questions and "an open-mindedness toward literary and humanistic culture" that stood in sharp contrast to the narrow intolerance of its Swedish counterpart.[18]

Swedish literary life was at low ebb during the mid-nineteenth century, up at least to the 1890s. The Norwegian Lorenz Dietrichson, who came to Uppsala University to teach Danish and Norwegian literature in 1869, dismissed it as simply "echoes of Tegnér, empty patriotic bombast, and great self-satisfaction." "I was altogether too spoiled," he went on, "when it came to hearing the words of writers of genius, Welhaven's finely formed, brilliant conversation, or Bjørnson's rushing cascades of new ideas, or Ibsen's fine sarcasms."[19]

The Swedish literature of that time could hardly provide the same inspiration to Swedes in America as the fresh winds that came to Norwegian Americans from their homeland; with some significant exceptions, Swedish American literature was correspondingly rather insubstantial. It reveals, according to Dorothy Skårdal—herself of Swedish descent—a pessimistic "general assumption that culture belongs only to the upper classes, and the ordinary people have none." Only later would the poet Carl Sandburg lead a second, English-speaking generation of Swedish Americans into the realm of American literature.[20]

Norwegians and Swedes were both among the most historically minded immigrant groups in the New World. The earliest of their ethnic historians— amateurs all at first—were Norwegian, beginning in the 1870s, in keeping with their earlier presence in nineteenth-century America. By the 1880s and '90s, however, accounts of the Swedes in the new land appeared in growing numbers. In recounting their histories, these early historians proudly stressed the uniquely vital role of their groups in American society, based on their early presence, their heroism in the nation's wars, and the allegedly unique similarities between the essential values of their old and new homelands. Naturally, there was close interaction between their immigrant ideologies. They even went so far as to claim that the basic Anglo-Saxon values ultimately derived from the Scandinavian North.[21]

By the early twentieth century, academic scholars from both groups began to enter the historical field. The Swedes were the first to organize a historical society; after a false start in 1888, the Swedish Historical Society of America was established in 1905. The Norwegian-American Historical Association was not founded until 1925. One might speculate, at least, that the Swedish Americans' earlier organizational initiative reflected the more strongly institutionalized patterns of Swedish society at the time. The second-generation Swedish American historian George M. Stephenson and his second-generation Norwegian

Norwegian Ski Club of Stillwater, Minnesota, in 1888. Left to right, top row,
Martin Olstad, Emil Grant, Pete Foss, John Johnson, Mikkal Thon, Nels Paulson,
and Bert Johnson. Bottom row, Ole H. Olsen, Hans Olsen, Nick Bakke, Jens Olsen,
John Anderson, and Mikkal Hemmingstvet. Photographed by J. M. Kuhn.

Collected by John Runk, photographer, Stillwater, Minnesota U.S.A.
Historical Collection No.414

Norwegian Ski Club of Stillwater, Minnesota

American colleagues Theodore A. Blegen and Marcus Lee Hansen achieved
particular distinction as pioneers of American immigration history, as well as
the histories of their own ethnic groups.[22]

In the end, what were the essential differences between Norwegians and
Swedes in America? It is again worth emphasizing that the similarities were
always greater than the differences. This is borne out early by the large number
of Scandinavian clubs and societies of all kinds in the United States until the
later nineteenth century. Thereafter, these were almost entirely supplanted by
separate organizations for each group as their total numbers increased and tensions mounted back home within the Norwegian-Swedish union. Ethnic leaders, particularly newspaper editors, sought to stand forth as uncompromising
homeland patriots by deliberately stirring resentments. The crisis surrounding
the end of the union in 1905 left long-lingering, exaggerated *perceptions* of basic
differences between Norwegian and Swedish Americans.[23]

The Norwegians had a head start over the Swedes, both because of the more
lively involvement of the peasantry in public life in the homeland and because
of their earlier immigration in force. Norway was on one hand more archaic than

Sweden as regards its rich folk life—but on the other hand it was more modern due to its democratic constitution and its lack of an aristocracy and of other venerable encumbrances from the past. This freed the Norwegians during the nineteenth century to strike out in new directions with the unbridled energies of a new nation confidently facing its future. It was far more difficult for Sweden to free itself from the "dead hand" of the past. This vital difference could not but have its effects upon the immigrants of both nationalities in the New World.[24]

In the United States both groups brought to bear their respective strengths, based on conditions and traditions in their native lands. Norwegians stood out especially in politics and in literature; Swedes were notable in science, technology, business, and the visual arts. Both gained from their constant interaction— as did their home countries during the same period. At this point, it must be admitted, one begins to enter into the realm of pure speculation. The differences between Norwegians and Swedes in the New World seem apparent. How to explain them all is far less so.[25]

Notes

1. For background, see H. Arnold Barton, *Sweden and Visions of Norway: Politics and Culture, 1814–1905* (Carbondale: Southern Illinois University Press, 2003), H. Arnold Barton, "Partners and Rivals: Norwegian and Swedish Emigration and Immigrants," *Swedish-American Historical Quarterly* (hereafter *SAHQ*) 54 (2003): 83–110, reprinted in H. Arnold Barton, *The Old Country and the New: Essays on Swedes and America* (Carbondale: Southern Illinois University Press, 2006), 166–91.

2. Lars Ljungmark, *Swedish Exodus,* 2nd ed. (Carbondale, IL: Swedish Pioneer Historical Society, 1996), 10–11; Odd S. Lovoll, *The Promise of America: A History of the Norwegian-American People* (Minneapolis: University of Minnesota Press, 1984), 28. For a broad regional survey, see Hans Norman and Harald Runblom, *Transatlantic Connections: Nordic Migration to the New World after 1800* (New York: Oxford University Press, 1988).

3. Amandus Johnson, *The Swedish Settlements on the Delaware, 1638–1664,* 2 vols. (Philadelphia: University of Pennsylvania Press, 1911); Alf Åberg, *The People of New Sweden: Our Colony on the Delaware River, 1638–1655* (Stockholm: Natur och kultur, 1988); and H. Arnold Barton, "Pre-Dawn of the Swedish Migration: Before 1846," *SAHQ* 48 (1997): 117–29.

4. H. Arnold Barton, "Peter August Gödecke, den svenska folkhögskolan och Norge. Progressiv liberalism och fornnordisk romantik," *Personhistorisk Tidskrift* 98 (2002): 5–20, esp. 13; Paul Peter Waldenström, *Nya färder i Amerikas Förenta Stater* (Stockholm; Aktiebolaget Normans förlag, 1902), 50. Knut Hamsun, *The Cultural Life of Modern America,* trans. Barbara G. Morgridge (Cambridge, MA: Harvard University Press, 1969), 10.

5. Odd S. Lovoll, *The Promise Fulfilled: A Portrait of Norwegian Americans Today* (Minneapolis: University of Minnesota Press, 1998), esp. 1–4, and Odd S. Lovoll, *Norwegians on the Prairie: Ethnicity and the Development of the Country Town* (St. Paul: Minnesota

Historical Society Press, 2006), 264; David E. O'Connor, "Who Are We? Swedish Americans and the 1990 Census," *SAHQ* 48 (1997): 60–90; Byron J. Nordstrom, [editor's introduction], *SAHQ* 53 (2002): 160. It should be noted that these figures were extrapolated from the long census forms sent to one out of six heads of households.

6. See H. Arnold Barton, "From Warfare to Welfare State: Sweden's Search for a New Identity," *Scandinavian Studies* 77 (2005): 315–26.

7. Lovoll, *The Promise Fulfilled*, 14–15, 142–414, and *Norwegians on the Prairie*, 7. *Rural*, as described by the U.S. Census Bureau, meant communities with a population of less than 2,500. The Germans were the third most rural ethnic group, with the corresponding figures 38 percent German born and 43 percent of their children, respectively.

8. See esp. Lovoll, *Norwegians on the Prairie*, 65–71. The railroads meanwhile encouraged settlement on their lands by colonies. See Gilbert C. Fite, *The Farmers' Frontier, 1865–1900* (Albuquerque: University of New Mexico Press, 1974), 49. Cf. Jon Gjerde, *From Peasants to Farmers: The Migration from Balestrand, Norway, to the Upper Middle West* (New York: Cambridge University Press, 1985). Nonetheless, Swedes too tended to settle together with others from their home localities. See Robert C. Ostergren, *A Community Transplanted: The Trans-Atlantic Experience of a Swedish Immigrant Settlement in the Upper Midwest, 1835–1915* (Madison: University of Wisconsin Press, 1988).

9. See Odd S. Lovoll, *A Folk Epic: The Bygdelag in America* (Boston: Twayne Publishers, 1975); H. Arnold Barton, *A Folk Divided: Homeland Swedes and Swedish Americans, 1840–1940* (Carbondale: Southern Illinois University Press, 1994), 211–12; Sten Carlsson, "Flyttningsintensiteten i det svenska agrarsamhället," *Turun historiallinen arkisto* 28 (1973): 189–210; Einar Anderson, "Våra hembygdsföreningar," *Svenska Kulturförbundets Minneskrift* (Chicago, 1938); and Einar Anderson, ed., *Hembygden. Historik av Chicagos svenska hembygdsföreningar: A Century of Progress* (Chicago, 1933).

10. Cf. Henry Bengston, *On the Left in America: Memoirs of the Scandinavian-American Labor Movement* (Carbondale: Southern Illinois University Press, 1999). The Norwegian-born Andrew Furuseth meanwhile headed the Sailors Union of the Pacific Coast.

11. Helge Nelson, *The Swedes and the Swedish Settlements in North America*, 2 vols. (Lund, 1943; repr. New York: Arno Press, 1979); and Carlton C. Qualey, *Norwegian Settlement in the United States* (New York: Arno Press, 1938).

12. Sverre Arestad, "What Was Snus Hill?" in *Makers of an Immigrant Legacy: Essays in Honor of Kenneth O. Bjork* (Northfield, MN: Norwegian-American Historical Association, 1980), 159–72; Lovoll, *Norwegians on the Prairie*, 197.

13. See esp. John Wefald, *A Voice of Protest: Norwegians in American Politics, 1890–1917* (Northfield, MN: Norwegian-American Historical Association, 1971); Lowell J. Soike, *Norwegian Americans and the Politics of Dissent, 1880–1924* (Northfield, MN: Norwegian-American Historical Association, 1991); Jørn Brøndal, *Ethnic Leadership and Midwestern Politics: Scandinavian-Americans and the Progressive Movement in Wisconsin, 1890–1914* (Northfield, MN: Norwegian-American Historical Association, 2004). Cf. Daron Olson, "Norwegian Socialism and the Non-Partisan League in North Dakota, 1904–1920: How Red Was Their Protest?" (master's thesis, University of North Dakota, 1993), which criticizes Wefald.

14. See Ernst Sars, *Udsigt over den norske Historie*, 4 vols. (Christiania: A. Cammer-

meyer, 1879); Halvdan Koht, *Norsk bondereising. Fyrebuing til bondepolitikken* (Oslo: H. Aschehoug & co. [W. Nygaard], 1926); Ottar Dahl, *Norsk historieforskning i 19. og 20. århundre*, 3rd. ed. (Oslo: Universitetsforlaget, 1976), esp. ch. 6.

15. Sten Carlsson, "Swedes in Politics," in *From Sweden to America: A History of the Migration*, ed. Harald Runblom and Hans Norman (Minneapolis: University of Minnesota Press, 1976), 291–300; Lars Ljungmark, "First Generation of Swedes and Norwegians in Minnesota: Rivalry and/or Cooperation—a Case Study," in *Scandinavians in America: Literary Life*, ed. J. R. Christianson (Decorah, IA: Symra Literary Society, 1985), 59–74; Lovoll, *The Promise Fulfilled*, 199–200.

16. The Norwegian American Colleges and Universities are Augustana (Sioux Falls), Luther, Augsburg, Concordia, Pacific Lutheran, and California Lutheran; the Swedish American are Augustana (Rock Island), Gustavus Adolphus, Bethany, North Park, and Bethel.

17. On literary life, see esp. Dorothy Burton Skårdal, *The Divided Heart: Scandinavian Immigrant Experience through Literary Sources* (Lincoln: University of Nebraska Press, 1974); Orm Øverland, *The Western Home: A Literary History of Norwegian America* (Urbana: University of Illinois Press, 1996). There is no comprehensive study specifically of Swedish American literature. See, however, Ernst Skarstedt, *Pennfäktare* (Stockholm: Åhlén & Åkerlunds förlag, 1930); Göran Stockenström, "Sociological Aspects of Swedish-American Literature," in *Perspectives on Swedish Immigration*, ed. Nils Hasselmo (Chicago: Swedish Pioneer Historical Society, 1978), 256–78; and Eric Johannesson, "Scholars, Pastors, and Journalists: The Literary Canon of Swedish America," in *Swedish Life in American Cities*, ed. Dag Blanck and Harald Runblom (Uppsala: Centre for Multiethnic Research, 1991), 95–109. On the press: Anna Williams, *Skribent i Svensk-Amerika. Jakob Bonggren, journalist och poet* (Uppsala: Avdelningen for litteratursociologi vid Litteraturvetenskapliga institutionen, 1991), 31. Both Rølvaag's and Moberg's novels had sequels: Rølvaag's *Peder Victorious* (1929) and *Their Fathers' God* (1931), and Moberg's *Unto a Good Land* (1954), and *The Last Letter Home* (1961). Moberg's series has since come out in a four-volume edition.

18. The most comprehensive study of the Scandinavian folk high schools is Erica Simon, *Réveil national et culture populaire en Scandinavie: La genèse de la højskole nordique 1844–1878* (Paris: Presses Universitaires de France, 1960). Cf. Barton, "Peter August Gödecke," 13, 16; Dorothy Burton Skårdal, "Grundtvigianism in Danish-American Literature," in *Grundtvig's Ideas in America: Influences and Parallels* (Copenhagen: Danske Selskab, 1983), 109–21, esp. 113, and letter to the author dated May 7, 2003.

19. Lorenz Dietrichson, *En norrmans minnen från Sverige*, 2 vols., trans. Klara Johansson (Stockholm: Wahlström & Widstrand, 1901–2), I:61–62.

20. Skårdal, "Grundtvigianism in Danish-American Literature," 119–20.

21. Barton, "Partners and Rivals." Cf. Orm Øverland, *Immigrant Minds, American Identities: Making the United States Home, 1870–1930* (Urbana: University of Illinois Press, 2000), and Victor R. Greene, *American Immigrant Leaders, 1800–1910: Marginality and Identity* (Baltimore, MD: Johns Hopkins University Press, 1987), which show the essential similarities in most immigrant ideologies.

22. See H. Arnold Barton, "Historians of the Scandinavians in North America," in

Scandinavians in America, ed. Christianson, 26–38 (also in Barton, *The Old Country and the New,* 1–16); O. Fritiof Ander, "Four Historians of Immigration," in *In the Trek of the Immigrants: Essays Presented to Carl Wittke,* ed. O. Fritiof Ander (Rock Island, IL: Augustana College Library, 1964); Daron W. Olson, "Norwegian-American Historians and the Creation of an Ethnic Identity," *Scandinavian Studies* 79 (2007): 41–56. George M. Stephenson's *A History of American Immigration, 1820–1924* (New York: Ginn and Company, 1926) is considered the first academic study of the subject as a whole.

23. Ulf Beijbom, *Swedes in Chicago: A Demographic and Social Study of the 1846–1880 Immigration* (Uppsala: Läromedelsförlagen, 1971), 266–87; John R. Jenswold, "The Rise and Fall of Pan-Scandinavianism in Urban America," in *Scandinavians and Other Immigrants in Urban America: The Proceedings of a Research Conference, October 26–27, 1984* (Northfield, MN: St. Olaf College Press, 1985), 159–70; Odd S. Lovoll, *A Century of Urban Life: The Norwegians in Chicago before 1930* (Urbana: University of Illinois Press, 1988), 66–67, 90–96, 132–33, and "A Scandinavian Melting-Pot in Chicago," in *Swedish-American Life in Chicago: Cultural and Urban Aspects of an Immigrant People, 1850–1930,* ed. Philip J. Anderson and Dag Blanck (Urbana: University of Illinois Press, 1992), 60–67.

24. See Barton, *Sweden and Visions of Norway,* 174. Cf. Arne Lidén, *Den norska strömningen i svensk litteratur under 1800-talet* (Uppsala: Almqvist & Wiksell, 1926), 292.

25. Cf. esp. Barton, "Partners and Rivals," and *Sweden and Visions of Norway.*

Culture

CHAPTER 3

Preserving a Cultural Heritage across Boundaries

A Comparative Perspective on Riksföreningen Sverigekontakt and Nordmanns-Forbundet

ODD S. LOVOLL

"Immigration," Nancy L. Green and François Weil wrote, "has come to be seen as a litmus test for how nations define themselves." Indeed, historians have traditionally directed major attention to the countries of immigration and how the immigrants integrated into a new society and influenced national self-definitions. The historically considered monocultural Nordic countries currently defining themselves as multicultural societies are an illustrative case in point. A 2003 published three-volume work on Norwegian immigration history from 900 to 2000 and its contemporary relevance might be viewed as symptomatic of prevailing scholarly inquiry. The intent of the study, as declared in the introduction, is "to show that immigration is not a new phenomenon." "Historically Norwegians have not," the authors insisted, "been as uniform as some versions of their history maintain." Norway has, in other words, always been a country of the immigration experience. Nevertheless, the historical path tracked through eleven hundred years concludes with a chapter titled "The Multicultural Norway," covering the final quarter of the twentieth century and the so-called new emigration from third-world countries. In its 1996–97 parliamentary report, the Norwegian Storting stated explicitly "that Norway now is a multi-cultural society." The following caption to a photograph of dark-skinned youth carrying Norwegian flags suggests a common scholarly reading of how immigration redefines national identities: "Newcomers have through time functioned as a mirror for the permanent residents, people one could define oneself in comparison to. And the newcomers altered the concept of what is 'Norwegian.'"

Green and Weil, editors of the anthology, titled *Citizenship and Those Who Leave,* proposed in the introduction "to reverse this perspective in order to examine how nations also have defined themselves by their attitudes toward those who leave." The volume, which contains fourteen separately authored chapters, "casts an eye to emigration and expatriation worldwide." The emigration perspective—the relations nations seek to maintain with their citizens and their descendants abroad and why—may be considered from economic, political, and cultural points of view. A comparative analysis will be presented of two organizations, one Swedish, the other Norwegian, of how they reached out to citizens who had left the country, permanently or as temporary expatriates.[1]

The Founding of Swedish and Norwegian Societies

Nordmanns-Forbundet—or the Norse Federation, the current official English name—was formally organized in Oslo (Kristiania) on June 21, 1907. Riksföreningen Sverigekontakt—its name from the 1970s, rendered in English as the Royal Society for Swedish Culture Abroad—saw the light of day in Gothenburg on December 3, 1908, as Riksföreningen for svenskhetens bevarande i utlandet (National Society for the Preservation of Swedishness Abroad). The new name will be employed throughout this chapter. The two organizations appeared during a period of heightened nationalism in both Norway and Sweden as well as on the European continent in general. No fewer than ten new European nation states appeared during the two first decades after 1900.

The founding of the Swedish and Norwegian societies reflected the nationalistic spirit of the time, which was not unique to the two Nordic nations. Other national organizations with similar aims in time came into being. Foreningen Dansk Samvirke (The Society for Danish Joint Action), now Danes Worldwide, made its appearance in 1919; Finland Samfundet—in Finnish Suomi Seuro (The Finland Society)—was organized in 1927; and Utenlandssvenkarnas förening (The Expatriate Swedes' Society), since 1988 Föreningen Svenskar i Världen (The Society Swedes in the World), was organized in 1938. The different Nordic groups cooperated and arranged joint meetings.[2]

The histories of the five organizations identified above are intertwined; only two, Nordmanns-Forbundet and Riksföreningen Sverigekontakt, will be considered. Both have passed the hundred-year mark and will be viewed through a century of activity. A comparison of purpose, activity, and results can be viewed in historical space that witnessed great changes in national attitudes and worldwide communications.

The spirit of the time, as historian Lennart Limberg submits, was also influenced by the restlessness and anxiety brought about by the loss of citizens through emigration. The impressive twenty-volume analysis (Emigrationsutredningen) of the nature and cause of Swedish emigration by the statistician Gustav Sundbärg, published during the years 1908–14, emanated from diverse actions to hinder the nation from becoming impoverished of human resources from the departure of "the young and progressive who disappeared across the ocean." In both Sweden and Norway societies were founded in the early twentieth century to limit emigration; these promoted home colonization as a means of keeping the young from leaving. Like Sundbärg, their proponents saw the agricultural crisis and the poor use of land as the cause of emigration; they urged retention of labor in agriculture. In other areas of the economy there was notable progress. The organized efforts to stop emigration may be viewed against the background of nationalistic economic expansion and a continued high rate of emigration.

Official Contact between Emigrants and Homeland Governments

The loss of citizens through emigration affected Sweden and Norway greatly in the nineteenth and early twentieth centuries. Those who left the homeland may be classified in different ways; they had a variety of motives for seeking their fortunes in a different part of the world. Between 1836 and 1915 about 755,000 Norwegians and between 1841 and 1915 about 1,105,000 Swedes moved overseas. The Nordic emigration intensity from 1866 to 1910 was to a pronounced degree greater than that in the rest of Europe.

The favored destination for Swedish and Norwegian emigrants in the nineteenth century was by far the United States, inasmuch as it accounted for from 97 to 99 percent of the total registered emigration volume; after 1900, Canada received an increasing number of immigrants from the two Nordic nations. Others departed for European nations; Swedish minorities lived in Finland, Estonia, and Ukraine. In addition, many Swedes and Norwegians were employed outside the two homelands: individuals in international business and trade; those employed in the merchant fleet—the latter especially large in Norway's case; as well as those who participated in "the holy emigration wave" and served as missionaries in distant lands. A coterie of Scandinavian diplomatic representatives were also stationed throughout the world. All these were national points of contact in the world community.

Until June 2007, when Nordmanns-Forbundet decided to establish a Norwegian expatriate parliament (Utenlandstinget), of the Nordic nations only Finland had formalized relations between national authorities and organizations and individuals outside the country through a separate body established in 1997 and given the name Utlandsfinländarparlamentet (UFP, Finnish expatriate parliament). The Norwegian expatriate parliament, as reported in May 2009 "for the present suspended," was intended when fully operational to be a representative organ for debate and mediation of opinions between individuals of Norwegian descent abroad and Norwegian authorities. Thus no formalized contact exists between official Norway and immigrants and their descendants. Denmark and Sweden also lack a formalized contact between the country's authorities and their citizens living abroad; these two countries and Norway have adopted different ways of cultivating relations between the homeland and those who left. The voluntary organizations under consideration—Nordmanns-Forbundet and

Riksföreningen Sverigekontakt—are significant partners in the international outreach of their respective countries in building bridges among compatriots worldwide.[3]

Nordmanns-Forbundet: The Norse Federation

Nordmanns-Forbundet was founded in 1907 as a direct result of the dramatic events that in 1905 dissolved the Swedish-Norwegian Union and created a national monarchy; from the beginning, it consequently played a unique national role. Norwegian historian Jacob S. Worm-Müller—prone to employing flowery speech—eloquently insisted, "Nordmanns-Forbundet originated in the gratitude a whole nation felt for the love our countrymen throughout the world had shown their old homeland." F. G. Gade, a prominent microbiologist and Nordmanns-Forbundet's founder, stated that during the union conflict, homeland Norwegians "discovered that thousands of our emigrated countrymen from their new homes round about the globe showed interest in the old country, its people and its circumstances with warm affection and sympathy, and we in turn in gratitude felt that Norway thereby became greater." The romantic concept of "a greater Norway" appeared regularly and was expressed with some passion on festive occasions. It enhanced Norway's newfound position in the international community.

Nordmanns-Forbundet was organized as a worldwide federation and cultivates close contact with Norwegian "colonies" across the globe. Its major operation and support, as one surely would anticipate, come from Norwegian expatriates and people of Norwegian descent in the United States. A Norwegian America—a popular concept of the Norwegian immigrant community—blossomed between 1895 and toward the end of the 1920s. The federal U.S. Census shows that in 1910 nearly every third Norwegian, counting only the immigrants and their American-born children—the two first generations—resided in the United States. They were about a million strong, more than 80 percent of them living in the states of the Upper Midwest. It was a productive field to cultivate: keeping Norwegians in America in touch with Norway would surely promote the notion of "a greater Norway."

The San Francisco Norwegian-language newspaper *Pacific-Posten* (The Pacific Post) in its January 8, 1906, issue, reprinted from the Oslo journal *Verdens Gang* (The Way of the World) an appeal to form a Norwegian world association—a union of all Norwegians. The article was written by Halvard Backhe, who later became Norwegian diplomatic minister to Washington, DC. *Pacific-Posten's* editorial rejoinder to the idea as a representative opinion of the Norwegian ethnic press gives insights into the nature of the relation between "home Norwegians"

"Greetings from Norway" sent by Nordmanns-Forbundet

and "abroad Norwegians." "Remarkable, indeed," the editorial noted, was the fact that "the Idea this time comes from Norway, as one can see by reading Halvard Bachke's article in *Verdens Gang*, reprinted on *Pacific-Posten*'s front page."

"Overtures from this side of the Atlantic to the fatherland," the editorial continued, "are common enough; on the other hand, there has been little reciprocation from the other side." The editorial then emphasized the love for the homeland harbored by those who left, evidenced in the establishment of Norwegian schools, churches, societies, and newspapers in the United States and by frequent visits "back home, and generous monetary gifts, not only to relatives in Norway, but also to the furtherance of public initiatives and the relief of ordinary need following disasters that have struck the country." Official Norway as well as organizations and societies, church groups and associations were slow in trying to create a closer and more systematic contact with Norway; Bachke's agitation for a league of Norwegians worldwide would understandably be seen by the immigrant columnists as a radical and welcome departure from previous attitudes. "We will not say anything about how much gratitude there might have been from individuals," the editorial concluded, "but we do know that there in the [Norwegian] press has been uttered little appreciation; there has likewise been very little interest for Norwegian American circumstances."

The editorial then emphasized its point by comparing Norwegian attitudes to those it found in Denmark. "If we are not mistaken," the editorial affirmed, "in Denmark there is quite a different interest in emigrated compatriots." The reason given was the greater unity evidenced among Danes in America than among Norwegians, "whose strong suit was hardly solidarity." In all fairness it should be noted that Lutheran and other religious divisions existed among the Danes as well as among the Norwegians, alongside political and cultural controversies. It was a smoothly running Danish American organizational life, *Pacific-Posten* argued, that encouraged people in Denmark to publish *Vore Landsmænd i Udlandet* (Our Countrymen Abroad), devoted entirely to "news about Danes from all parts of the world."

"In Norway," the editorial deplored, "there has been painfully little of that sort." But things were looking up, powered by an expanded Norwegian nationalism created by "the now past [union] crisis," which opened the eyes of Norwegians at home for "what splendid brothers they really had in their emigrated countrymen." These developments boded well for a Norwegian world federation to become a reality.[4]

A prevalent national self-image of disunity was expressed as well by those who organized Nordmanns-Forbundet. The initial issue of the federation's magazine *Nordmanns-Forbundet*, dated October 1907, stated that the purpose of the newly founded organization was to make Norwegians abandon their parochial and provincial loyalties and make Norwegians inside and outside Norway feel a stronger interdependence—in other words, become a part of a greater Norway.

The federation's bylaws determined that its mission was to create a league of Norwegians worldwide and unite them in a common effort for Norwegian culture and Norwegian interests. It would work for its objective by organizing societies of men and women of Norwegian birth and descent in all countries, by publishing a journal and other communications, by correspondence, by arranging meetings, lectures, and exhibits, by dispatching representatives, by organized collection of information about where Norwegians lived, their work and circumstances, and by giving support and guidance to compatriots in foreign lands who returned to the homeland. It was an ambitious goal.

The federation's first elected president was Carl Berner, who had been the president of the Storting during the politically stormy days centering on Norway's unilateral declaration on June 7, 1905, that the Norwegian throne was vacant and the union with Sweden dissolved. The elite leadership assured international success of the organization. The leaders were men of stature and influence who were well connected at home and abroad. They were generally members of the Conservative Party (Høyre), many of them politically active, such as C. J. Hambro. Hambro was one of Norway's major political leaders and statesmen of the last century. A political motive, one may surmise, had a hand in the federation's founding and activities.[5]

Riksföreningen Sverigekontakt: The Royal Society for Swedish Culture Abroad

The forces that propelled the founding of Riksföreningen Sverigekontakt, as with Nordmanns-Forbundet, arose out of a renewed national spirit and patriotism. Riksföreningen, Lennart Limberg suggested, appeared as a result of "the resurgence of Swedish nationalism, following on the heels of the dissolution of the union between Norway and Sweden in 1905." "The crisis in 1905," Limberg explained, "led to a demand for unification in national circles and an affirmation of that which is authentic Swedish." He further asserted, "this movement away from the Scandinavian became noticeable also among Swedes abroad."

In proving his point, Limberg noted that Scandinavian societies abroad, between 1905 and 1910, were transformed into purely Swedish organizations, and many new exclusively Swedish societies were also organized. An urban Scandinavianism in American cities carried forward by a Nordic urban elite ended in the tumultuous 1890s, not only because of the union conflict but also as the result of ethnic self-sufficiency as members of each nationality increased in number. Still, the constitutional crisis, to paraphrase from an earlier article by the author, fueled enmity most clearly by Norwegian American anti-Swedish sentiments and much less by Swedish American dissatisfaction with Norwegian national assertion. Norwegian Americans came to harbor strong hostilities toward Swedish Americans and Sweden; organizations, societies, and activities with joint Swedish Norwegian participation were discontinued or split along national lines, resulting in the creation of separate national entities. In 1893, the politically liberal weekly *Svenska Amerikanaren* (Swedish American), which earlier actually had shown sympathy for the Norwegian cause, reported that the Swedish singers had withdrawn from the joint Scandinavian singing society, consisting of Swedish, Norwegian, and Danish male choirs. The Swedish Americans formed their own group because of the hatred it maintained Norwegians had toward Swedes.

While the joint Scandinavian organizations were not restored, tensions between Swedes and Norwegians in America faded rapidly after 1905; it was especially the case in urban areas, where Swedes, Norwegians, and Danes frequently resided together in close-knit neighborhoods and met at public events, at Saturday night dances, and at many other venues, including religious services. The pro-Scandinavian Norwegian weekly *Everett Ekko* (Everett Echo) in Washington State urged Scandinavian unity in political affairs and praised Scandinavians in Minnesota and Wisconsin for pulling together politically. And there were additional moves toward unity. In 1911, the *Sioux Falls-Posten* (The Sioux Falls Post) reviewed how Swedes and Norwegians gathered in Webster, South Dakota, for "A Big June 7th Festival" to celebrate a peaceful separation.[6]

A number of the Swedish societies organized outside Sweden were associated with Riksföreningen's founding. "For almost a century," Lennart Limberg wrote in 2004, "this organization has worked not only to maintain contact with Swedes and Swedish descendants living around the world, but also . . . to preserve the Swedish language and its foothold abroad." Many of Riksföreningen's goals naturally coincided with Nordmanns-Forbundet's ambitions; there were also major differences in how the two organizations defined their international mission. This chapter will next shed light on the early years of Riksföreningen and the ideology of its founders before looking more closely at Nordmanns-Forbundet's approach in its efforts to maintain contact with expatriate Norwegians and their descendants.

The Goals and Activities of Riksföreningen Sverigekontakt

The Swedish stock in the United States, the foreign born and individuals of foreign or mixed parentage, in 1910 numbered 1,417,878; of these 665,183 were born in Sweden. Like the Norwegians, Swedes were highly concentrated in the north central states but with great visibility also in the eastern states. The population represented a potentially rich field of operation for Riksföreningen Sverigekontakt. The organization's reach was, however, global.

The term *svenskhet* (Swedishness) was interpreted by Riksföreningen's architect Vilhelm Lundström to mean the Swedish language; the language was, for him, the essence of his nationalism and Swedishness. Consequently, a major component of the organization's work centered on support of Swedish schools in foreign lands, teaching the Swedish mother tongue to children of Swedes residing there, and the instruction of the Swedish language outside Sweden in general. Lundström and the other leaders of Riksföreningen were of the opinion that an increased international interest in Swedish language would strengthen the self-confidence and the pride among emigrated Swedes and thereby reinforce their desire to maintain their Swedish connection and culture.

Lundström was not only one of Riksföreningen's founders but also its driving force during the first thirty years of its existence. He was a professor of Greek and Latin and, in addition, a linguistic nationalist. Lundström enthusiastically held that the Swedish language was a completely adequate and beautiful language, a language in which Swedes ought to show pride. Bengt Bogärde, Lundström's biographer, described him as "a champion of Swedishness during the first decades of the 1900s." Lindström founded Riksföreningen with the Reverend Per Pehrsson. Pehrsson was born in Gävle, Sweden, and studied theology at the University of Uppsala; he served two periods in the second chamber of the Riksdag. In that capacity, in 1907 he made a legislative motion to establish a national employment agency for Swedes residing abroad who wished to return to the homeland. Riksföreningen—or as organized in Gothenburg in

December 1908 as the National Society for the Preservation of Swedishness Abroad—emanated from an interest in retaining contact with compatriots outside Sweden and the promotion of Swedishness abroad, an interest, according to Lennart Limberg, that was stronger in Gothenburg than in the country's capital, Stockholm. The elite leadership of the Swedish organization resembled that of its Norwegian contemporary, Nordmanns-Forbundet. Both Lindström and Pehrsson, as charter members, served on Riksföreningen's board of directors, Lindström until his death in 1940 and Pehrsson until 1948.[7]

Vilhelm Lundström, founder of Riksföreningen

The Swedish school (*Svenska Skolan*) in Berlin was the first recipient of financial support from Riksföreningen. Pastor Pehrsson became a central figure in the relationship with Swedes in Germany, where the new Swedish national spirit, as Limberg explains, was especially high, relating to the regular celebration of King Gustavus Adolphus and the commemoration of his death at the battle of Lützen on November 6, 1632. The event was much celebrated among Swedes in America as well. Gustavus Adolphus, the heroic defender of the Protestant faith in the Thirty Years' War, became a symbol of both Lutheranism and Swedish identity and was celebrated more and more throughout the main Swedish ecclesiastical communion, the Augustana Synod. By so doing, historian Dag Blanck—citing from the synod's official organ *Augustana*—wrote, "Swedish Americans would combine a pride in their 'ancestral faith' with 'the glorious history, language, and literature' of their ancestral country."[8]

The maintenance of the Swedish language and Swedish schools, as Pehrsson insisted, were major components in preserving national identity. The large Swedish emigration to the United States resulted in Swedish language being taught not only at the elementary level but at institutions of higher learning as well as in the training of teachers and pastors. In 1917, the Swedish language was offered as an academic subject at as many as eleven American universities—including the Swedish American colleges—in addition to high schools. Vilhelm Lundström was widely traveled within Europe; only in 1938, however, did he visit the United States. It became Per Pehrsson's task to strengthen the bonds of Swedishness in America; his close relationship with the clergy of the Augustana Synod made him an important resource for Riksföreningen in this endeavor.

Professor Limberg described how Pehrsson's personal contact developed, his active role in founding Allmänna Svenska Prästföreningen (Swedish Pastoral Association), and its collaborative efforts with the synod. Pehrsson attended the fiftieth anniversary of the Augustana Synod in Rock Island, Illinois, at its annual meeting in June 1910 as a representative for Prästföreningen. He made abiding contacts with Swedish American pastors. Strengthened by family ties, he developed a concern for the welfare of Swedish immigrants and was an engaging speaker. At this meeting, Riksföreningen för svenskhetens bevarande i Amerika (Society for the Preservation of Swedish Heritage in America) came into being. It never fulfilled its anticipated promises, but its creation obviously suggested the necessity of an organized effort, if the goal was to preserve a sense of Swedish nationality among Swedes abroad. The society exists today as Svenska Kulturförbundet (The Swedish Cultural Alliance).[9]

The Great War made it difficult to retain non-English languages in America. Nordmanns-Forbundet and Riksföreningen Sverigekontakt both consequently faced additional challenges in their individual efforts to advance national cultures among their emigrated citizens. Even though both organizations had world-wide ambitions, major activity continued in the United States. Riksföreningen focused its efforts on Europe and promotion of Swedish-language teaching. It should be noted that World War I, contrary to what might have been anticipated, did not impede the creation of new academic positions of Swedish language and literature in Germany, Great Britain, and elsewhere in Europe; in fact, these roles expanded greatly in the postwar years. Riksföreningen, from its inception, had involved itself greatly in the academic teaching of Swedish—financing its efforts with a variety of fundraising strategies.[10]

Despite the extreme nativism of the war years muffling its use, Swedish language in the United States held its own as an academic subject in the postwar era, as reported in Riksföreningen's organ *Allsvensk Samling*. The journal's name was changed during the 1970s to *Sverigekontakt*. The magazine, unaffected by changing mastheads, continues to be printed entirely in Swedish; it represents a major historical source for Riksföreningen Sverigekontakt. Its Swedish-language dress denotes the organization's main cultural mission and the fact, to cite an e-mail message from Lars Björkman, Riksföreningen's secretary general, that "a very large percentage of our members are teachers who teach the Swedish language but who are not necessarily Swedish and some possibly not conversant in English." "We therefore," Björkman concluded, "find it important to use the Swedish language as much as possible."[11]

Professor Limberg kindly provided me with a number of recent issues of *Sverigekontakt*. The journal has changed in focus over the years. The shift reflects adjustment to altered circumstances in a rapidly changing international community and Riksföreningen's sense of its mission as a major advocate of Sweden's cultural position abroad. Vilhelm Lundström viewed Swedish emigrants "as ambassadors for Sweden with its language and culture in their respective countries where they settled" who would maintain contact with the homeland and expand a Swedish presence worldwide. He was praised after his death by the Swedish press for his promotion of Swedish culture as a person who sought to rebuild the razed "great-power-Sweden" in the cultural field. At present, however, Riksföreningen's main concern is the teaching of the Swedish tongue all over the world. In its annual report for 2005, printed in *Sverigekontakt* (March 2006), Riksföreningen viewed its activities on the whole as having prospered greatly during the past year. The report pointed to improved financial resources, book gifts to Swedish schools abroad, support to teaching Swedish in many parts of the globe, scholarships to foreign students to enroll in Swedish folk high schools, and the aid given by Riksföreningen's twelve local chapters, almost all in Sweden. The local societies had played a significant role in Riksföreningen's mission; in 1927 twenty-seven such local groups existed in Sweden, and in 1934 twenty-five of the local societies had more than a hundred members. Financial contributions filled Riksföreningen's account and also supported individual educational ventures abroad. Yet the reality for Riksföreningen, shared with Nordmanns-Forbundet, suggested that ambitions frequently exceeded resources.[12]

The Goals and Activities of Nordmanns-Forbundet

Outreach to compatriots abroad had been a founding principle of both Riksföreningen Sverigekontakt and Nordmanns-Forbundet. They cultivated interorganizational relations, were represented at the annual meetings of each other's societies, and exchanged publications. The stated mission of Nordmanns-Forbundet at its founding in 1907, as suggested earlier, was bridge-building between "home Norwegians" and "abroad Norwegians." C. J. Hambro not only viewed expatriate Norwegians as ambassadors, as Lundström did, but also expressed the idea that each Norwegian abroad was "a Norwegian flag in a foreign land." It was a romantic notion cited on many occasions.

The Norwegian language, as the Swedish language was for Riksföreningen, constituted an essential cultural component of Nordmanns-Forbundet's contact with people of "Norwegian birth or blood" living outside Norway. It did not, however, result in a worldwide support of schools teaching Norwegian or the organization of separate Norwegian schools in the manner of Riksföreningen's "Swedish schools" in places like Wellington (New Zealand), Cairo (Egypt), Kassel (Germany), and Dublin (Ireland). Yet, Nordmanns-Forbundet—although not nearly as systematic or extensive as Riksföreningen Sverigekontakt—did promote academic exchanges and the financing of visiting lectureships in Norwegian at academic institutions outside Norway. It gave high priority, however, to student exchanges between Norway and the United States. In comparison, by World War II some fifty universities—mainly in Europe and the United States—had established Swedish lectureships; the practice was reinstituted after the years of hostilities, which had largely destroyed the program.

In Norway, complex language issues affected its teaching and use by Norwegians abroad. What constituted a Norwegian literary language? The very year of Nordmanns-Forbundet's founding saw the first orthographic reform of the literary Dano-Norwegian to bring it closer to urban Norwegian speech habits. A second linguistic reform took place in 1917. These changes distanced the Norwegian language from the literary forms employed by immigrant publications, most especially in the United States, during the decades generally termed the golden years of Norwegian America. Most Norwegian American newspapers and other periodicals initially ignored the reforms, in part out of concern for losing Danish subscribers but mainly because they viewed the reforms as a betrayal of a shared literary cultural heritage.

Norwegian-language studies in the United States emanated from a Norwegian American cultural world rather than from initiative in the homeland. Immediately before World War I, eight universities and nine colleges in the United States offered Norwegian-language instruction. The nationalistic and social forces that powered the linguistic reforms in Norway were difficult to comprehend for those who were no longer a part of Norwegian society. Not until after the major linguistic reform of Norwegian in 1938, at a time when the number of Norwegian speakers in America was rapidly declining, did teachers of Norwegian decide in principle to follow the literary forms established by law in Norway and abandon the traditional standards employed by Norwegian American publishers.

During the interwar years, most Norwegian American publications made some accommodation to the 1917 standard, though few would consider the radical 1938 changes in the homeland's book language. *Nordmanns-Forbundet,* the organization's journal, followed suit and retained the conservative orthography of immigrant periodicals until the early 1930s. C. J. Hambro, then Nordmanns-Forbundet's president, reminded the organization that "emigrants are always conservative linguistically . . . in consideration of our emigrated countrymen one must therefore take care not to make hasty changes [in the language that is] familiar [to them]." Beginning with its January 1932 issue, *Nordmanns-Forbundet* abandoned the 1907 forms and adopted the 1917 changes.[13]

Nordmanns-Forbundet's loyalty to the Norwegian language—whatever

Lasse Espelid, secretary general of Nordmanns-Forbundet

literary changes were enacted—is evidenced in the persistent postponement of adopting English in its publications, even as it endeavored to attract emigrated members. Its fiftieth anniversary history in 1957, *De tok et Norge med seg* (They Took a Norway with Them) was published entirely in Norwegian. Not until the 1960s did it launch the English-language periodical *Norseman* alongside the Norwegian-language *Nordmanns-Forbundet*. Only the English-language magazine is currently published, from September 2011 titled *Norwegians Worldwide*.

Nordmanns-Forbundet had from the time of its founding invited individuals of Norwegian descent to join one of its local chapters outside Norway, most organized after World War II. The organization also arranged tours to the ancestral sod for those born to Norwegian immigrant parents. Nordmanns-Forbundet's chapters, inside and outside of the homeland, had a somewhat different mission than Riksföreningen's local societies, though those organized in Norway—like their Swedish counterparts—served as welcoming and reception stations for visiting and returning compatriots to the homeland. By the 1950s seven local chapters existed in Norway itself. Eleven chapters had been established outside Norway, a number that in the following decade grew to twenty. Most existed in the United States, which in 1985 boasted twenty-three chapters from coast to coast. The first chapter, however, came into being on May 17, 1909, among Norwegian missionaries on the island of Madagascar; the second chapter was organized in 1915 in Grand Forks, North Dakota; only in the 1920s and 1930s was there a further increase in new chapters.[14]

The local chapters outside Norway were for Nordmanns-Forbundet "of central importance to our task out there in the world." An analysis of the organization's activities, most visible during its first fifty years of existence, demonstrates that Nordmanns-Forbundet sought to integrate expatriate Norwegians and their descendants into Norway's national history; it encouraged a collective historical narrative—a common historical memory if you will. Motives may have varied, but augmenting the nation's population by Norwegians residing in foreign lands would enhance Norway's influence and standing in the world. In 1914, Nordmanns-Forbundet determined that the "Norwegian race" (*folkestamme*), as it was romantically defined, had 2,462,358 members in Norway and 2,079,782 beyond Norway's boundaries, for a total of 4,542,140 members—indeed a greater Norway.[15]

Nordmanns-Forbundet pursued its ambitious goals by close association with Norwegian societies and organizations, missionary stations, shipping firms, and prominent Norwegians living abroad. Until 1925, members in affiliated organizations were counted as members of Nordmanns-Forbundet as well. Nordmanns-Forbundet encouraged a celebratory national and ethnic identity associated with significant anniversaries, historical events, and historical heroes. The historical narrative created was gloried and constantly positive.

Observances of May 17, Norway's Constitution Day, were the most prominent of all Scandinavian celebratory ethnic events worldwide. Monuments to Norwegian Americans, like the hero of Civil War fame Colonel Hans Christian Heg, politician Knute Nelson, and football coach Knute Rockne, were raised in Norway. Norwegian Americans unveiled statues and busts of Norwegian historical and cultural figures, from the brave Norseman Leif Eriksson to the poet Henrik Wergeland and the man of letters Bjørnstjerne Bjørnson. These memorials, with heavy involvement of Nordmanns-Forbundet, reinforced and symbolized a sense of a common Norwegian peoplehood and a shared historical experience.

Norwegian America, in the minds of many, represented the other half of the Norwegian nation; its success clearly bolstered Norway's international reputation. The appearance in 1941 and 1950 of two pioneering volumes, *Veien mot vest* (The Way West) by historian Ingrid Semmingsen—initiated and supported by Nordmanns-Forbundet—integrated disparate Norwegian immigrant communities. The publications validated the immigrants as true Norwegians, not only in the United States but wherever they resided on the globe, and made them an integral part of Norway's national history.[16]

The Legacy of Riksföreningen Sverigekontakt and Nordmanns-Forbundet

Riksföreningen Sverigekontakt and Nordmanns-Forbundet were both motivated by patriotism and nationalistic fervor. Both were led by prominent individuals with vision who saw the emigrants in a positive light as a national asset. *Nordmanns-Forbundet*'s editor pointed out a clear national advantage to emigration: it formed "the natural and, one can say, the necessary connecting link to foreign nations." Lundström viewed the emigrants as ambassadors and carriers of a Swedish cultural heritage; the idea was replicated by those who spoke for the cultural influence of Norwegians in their new environments abroad. The two organizations sought to gain worldwide recognition of the intrinsic value of their individual national cultures and to enhance Sweden's and Norway's position and prominence in the international community. Of the two, Nordmanns-Forbundet has pursued its goals more broadly and with a more specific objective to maintain and strengthen contact with people of Norwegian ancestry residing outside Norway. Historically, its network of chapters beyond the homeland's borders has been a significant dimension in this regard. How, then, did the two organizations influence their respective national identities?

Sweden and Norway lost hundreds of thousands of citizens to emigration. All the same, one may conclude that neither country has defined itself as a "nation of emigrants." The nationalistic movements that created and shaped Sweden and Norway were not limited to human mobility. But the two organizations at a time of heightened nationalism indeed sought to promote cultural retention among their emigrants. In both countries they advanced, to cite *Citizenship and Those Who Leave*, "positive evaluations of emigration focused on the notion that the mobile 'carried their culture' along with them . . . [and] dreams of national expansion." That is of course the essence of the emigration perspective.[17]

Notes

1. Nancy L. Green and François Weil, eds., *Citizenship and Those Who Leave: The Politics of Emigration and Expatriation* (Chicago: University of Illinois Press, 2007), ix, 1–2; Erik Opsahl and Sølvi Sogner, *Norsk innvandringshistorie* (Oslo: Pax Forlag A/S, 2003), 14ff., quote 15 (author's translation); Hallvard Tjelmeland and Grete Brochmann, *Norsk innvandringshistorie* (Oslo: Pax Forlag A/S, 2003), 3:374–87; see *Stortingsmelding* 17 (1996–97).

2. Lennart Limberg, ed., *Internationell nationalism. Riksföreningen 100 år* (Gothenburg: Riksföreningen Sverigekontakt, 2008), 7–8, 15–20; *Hjemme og Ute* 2 (2007);

Nordmanns-Forbundet, Jan., Feb. 1924, Dec. 1963. I am most grateful to Lennart Limberg for the literature and advice he provided on Riksföreningen's history.

3. Limberg, *Internationell nationalism*, 15; Andres A. Svalestuen, "Nordisk emigrasjon— en komparativ oversikt," in *Emigration fra Norden indtil 1. Verdenskrig* (Copenhagen: Fr. Bagges Kgl. Hofbogtrykkeri, 1971), 12, 16, 50ff.; *Hjemme og Ute* 2 (2007); *The Norseman* 2 (2009): 66. Utenlandstinget is still not operational in 2011.

4. Odd Sverre Lovoll, *Celebrating a Century: Nordmanns-Forbundet and Norwegians in the World Community 1907–2007* (Oslo: Nordmanns-Forbundet, 2009), 8–34; *Pacific-Posten*, Jan. 8, 1906; U.S. Bureau of the Census, *Thirteenth Census, 1910*; George R. Nielsen, *The Danish Americans* (Boston: Twayne Publishers, 1981), 70–86.

5. *Nordmanns-Forbundet*, Oct. 1906; Lovoll, *Celebrating a Century*, 8–10, 19. The original name of the organization and its magazine was spelled *Nordmands-Forbundet* until the early 1930s, when it was altered to *Nordmanns-Forbundet*. The latter spelling is used throughout the essay.

6. Lennart Limberg, "Almost a Century's Work: Preserving Swedishness Outside Sweden," in *Scandinavians in Old and New Lands: Essays in Honor of H. Arnold Barton*, ed. Philip J. Anderson, Dag Blanck, and Byron J. Nordstrom (Chicago: Swedish-American Historical Society, 2004), 126; Limberg, *Internationell nationalism*, 17ff., quote 17 (author's translation); Odd S. Lovoll, "Unionoppløsningen og det norske Amerika," in *100 år— var det alt?* ed. Øystein Rian, Harriet Rudd, and Håvard Tangen (Oslo: Nei til EU, 2005), 92–99; Odd S. Lovoll, "The Changing Role of May 17 as a Norwegian-American 'Key Symbol,'" in *Nasjonaldagsfeiring i fleirkulturelle demokrati*, ed. Brit Marie Hovland and Olaf Aagedal (Copenhagen: Nordisk Ministerråd, 2001), 65–78, paraphrase 66; *Everett Ekko*, Dec. 7, 1906, Feb. 22, 1907; *Sioux Falls-Posten*, May 25, 1911. The last paragraph paraphrases from ch. 6 in the author's *Norwegian Newspapers in America: Connecting Norway and the New Land* (St. Paul: Minnesota Historical Society Press, 2010).

7. Limberg, *Internationell nationalism*, 16, 17, 20–21, 24; Limberg, "Almost a Century's Work," 125; Helge Nelson, *The Swedes and the Swedish Settlements in North America* (1943; reprint: New York: Arno Press, 1979), 45–51, 53; Bengt Bogärde, *Vilhelm Lundström och svenskheten* (Gothenburg: Riksföreningen Sverigekontakt, 1992), 7–8; Lennart Limberg, "Undervisning i svenska språket utanför Sverige" (manuscript of work in progress kindly provided by the author).

8. Limberg, "Almost a Century's Work," 127–28; Limberg, "Undervisning I svenska språket utanför Sverige"; Dag Blanck, *The Creation of an Ethnic Identity: Being Swedish American in the Augustana Synod, 1860–1917* (Carbondale: University of Illinois Press, 2006), 83, 178–81, quote 180.

9. Limberg, *Internationell nationalism*, 16; Limberg, "Almost a Century's Work," 139–43; Limberg, "Undervisning i svenska språket utanför Sverige."

10. Limberg, "Undervisning i svenska språket utanför Sverige."

11. Limberg, "Undervisning i svenska språket utanför Sverige"; Lars Björkman, "Why we use the Swedish language," e-mail message to author, Jan. 24, 2007.

12. Björkman, Jan. 24, 2007; *Sverigekontakt*, Mar. 2006; Limberg, *Internationell nationalism*, 170–73, 208, 213–14; Bogärde, *Vilhelm Lundström och svenskheten*, 123.

13. Lovoll, *Celebrating a Century*, 67–99; *Sverigekontakt*, Mar. 2006; Limberg,

Internationell nationalism, 468–69. Consideration of written forms does not take into account the literary language, *Landsmaal* (countrywide language), created by the Norwegian linguist Ivar Aasen, or present-day *Nynorsk* (New Norse), since this written standard was to a great extent rejected by the Norwegian expatriate community. *Landsmaal* gained equal status with the standard Danish forms in 1885, the current *Bokmål* (book language).

14. Lovoll, *Celebrating a Century*, 16, 58–70, 101–36, 145; Johan Hambro, ed., *De tok et Norge med seg. Nordmanns-Forbundets saga gjennom 50 år* (Oslo: Dreyers Forlag, 1957).

15. Lovoll, *Celebrating a Century*, 28–29, 105.

16. Lovoll, *Celebrating a Century*, 15–16, 35–66.

17. Lovoll, *Celebrating a Century*, 24; Donna R. Gabaccia, Dirk Hoerder, and Adam Walaszek, "Emigration and Nation Building during the Mass Migration from Europe," in *Citizenship and Those Who Leave*, 63–90, quote 80.

CHAPTER 4

Freedom, Identity, and Double Perspectives

Representations of the Migrant Experience in the
Novels of Vilhelm Moberg and O. E. Rølvaag

INGEBORG KONGSLIEN

The emigrant and immigrant epics written by the novelists Vilhelm Moberg and Ole Edvart Rølvaag respectively have contributed important depictions and interpretations of the Scandinavian emigrant and Scandinavian American immigrant experience. These novels are cultural representations of migrant movements, their historical, sociological, psychological, and existential aspects. They have been widely read over the years on both sides of the Atlantic. Moberg's books are still read to some extent in the United States as translations but are particularly popular in the Swedish originals, which are very much part of the literary canon in Sweden. Rølvaag is still read in the United States, mainly the first volume of the English version, less so volumes two and three. The original novels in Norwegian are today rarely read.

Rølvaag's epic—in the original Norwegian version a tetralogy consisting of *I de dage* (1924), *Riket grundlægges* (1925), *Peder Seier* (1928), and *Den signede dag* (1931)—was first published in Norway. He was one of the very few writers of the Norwegian American literary tradition who succeeded in being published in Norway. The series was widely read in Norwegian American communities as well as in Norway for several decades after its publication. After the first two volumes were translated into English and published together as *Giants in the Earth* (1927), it entered the American literary realm and was recognized as the ultimate depiction of settling on the prairie. It has appeared on high school reading lists for several decades. Frank McCourt's 1999 novel, *'Tis*—a sequel to *Angela's Ashes*—chronicled his teaching experience in a New York suburban high school in 1959, where the students read *Giants in the Earth* as one of their required texts. They are not appreciative though, and call it a boring book about "those depressed Europeans on the prairie." The other two volumes in the series were translated into English as *Peder Victorious* and *Their Fathers' God,* respectively. Rølvaag had written and published fiction prior to the immigrant epic, but his literary legacy rests on *Giants in the Earth,* which is the only one of his books that is continually reprinted.

Moberg was an established writer and important figure in Swedish literary and cultural life when, after World War II, he turned his attention to the history of emigration from his country. The four-volume novel series—*Utvandrarna* (1949), *Invandrarna* (1952), *Nybyggarna* (1956), and *Sista brevet till Sverige* (1959)—was an immediate success both with readers and critics, despite some early criticism of his starkly realistic descriptions. Already a highly merited writer at the time he undertook this theme, Moberg published this emigrant epic at the high point of his prolific literary career. The novels were translated into English as *The Emigrants, Unto a Good Land, The Settlers,* and *The Last Letter Home,* respectively, and thus acquired an audience outside of Sweden, as well— in particular, of course, in the United States. The emigrant epic belongs to the classical canon of Swedish literature; the English version is also continuously in print. At the turn of the millennium, *Utvandrarna* was voted the most popular Swedish literary work of the twentieth century.

Time, Place, and History

Both novel series are based on extensive knowledge about Scandinavian emigration and immigration; both are firmly rooted in historical details as bases for their fictional depiction and interpretation of the migration movement. Rølvaag's trilogy (as it will be referred to in the following, i.e., the English edition) was published between 1924 and 1931 and depicts the years 1873 to 1896: June 6, 1873, was the date on the characters' paper land deed, and the final book takes place during the presidential election of 1896. The place is in the southeastern corner of today's South Dakota. Historical-documentary aspects essential for character description and plot development are, for example, the grasshopper plague of the mid-1870s, the heavy snowstorms of the winter of 1880–81, the discussions regarding the establishment of the two states, North and South Dakota in 1889, and the elections of 1892 and 1896. Moberg's tetralogy was published between 1949 and 1959 and depicts the background in Sweden and reasons for the 1850 emigration. It details the years up to 1862, gives glimpses from those years until 1875, and rounds off with an epilogue from 1890. Historical-documentary aspects integrated in the narrative are, for example, the emigrants becoming citizens in 1858 when Minnesota entered the Union, the Dakota War of 1862, and the Civil War. Rølvaag's epic spans twenty plus years and is based entirely in the American Midwest. Moberg's epic spans close to a half century and is set in Sweden and America, Småland, where the emigrants come from, and Chisago in Minnesota, where they settle.

The oeuvres of both Moberg and Rølvaag are historical novels. A historical novel will always have a double time reference—the time when it is written and the time described—and there will be a distance between the two. Plot and characters are anchored in a certain historical, social, and cultural setting;

a realistic novel will strive to give a picture that is believable and convincing for the time and setting chosen. Both Moberg and Rølvaag base their narratives on intimate insights into the emigration movement of their respective peoples. Through their fictional accounts with plot and characters, they give us the individual experiences and, thereby, interpretations of the process of migration. Despite these common bases and principles, the authors' individual narratives contain noticeable differences.

Rølvaag, writing in the 1920s, places his immigrants about a generation back: the 1870s to the '90s. He begins with the immigrants heading west and describes in detail the first generation's pioneers settling on the open prairie, how they start from scratch to cultivate the prairie and build homes and communities, including schools and churches. The second half of his epic concerns the second generation and generational relationships. Rølvaag was an immigrant and a participant in the Norwegian American community and thus had a personal, direct connection to his topic. Moberg wrote from his perspective in Sweden and that of a hundred years back from his time of writing. He provides a broad outline of the reasons for emigrating through the stories of his individual characters. He details the journey across the ocean and into Minnesota, where the immigrants establish their new homes, build farms, and develop their community. Moberg's epic focuses on first-generation immigrants and follows them to the end of their lives in the new country. For both works, the double perspective is an important feature; in Rølvaag's narrative, the emphasis is on the psychological and cultural aspects, and in Moberg's books it is on the sociological and historical features.

Moberg and Emigration

The stony fields of Småland and the meager income of the farmer Karl Oskar's family constitute important impetus to emigration. The attraction of America one day comes to him through a newspaper picture of "A Wheat Field in North America": "An even field was visible, an endless field without borders or fences. The wheat field had no end at the horizon, it stretched beyond the place where sky met the earth. Not a single stone or heap of stones, no hillock or knoll was visible on this whole wide field of wheat stubble . . . It was the fruit of the earth he saw here, an unmeasurable quantity of bread for man: 'A Wheat Field in North America.'" The very contrast to his fields in Sweden promises him a new life and new possibilities to provide for himself and his family, and a picture cannot lie![1]

The small farmer turning emigrant is a frequent literary character in this type of fiction and embodies one of the most frequent reasons for emigration from the Scandinavian countries. Karl Oskar's brother, Robert, a sensitive young man longing for freedom and escape from the social hierarchy of his home place explains their situation to his friend: "Robert held up his right hand and counted on his fingers. For every lord and master he bent one finger. First was the King, then the Governor, below the King; the third was the Crown Sheriff, who came under the governor. The fourth was Sheriff Lönnegren, and the fifth was the sheriff's hired hand. The sixth was the dean, their spiritual authority, and the seventh their own master, Aron of Nybacken . . . There were seven superiors and masters in all."[2]

His friend's reaction is this: "Jesus Christ! What a lot of masters!" These two texts illustrate the main motif in Moberg's emigrant novel: namely, freedom. Karl Oskar searches for freedom to *förkovra sig* (to improve one's lot), that is, to provide for himself and his family by his work, something that is not possible given his small and stony holdings in Småland as his family is expanding. Robert wants freedom from the social hierarchy of his homeland. A focused group of people in the first volume of this emigrant epic illustrates different emigrant motifs; together they give a broad and nuanced picture of reasons for leaving Sweden. When the emigrants embark on their journey, each character voices his or her particular motivation. Karl Oskar says, "I seek a land where through my work I can help myself and mine." Kristina, his wife, says, "I go with my husband, but I do so with hesitation and half in regret." Robert says, "I do not like masters." Ulrika, the orphan who became the parish whore, says, "Sweden—this hellhole." And Danjel, a true Christian who puts his beliefs into social practices and, therefore, resists the strict hierarchical state church, says, "I wish freely to confess the God of the twelve apostles in the land He shall show me." Two of these emigrants want freedom *to;* two of them want freedom *from.* Together, they represent the main reasons for emigrating from Sweden as well as from other countries in Europe at the time: material need and social and religious oppression.[3]

The central theme in the epic is how the poor Swedish farmer can gain freedom and build a meaningful life in the New World where he has access to land: an implied criticism of the Swedish class society of the mid-nineteenth century. The two main characters appropriate the new space from different perspectives:

"The land is easy to cultivate," Karl Oskar said. "You can't find anything better . . ."

"A beautiful place you have found, Kal Oska. It is almost as wonderful as at home in Duvemåla . . ."

Karl Oskar showed her: "This deep is the fertile top soil—this deep all over the place."

"—What beautiful flowers grow in the field," Kristina said.

Karl Oskar's main concern is to turn the land into fertile grounds for crops; Kristina's is to establish a new home, one that can remind her of home in the old country.[4]

With the concept of freedom at the center of Moberg's interpretation of the migrant process, the continuous criticism of Sweden, with its exploitation of the poor and weak by the rich and powerful, is developed as the novels describe the characters' lives and destinies in the United States. Karl Oskar gets his farm in Minnesota, which enables him to provide for his family. Thus, he is able to employ his freedom *to* fulfill his visions, though it takes a lifetime of hard work and all his physical strength. Ulrika started out with a strong wish expressed as freedom *from* her humiliating life in Sweden. Now in America, her strong personality, wit, and energy help her carve out a new existence for herself, becoming a Baptist pastor's wife and, more importantly, a respected person among her Swedish peers. Her freedom *from* was transformed into a freedom *to,* that is, to realize her great potential that never was possible for someone like her in Swedish society. The hat she buys in the new land is symbolic of her new status and brings out the contrast: "In Sweden I had no right to wear a hat. But in America I've become a free person." Ulrika and Karl Oskar, in a comparison of their lives in the United States with the Swedish past, together express the epic's criticism of the homeland. The structural element of the double perspective, so typical in novels of migration, here bears on the relationship between the individual and society, especially the sociological aspects.[5]

The other two central characters in the novels, Robert and Kristina, relate to the aspect of the double perspective in a different way. Robert obtains his wish for freedom *from* his masters as he leaves Sweden. But his life in America, where he pursues gold in California as a way to be free, is disappointing, and he returns to his brother's farm in Minnesota to become reconciled to his fate and die— whereupon Robert achieves a sort of freedom. In this, he shares his experiences with Kristina. She was initially hesitant to emigrate but followed her husband to America. The couple is at the center of the novel series as it moves from a primarily group focus to one that is more individual. Kristina shares with Robert the experience that one has to *forlika sig,* that is, to reconcile oneself with one's fate, as was his way of being free. For the devout Kristina, the double perspective manifested itself in her *där hemma—här borta* (there at home—here away from home) perspective, a switching of places and concepts. Her faith in God and acceptance of God's plan for her life meant that she had to reconcile herself to her life in the United States despite her homesickness. The double perspective for Kristina, which for Karl Oskar and Ulrika was sociological in nature, was spiritual and existential. In a departure from the linear thematic structure, at the end of their lives all of the characters think back to their youth in Sweden, which gives the epic a cyclical effect. This evinces, on the one hand, the realization of

Vilhelm Moberg welcomed at O'Hare Field, Chicago, by Consul General
B. G. Järnstedt and leaders of the Swedish Pioneer Historical Society, professors
Franklin Scott and E. Gustav Johnson, January 27, 1966

potential, as in the case of Karl Oskar and Ulrika, and, on the other, the recon-
ciliation of one's fate in order to accept it—as with Kristina and Robert.[6]

The fate and description of the American Indians constitute an interesting
element in Moberg's emigrant novels. The rock called "The Indian Head" is a
visual symbol that to some extent comes to represent the decline of this people,
but their presence also contributes to the characterization of the individual
immigrant in the way each of them relate to the indigenous people. Robert
admires them for the way they seem to epitomize freedom, while Karl Oskar, the
hardworking farmer, thinks they are lazy. Kristina pities them for not knowing
about God and feels sorry for their material condition. The way Moberg brings
the real Dakota War of 1862 into his story enables him to balance his picture of
the natives by depicting their cruelties while underscoring the unjust treatment
and their victimization. The motif of the indigenous people of North America
though also has a direct bearing on the main theme of the epic, that of freedom
to build a new life. The tiller of the soil from the Old World, Karl Oskar, has not

come to an empty space, although he thinks he has, and the authorities tell him it is so. The emigrants from Europe have come to the land of the nomad, and thus "two different ways of life met head on." The hunter, Nöjd, a man situated between farmer and nomad, reminds Karl Oskar that "all the land is stolen from the Indians!" but the immigrant turned American farmer justifies his land taking: "Only prairie weeds grew here when I came! What grows here now? Crops to nourish us as well as others." Two opposite views of land are in focus: the American Indian's, that man cannot own the land, and the farmer's, that using land to feed humans entitles him to it. The greatness of Moberg's representation is that his epic demonstrates the unsolvable opposition—between the tiller of the soil who gets a second chance in the New World and the native nomad who has his space invaded and exploited—without giving the blame to either side. The author shows us how the forces of history work.[7]

Rølvaag and Immigration

Rølvaag's *Giants in the Earth* has acquired a place in the history of American literature as well as its place in Norwegian American and Norwegian literary history. Where Moberg's emphasis was first on the sociological aspects and second on the existential, Rølvaag was more concerned with the psychological and cultural aspects of the immigration theme. By bringing his story into the second generation and examining generational conflict, questions of language and identity are at the forefront. A discussion regarding assimilation versus preservation of the cultural heritage runs as a leitmotif through the second and third volumes.

Giants in the Earth presents the westward movement and the settling and building up of a new life on the Dakota prairie. The two main characters, Beret and Per Hansa, who have emigrated from northern Norway, display two very different views of and reactions to the prairie:

> As Per Hansa lay there dreaming of the future it seemed to him that hidden springs of energy, hitherto unsuspected even by himself, were welling up in his heart. He felt as if his strength were inexhaustible . . . His heart sang as he thought how he would have to hurry! Here there was nothing even to hide behind! . . . He certainly would soon find out for himself that a home for men and women and children could never be established in this wilderness . . . And how could she bring new life into the world out here! . . . Beret could not go to sleep for a long time that night.[8]

Per's reaction to the prairie is that it is a challenge that summons the use of all your talents to conquer; to him this is inspiring and exhilarating. In Beret's view, the prairie may corrupt and destroy you. The contrast between these two characters, placed on the South Dakota prairie to depict the settling and the process of creating a new society, makes for a rather dramatic story. Breaking the soil, building houses, living through harsh winters and grasshopper plagues for the two of them and the small group of people around them provide a narrative that has many of the typical elements of the immigrant novel. The double perspective is an important feature on many levels; for example, Per Hansa compares sailing on the stormy ocean back home in northern Norway with traveling in a snowstorm on the prairie—and as experiences from his old life that help him master new challenges. This perspective is even more prevalent on the psychological level, however, in particular relating to Beret with her homesickness and her feeling of foreignness and the angst that the landscape inflicts on her. When Per Hansa perishes in a snowstorm after seven pioneering years, it is a result of the harsh winter on the prairie in 1880–81—a historical fact Rølvaag has included in his novel—and of Beret's fear that their life on the prairie has left them spiritually barren. She had insisted that he go out, in spite of the forbidding weather, to get a minister for his dying friend.

As the story moves on to depict the second generation, the double perspective also has bearings on the epic's cultural theme. After Per Hansa's death, Beret has to shoulder the responsibility of running the farm according to the plans he had outlined, something she masters skillfully despite her earlier reservations. Also at the core of the last two volumes is the question of preserving the cultural heritage of language, religion, and values in their immigrant lives versus assimilation and Americanization. Peder, a second-generation Norwegian American boy, is born on the prairie. He learns the ways of his new homeland and is attracted to the prospects and promises he sees, while his mother Beret sees it as her moral duty to preserve the Norwegian cultural heritage. All this is put to a test, in general with the rapid changes and with the immigrant community becoming increasingly part of the larger American society, and in particular when the Norwegian American Lutheran boy Peder falls in love with, and eventually marries, the Irish Catholic Susie. A leitmotif is Beret's belief that the mixture of people across ethnic and religious boundaries is a bad thing. She has warned Peder that "you are Norwegian and they are Irish," which seems to express an essentialist understanding of the concept of ethnicity and identity, an understanding that these matters are fixed and not subject to change. And when she listens to her children's talk, she feels that they are changing and moving away from her and thus from their Norwegian cultural heritage. Preservation of language and culture, including religion, is to her a prerequisite for cultural and spiritual growth:

But they are of another kind. They have another faith. And that is dangerous.

Ole Rolvaag writes in the backyard of his Northfield, Minnesota, home, 1928

For it is with such things as with weeds . . .—you can't mix wheat and potatoes in the same bin.

At times, as she listened to their talk she would fall to wondering whether she actually was their mother . . . each did not bring forth after its own kind . . . Wheat did not yield wheat; nor cattle beget cattle . . . Had nature's laws been annulled altogether in this land?[9]

The use of biological metaphors in describing human relations and developments is a bit disturbing to a modern reader but fits in the context of the time the books were written and the concepts that were used. Rølvaag's literary text is a realistic novel that presents the second generation, that is, Peder's development: he becomes increasingly more interested in, and influenced by, the larger American society, through school and later also social and political life. For example, Rølvaag brings into the story the actual discussion about statehood in 1889, when North and South Dakota entered the Union, to underline its authenticity and to demonstrate how strong the pull is for the young man to become fully involved in this society and its future. *Peder Victorious* ends with Peder and Susie, his friend Charley's sister, getting married. Reality has overcome Beret's objections, and Peder sees the future as an American future, without authorities from the respective backgrounds: "You and I are Americans, Charley. Popes and kings mean darn to us."[10]

The final volume concludes Beret's story, particularly focusing on her efforts to preserve the cultural heritage, which for her implies a deep concern for morals and values. It also tells the story of the young couple moving from bliss to disaster as their marriage disintegrates. This can be interpreted as giving Beret's views precedence, recalling her often-repeated statement that "you cannot have wheat and potatoes in the same bin." This view is also underscored by some of the characters who represent church and religion:

> These mixed marriages are the greatest bane, the greatest danger, confronting the Church.

> *A people that has lost its traditions is doomed!*

> May I ask you, does the leopard change his spots by coming into new pastures? . . . If we're to accomplish anything worth while, anything at all, we must do it as Norwegians.[11]

The first quotation above is from Father Williams, the Catholic priest; the other two are from the Norwegian Lutheran minister. Beret feels great joy, especially when she hears her pastor's support of her own reflections about culture and heritage. He has often been interpreted as Rølvaag's spokesperson in the novel, since his views correspond so much to what the author himself put forward in his many speeches and articles. But they should not be used directly as keys to interpreting his fiction; the theme and message of the immigrant epic are expressed through the literary text as a whole—plot, characters, historical elements, and narrator's voice. The depiction of the immigrant experience is complex, showing that it includes both trials and triumphs, that the costs were high both physically and mentally, that the generational relationship in particular is challenging, and that (in this narrative's special take on it) preservation of cultural heritage is vital for human beings.

Moberg and Rølvaag—A Comparison

A comparison between the writers and their oeuvres is of great interest, since the two have obvious similarities but many differences, as well. Moberg was an established and prolific Swedish writer; his emigrant epic is one among many works, albeit the high point of his carrier. Rølvaag was an immigrant living and working in Norwegian America—an educator and writer who published several books—but his literary "fame" rests on the immigrant epic alone. The differences in place and in worldview determines the structure: Moberg depicts the emigration process from a background of oppression and the vision of a better life, details the journey, the establishment of new homes, and the acculturation process, following the emigrants to the end of their lives. Rølvaag depicts the process as the immigrants begin their journey west on the prairie, the establishment of new homes, and the acculturation process that includes the second generation born on the prairie and complex generational relations. Both have groups as well as individuals in focus, but with different emphases and focal points. Moberg's are Swedish, which brings forward an examination of why the emigrants left and how they fared. Rølvaag's are American within a Norwegian immigrant community, the story written in the immigrant language for and about this group to clarify their lives between countries and cultures.

These differences—along with Moberg's historical and sociological and Rølvaag's cultural and psychological interests—account for the varying interpretations of the migrant experience. The migrant experience portrayed in Rølvaag's epic is an American experience but confined to the immigrant group that faced the question of finding a balance between the preservation of cultural heritage and assimilation. Rølvaag's personal engagement as an immigrant strengthened the didactic element, particularly apparent in the last two volumes. This was for him a strongly held commitment, but it marred the literary quality. Moberg's political engagement in Swedish society and his view of history directed his depiction of the migrant experience toward explaining the reasons for emigrating, the social and economic aspects, and, through the double perspective, toward promoting a continuous criticism of Swedish class society. The emigrant experience, including both *förkovra sig* and *förlika sig* (to improve one's lot and to be reconciled), also provided opportunities for human growth.

Moberg's incorporation of American Indian themes lends authenticity to his description and helps in characterizing the individual immigrants according to how they look upon the Indians. It also adds yet another layer to the epic. The farmer protagonist Karl Oskar, who breaks the land and provides food for his family and other people, is contrasted to the nomad whose land he has cultivated. For the hungry and oppressed of the Old World to have a better life—the very raison d'être behind the emigration—the peoples of the New World had their existence and way of life destroyed. Moberg's literary project is to depict the liberating aspect of the emigration movement, but it includes the larger picture and its costs as well.

The two series of books can both be characterized as realistic, historical novels. Both writers had knowledge and insight about the facts of migration with a difference in focus. They also differ in terms of what space—time period, geography, culture—they write within as well as the temporal difference between narrated time and narrator's time. One can see elements of Moberg's engagement in the political discussions and his critical views of the Swedish establishment in the 1940s and '50s, the time he wrote the novels, and in his depiction of Sweden of the 1840s and '50s, the time that the emigrants left. Rølvaag wrote his immigrant novels in the 1920s, and his depiction of the discussions regarding culture and heritage that he attributed to the 1880s and 1890s seems more valid for the 1920s when he wrote the novels and was himself active in these discussions than it was for the 1880s and 1890s. This accounts for the rather heavy didactic element in the second half of his epic.

Moberg's and Rølvaag's narratives are not historical accounts. The works are fiction, yet as historical-realistic novels by writers with great knowledge of and insights into Scandinavian emigration and immigration history, they present reliable and believable depictions. As novels, they can dramatize and individualize the process and thereby grant the reader a deeper understanding of the emotional and existential aspects of the migrant experience. As this chapter has demonstrated, the two epics possess many similarities, rooted in the times and material that are the bases of their narratives. There are, as well, major differences in their interpretations, because of differences in time, space, and perspectives but mainly the result of differences in worldview. Some scholars argue that Rølvaag's work represents the most genuine understanding of the psychological and cultural aspect of the migrant experience because he himself was an immigrant, although that depends on how such an insight is established in the literary text. Others will argue that Moberg's works demonstrate a wider understanding of the societal aspect of the migration process as well as the larger context, comparing his narratives to the epics of biblical and classical times and pitting his individual emigrants from Sweden against the indigenous peoples of the New World. Both views can claim some validity. As belles lettres, however, the literary and artistic quality of the works are decisive. Rølvaag's work demonstrates the intimacy of personal experience while Moberg's convinces with its richness of style, from poetic to starkly realistic, its nuanced character descriptions, and its sociological span, all within the larger context of time and space. These works of fiction have been important in shaping people's understanding of the migrant processes: they have been widely read, are well written, and are good complements to historical accounts of migration.

Notes

1. Vilhelm Moberg, *The Emigrants* (New York: Fawcett Popular Library, 1971), 107, 108.
2. Moberg, *The Emigrants*, 56.

3. Moberg, *The Emigrants,* 56, 189.

4. Moberg, *Unto a Good Land* (New York: Fawcett Popular Library, 1971), 234.

5. Moberg, *The Settlers* (New York: Fawcett Popular Library, 1971), 46.

6. Moberg, *Unto a Good Land,* 278, 405, 406.

7. Moberg, *The Settlers,* 46; Moberg, *The Last Letter Home* (New York: Fawcett Popular Library, 1971), 68, 69.

8. Ole Edvart Rølvaag, *Giants in the Earth* (New York: Harper Perennial Classics, 1927), 36, 38, 41, 45, 46.

9. Rølvaag, *Peder Victorious* (Lincoln: University of Nebraska Press, 1929), 104, 179.

10. Rølvaag, *Their Fathers' God* (Lincoln: University of Nebraska Press, 1931), 11.

11. Rølvaag, *Their Fathers' God,* 131, 207, 209.

Bibliography

Vilhelm Moberg, *Utvandrarna* (1949), *Invandrarna* (1952), *Nybyggarna* (1956), and *Sista brevet till Sverige* (1959). All were published in Stockholm by Bonniers.

———. *The Emigrants, Unto a Good Land, The Settlers,* and *The Last Letter Home.* New York: Fawcett Popular Library, 1971. These have been reprinted and published by the Minnesota Historical Society Press.

O. E. Rølvaag, *I de dage* (1924), *Riket grundlægges* (1925), *Peder Seier* (1928), and *Den signede dag* (1931). All were published in Oslo by Aschehoug.

———. *Giants in the Earth* (New York: Harper, Perennial Classics, 1927).

———. *Peder Victorious* (Lincoln: University of Nebraska Press, 1929).

———. *Their Fathers' God* (Lincoln: University of Nebraska Press, 1931).

CHAPTER 5

"Ar Du Svensk?"—"Norsk, Norsk!"

Folk Humor and Cultural Difference in Scandinavian America

JAMES P. LEARY

I was born in 1950 and raised in Rice Lake, a farming and logging town in north-western Wisconsin. Like some in the area, we were Irish, but the community also included Ojibwes, French Canadians, Germans, Swiss, assorted Slavs, Italians, and especially Scandinavians—Swedes aplenty but even more Norwegians. Like my dad who had grown up there in the 1920s, I have known the following comic folk taunt for almost as long as I can remember:

Ten t'ousand Svedes	[Ten thousand Swedes
ran t'rough da veeds—	ran through the weeds—
chased by von Norvegian!	chased by one Norwegian!]

More than a half century ago, this rhyme appealed to me because of its playful reliance on a broken-English dialect that only slightly exaggerated actual speech I sometimes heard on the street from immigrants and their offspring. But the improbable image of hordes scampering from the onslaught of a single pursuer was just as intriguing. As an Irish American who, even then, knew something of Ireland's struggle for independence from England, I began to wonder why an upstart Norwegian was tangling with so many Swedes.

Peter Munch provided answers in 1960, although it would be twenty years before I read his classic essay, "Ten Thousand Swedes: Reflections on a Folklore Motif." A Norwegian-born sociologist on the faculty of Southern Illinois University, Munch was well aware of "numerous wars between Denmark-Norway and Sweden," of Sweden's political reign over Norway from 1814 until 1905, and of long-standing Norwegian conceptions "of 'the Swede' as the traditional enemy" when he systematically investigated versions of the "Ten Thousand Swedes" rhyme, along with eight related origin stories gathered from tellers in Michigan and Minnesota for the Folklore Archives at Indiana University. All of the tellers shared legendary accounts linking the rhyme to an actual battle involving the rout of Swedes by outnumbered Norwegians. Yet despite such uniform claims, Munch provided convincing evidence that "Ten Thousand Swedes" emerged in the United States. Furthermore, he argued, it was likely an American adaptation of an English-language taunt celebrating the English defeat of Irish rebels at the Battle of the Boyne in 1790:

> Ten thousand micks
> Got killed with picks—
> At the Battle of Boyne Waters.

Munch offered a series of important observations about folk humor featuring Norwegians and Swedes in America, albeit from a Norwegian American perspective.[1]

Most significantly, Munch contended that as fellow immigrants Norwegians and Swedes in the United States were on relatively equal footing politically and shared common allegiance to their new nation. Hence actual "military achievements of the one group over the other were hardly meaningful anymore." Indeed, as fellow Scandinavians, Norwegian and Swedish newcomers—sharing many linguistic, customary, religious, and other cultural practices—frequently relied on one another to establish community in the New World. At the same time, the immigrants could not forget relationships between their respective homelands, especially since, for example, the major periods of Norwegian exodus "in the 1860s and 1880s coincided with periods in which the political tension between the two countries was particularly high." Consequently, "a milder form of expression of group differentiation, not entirely unfamiliar to the immigrant, was offered by the culture of the frontier in the deriding joke," which had the advantage of being "obviously made up, with no pretension of relating to actual events." Useful as expressive forms that were at once residual and transformed, at once of the Old World and the New, deriding jokes distinguishing Norwegians and Swedes in America not only served these groups but also provided a means to assert distinct ethnic identities contrary to larger American inclinations "to lump . . . Norwegians and Swedes together as 'Scandinavians.'" The fourth volume of the *Dictionary of American Regional English* fortifies Munch's final point with evidence that a jocular Americanized rendition of Scandinavian as "Scandihoovian"—alternatively Scandahoovian, Scandihuvian, Scandinoovian, and Skandihoovian—was circulating as early as 1901, particularly in association with Norwegian and Swedish loggers in the Upper Midwest and Pacific Northwest.[2]

Rich in insights, Munch's landmark essay is scant regarding illustrative examples. The only joke he mentions involves a "Norwegian who was mistaken for a Swede because he had just gotten out of the hospital after a long illness." Likewise his focus on the "Ten Thousand Swedes" rhyme, necessarily emphasizing the Norwegian American experience, gave short shrift both to the Swedish side of the inter–Scandinavian American rivalry and to the perspectives and participation of non–Scandinavian Americans. My task here is to extend Munch's keen observations on Norwegian and Swedish folk humor in the United States through an inclusive consideration of Norwegian, Swedish, and non–Scandinavian American participants, with particular attention to three interrelated phenomena: oral tradition and informal joking; joke books; and the public performances of semiprofessional Scandinavian American humorists.[3]

Oral Tradition and Informal Joking

Folklorists and other ethnographers did not begin to record the jocular oral traditions of Scandinavian immigrants until roughly the middle of the twentieth century, yet we can begin to glimpse the earlier nature and purpose of joking across ethnic lines from letters, reminiscences, and especially the memories of older joke-tellers regarding tales acquired in their youth. Some of the complexities of jokes concerning Norwegians and Swedes in America are most apparent when considering the particular uses of different versions of the same joke by several tellers.

On August 12, 1946, for example, folklorist Richard Dorson recorded the following joke from Wallace Cameron in Gladstone, a village in Michigan's Upper Peninsula not far from the north shore of Green Bay.

> A Swedish farmer at Ensign staggers home from a Grange meeting—his wife had left him because of his drinking—and falls asleep in a neighbor's pigpen. In the morning cool breezes wake him up, he blinks and finds his arm wrapped around a pig.
> "Ar du Svensk?" [Are you Swedish?] he asks.
> The pig rustles a little bit, grunts, "Norsk, norsk" [Norwegian, Norwegian].[4]

Intriguingly, Cameron appended his Scandinavian performance with a French Canadian variation.

> The Frenchman, in a similar position, says "Good morning, mistaire, what time is eet?" Pig says, "Neuf, neuf" [Nine, nine]. "Jesus Chris'! That late alreadee." The little pig alongside says, "Oui, oui" [Yes, yes]. Frenchman says, "Tank you, mistaire."

Apparently, Dorson did not discover when this joke was first learned, nor did he offer any evidence establishing whether the Scandinavian or the French Canadian rendition came first, nor did he provide biographical information. The teller's Scottish first and last names argue, however, that he was neither Swedish nor Norwegian nor French Canadian, as do his prefatory remarks to the double telling: "The Scandinavians are very proud of their native heritage . . . A Swede does not like to be called Norwegian and so on." Perhaps like George T. Springer, a fellow non-Swede Gladstone-born teller of Scandinavian jokes, about whom more will be said, Cameron acquired the Svensk-Norsk joke amid the many Swedes who farmed, logged, and worked as domestics throughout Delta County in Michigan's Upper Peninsula.[5]

We know much more about I. S. "Mox" Lindquist (1881–1965), who, in 1958 on the occasion of Minnesota's centennial, published *Manasota Folklore: Scandinavian Stories,* the first of a series of six collections of regional jokes and poems mostly in Scandinavian dialect that were laced with personal reminiscences. Piecing together biographical fragments from various pamphlets, we learn that Lindquist, a 1908 graduate of Ohio's Oberlin College, subsequently moved to Minneapolis to begin a fifty-year career with the agricultural seed company Northrup King. He was, however, born and raised in Marinette, Wisconsin, a logging town on Green Bay, some fifty miles from Gladstone, Michigan. His parents, John Oscar Lindquist and Inger Marie Westman, were, as revealed in the preface to his first collection, Scandinavian immigrants of differing national origins: "My father hailed from Stockholm, Sweden, and my mother came from Larvic [*sic*], Norway. I deeply cherish the memory of their ability to laugh and enjoy a good joke even when the joke was on themselves. A very noticeable trait found among the Scandinavians that we admire and we love them for it." Many of the jokes in his collection are attributed to the tellings of particular friends, while more are jokes that have circulated long and widely in oral tradition, including this version of the Svensk-Norsk story.

> One reason why Sven and Pete are having a hard time making a go of their farm is Pete's habit of going to town every Saturday night and coming home drunk.
>
> One night he was so drunk he had a hard time finding his way home. He finally landed in the pig pen where he fell into a drunken stupor. In the night he was awakened in his sleep and he felt a warm body back to back and drowsily he said, "Are du Svensk?" and the answer he received was–"Norsk, Norsk, Norsk."

It is impossible to know exactly how and when Lindquist acquired his version of this dialect joke. Perhaps he learned it in the Minneapolis area. Yet given his parents' origins and inclination to "enjoy a good joke . . . on themselves," the abundance of Swedes and Norwegians in Marinette, and the community's rural surroundings, he may also have heard it at home in the late nineteenth or early twentieth century.[6]

We can be more precise about a third version that I recorded from Edwin Pearson on July 29, 1987:

> This Swede went and got drunk and couldn't find his way into the house. So he got down into the hoghouse and opened the door and lay down in the straw and went to sleep. And he woke up. He thought somebody was sleeping alongside him. It was a big sow.
> So he poked it with his elbow and said, *"Ar du Svensk?"*
> And the old sow says, *"Norsk, norsk."*

Pearson's father, Axel, emigrated in 1906 from Småland to the Swedish settlement of Wahoo on the prairie of eastern Nebraska. He had soon saved enough to bring over his wife, Bertha, and Edwin (1911–91) was born in Wahoo. When the family could not afford to buy the farm they rented, they took the train in 1920 with several fellow immigrant families to establish their own farms in the Cloverland area near Maple in northwestern Wisconsin's Douglas County. Eventually Ed farmed, was active in town government, and even ran as a Progressive Party candidate for state assembly in the 1930s. Possessing a dry wit and deadpan delivery, he was also renowned as a joke-teller. He learned the foregoing joke, perhaps the oldest in his considerable repertoire, in the early 1920s as one that his parents told and that "was popular" locally.[7]

These three renderings of the same joke are among the earliest instances of folk humor focused on the interrelationships of Swedes and Norwegians in the United States. Presumably originating in the Upper Midwest—possibly in the Michigan-Wisconsin borderland—in the early twentieth century, set in a rural community, told mostly in English but with key words and phrases in Swedish and Norwegian, the joke has clearly circulated among non-Scandinavian neighbors of Swedes and Norwegians, among Americans of mixed Swedish and Norwegian ancestry, and among Swedish Americans. Casting a Swede as a drunken farmer, the joke alludes to larger stereotypes of male immigrant Scandinavians as agrarian workers fond of drink while likewise reflecting social realities of the late nineteenth- to early twentieth-century era that spawned a vigorous temperance movement. The presence of a pig imagined as a Norwegian connotes the supposedly bestial nature of Norskies through the homophony between animal and human languages, that is, a teller's successful pronunciation of "Norsk" requires a snorting inhalation onomatopoeically equivalent to a porker's grunt. Most of all, however, the joke serves to distinguish Norwegians from Swedes since in America they are often mistaken for one another. In sum, the Norsk-Svensk joke has been used chiefly to perform cultural difference by competing Scandinavian Americans bent on maintaining internal ethnic borders, by cooperating Scandinavian Americans concerned that ethnic outsiders

recognize their unique national origins, and by curious neighboring ethnic outsiders keen to demonstrate an insider's understanding.

Additional examples from oral tradition substantiate the notion that humorous jokes and jibes juxtaposing Norwegian and Swedish Americans are not
simply comic extensions of an Old World family feud; rather, they address
decidedly New World experiences and issues situated in culturally diverse contexts. To cite a significant early instance, in 1909 George F. Erickson emigrated
from Västmanland to find work in an iron ore mine in Stambaugh, a hamlet
in Michigan's Upper Peninsula. The following June he heard a joke compelling
enough to reiterate in a letter sent to Sweden:

> I heard a good story the other day, there was a man who told it to me
> in English. There was a Swede and an American, who stood and talked,
> and the American told the Swede about everything in this country,
> but to everything he told about the Swede said, "We have exactly the
> same thing in Sweden." Finally the American got mad and said, "I know
> one thing which you still don't have in Sweden, you don't have any
> Indians." But the Swede was not without an answer and replied immedi-
> ately, "We have Indians in Sweden too, but we call them Norwegians."

Here we have an English translation of a letter in Swedish concerning a joke in
English—told by (presumably) an American or at least a non-Swede—that was
written to a Swede concerning Swedes, Americans, American Indians, and Norwegians. Although the original teller's intentions can only be guessed, the joke
clearly goes well beyond the simple recognition that Swedes and Norwegians
are distinct. Instead, the teller seems to suggest that Swedes are just as good as
Americans—perhaps better since the quick-thinking Swede gets the last word.
Such egalitarianism is limited, however, by the implication that both Americans
and Swedes are superior to the supposedly kindred and savage Native peoples
and Norwegians over which their respective home nations have had dominion.[8]

As we shall see when considering joke books and contemporary performers
of Scandinavian American humor, the theme of urbane, sophisticated Swedish
snootiness and rustic, uncouth Norwegian resentment remains prominent.
Within the everyday contexts of joke telling among diverse Scandinavian friends
and neighbors, more fully egalitarian raconteurs like Edwin Pearson were aware
of, and at pains to minimize, Norwegian-Swedish friction. When telling me a
joke he had first heard concerning a proverbially "stubborn Norwegian," Pearson
modified his telling so as not to be perceived by a Scandinavian American outsider as a Swede lampooning Norwegians: "Then there was one I heard a while
ago that I think is really pretty good, but it's had a lot of circulation in the country
already. A Norwegian came in the bank. Well, I'll say a Scandinavian, being I'm a

Swede, so I'll include Swedes." Of course, given Pearson's genial personality and sly sense of humor, I could easily imagine him, in the presence of Norwegian friends, performing this story teasingly in the version he had originally heard—with the expectation that his audience would respond in kind.[9]

A joking relationship characterized by friendly egalitarian teasing across ethnic lines has long been common in culturally diverse contexts wherein neighbors and fellow workers must rely on one another. Bonds are forged through testing, give and take, and inversion as participants signify friendship through the inoffensive exchange of mock insults. Born in 1912, George Dybedol of Mason, Wisconsin, was raised speaking Norwegian and playing Lutheran hymns on guitar. In the 1970s, after retiring from work as a welder and logger, he performed with other Norwegians in the Moland Lutheran String Band, but he also crossed religious and ethnic lines as the lone Norwegian and lone Lutheran member of Mason's Bethany Baptist Swedish String Band. Perhaps in this instance, supposed Swedish superiority over Norwegians was neutralized by the recognition that Scandinavian Lutherans lord it over Scandinavian Baptists. In any case, George Dybedol was often razzed affectionately for being Norwegian, not only because he could take it but also because he could be expected to dish it out. On February 21, 1981, I recorded the Swedish String Band as part of a project to document ethnic music traditions. Over coffee and cake in the church basement, someone remarked on the presence of a Norwegian among so many Swedes. Dybedol rose to the bait by telling this joke: "Christ was walking along the road to Galilee. He met all these different people along the way. Finally he met a man who was weeping. Jesus said, 'Why do you weep?' The man told him, 'I'm weeping because I'm a Swede.' And the Lord sat down and wept with him." George grinned, and his audience whooped with laughter.[10]

Joke Books

Unlike orally told jokes that flourished alike in church basements, kitchens, saloons, ethnic halls, and worksite break rooms, be they rural or urban, the joke books of the late nineteenth and early twentieth centuries required a combination of literacy, capital, equipment, professional training, marketing, distribution, and a paying clientele found mainly in large cities. Midwestern urban centers such as Chicago and Minneapolis, with their substantial ethnic enclaves, performance venues, and technological facilities, also fostered opportunities for professional comedians not only to entertain on stage but also to further their careers through sound recordings and books. As might be expected, Norwegian and Swedish American newspapers published comic cartoons, humorous anecdotes, and occasional jokes concerning immigrant life between the 1890s and the 1920s, while performers like the Minneapolis-based Hjalmar Peterson adopted the stage name Olle i Skratthult (Ole from Laughtersville) to perform under the lights, make 78 rpm recordings, and peddle books including his witty signature songs and routines. The jokes and humor of this era's Scandinavian American newspapers and of performers like Peterson, however, were in the languages of their respective homelands and not intended for either inter– or extra–Scandinavian American consumption.[11]

Meanwhile, the earliest full-fledged books featuring Scandinavian American humor, published in Scandihoovian English and thus accessible to mainstream audiences, nonetheless avoided Norsk-Svensk interaction to focus exclusively on the misadventures of either Norwegians or Swedes in the New World. Moreover, although decidedly jocular, such publications as *Yust Yokes bae Yansen* (Anonymous, ca. 1915), concerning a bumbling Swede in "Minaplis, Unitestates," and *Yust for Fun: Norwegian-American Dialect Monologues* by the Chicago-born sisters Eleanora and Ethel Olson, were not joke books in the sense of presenting a series of discrete, relatively short comic narratives concluding with a punch line. We know nothing, unfortunately, about the author of *Yust Yokes bae Yansen,* but in the case of the Olson sisters, their extended solo performances were honed by entertaining diverse audiences mostly in Iowa, Minnesota, North Dakota, and Wisconsin on the Chautauqua and Lyceum circuits beginning in 1905 and by recording thirty-five dialect monologues for several record labels from 1918 to 1923. Newspaper accounts, commercial recordings, and *Yust for Fun* confirm their consistent preoccupation with the inadvertently comic escapades of wide-eyed immigrant women from rural Norway as they encountered American city life by visiting the photographer and the beach, taking in a baseball game and the movies, and using the telephone.[12]

The first Scandinavian American joke book to go beyond mono-ethnic limitations was George T. Springer's *Yumpin' Yimminy: Scandinavian Dialect Selections,* published just outside of Minneapolis in 1932. Born in Gladstone, Michigan, of German heritage, Springer (1889–1981) graduated from Gladstone High School in 1907 and then attended the University of Michigan before moving to Minnesota, where he earned a degree from the St. Paul College of Law in 1915. After a stint in Montana, Springer settled permanently in Minneapolis, working as an attorney for Griggs, Cooper & Company, a wholesale grocery business, until his retirement in 1953. He had a lifelong interest in journalism and wrote for his hometown paper while in high school. Besides work on dialect humor, Springer produced a spate of publications over a forty-year period on Gladstone football and lumberjack sports.[13]

Springer regularly returned to Gladstone, where folklorist Richard Dorson met him while doing field research for two of his most influential publications: "Dialect Stories from the Upper Peninsula: A New Form of American Folklore"

George T. Springer's joke book Yumpin' Yimminy

and *Bloodstoppers and Bearwalkers*. Dorson reported on Springer's adeptly performed dialect jokes, while his book made considerable use of both jokes circulating in oral tradition and others lifted from print: "When I met Mr. Springer
in Gladstone, August 22, 1946, he gave me a nice copy of this little yellow paper-
backed book, read me selections from it in his superb Swedish dialect, and
then, at my request, indicated those which he had heard as traditional in Upper
Michigan, as distinct from the majority of stories which were reprinted from
books and periodicals."[14]

Several years later, through a tape recording that he made for and sent to
Richard Dorson, Springer confirmed that he acquired his interest in jokes while
growing up in Gladstone, where Scandinavians predominated: "My family on
both sides were German, but I found I possessed a natural talent for imitating
the Scandinavian. I began collecting Scandinavian dialect stories whenever I saw
or heard them." Indeed, beyond oral tradition Springer's impressive collection
of Scandinavian American sheet music, sound recordings, vaudeville sketches,
and books, including the only known copy of *Yust Yokes bae Yansen*, testifies to
an interest in Scandihoovian dialect humor that preceded and persisted well
beyond the publication of his joke book in 1932.[15]

Regarding the dialect jokes included in *Yumpin' Yimminy*, sixty-four mention
Swedes, five concern Norwegians, twenty-three adopt a neutral or interchange-
able Scandinavian, and only one specifically invokes both groups. The presence of
more than twelve times as many Swedish as Norwegian jokes is probably attribut-
able to three factors evident in the late nineteenth and early twentieth centuries: the
far greater population of Swedes relative to Norwegians in Springer's Gladstone
and Minneapolis homes; the dramatic upsurge of urban Swedish Americans in
contrast to the less urban and far greater rural presence of Norwegian Americans;
and the shift of Swedish immigration from the Midwest to East and West Coast
cities, where the theater and music publishing industries began to feature comic
Swedish stage performers and songs. Indeed, a Norwegian has only a phantom
presence in Springer's sole Norwegian-Swedish joke:

> A badly battered Swede was sitting in front of a saloon and a passerby
> noticed his plight. The wreck was laughing hilariously through a badly
> damaged mouth.
> "What's the matter?" asked the passerby.
> "Dar ban faller kom op to me en hae giv me soaker en hae say, 'Tak
> det ju Norvegan,' en hae giv me black eye en hae soak me on nose
> en hae say, 'Tak det ju Norvegan,' en hae kick me aut door. Ho! Ho!
> Ha! Ha!"
> "I do not see anything so very laughable about that," was the reply.
> "Vell, ay ban Svede," grinned the wreck.

Powers Moulton's *2500 Jokes for All Occasions*—an Eastern, urban, catchall anthology culled chiefly from prior publications rather than oral tradition— included a very similar version.[16]

Scant though it was in encompassing jocular Norsk-Svensk rivalries flour- ishing in the Upper Midwest for decades, Springer's pioneering book nonethe- less drew significantly on regional oral tradition and eventually inspired Paul F. Anderson's dual publications roughly a half century later. The great-grandson and grandson of successive Swedish immigrants to Minnesota, the Minneapolis- based Anderson was born in 1951 and has been immersed in Scandinavian American music and humor since the early 1970s as a performer, researcher, writer, and publisher. While working behind the scenes at the Snoose Boulevard Festival, a key event in the upper midwestern revitalization of Scandinavian American music and song, Anderson met George T. Springer:

> He was an 88-year-old retired lawyer when I met him in 1977. We
> became friends, and he later sold me several items from his collection
> of Scandinavian dialect humor, dating back to 1905 . . . *Yumpin' Yimminy*
> inspired me to publish my own joke books. These were intended as a
> lighthearted look at yesteryear. Springer gave me permission to use his
> material, and in all I took fourteen jokes from his collection. Nearly all
> of my jokes came from American sources. As an editor I was guided
> by the books, recordings and performers who had gone before me . . .
> Names, locations, occupations, situations and subject matter were
> chosen to give the jokes an old time Scandinavian feel.

Anderson published *Scandinavian Yokes* in 1978, revising it a year later, and then produced a second anthology, *Scandimania: A Smorgasbord of Fun* in 1985.[17]

Very much part of the tradition of prior joke books, Anderson's produc- tions are also retrospective appreciations of old-time Scandinavian heritage, late twentieth-century assertions of Scandinavian American identity, and well- informed considerations of the broad range of Scandinavian American humor. Regarding the latter point, Anderson's joke books innovatively featured several jokes about Finns and a few concerning Danes, had a much more equivalent balance of Norwegian and Swedish jokes, and included nine setting Norwegians against Swedes in an American context. One of them was the cheerful battered Swede figuring in Springer's anthology, but the others departed from *Yumpin' Yimminy* while at the same time invoking such common themes from oral joke telling as the urbane, superior Swede versus the stubborn, rustic Norwegian:

> A new neighbor moved in across the street from Anders Soderberg,
> and like a good Swede Anders went over to greet the newcomer and

welcome him to the area. When Anders heard that the man's last name was Olson, he said, "I suppose you must be a Svede den?"

"I should say not," said the other man indignantly. "I vas born and raised in Norvay. I'm a Norvegian still. And I'll die a Norvegian."

"Vell, goodness sakes, man," said Anders, "don't you ever vant ta improve yourself?"

The aforementioned self-described Norwegian-Swedish "half-breed," I. S. "Mox" Lindquist, whose books are strewn with dialect jokes and historical observations, liked the previous story so much that he included two distinct versions among the six overtly Svensk-Norsk jokes he published. In the first, the Swede Yon Person rebukes the Norwegian Ole Vigard. In the second, Sven the Swede confronts Olaf the Norwegian, with Olaf hailing from Lindquist's mother's hometown, Larvik.[18]

Public Performers of Norsk-Svensk Humor in the United States

Public performers of inter–Scandinavian American humor, typically garbed as rustic frumps, have drawn to varying degrees on jokes circulating in oral tradition, on joke books, and on their own experiences to fashion comic routines delivered to mixed audiences in Scandihoovian dialect. We do not know exactly when this phenomenon first occurred, but it was flourishing by 1925. In the fall of that year, Lawrence Welk, a German Russian accordionist from North Dakota, joined the Peerless Entertainers, led by the Irish American comedian George T. Kelly, to barnstorm the eastern Dakotas, northern Iowa, and western Minnesota. As Welk recalled:

> [Kelly] did a character called Ole the Swede, and since we toured through a part of the country heavily populated by Swedes and Norwegians, they all loved him. If George was playing to a Norwegian audience, he'd come out in his "Ole" costume—loud checked pants, lumberman's boots, flannel shirt, knitted cap with a tassel on the end of it—and with a wink at the audience, he'd say in his outrageous accent, "You all know what a Svede is, don't you? . . . Yah, sure, that's a Norwegian with his brains knocked out!" The Norwegians would roar with laughter. Next night he might be playing to the Swedes and he'd reverse the line and the Swedes laughed just as hard. They all recognized themselves in George's impersonations and laughed at their own quirks.

Like the Scottish joke-teller Wallace Cameron and the German joke book publisher George T. Springer, the Irish Kelly was an ethnic outsider demonstrating to insiders his awareness of inter–Scandinavian American similarities and distinctions. He was also sufficiently savvy to shift ethnic allegiance depending on the situation. Critically, he endeared shifting audiences enough for them to accept him as one of their own and, thanks to that willing suspension of disbelief, assorted Norwegians and Swedes "recognized themselves" and "laughed at their own quirks."[19]

In 1989, concerned with maintaining the Czech hall in his hometown of Haugen, Wisconsin, Robert Heinze formed the Mighty Uff Da Players, a nominally Scandinavian but actually more Czech (Bohemian) and German aggregation trading on the familiarity of upper midwestern audiences with public performances of Scandihoovian humor: "I don't know how it would float if we tried to run Bohemian humor. Of course there isn't a lot that's out there to begin with. With Scandinavians, generally speaking, there's definitely a sober side to them too. But for some reason they just seem to be not just fair game but very good natured about it."[20]

Norwegians from surrounding Barron County, Swedes from nearby Polk and Burnett counties, and many others of decidedly non-Scandinavian descent persist to the present in thronging Haugen's Czech hall for the Mighty Uff Da Players' semi-annual shows. Their appreciation of humor targeting Scandinavians generally, Norwegians and Swedes individually, and the Norsk-Svensk rivalry, combine as elements of a common regional culture accessible to diverse upper midwesterners.

Although far from unusual, faux Scandinavian performers such as the Mighty Uff Da Players, as well as George T. Kelly, have been considerably outnumbered by such counterparts of actual Swedish or Norwegian descent as the contemporary performers Bruce Danielson and Suzann Johnson Nelson. Born in South Minneapolis in 1949 to a father who was a "full-blooded Swede," Danielson grew up entertained by media personality Clellan Card in his guise of the Norsky buffoon Axel Torgeson. Card (b. 1903) debuted his zany dialect-spouting Axel character in the late 1930s over WCCO radio, then hosted a popular kids cartoon show, "Axel's Treehouse," on WCCO television from 1954 until his death in 1966. A comic stage performer in high school plays, Danielson eventually became a high school theater teacher in the heavily Swedish community of Cambridge, Minnesota. In the mid-1980s he teamed with fellow Swede Ann Berg to launch a variety show fundraiser for school activities. Seeking regional appeal and inspired by both Card and Red Stangland, whose highly successful *Norwegian Jokes* was followed by a spate of Ole and Lena joke books, Danielson and Berg assumed the personas of Ole and Lena to masquerade as Norwegian bumpkins. Innocently unaware until informed by a lone cast member of Norwegian descent that Norskies might be riled if the continuous butt of jokes by uppity Swede impersonators, Danielson and Berg soon changed their ways: "Oftentimes we

Bruce Danielson, glasses askew, assumes the guise of Ole while showing off the illustrated humor book he produced with Ann "Lena" Berg, Cambridge, Minnesota, 2008

will start our act by asking how many Norwegians do we have? How many Finns? How many Danish? And we usually end with how many Swedes, because there are usually so many. And then we say, 'Oh, that's good to know. Now we'll tell the jokes a little slower.'"[21]

Inversely akin to the West Coast's Harry (Skarbo) Stewart, a Norwegian adopted by Scots who took the stage name Yogi Yorgesson, the Swedish Swami, Danielson and Berg were Swedes disguised as Norwegians making fun of Swedes. Entering into what was effectively an egalitarian joking relationship with themselves, they stumbled on a complex humorous tactic enjoyed not only by their decidedly Swedish hometown audience but also by the Norwegians and other upper midwesterners they entertained on tours through the Dakota, Minnesota, and Wisconsin hinterlands.

Janet Letnes Martin and Suzann Johnson Nelson, who form the Lutheran Ladies comic duo, often begin their act similarly, as evident from their CD *Those Lutheran Ladies: Live in Medora!*

Suzann: Now that you know who we are, we want to find out who you are up there. Do we have any Norwegians here? [Loud assertive whooping and clapping.]

Janet: Are there any of those stiff Swedes here? [Laughing.]

Suzann: Do we have any Norwegians who married one of those stiff Swedes? [More laughter.] How does that work? [Laughter continues.] Mixed marriage. [Laughter.]

Janet: Are there any of those arrogant Germans here? [A LOT of whooping.]

Suzann: Yeah, do we have any of those arrogant Germans who think they're better than the Norwegians and Swedes? [Laughter.]

Janet: Are there any Lutherans here? [Whooping.]

Nelson and Martin went on to ask if any Catholics were present, then if there were any Lutherans who turned Catholic, or Catholics who turned Lutheran, thus extending the Norwegian-Swedish rivalry to a Scandinavian-German rivalry, and then, since German Catholics and Lutherans are equally abundant, to a Lutheran-Catholic rivalry. Far more playful than serious, perhaps more fictitious than real, such "rivalries" in the twenty-first century nonetheless conjure memories, break the proverbial ice, and prompt spirited interaction across ethnic and religious lines.[22]

Born in 1946 on a farm near Evansville, in western Minnesota between Alexandria and Fergus Falls, Suzann Nelson grew up in a conservative Norwegian Lutheran community: "Where I grew up a mixed marriage was a Swede and a Norwegian. Seriously. And, for crying out loud, 'If he marries her are they going to get married in the Swedish Lutheran church or the Norwegian Lutheran church?' And if it's the Swedish Lutheran church, 'I'm not bringing a pan of bars to her shower.'" A graduate of Augsburg College and possessed of a rich, mischievous, edgy sense of humor, Nelson is not a joke-teller but a humorist who draws on deep personal experience and cultural insights to create comedy by, in the manner of an astute ethnographer, calling attention to and challenging the peculiarities of socially ingrained patterns and perspectives—a playful, provocative talent that is not confined to stage performances.[23]

On Sunday, June 29, 2008, as I sat with Nelson taping an interview in Moorhead, Minnesota, at the close of that weekend's Norsk Hjemkomst festivities, a plump, smiling, and very blond middle-aged woman walked by. Recognizing her, Suzann called out, "She's Swede and blond and sits in the front pew at church." The woman laughed and then said, "That was the best. Thank you. It's true." Referring to her stage performance that morning as a 1950s-era Norwegian-Lutheran farm woman in her sensible Sunday best, Suzann elaborated for the benefit of us both, subtly invoking the class connotations of punctuality and seating in old-time churches:

See, I don't do fiction. I do nonfiction.

She came in there and I said, "I'm having church service." And I had just said, "You're obviously all Norwegian—the front row is empty." She comes late, she sits down. I said, "Do you always come late to church?"

And she said, "Yeah, I'm Swedish."

I said, "I can tell because you're blond and you're sitting in the front pew. We don't do that."

[Suzann and the woman both laugh, and the woman replies.] "It's perfect. It's so true."

On a half-facetious, half-factual roll after the woman had walked away, Suzann brilliantly wed Swede mockery with self-mockery firmly situated in America's Upper Midwest, past and present:

Yah! Swedes aren't funny at all. They're kind of pathetic. Pathetic people, blond people. [Sighs.] They're stubborn . . . We [Norwegian] Lutherans are meek, mild, we don't want to stand out. That's why we all drive grey cars so you won't see us on the highway. Yeah, there definitely is a difference between Norwegian and Swedish Americans . . . Swedes stayed in Minneapolis. Took the train from Chicago to St. Paul and stayed there, moved to Minneapolis when they had a few cents. But the Norwegian took the train from Chicago to Minneapolis and the ox cart to St. Cloud and then went out in the country where they belonged.[24]

Cast in such forms as rhymes, jokes, banter, and personal experience stories, variously sustained through informal oral tradition, joke books, and public performances, Norsk-Svensk folk humor in America hearkens to the old country but has more to do with New World conditions, those in the Upper Midwest especially. Initiated, understood, and enjoyed by Scandinavians and non-Scandinavians alike, it has been used for all of the following purposes: to distinguish Swedes from Norwegians in America; to express ethnic stereotypes and assert both superiority and resistance thereto; to engage in playful teasing by establishing an egalitarian joking relationship; to identify the prevailing presence of urban Swedes and rural Norwegians; to constitute a niche market through commercial productions; to express ethnic, interethnic, and regional cultural heritage; and to foster dynamic interaction by getting a rise out of diverse audiences large and small. In existence since at least the late nineteenth century and still going strong in the twenty-first, will Norsk-Svensk folk humor prevail in the decades to come? I am convinced that the answer is Yah, shure, you betcha!

Notes

This chapter could not have been completed in its present form without the assistance of Paul F. Anderson, who provided essential copies from his collection of Olson Sisters and George T. Springer materials while offering insights into his own experience as a joke-book compiler. The contemporary Scandihoovian dialect performers Bruce Danielson, Robert Heinze, and Suzann Nelson likewise generously shared valuable experiences and insights.

1. Peter Munch, "Ten Thousand Swedes: Reflections on a Folklore Motif," *Midwest Folklore* 10.2 (1960): 61–69. Reprinted in *Wisconsin Folklore*, ed. James P. Leary (Madison: University of Wisconsin Press, 1998), 62–71.

2. Munch, "Ten Thousand Swedes," 68–69. Odd Sverre Lovoll, *A Folk Epic: The Bygdelag in America* (Boston: Twayne Publishers, for the Norwegian-American Historical Association, 1975), 49–50. Joan Houston Hall, chief editor, *Dictionary of American Regional English*, vol. 4 (Cambridge, MA: Harvard University Press, 2002), 772.

3. Munch, "Ten Thousand Swedes," 63.

4. Richard M. Dorson, *Bloodstoppers and Bearwalkers: Folk Traditions of Michigan's Upper Peninsula*, 3rd ed., ed. and with an introduction by James P. Leary (1952; reprint, Madison: University of Wisconsin Press, 2008), 354.

5. Dorson, *Bloodstoppers and Bearwalkers*, 354.

6. I. S. "Mox" Lindquist, *My Manasota Pals: Ole, Olaf, Oscar an Yon* (Minneapolis, MN: The author, 1959), 1, 47; I. S. "Mox" Lindquist, *Ya! Ya! Another Trip Around Minnesota with Ole, Olaf, Oscar, an' Yon* (Minneapolis, MN: The author, 1961), 1; I. S. "Mox" Lindquist, *Mr. Mox Rides Again!* (Minneapolis, MN: The author, 1963), inside cover. I. S. "Mox" Lindquist, *Manasota Folklore: Scandinavian Stories* (Minneapolis, MN: E. C. Boynton Printing Co., 1958).

7. James P. Leary, *So Ole Says to Lena: Folk Humor of the Upper Midwest* (Madison: University of Wisconsin Press, 2001), 66, 210; Jane A. Pearson Grimsrud, *Who Are These People* (Self-published electronic manuscript, 2009), 300.

8. H. Arnold Barton, *Letters from the Promised Land: Swedes in America, 1840–1914* (Minneapolis: University of Minnesota Press, for the Swedish Pioneer Historical Society, 1975), 269–70.

9. Leary, *So Ole Says to Lena*, 76.

10. George Dybedol, conversation following Swedish String Band concert, Feb. 21, 1981.

11. Anne-Charlotte Harvey and Richard Hulan, *Teater, Visaften och Bal: A National Tour of Theater, Music and Dance Traditions of Swedish Americans* (Washington, DC: National Council for the Traditional Arts, 1982), 6; see also Ann-Charlotte Harvey, "Swedish-American Theater," in *Ethnic Theater in the United States*, ed. Maxine Schwartz Seller (Westport, CT: Greenwood Press, 1983), 491–524; Anne-Charlotte Harvey, "Holy Yumpin' Yiminy: Scandinavian Immigrant Stereotypes in the Early Twentieth Century American Musical," in *Approaches to the American Musical*, ed. Robert Lawson Peebles (Exeter: Exeter University Press, 1996), 55–71; and Anne-Charlotte Harvey, "Performing Ethnicity: The Role of Swedish Theatre in the Twin Cities," in *Swedes in the Twin Cities: Immigrant Life and Minnesota's Urban Frontier*, ed. Philip J. Anderson and Dag Blanck (St. Paul: Minnesota Historical Society Press, 2001), 149–72.

12. Anonymous, *Yust Yokes bae Yanson* (St. Paul, MN: no publisher listed, 1915); Eleanora and Ethel Olson, *Yust for Fun: Norwegian-American Dialect Monologues* (1925; reprint, with preface by Paul F. Anderson, Minneapolis: Eggs Press, 1979). Anonymous, "Scandinavian Fun: Notes about the Olson Sisters, Popular Entertainers from the Northwest," *The Voice of Victor: The Trade Journal of the Victor Talking Machine Company* (Aug. 1924); Richard K. Spottswood, *Ethnic Music on Records: A Discography of*

Ethnic Recordings Produced in the United States, 1893–1942, vol. 5 (1990), 2627–31; Paul F. Anderson, e-mail communication, Feb. 2. 2009.

13. George T. Springer, *Yumpin' Yimminy: Scandinavian Dialect Selections* (Long Prairie, MN: The Hart Publications, 1932). Anonymous, "Historic Papers Donated to Library: George Springer Collection," *Delta County Reporter,* Mar. 28, 1979.

14. Richard M. Dorson, "Dialect Stories from the Upper Peninsula: A New Form of American Folklore," *Journal of American Folklore* 61.240 (1948): 113–50.

15. George T. Springer, homemade tape recording (Minneapolis, ca. 1950); copy in Richard M. Dorson collection (Bloomington: Lilly Library, Indiana University).

16. Ulf Beijbom, "Swedes," in *Harvard Encyclopedia of American Ethnic Groups* (Cambridge, MA: Harvard University Press, 1980), 973–74; Harvey, "Swedish-American Theater"; Landis K. Magnuson, "Ole Olson and Companions as Others: Swedish-Dialect Characters and the Question of Scandinavian Acculturation," *Theatre History Studies* 28 (Tuscaloosa: University of Alabama Press, 2008), 64–111. Springer, *Yumpin' Yimminy,* 52–53. Powers Moulton, *2500 Jokes for All Occasions* (Philadelphia, PA: The Blakiston Company, Circle Books, 1942), 368.

17. Paul F. Anderson, e-mail communication, Sept. 14, 2009. Paul F. Anderson, *Scandimania: A Smorgasbord of Fun* (Minneapolis, MN: Eggs Press, 1985).

18. Paul F. Anderson, *Scandinavian Yokes* (Minneapolis, MN: Eggs Press, 1978, revised 1979), 31. Lindquist, *My Manasota Pals,* 55. I. S. "Mox" Lindquist, *Mr. Mox Stays Home* (Oberlin, OH: The author, 1965), 43.

19. Lawrence Welk, *Wunnerful, Wunnerful! The Autobiography of Lawrence Welk* (Englewood Cliffs, NJ: Prentice-Hall, 1971), 83.

20. Robert Heinze, tape-recorded interview with James P. Leary (Rice Lake, WI, July 14, 2008).

21. Julian West, *What a Card! The Story of Clellan Card and Axel and His Dog* (Edina, MN: Beaver's Pond Press, 2008), and Anonymous, "Clellan Card," *Wikipedia,* http://en.wikipedia.org/wiki/Clellan_Card. Red Stangland, *Norwegian Jokes* (Sioux Falls, SD: Norse Press), 1979. Bruce Danielson, interview, 2008.

22. Janet Letnes Martin and Suzann Nelson, *Those Lutheran Ladies: Live in Medora!* (Caragana Press CD E-2824, 2005), tracks 1 and 2.

23. Suzann Johnson Nelson, tape-recorded interview by James P. Leary (Moorhead, MN, June 29, 2008).

24. Nelson interview.

CHAPTER 6

Long after the Immigrant Language Shift

Swedish and Norwegian in Heritage Communities

ANGELA FALK

When Swedish and Norwegian emigrants left their home parishes to migrate to the United States, the status of their native languages for them and their families was no longer the same. The language contact they experienced with English as individuals and as groups set into motion a dynamic state of affairs that is still perceptible today in some communities. This chapter compares dimensions of the Swedish and Norwegian language-shift experiences and traces the basic trajectory for the two languages transplanted in the United States. Swedish and Norwegian, once immigrant languages spoken by hundreds of thousands of people across the United States in the 1800s and 1900s, have now also gained the status of so-called heritage languages.[1]

The Dynamism of Immigrant and Heritage Languages

To define the concept *heritage language,* it is useful to examine its semantics in relation to other terms frequently used for *languages other than English* (LOTES). The terminology for languages in the United States that are not English is numerous. Foreign language as a concept certainly amplifies the difference between English (the dominant language) and all others. In the educational world, the term *foreign language* brings to mind associations with, for example, courses in Spanish, French, German, and Latin that must be taken to satisfy degree requirements. At first glance *minority language* seems like a transparent term simply relating to any language that is not English and, by extension, any language spoken by fewer persons than English. Close inspection of U.S. Census figures (selecting results for "language spoken at home"), however, will reveal that minority languages actually are spoken by the "numerical majority" in many communities, including, for example, Hialeah, Florida; Laredo, Texas; East Los Angeles, California; and Brownsville, Texas. The United States and immigrant languages may be thought to go hand in hand, immigrant language here being linked with the (native) languages that are not English and that are spoken by people who seek residency in the United States. LOTES, used by Michael Clyne, has wide applicability thanks to the neutrality of the expression, but the term does not capture the dimension of identity formation for those who speak or wish to speak the LOTE. The term *heritage language* has been given considerable attention over the last decade by linguists and language education activists in the United States. As in the case of some of the terms above, the term *heritage language* encompasses linguistic as well as social dimensions. Joy Kreeft Peyton and Ann Kelleher defined it as a language "used to describe any of these connections between a non-dominant language and a person, a family, or a community."[2]

In focusing on the individual, Peyton wrote that the term *heritage language learner* "is used to describe a person studying a language who has proficiency in or a cultural connection to that language." In considering the phenomenon of heritage languages from the vantage point of an individual user, Guadalupe Valdés emphasized that "It is the historical and personal connection to the language that is salient and not the actual proficiency of individual speakers." Valdés's perspective is highly relevant in post-immigrant settings. She exemplified her viewpoint by identifying some types of heritage language learners. One type includes persons "raised in a home where a non-English language is spoken, who speak or only understand the heritage language, and who have some proficiency in English and the heritage language." This definition of heritage language learners is a broad mantle that readily accounts for numerous scenarios. It is worth identifying a range of heritage language proficiencies. One such example of this type of heritage language learner includes young adults—native speakers of English—who are bilingual to a great extent in Spanish thanks to their family life and who now study Spanish in a university classroom with the goal of acquiring greater proficiency in standard written and spoken Spanish. Another way to define heritage language learning is "the study, maintenance, and revitalization of non-English languages in the United States." The latter general definition does, of course, include learners with a high degree of functional proficiency, as in the case of the Spanish speakers described above, but it can also account for learners who have a high degree of connection, awareness, and self-affiliation to their heritage yet simultaneously relatively little observable proficiency in the heritage language itself. As will be discussed below in the section devoted to heritage language communities, the Swedish and Norwegian languages certainly function as heritage languages in places such as Lindsborg, Kansas, and Decorah, Iowa. Thus, for the vast majority of most individuals who have grown up in Swedish and Norwegian heritage communities, academic study of the heritage language would typically require focused effort to learn the fundamentals of grammatical patterns, even though the heritage learners may already have some passive knowledge and incipient linguistic skills that allow them to participate in a bilingual setting.[3]

Both types of hypothetical language students—persons already highly proficient in spoken Spanish but wishing to move toward greater bilingualism and

TABLE 6.1												
Real Bilinguals: A Continuum												
MONOLINGUAL						MONOLINGUAL						
Language "A" Example: Spanish Norwegian Swedish						Language "B" Example: English English English						
A	Ab	Ab	Ab	Ab	Ab	aB	Ba	Ba	Ba	Ba	Ba	B

the incipient speakers of Swedish and Norwegian—can be discussed within the framework of heritage language education, but a nuanced perspective of the definition of bilingualism is needed for a departure point. Valdés finds little support for perfectly matched bilingual proficiencies ("two monolinguals in one") within one individual. In her view, bilingualism nearly always exists in uneven or slightly uneven proportions within an individual. Table 6.1 is an adaptation of her conceptual model that characterizes real rather than mythical bilinguals.[4]

The Spanish speakers described above may be placed close to the midpoint of the bilingualism continuum as they indeed can have nearly dual abilities in two languages. In most cases, the Swedish Americans and Norwegian Americans who study their respective heritage language begin functionally at or near the "B" point of the continuum. Many of the students are monolingual speakers of English when they begin a course in Swedish or Norwegian. At the same time, however, their personal association with the heritage language may accelerate their already strong instrumental motivation, possibly propelling the heritage language learners closer to the midpoint, modeled in table 6.1, for Swedish or Norwegian proficiency. If we had applied this conceptual model to the Swedish American and Norwegian American communities in the 1910s and 1920s, when proportionately many more immigrant language speakers were alive in the ethnic communities, then young persons studying Swedish and Norwegian at college and university levels would undoubtedly have possessed similar bilingual proficiency as the hypothesized Spanish students described above. Now, nearly a century after the major language shift in Swedish American and Norwegian American communities, the Swedish and Norwegian languages for young adults are less commonly first-generation immigrant languages; U.S. Census figures surveyed in the following sections will provide support for this interpretation. Swedish and Norwegian languages are nonetheless something more than objects of foreign language study. In the next section, we will examine the language shift, with milestones in the 1910s and 1920s, that radically altered the ethnic communities and set the stage for heritage language maintenance.

Historical Dimensions of Heritage Language Formation in Norwegian American and Swedish American Communities

Joshua A. Fishman enumerated three categories of heritage languages in the United States: *indigenous heritage languages, colonial heritage languages,* and *immigrant heritage languages.* Applying his terminology to the Swedish American and Norwegian American community contexts is a fairly straightforward task. Neither language was, of course, an indigenous language in the United States. Swedish can claim—but only very tenuously—the status of a colonial heritage language because of the establishment of the New Sweden Colony in 1638 along the Delaware River near Wilmington, Delaware. Even so, the rubric *colonial heritage language* to designate the place Swedish has held in the United States pales considerably in importance when we turn to its status as an immigrant heritage language, as both Swedish and Norwegian have held in the United States. The number of Swedish immigrants approximated 1.2 million persons between the years 1850 and 1930, and the number of Norwegian immigrants approximated 810,000 persons between the years 1825 and 1925, the time frame when most of the organized immigration took place.[5]

With such expansive and protracted immigration, intergenerational transmission of the heritage languages has not only been observable on a family basis but also readily perceived on a community basis and readily tracked nationally. Thanks to older records in the U.S. Census, chiefly those that categorized foreign-born residents according to their mother tongues, national trends are traceable. Fishman and John E. Hofman examined the "U.S. Census of Population 1960: General Social and Economic Characteristics," deriving a table in which they presented the number of foreign-born white persons in the conterminus United States classified by mother tongue. Examining data across a fifty-year range, decades 1910 through 1960, Fishman and Hofman noted a pattern that affected many immigrant nationalities:

> Since 1930 most languages have consistently revealed declining numbers of claimants. Even the few departures from this general rule usually require no additional explanatory concepts. For example, in some cases the decline becomes apparent in 1920, although mass immigration was still underway during the previous decade. Thus Norwegian, Swedish, French, and German were less frequently claimed as mother tongues by foreign-born individuals in 1920 than in 1910. This is understandable in

terms of the relatively early northern and western European immigra-
tions which brought speakers of these languages to the United States.
During the second decade of the present century and even before, these
early immigrants who had arrived in large numbers between 1840 and
1860 were dying out. Mother tongue data for 1910 and 1920 undoubtedly
reflect this natural generational turnover in the case of northern and
western European languages.[6]

Already here it is useful to consider the dynamic language situation that
affected various generations of Swedes and Norwegians in the midst of their
protracted migration to the United States and to note the respective peaks and
dips in the numbers of speakers. Looking at table 6.2 below, one can see that the
number of Swedish mother-tongue claimants is higher than the number of Norwegian mother-tongue claimants in every column, that is, 1960, 1940, 1930, 1920,
and 1910. Despite the obvious numerical difference in every column between the
Swedish and Norwegian speakers, we can note an important correspondence:
the peak number of claimants in this table for Swedish speakers was recorded in
1910 (with 683,218 claimants), and the peak number of claimants for Norwegian
speakers in this table was also recorded in 1910 (with 402,587 claimants). The
lowest number of respective speakers on this table is reported in 1960, when
the total number of Swedish speakers falls to 211,597 and the total number of
Norwegian speakers falls to 140,774.[7]

While these numbers readily summarize the census trends in immigrant communities over five intervals, it is only when we examine the richly contextualized

TABLE 6.2

**Mother Tongue of the Foreign Born, for the United States, Urban and Rural, 1960,
and of the Foreign-Born White for Conterminous United States, 1910 to 1940**

	United States—Total foreign born, 1960				Conterminous United States Foreign-born White			
MOTHER TONGUE	TOTAL	URBAN	RURAL NONFARM	RURAL FARM	1940	1930	1920	1910
Total	9,738,143	8,510,152	1,007,621	220,370	11,109,620	13,983,405	13,712,754	13,345,545
English	1,852,992	1,614,686	213,976	24,330	2,506,420	3,097,021	3,007,932	3,363,792
Norwegian	140,774	107,902	24,332	8,540	232,820	345,522	362,199	402,587
Swedish	211,597	171,062	31,897	8,638	423,200	615,465	643,203	683,218
Danish	79,619	61,035	13,331	5,253	122,180	178,944	189,531	186,345
Dutch	123,613	97,686	17,394	8,533	102,700	133,142	136,540	126,045
French	330,220	278,125	45,533	6,562	359,520	523,297	466,956	528,842

Source: Mother tongue claimants, Fishman and Hofman, *Mother Tongue and Nativity in the American Population*, 36.
Note that only a portion of Fishman and Hofman's original table is reproduced here.

analyses performed by Nils Hasselmo and Einar Haugen that we can appreciate how the language shift affected networks of speakers of Swedish and Norwegian. Hasselmo and Haugen conducted expansive and thoroughgoing fieldwork in the Swedish American and Norwegian American communities, respectively. The linguists followed the so-called language question that was publically discussed and debated in the congregations of the Swedish and Norwegian immigrant communities. The patterns of language shift uncovered by Hasselmo's and Haugen's work are strikingly similar. By the 1920s, the public use of the respective immigrant languages dropped dramatically and the use of English surged ahead. Both scholars traced evidence for the language of publications (for both the church and secular worlds). When looking at archival materials available for the Swedish American Lutheran church community, Hasselmo uncovered, for example, publication evidence available for the Augustana Synod (with its home in Rock Island, Illinois) and the Augustana Book Concern, and he examined data from the 1890s through approximately the middle of the 1950s. For books, he tracked the numbers of titles in each language as well as the size of the edition for each title; for serial publications, he tracked the number of subscribers of the publications *Augustana* (in Swedish) and the *Lutheran Companion* (in English). Obvious trajectories for publications in Swedish and English are readily perceptible in the figures Hasselmo prepared based on the publication data. The number of Swedish publications and the sizes of these editions reached their peak between the years 1910 and 1915. The number of subscribers to the Swedish *Augustana* also reached its peak by 1915. While spoken Swedish is more difficult to estimate and express in precise numbers for this time period, Hasselmo found that as many as 85 percent of the sermons in the sanctuaries of the Augustana Synod were still given in Swedish by 1921. This sizeable percentage in itself gives the impression of linguistic stability in favor of retaining the Swedish language in a formal, institutional setting, but only four years later the synod adopted its first complete order of service in English. Concerning the Augustana Synod in the United States, Hasselmo wrote, "Although no decision to adopt English as the language of the Synod was ever made, English must be considered its official language after the middle of the 1930s." By looking at records for Sunday schools and Swedish language schools, especially in Minnesota, the location of some of the most tightly knit Swedish settlements, Hasselmo was able to say that "By the end of the 1920s, very few children were learning the language of their ancestors."[8]

Not surprisingly, this generational and linguistic shift was the topic of commentary published by church and cultural leaders in the 1920s. Gustav Andreen, then president of Augustana College, Rock Island, Illinois, was one of the contributors to chapters appearing in a massive, two-part volume entitled *Svenskarna i Amerika: Populär historisk skildring* published in Stockholm in 1926. Andreen wrote a lengthy survey of the Augustana Synod and its activities:

Ett ord torde tarvas om språkfrågan. Det svenska språket brukas som gudstjänstspråk, omväxlande med engelskan, i över ett tusen av våra församlingar. I något hundratal församlingar nyttjas enbart engelskan. Den frågan ställes ofta till oss: Kommer ej svenskan i Amerika att leva till evärdelig tid? Det våga vi ej tro. Den övertygelsen tränger sig på var och en, som undersöker amerikanska förhållanden, att i längden engelskan nog kommer att bliva det allenahärskande språket. Och i stort sett är kanske ej annat att önska.

One word would need to be said on the language question. The Swedish language is used as the language of church services alternating with English in over one thousand of our congregations. There are a few hundred or so congregations that use only English. The following question is frequently asked of us: Will the Swedish language in America not live an eternal life? We dare not believe so. The realization hits each and every person who examines the conditions in America that English will probably become the completely dominant language in the long run. And on the whole there would perhaps not be any other outcome to hope for.[9]

In the same volume, G. N. Malm contributed a sketch with the title "En sommardag på Jan Swansons farm." In the piece rich with dialogue—undoubtedly influenced by Malm's thorough connections to Lindsborg, Kansas—the parents speak Swedish combined with ample lexical items in English. Members of the younger generation answer their elders in English. In describing some of the linguistic characteristics, low status, and incipient demise of the immigrant mixed language used by the parents, Malm wrote:

Det är ett besynnerligt språk, detta blandspråk, vars tillvaro ofta förnekas, t.o.m. av dem, som själva begagna sig därav. Nöden är ju ofta uppfinningarnas moder, och det hederliga svensk-amerikanska språket har nog tillkommit av nöd. Ytterst få av de invandrade farmarna i västern ha någonsin talat rikssvenska, och deras ordförråd var, då de togo det stora steget, ej vidare stort. [...] I mån som han kommit i kontakt med nya föremål, termer och tankar, har hans språk blivit en behändig blandning av småländska, västgötska, skånska, dalska och engelska ord, och som grammatiken har djupa rötter, så ha orden fått svensk böjning och satsbildningen blivit svensk. Detta har gjort ett lika befängt som invecklat språk, som, populärt och användbart, nu fått tjänstgöra i två generationer. Huru länge det kommer att leva, är svårt att avgöra, men det är nu, sedan den tredje generationen kommit att ta ledningen, på stark upphällning och kommer väl att läggas på hyllan, det som allt annat obrukbart, när den tiden kommer.

It is a strange language, this mixed language, whose existence is often denied, even by the ones who use it. As necessity is the mother of invention, the decent Swedish-American language has probably emerged out of necessity. Very few of the farmers who immigrated to the West have ever spoken Standard Swedish, and their vocabulary was not all that large when they took the great step to come here . . . To the extent that the farmer came into contact with new items, terms, and thoughts, his language became a handy mix of Småländska, Västgötska, Skånska, Dalska, and English words, and because grammar has such deep roots, the words have gotten Swedish endings, and the sentence structure has stayed Swedish. All this has made a language just as absurd as it is complicated; popular and useful, it now has gotten to do its duty for two generations. How long it will survive is difficult to determine, but (it is) now when the third generation has come to take leadership that the language is on a steep decline and will probably be put aside, just as everything else that is not of use, when that time comes.[10]

Certainly the bilingualism in Lindsborg and in similar places always existed as fluctuating proportions of Swedish and English linguistic elements, as Malm suggested. Malm's description and depiction of mixed Swedish and English readily exemplifies a cross-generational progression of table 6.1 presented in the section above. The first generation of Swedish immigrants was faced with new concepts in the United States and therefore expanded its lexicon, deriving a functional vocabulary comprised of lexical elements from native regional dialects and English. One could say that from the starting point /A/, all Swedish, they rapidly moved to /Ab/. Despite the mixed language origin of the vocabulary, it was adapted to fit morphological patterning of Swedish. Malm suggested that the mixed language had been functional for two generations but by the third generation had diminished. Extrapolating from Malm's observations, we could say that the third generation, now clearly more proficient in English, can be modeled in the /Ba/ range of the continuum depicted in table 6.1.[11]

The language shift chronology traced above for the Swedish American communities bears striking similarity to the language shift patterns in the Norwegian American communities. Tracking the language shift in Norwegian networks, including Norwegian Lutheran congregations, Haugen had surveyed the language question vantage points similar to those used by Hasselmo. Haugen's research reveals, for example, that approximately 22 percent of the sermons given in the Norwegian Lutheran churches were in English already by the year 1915. Even if by extension this means that nearly 80 percent of the sermons in the congregations were still given in Norwegian at this time, one could reasonably argue that the language used in sermons and the official order of service may actually reveal more about the exposure adults had in a given congregation than did their children. From 1915, according to Haugen, the language shift in the Norwegian churches took place with great pace. The watershed year appeared a decade later in 1925, when the Norwegian Lutheran Church first used the English language more frequently in their services than Norwegian. Individual congregations navigated the language question in a series of moves that Haugen summarized with great clarity:

> The decision in each congregation was reached by a vote of the members, with each change fought through by the younger members against a certain opposition from the older ones. While the precise course of this change was different in each congregation, the typical pattern was to begin with the introduction of an occasional English service, on Sunday afternoon or evening. Then would come parallel services, and a gradual fading out of the attendance at the Norwegian ones. In time the Norwegian services became the occasional ones, held at scattered intervals and inconvenient times.[12]

Haugen also consulted records revealing the language use of Sunday schools and confirmation classes, discovering that the year 1928 is the point when one can say with great certainty that Norwegian was no longer being used as the language of instruction. That date is very significant, because it proved to be the year that official documents of the Norwegian Lutheran Church were published in English rather than Norwegian. Interestingly, the language question in the secular sectors of Norwegian American society was apparently not firmly settled until later in the century. It was not until 1942, according to Haugen, that the fraternal organization Sons of Norway changed the language of its publications to English. The results for the church world and its related organizations are particularly fascinating for an apparent paradox: a massive organization with a high amount of formalized governance and infrastructure was nonetheless amenable to change. Ultimately it looked to strategies for prosperity and survival.[13]

As Haugen and Hasselmo tracked the presence over time of the immigrant languages in the ethnic communities, they were, in effect, identifying and measuring the "tempo of assimilation," chiefly the trajectory that the immigrant languages followed as community groups turned to English for an increasing number of functions. Already by the 1950s, Haugen was thinking in terms of ethnic-linguistic comparative bases. Haugen's investigation of this trajectory, in his words, monitored the "linguistic retentiveness" of Norwegian, especially in the Upper Midwest; he even went so far in his analysis to consider and compare the linguistic retentiveness of the Norwegians in the United States with other European American groups, including the Swedes. In order to accomplish this, he considered the feasibility of calculating ratios of persons of a specified immigrant background and their language use to come up with an *index of retention*. Even though he identified and described some emerging patterns, he was cautious about drawing any sweeping conclusions, explaining, "It appears that linguistic retentiveness is correlated with such factors as rural, i.e. isolated settlement; recency of arrival; size of group; religious separatism; social visibility. But exceptions occur to all of these factors to such an extent that it is not always easy to see just why a given nationality should be placed where it is in the scale." A bit later in his text he wrote "It is obvious that such conclusions would be more convincing and concrete if they were bolstered by studies of local communities where various ethnic groups could be directly compared."[14]

The quantitative evidence presented in Fishman and Hofman, as well as the fine-tuned analyses of quantitative and qualitative data performed by Hasselmo and Haugen, clearly revealed the similar trajectories of Swedish and Norwegian as immigrant languages in the United States. The following section presents some basic contemporary data extracted from the U.S. Census in order to prepare the backdrop for discussion of the current presence of the Swedish and Norwegian languages in two communities.

Census Data: Comparisons between Swedish Americans and Norwegian Americans

Over the decades of the 1900s, the number of claimants in the U.S. Census who reported Swedish and Norwegian language use dropped remarkably. The numbers of respective mother-tongue claimants in 1960, according to the figures presented by Fishman and Hofman, were below half of what they had been in 1910 (see table 6.2). In the 1990 Census, the number of claimants of Swedish and Norwegian (languages used at home) was well below half of the number identified in 1960. Even so, Swedish and Norwegian have continued to figure relatively prominently in the census with regard to the categories pertaining to *languages* and *ancestry*. By consulting one of the major tables published as part of the 1990 U.S. Census, one finds that the Swedish and Norwegian languages rank very similarly, as both are included in the group of languages referred to as "the 50 languages with greatest number of speakers." In that particular census report, Norwegian held thirty-first place; Swedish held thirty-third place.[15]

Ancestry is defined by the U.S. Census Bureau "as a person's ethnic origin, heritage, descent, or 'roots,' which may reflect their place of birth, place of birth of parents or ancestors, and ethnic identities that have evolved within the United States." Respondents to the U.S. Census questionnaire may state up to two answers pertaining to their ancestry or ethnic origin. Before we consider additional details in census reports concerning ancestry and its relationship to language, some caveats should be mentioned. Ancestry and linguistic use are not synonymous. The language people speak at home is not always synonymous with their ancestry. Persons without Swedish or Norwegian heritage might, of course, speak these languages at home if various educational and social paths in their lives have brought them into close contact with the languages. As we can deduce from the numbers of claimants for the two ancestries, the vast majority of persons with Swedish and Norwegian heritage do not speak these languages at home.[16]

Data pertaining to ancestry for Americans can be readily obtained in the U.S. Census reports for 1980, 1990, 2000, and beyond, and it is possible to make some general comparisons between claimants' answers concerning Swedish and Norwegian ancestry. Claimants for both groups have hovered around the four million person point, which has the consequence that the two ancestries maintain positions in the so-called largest ancestry groups in the United States. Persons claiming Swedish ancestry were more numerous than Norwegians in the 1980 Census report (Swedish ancestry: 4,345,392; Norwegian ancestry: 3,453,839). In the 1990 U.S. Census report, Swedish was again claimed more times than Norwegian in the ancestry question (claimants of Swedish ancestry numbered 4,680,863; claimants of Norwegian ancestry, 3,869,395). The trend was reversed a decade later. The 2000 Census revealed that more persons claimed Norwegian than Swedish ancestry (claimants with Norwegian ancestry: 4,477,725, equivalent to 1.6 percent of the total U.S. population; claimants with Swedish ancestry: 3,998,310, equivalent to 1.4 percent of the total U.S. population). These slight differences aside, it is nonetheless the case that claimed Swedish and Norwegian ancestries continue to appear in the largest ancestry groups, comprising the groups whose ancestry is claimed by approximately four million or more persons. More recently, data available from the *Statistical Abstract of the United States* confirm a similar trend in which slightly higher numbers of persons have reported Norwegian ancestry (approximately 4,656,000 individuals) compared to Swedish ancestry (approximately 4,340,00 persons). Even so, the differences are even slighter than before.[17]

The final part of this chapter will identify some of the main ways that the Swedish and Norwegian languages in the United States serve as heritage languages for many speakers. My examples are selected from two communities: one in Kansas and the other in Iowa. I will consider the extent to which Swedish Americans and Norwegian Americans as speaker groups reveal similar phenomena and processes with respect to heritage languages. As we will see, ample evidence suggests that the communities have responded to the immigrant language shift in some similar, but not identical, ways.

Heritage Language Communities: Lindsborg, Kansas, and Decorah, Iowa

This chapter heretofore has traced language shift generally in the Swedish American and Norwegian American communities. It proceeds now to focus on Lindsborg, Kansas (population 3,251), and Decorah, Iowa (population 7,865). Both towns are the homes of private, liberal arts colleges founded by Swedish and Norwegian Lutherans: Bethany College in 1881 and Luther College in 1861. Both colleges readily highlight their ethnic origins on their homepages. An additional and striking similarity between the two communities is their large-scale public festivals with obvious Scandinavian heritage themes. Lindsborg observes Svensk Hyllningsfest biannually in October, coinciding with the homecoming festivities of Bethany College. Decorah holds its Nordic Fest annually in July. Some of the heritage language elements of these community-wide festivals will figure below.[18]

According to the *2005–2009 American Community Survey 5-year Estimates,* a relatively large percentage of residents in these communities claimed Swedish and Norwegian ancestry, respectively. During this time frame, more than 1,069 residents of Lindsborg claimed Swedish ancestry, equivalent to 32.9 percent of the population. In fact, this percentage is higher than any other community where a Swedish American Lutheran college is located. In Decorah, more than 2,673 residents claimed Norwegian ancestry, equivalent to 34 percent of the population. Concerning claimed Norwegian ancestry, Decorah stands well ahead of all other communities with Norwegian American Lutheran colleges.[19]

Many linguists and language educators work tirelessly to encourage institutional support for heritage languages and to promote multilingualism in the face of the globalization of English. In the small towns of Lindsborg and Decorah, it is not possible to claim that wide-scale institutional support has been mobilized to teach fluent use of the heritage languages, but numerous opportunities do exist for individuals and groups to express affiliation with Swedish and Norwegian heritages, respectively. Simultaneously, the Swedish and Norwegian languages are given a position of respect, even if the reverence is not typically accompanied by community proficiency on a wide scope. Space limitations do not permit a highly detailed catalogue of the numbers of speakers and their estimated proficiencies. Instead, this section identifies some of the ways that the heritage languages survive and receive attention from community organizations, public schools, and the colleges.[20]

Lindsborg shows robust signs of community acknowledgement of Swedish, and this support comes from various sources. On one hand, there is a highly concerted effort on the part of the chamber of commerce, various retail merchants, and the local newspaper, the *Lindsborg News-Record,* to use Swedish lexical items regularly and on a large scale. For decades, at least one very prominent Swedish

word has been emblazoned on billboard signs along interstate and state highways leading to Lindsborg. One of them declared "Välkommen / Lindsborg /
Little Sweden USA." As mentioned above, the town organizes large public festivals, one bearing a Swedish-language name, Svensk Hyllningsfest. Visitors to
the town cannot help but notice that many businesses have Swedish names
(Öl Stuga, Apotek, Hemslöjd, Axel's) and that certain community-wide services are identified with Swedish names or partial Swedish names (for example,
Biblioteket and the Välkommen Trail, "Lindsborg's 2.5 mile bicycle and pedes-
trian trail," with membership possibilities to join the Vandringsklubb [walking
club]). Many other businesses, community services, and community facilities
identify themselves with dual English and Swedish names on their signs (one
such sign reads Bethania Kyrka Parkering/ Bethany Church Parking Lot).

The individual lexical items on signs and in print advertising must also be
seen in relation to some other heritage language efforts, many of them less
obvious to tourists. One active social club, Svenska Vänskapsgruppen (The
Swedish Friendship Group), places the Swedish language and topics concerning
Scandinavia foremost on their agenda. The group, consisting of approximately
twenty-five regular members, holds weekly meetings and works together on
Swedish lessons focusing on grammar and vocabulary. At nearly every meeting,
the group members recite the Lord's Prayer in Swedish *(Fader Vår)*, and when
visitors from Sweden are present at meetings, the members sing the national
anthem, *Du Gamla Du Fria*. Svenska Vänskapsgruppen exists entirely as a volunteer phenomenon and has maintained steady membership thanks to the link
participants feel toward their heritage language. Some of the very oldest members
learned to speak Swedish as children growing up in the Lindsborg area, and a few
of the members were born in Sweden. Membership in this club is certainly open
to anyone who expresses an interest in Swedish and Scandinavia, but the majority of the participants are in their seventies, eighties, and nineties, free to attend
the regular meetings held 10:00 on Friday mornings in the Martin Luther meeting room of Bethany Lutheran Church. Svenska Vänskapsgruppen is also highly
involved in organizing an annual worship service in Swedish, the *Annandag Jul*
service (observed the day after Christmas), held at Bethany Lutheran Church.[21]

Younger residents in Lindsborg also have some regular opportunities to learn
Swedish beyond simply the lexical items printed on signs and in local advertisements. All pupils at Soderstrom Elementary School are taught Swedish songs
(among them the hymn *Tryggare Kan Ingen Vara* and the national anthem), many
of which are performed at the official opening ceremony of Svensk Hyllningsfest
and at various school-organized holiday visits to Bethany Lutheran Church and
to Bethany Home. Likewise, they learn vocabulary for food items, also part of seasonal preparations. Swedish is no longer taught in the local high school, although
it was many decades ago. Teenagers who are interested in Swedish and Swedish

heritage may join the Lindsborg Swedish Folk Dancers, billed as an ambassador group for the community. At regular intervals, approximately every three or four years, the group travels to Sweden to perform at various summer events and festivals. The official 2010–11 course catalog for Bethany College included *Elementary Swedish I* and *Elementary Swedish II,* but the college does not offer a program of major study in Swedish or Scandinavian studies (see, however, the discussion of Luther College, below). Even so, a relatively recent donation to the college has created the Pearson Distinguished Professor of Swedish Studies, a rotating professorial chair that brings Swedish scholars from various disciplines to Bethany for an extended period of residency. The Bethany College Choir plans regular tours to Sweden, the most recent having taken place during 2008.[22]

Up to this point in the inventory of Swedish as a heritage language in Lindsborg, the reader may have the clear impression that conversational abilities in Swedish are highly age graded—that proficiency in Swedish is linked in a predictable way with generational categories. So too might Swedish as a heritage language seem explicitly Lutheran from an organizational standpoint. These two observations certainly lend themselves to empirical testing. However, some additional details will give a more comprehensive view of Swedish in Lindsborg. These details involve some individual family constellations that have provided for intergenerational transmission of Swedish as well as some supralocal opportunities.

In a few cases, the transmission of Swedish still occurs within a couple of families across generations. Some relatively recent immigrants to Lindsborg (recent in the sense of some decades ago) have in turn raised their children to be bilingual—islands of bilingualism in the heritage language community. In other cases, a couple of Swedish Americans in the third or fourth generation have been sufficiently motivated to learn Swedish to the extent that they have built upon their initial, basic exposure in Lindsborg by expanding it greatly through guided self-study, study abroad, and regular visits to Sweden. These third- or fourth-generation Swedish Americans have clearly made use of supralocal opportunities. Such Swedish Americans might have felt strong affiliation to Swedish because of the values held by their parents and grandparents, but they have gained linguistic proficiency in Swedish thanks to some educational opportunities that they themselves have pursued. Furthermore, as they live in Lindsborg, they have peripheral support when they practice Swedish with community residents who are members of Svenska Vänskapsgruppen or members of the families mentioned previously. In addition, steady streams of Swedish visitors come to Lindsborg. The professorial chair at Bethany adds a layer of support, as do the many groups of Swedish musicians and folk dancers who perform at Svensk Hyllningsfest and at the annual midsummer festival.

In 2009 the *Lindsborg News-Record* began to feature some opportunities for supralocal support for the Swedish language in Lindsborg. Readers may have noticed a brief article providing details on how young persons could apply for a scholarship to attend the Swedish language camp known as Sjölunden and operated in Minnesota by Concordia Language Villages. Approximately one month later, the *Lindsborg News-Record* ran another brief article, this time reporting that the Svensk Hyllningsfest committee had received grant money to support a program item identified as "Swedish in 30 minutes." The brief article, which accompanied a photo, read as follows:

HYLLNINGSFEST CLASS RECEIVES GRANT
[A] representative of the Smoky Valley Community Foundation, attended the May Svensk Hyllningsfest committee meeting to present the check for the spring 2009 Heritage Fund Grant that the committee received. The funds will go toward a special "Swedish in 30 minutes" class that will be taught throughout Hyllningsfest weekend. Receiving the check were festival co-chairs . . . [23]

The expression of heritage language phenomena and affiliation in Lindsborg appears to be multifaceted. A survey of heritage language phenomena and affiliation is clearly multifaceted in Decorah as well. In Decorah, ample printed lexical evidence of Norwegian linguistic heritage meets the eyes of visitors. As in Lindsborg, the community clearly affirms its ancestry, in part through popular, public festivals. The Nordic Fest (forty-fifth annual as of July 2011) produces an extensive printed program that contains not only relevant logistic information concerning what to see and do but also a few Norwegian texts. The lyrics of the Norwegian national anthem are contained there along with a fairly long glossary of Norwegian items. Elsewhere in the program, Norwegian lexical items are used to name sporting events (*Kanoløpet* [canoe race]; *Elveløpet* [river run]; and Lutefisk Eating Contest), to distinguish various styles of painting that will be demonstrated (rosemaling, categorized by some Norwegian place-names including Telemark-style, Hallingdal-style, Valdres-style, and Agder-style), and to identify food items (see Glossary of Norwegian Terms listing, among other items, *Kranskake, Kringle, Krumkake, Lefse, Rømmegrøt, Sandbakkels,* and *Varme pølse*). Entertainment options include a number of clearly designated Norwegian-language offerings, the most striking: "Ethan Bjelland—will teach you 'Norwegian in a Nutshell' in a way that is easy and enjoyable for all." Multiple other performers sing in Norwegian. Of the many church services listed in the program, two stand out for their explicit connections to Norwegian as a heritage language: "Decorah Lutheran Church . . . Old Norwegian/English service from Black Hymnal . . ." and "First Lutheran Church . . . Traditional Norwegian Service in English."[24]

In addition to this annual festival, other Decorah organizations anchor or showcase the expression of Norwegian identity. Vesterheim Norwegian-American Museum does not teach courses in the Norwegian language but offers an extensive range of courses in Norwegian handcrafts. Many, if not most, of the handcraft traditions are identified with Norwegian lexical items. The regularly scheduled Children's Hour is known as *Barnetimen,* according to details provided on the homepage. Another Norwegian anchor in the community is Luther College, clearly a heritage language stronghold. Students can major in Scandinavian studies, which contains a core of multiple courses in Norwegian readily augmented by study abroad possibilities in Norway. Norwegian had been taught in Decorah High School until recent decades, but Spanish has replaced it on the curriculum. In cases where high school students are highly motivated to study Norwegian, they are eligible to enroll in the college-level courses at Luther, thanks to a cooperative arrangement with the local school district. Another possible way (a so-called supralocal option; see the Lindsborg discussion above) for young people to study Norwegian is in Minnesota, at the Norwegian camp organized by Concordia Language Villages. Elementary school pupils are not taught Norwegian, but the Vesterheim Museum arranges for a so-called immigration and pioneer unit, where children are exposed to some Norwegian lexical items. The focus of this unit, which is called an *immersion experience,* is not on language but on the pioneer lifestyle.[25]

Heritage Languages in Lindsborg and Decorah: Languages on Parallel Tracks

The perceptible presence of heritage languages many decades after language shift reveals a number of things, suggesting that Swedish and Norwegian are on parallel tracks. Heritage languages are important in the communities, which show signs of creative efforts to attract further interest in the languages. The presence of Swedish and Norwegian lexical items is readily noticeable. For the most part, the current state of the heritage languages is not so much maintenance or preservation of the languages as *full* linguistic systems that have been passed from one generation to another in a chain of unbroken linguistic transmission but generally *partial* linguistic systems. The possibility of such on a large, community-wide scale did indeed pass away many decades earlier, as we know from the passionate discourse that was part of the "language question" debate and from the quantitative data that clearly show the steep decline in the numbers of mother tongue speakers. It is true that some recent immigrants have settled, for example, in Lindsborg, and on this scale of individual families they have reinstituted unbroken linguistic transmission by using Swedish with their children, who are bilingual. But for the communities as a whole, heritage language transmission does not now result from inter-generationally transmitted vernaculars following the lines of the family tree without a break. Full linguistic systems are taught in college-level courses and spoken by, for example, some members of Svenska Vänskapsgruppen. Even so, on the wide-scale community levels of the two towns, the goal with the heritage language efforts appears to be to emphasize connections and fun. Some residents of the towns in several generations may indeed aim to become speakers with native-like proficiency, but motivation for many people to learn some portions of the languages seems to be fueled by the desire to connect with other people who also treasure their ancestral roots.[26]

Joshua A. Fishman, scholar of linguistic sociology who has advocated linguistic human rights for decades, has investigated language maintenance from a number of angles, including his own experience. In the preface to *In Praise of the Beloved Language: A Comparative View of Positive Ethnolinguistic Consciousness,* he writes about an exercise he has used over the years with numerous audience groups. He reports that, without fail, when he showed any audience a passage about language shift, audience members would identify the shifting language scene as their own:

> For years before I began teaching about language and ethnicity in this "insider" fashion, I began collecting bits of evidence (citations) revealing the positive things that people all over the world had said and were still saying about their traditionally associated "beloved" languages. Often I would read a citation about Language X to an advocate of Language Z and ask him or her to "Guess what language this is about." In almost all cases they would guess it was about their own "beloved language" (although it never was) and that gave me the idea that the content of language praises might really be quite parsimoniously structured the world over.[27]

When it comes to the heritage language expression of Swedish and Norwegian in the communities discussed in this article, the evidence examined to date suggests that the "beloved languages"—while different—nonetheless exhibit extremely similar phenomena.

Notes

1. I wish to thank Dag Blanck for numerous discussions that stimulated my thinking on this topic, Barbara Hoffman and Erik Falk for their support while I prepared the text, and Åke Eriksson for his technical help in preparing the tables. I am indebted to persons in Lindsborg, Kansas, and Decorah, Iowa, who not only answered my numerous queries but offered firsthand observations: Maj-Britt Hawk, Martha Griesheimer, and Rhonda

Thompson. I express my gratitude to the Department of English and Språkvetenskapliga fakulteten, Uppsala University, which supported my research with some teaching- and administrative-leave time in fall 2009.

2. Michael Clyne, *Dynamics of Language Contact*, Cambridge Approaches to Language Contact (Cambridge: Cambridge University Press, 2003), 17. Joy Kreeft Peyton, ed. (with Ann Kelleher), "Frequently Asked Questions about Heritage Languages in the United States," (Washington, DC: Center for Applied Linguistics, 2008), available: http://www.cal.org/heritage/research/faqs.html, p. 3.

Information on minority languages was extracted from the publication "Language Use and English-Speaking Ability, 2000: Census. 2000 Brief." See especially table 4: "Ten Places of 100,000 or More Population with the Highest Percentage of People 5 Years and Over Who Spoke a Language Other Than English at Home . . ." p. 9. See www.census.gov.

See, for example, links available on the homepage to the Center for Applied Linguistics (CAL) in Washington, DC: http://www.cal.org/heritage/research/index.html.

3. Quote from Donna Patrick, "Review of *Heritage Languages in America*," *Applied Linguistics* 25 (2004): 273–77; citing Valdés (p. 274), "Heritage Language Students." Available: http://applij.oxfordjournals.org/cgi/content/citation/25/2/273. See also: Peyton and Kelleher, "Frequently Asked Questions," 5. Guadalupe Valdés, "Heritage Language Students: Profiles and Possibilities," *Heritage Languages in America: Preserving a National Resource*, ed. Joy Kreeft Peyton, Donald A. Ranard, and Scott McGinnis (Washington, DC, and McHenry, IL: Center for Applied Linguistics and Delta Systems, 2001), 38, 39–40.

For studies focusing on conversational settings between highly proficient speakers of heritage languages and incipient bilinguals, see Nancy C. Dorian, "Defining the Speech Community to Include Its Working Margins," in *Sociolinguistic Variation in Speech Communities*, ed. Suzanne Romaine (London: Arnold, 1982), 25–33, and Angela Falk, "Narratives at the Crossroads of Generations and Languages," *Studia Neophilologica* 81.2 (2009): 145–60.

4. Valdés, "Heritage Language Students," 40.

5. Joshua A. Fishman, "300-plus Years of Heritage Language Education in the United States," in Peyton, Ranard, and McGinnis, eds., *Heritage Languages in America*, 81–87; cited also in Peyton and Kelleher, "Frequently Asked Questions," 2008: 3–4. See also Nils Hasselmo, *Swedish America: An Introduction* (New York: Swedish Information Service, 1976), 9–10; Axel Fredenholm, "Kolonien Nya Sverige," in *Svenskarna i Amerika. Populär historisk skildring*, ed. Karl Hildebrand and Axel Fredenholm (Stockholm: Historiska förlaget, 1926), 90–115.

Swedish migration for the time period of massive immigration to the United States is discussed in, for example, Hasselmo, *Swedish America*; Lars Ljungmark, *Swedish Exodus* (Carbondale and Edwardsville: Southern Illinois University Press, 1979); H. Arnold Barton, *A Folk Divided: Homeland Swedes and Swedish Americans, 1840–1940*, Studia multiethnica Upsaliensia 10 (Uppsala: Acta Universitatis Upsaliensis, 1994); Dag Blanck and Harald Runblom, eds., *Swedish Life in American Cities*, Uppsala Multiethnic Papers 21 (Uppsala: Centre for Multiethnic Research, 1991); and Dag Blanck, *Becoming Swedish-American:*

The Construction of an Ethnic Identity in the Augustana Synod, 1860–1917, Studia historica Upsaliensia 182 (Uppsala: Acta Universitatis Upsaliensis, 1997). See Einar Haugen, *The Norwegian Language in America: A Study in Bilingual Behavior,* 2nd ed. (Bloomington: Indiana University Press, 1969), 25–28, for analysis of Norwegian migration.

6. Regional and community contacts are detailed in, for example, articles in June Drenning Holmquist, ed., *They Chose Minnesota: A Survey of the State's Ethnic Groups* (St. Paul: Minnesota Historical Society Press, 1981), and Robert C. Ostergren, *A Community Transplanted: The Trans-Atlantic Experience of a Swedish Immigrant Settlement in the Upper Middle West, 1835–1915,* Studia multiethnica Upsaliensia 4 (Uppsala: Acta Universitatis Upsaliensis, 1988).

See "Table 2.1 Mother Tongue of the Foreign Born, for the United States, Urban and Rural, 1960, and of the Foreign-born White for Conterminous United States, 1910 to 1940," in Joshua A. Fishman and John E. Hofman, "Mother Tongue and Nativity in the American Population," in *Language Loyalty in the United States: The Maintenance and Perpetuation of Non-English Mother Tongues by American Ethnic and Religious Groups,* ed. Joshua A. Fishman (London: Mouton, 1966), 36, quote 35.

7. Fishman and Hofman, "Mother Tongue and Nativity in the American Population," 36.

8. Political pressures urging patriotism during the war years undoubtedly played a decisive role, speeding other social/generational changes along. See Nils Hasselmo, *Amerikasvenska: En bok om språkutvecklingen i Svensk-Amerika,* Skrifter utgivna av Svenska språknämnden 51 (Stockholm: Esselte Studium, 1974), 55ff., 65–67, and Haugen, *The Norwegian Language in America,* 255ff. Hasselmo, *Swedish America,* quotes 39–40, 42–44.

9. Gustav Andreen, "Augustanasynoden och dess verksamhet," in *Svenskarna i Amerika. Populär historisk skildring,* eds. Karl Hildebrand and Axel Fredenholm (Stockholm: Historiska förlaget, 1926) 104 (author's translation).

10. G. N. Malm, "En sommardag på Jan Swansons farm," in *Svenskarna i Amerika,* ed. Hildebrand and Fredenholm, 28–37, quote 30 (author's translation).

11. See Hasselmo, *Amerikasvenska;* Nils Hasselmo, "Language and the Swedish Immigrant Writer: From a Case Study of G. N. Malm," *The Swedish Pioneer Historical Quarterly,* Special Issue: Scandinavians and America: Essays Presented to Franklin D. Scott, 25 (1974): 240–53; Angela Karstadt [now Falk], *Tracking Swedish-American English: A Longitudinal Study of Linguistic Variation and Identity,* Studia multiethnica Upsaliensia 16 (Uppsala: Acta Universitatis Upsaliensis, 2003). See Haugen, *The Norwegian Language in America.*

12. Haugen, *The Norwegian Language in America,* 254, 263, 264.

13. Haugen, *The Norwegian Language in America,* 262, 276, 277.

14. Haugen, *The Norwegian Language in America,* 277ff., 283ff., and 291–92. Some studies that take into account *community* or *local* perspectives include, for example, Folke Hedblom, "Bishop Hill after a Century," in *Studies for Einar Haugen,* ed. Evelyn Scherabon Firchow, Kaaren Grimstad, Nils Hasselmo, and Wayne A. O'Neil, Janua Linguarum, Series Maior 59 (The Hague: Mouton, 1972), 281–95, for Bishop Hill, Illinois; Folke Hedblom, *Svensk-Amerika berättar* (Stockholm: Gidlund, 1982), for multiple Swedish American settlements; Per Moen, "The English Language of Norwegian-Americans in Four Midwestern States, with Special Reference to Syntax," *American Studies in*

Scandinavia 28 (1996): 1–22, for some linguistic data collected in Norwegian American communities in the Upper Midwest, including Decorah, Iowa; Blanck, *Becoming Swedish-American,* for detailed coverage of the Augustana Synod in Rock Island, Illinois; Odd S. Lovoll, *The Promise Fulfilled: A Portrait of Norwegian Americans Today* (Minneapolis: University of Minnesota Press, 1998), for multiple Norwegian communities in the Upper Midwest, including Decorah; Lizette Gradén, *On Parade: Making Heritage in Lindsborg, Kansas,* Studia multiethnica Upsaliensia 15 (Uppsala: Acta Universitatis Upsaliensis, 2003), for Lindsborg, Kansas; and Karstadt [now Falk], *Tracking Swedish-American English,* for Lindsborg, Kansas, and Minneapolis, Minnesota. These particular studies do not, however, compare phenomena *across* Swedish American and Norwegian American communities.

15. "Languages Spoken at Home and Ability to Speak English for United States, Regions and States: 1990" (1990 CPH-L-133), particularly Table A, "Language Spoken at Home and Ability to Speak English Ranked for Persons 5 Years and Over for United States, Regions, and States: 1990. For each area, the 50 languages with greatest number of speakers." The number of speakers, a calculation that is based on a sampling, was 80,723 Norwegian and 77,511 Swedish.

16. "Ancestry: 2000. Census 2000 Brief. Issued June 2004," available: www.census.gov. The specific instructions to claimants are reproduced in that particular census publication.

17. "Figure 2. Fifteen Largest Ancestries: 2000," U.S. Census Bureau, Census 2000 special tabulation. This information is based on a sampling of the census data. In rank ordering, containing the fifteen largest ancestries, we find the following groups: (1) German; (2) Irish; (3) African American; (4) English; (5) American; (6) Mexican; (7) Italian; (8) Polish; (9) French; (10) American Indian; (11) Scottish; (12) Dutch; (13) Norwegian; (14) Scotch Irish; and (15) Swedish. For more recent data, see "Table 52. Population by Selected Ancestry Group and Region: 2007," available: http://www.census.gov/compendia/statab/2010/tables/10s0052.pdf.

18. The population numbers were taken from the U.S. Census Bureau, American FactFinder, "Lindsborg city, Kansas" and "Decorah city, Iowa," available: http://factfinder.census.gov. Bethany College, Lindsborg, Kansas, www.bethanylb.edu; Luther College, Decorah, Iowa, www.luther.edu.

19. Starting from a list I constructed containing the names of Swedish American Lutheran colleges, I then consulted data available in the *2005–2009 American Community Survey 5-Year Estimates* for each host community to obtain the number and percentage of persons who claimed Swedish ancestry. For each community given below, I also report claimed Norwegian ancestry. (See http://factfinder.census.gov.)

- Home of Bethany College, **Lindsborg, Kansas** (32.9 percent Swedish). For Lindsborg city (population 3,251), the number of persons who claimed Swedish ancestry was 1,069, equivalent to 32.9 percent of the population. (The number of persons who claimed Norwegian ancestry was 36 persons, equivalent to 1.1 percent of the population.)
- Home of Gustavus Adolphus College, **St. Peter, Minnesota** (11.5 percent Swedish). For St. Peter city (population 10,844), the number of persons who

claimed Swedish ancestry was 1,248, equivalent to 11.5 percent of the population. (The number of persons who claimed Norwegian ancestry was 2,221 persons, equivalent to 20.5 percent of the population.)

- Home of Augustana College, **Rock Island, Illinois** (6.3 percent Swedish). For Rock Island city (population 38,106), the number of persons who claimed Swedish ancestry was 2,403, equivalent to 6.3 percent of the population. (The number of persons who claimed Norwegian ancestry was 740, equivalent to 1.9 percent of the population.)

The percentage of claimants for Norwegian ancestry in communities where Norwegian American Lutheran colleges exist are found below. For each community, I also report the claimed Swedish ancestry.

- Home of Luther College, **Decorah, Iowa** (34 percent Norwegian). For Decorah city (population 7,865), the number of persons who claimed Norwegian ancestry was 2,673, equivalent to 34 percent of the population. (Number of persons who claimed Swedish ancestry was 456, equivalent to 5.8 percent of the population.)
- Home of St. Olaf College, **Northfield, Minnesota** (20.7 percent Norwegian). For Northfield city (population 19,482), the number of persons who claimed Norwegian ancestry was 4,031, equivalent to 20.7 percent of the population. (Number of persons who claimed Swedish ancestry was 1,984, equivalent to 10.2 percent of the population.)
- Home of Augustana College, **Sioux Falls, South Dakota** (17.4 percent Norwegian). For Sioux Falls city (population 151,646), the number of persons who claimed Norwegian ancestry was 26,388, equivalent to 17.4 percent of the population. (Number of persons who claimed Swedish ancestry was 5,981, equivalent to 3.9 percent of the population.)
- Home of Augsburg College, **Minneapolis, Minnesota** (11.3 percent Norwegian). For Minneapolis city (population 379,499) the number of persons who claimed Norwegian ancestry was 42,722, equivalent to 11.3 percent of the population. (Number of persons who claimed Swedish ancestry was 30,892, equivalent to 8.1 percent of the population.)
- Home of Pacific Lutheran University, **Tacoma, Washington** (5.6 percent Norwegian). For Tacoma city (population 196,118), the number of persons who claimed Norwegian ancestry was 11,021, equivalent to 5.6 percent of the population. (Number of persons who claimed Swedish ancestry was 6,893, equivalent to 3.5 percent of the population.)

20. On promoting multilingualism, see, for example, Peyton, Ranard, and McGinnis, eds., *Heritage Languages in America.* Gradén, *On Parade,* and Karstadt [now Falk], *Tracking Swedish-American English,* offer analysis of Lindsborg; Lovoll, *The Promise Fulfilled,* offers some analysis of Decorah. On further avenues for research, see, for example, Russell N. Campbell and Donna Christian, "Heritage Language Education: Needed Research," in Peyton, Ranard, and McGinnis, eds., *Heritage Languages in America,* 255–66.

21. Maj-Britt Hawk, e-mail message to author, Aug. 15, 2009. The minutes of the club meetings regularly appear in the "Club News" section of *The Lindsborg News-Record.*

22. See http://www.svenskhyllningsfest.org/. Maj-Britt Hawk, e-mail message to author, Aug. 15, 2009. Bethany College 2010–11 Catalog, 141, available: http://www.bethanylb.edu/pdf/10-11-BethanyCollegeCatalog.pdf.

23. Quotation excerpted from the *Lindsborg News-Record,* June 25, 2009, p. 6. The earlier article was "Scholarship available to American Swedish Institute's Swedish Language Village": "The American Swedish Institute is offering a $1500 scholarship to be used this summer at Sjölunden, the Swedish language village. Sessions are offered for ages 8–18 starting July 27. Concordia Language Villages has been providing residential cultural and language immersion programs since 1961. No previous language experience is necessary and all levels of language learners are welcome at our culturally authentic Language Villages . . . The winners [*sic*] name will be posted on the Language Villages website concordialanguagevillages.org. Visit the website or call . . . for more information about Concordia Language Villages." (Excerpted from *The Lindsborg News-Record,* May 14, 2009, p. 9.)

24. See http://www.nordicfest.com/. As mentioned previously, Svensk Hyllnings-fest is celebrated biannually, with the most recent festival in Lindsborg having taken place in October 2009. In an effort to keep my presentation of the two festivals similar, I have drawn upon material in the festival program from the Nordic Fest in 2009. More on various Nordic Fest phenomena may be found in Lovoll, *The Promise Fulfilled.* See, for example, his overview, including a description of the parade, "where an eclectic confusion of earnest and silly ethnic expressions and characters compete for attention. A romanticized and popularized image of Norway and a Norwegian immigrant past is conveyed during the three days of the festival" (72).

25. Martha Griesheimer, e-mail message to author, Aug. 7, 2009. For a current list of courses and activities, see http://vesterheim.org/. On Luther's offerings, see http://www.luther.edu/academics/majors/scandinavian-studies/index.html. Regarding high school students studying at the college level, Rhonda Thompson, e-mail message to author, Aug. 9, 2009. The Norwegian camp, Skogfjorden, is operated by Concordia Language Villages. In fact, multiple course options of assorted lengths and targeted to various age groups are listed on the homepage, http://www.concordialanguagevillages.org/newsite/Languages/norwegian1.php.

26. See especially Gustav Andreen, *Det svenska språket i Amerika,* Studentföreningen Verdandis småskrifter 87 (Stockholm: Bonnier, 1900); Andreen, "Augustanasynoden och dess verksamhet"; Malm, "En sommardag på Jan Swansons farm"; Fishman and Hofman, "Mother Tongue and Nativity in the American Population."

27. Fishman, *In Praise of the Beloved Language: A Comparative View of Positive Ethnolinguistic Consciousness,* Contributions to the Sociology of Language 76 (Berlin: Mouton de Gruyter. 1997), preface, xviii–xix.

CHAPTER 7

Writing History Together

*Norwegian American and Swedish American
Historians in Dialogue*

MARK SAFSTROM

Is there a special relationship between Norwegian America and Swedish America? Participants raised this central question at the "Friends and Neighbors" conference at Augustana College in Rock Island, Illinois, October 19–20, 2007. Answering this broad question would require more time than the weekend conference allowed. What was addressed perhaps was that a special, time-honored relationship does seem to exist between the respective historical communities, the Norwegian-American Historical Association (NAHA), founded in 1925, and the Swedish-American Historical Society (SAHS), established in 1948. While Scandinavian perspectives, not to mention Scandinavianism, have frequently been applied in the histories of the various immigrant groups, the historians of these two societies have interacted more with each other than with any other ethnic history society in North America. Furthermore, when the scholars of each society have included comparative studies of ethnic groups other than their own, they have most often chosen each other as the comparative subject. This observation on its own does not prove that the relationship between Norwegians and Swedes in North America was any more special than the relationships with other Scandinavian groups. What it does suggest is that for many decades a high level of awareness, cooperation, and mutual respect has existed between NAHA and SAHS. If institutions play a central role in the life of ethnic communities in North America, then the relationship between these two societies does suggest that the ties between Norwegian America and Swedish America may have been stronger than those connecting the other migrants from the Nordic region, such as Danes and Swedish-Finns.

As the members of NAHA and SAHS have written articles and published books over the years, they have left a long trail of breadcrumbs for anyone looking to trace the interaction between Norwegians and Swedes, as well as the interactions of their historians. This chapter will present some of the highlights of this relationship, focusing on articles with Swedish-Norwegian relations as a major theme, comparative work and collaborations between historians from each group, and the general philosophies of ethnic history that have appeared over the years. What follows is thus a brief "history of the histories" produced by NAHA and SAHS that will draw some conclusions about the results of this relationship. The sources for this exploration are the full run of the journals of each organization as well as the commemorative book published by NAHA on the occasion of its fiftieth anniversary in 1975, *The Norwegian-American Historical Association 1925–1975* by Odd S. Lovoll and Kenneth O. Bjork. A comparable work for SAHS has not yet been published. The first of these journals to appear was that of NAHA, which has had three different versions of its title: it started as *Studies and Records* in 1926, was changed to *Norwegian-American Studies and Records* in 1931, and was shortened to *Norwegian-American Studies* in 1962. The journal of the Swedish-American Historical Society (known from its founding in 1948 to 1983 as the Swedish Pioneer Historical Society) has had two names, the *Swedish Pioneer Historical Quarterly*, launched in July 1950, and its present title, *Swedish-American Historical Quarterly*, which appeared first in January 1984.[1]

Trendsetters

Through the pages of these journals, certain people's names loom larger than others, in the amount of scholarship published, the positions held, and the years served. A few people have clearly been trendsetters in promoting collaboration between NAHA and SAHS. The earliest example of this impulse was already evident in the remarks of NAHA's first president, D. G. Ristad, in the very first volume of the journal. In describing the purpose of the organization, Ristad expressed the group's desire "to cooperate with all organizations that touch, in their activities, the broad field that the association seeks to cultivate—the Norwegian element both in its relations to its racial source and its special historical and cultural backgrounds and in its relations to the history and culture of the American people, of which it has gradually been becoming an integrant part." Several decades prior to the establishment of SAHS, the journal of NAHA was already engaged in questions of cross-cultural studies, particularly with Swedish American history. As soon as SAHS was born, members in both fields quickly expressed the desire for interaction.[2]

Leaders within the SAHS community also acknowledged the positive effect of cross-pollination between Swedish and Norwegian American historians that had already taken place before SAHS came into being and which helped that organization come to life. At a luncheon to celebrate the twenty-fifth anniversary of NAHA, Franklin D. Scott praised that organization, saying:

> The fair and balanced treatment of the data, including both the criticisms of disgruntled pioneers and the extravagant paeans of praise of others, indicates the maturity of the present generation, which can look

with equanimity on the opinions and activities of its ancestors. Honesty, thoroughness, and insight have characterized the work and have established ideals of scholarship to guide this Association and to challenge the best efforts of other groups. The newly formed Swedish Pioneer Historical Society is frankly inspired by the example this Association has set, and one hopes it can attain an equal scholarly status. The total result is more than building a body of knowledge, it is raising the standard of historical writing in a difficult but important field, it is placing truth above chauvinism. The romance of the great migration remains, but science is added to romance. It is scholarship with vitality.[3]

Both organizations have had similar origins, structures, and missions. The decisive moment for the establishment of NAHA came in the enthusiasm following the Norse-American Centennial Celebration of June 1925, although discussions had already been under way for several decades. The Swedish Pioneer Historical Society (SAHS since 1983) was formed also after the celebration of the centennial of the Swedish migration to North America, which was held in 1948. As evidenced by Scott's statements above, the formation of SAHS was based in no small part on the precedent set by NAHA. SAHS followed "best practices" of NAHA regarding scholarship and methodology, as well as those modeled by the earlier Swedish Historical Society of America (1905–34), led by distinguished immigration historians such as George M. Stephenson. The historians of SAHS also seemed to have been eager to continue the discussion of the relationship between Norwegians and Swedes in North America.[4]

As the muscles of the heart pump blood through a body, anniversaries have pumped new life into the organizations, both in terms of refocusing vision for each individual society as well as promoting cooperation between them. As the fiftieth anniversary celebration of NAHA approached, Kenneth Bjork made appeals to both societies to look to the future and to channel energy toward renewed cooperation. Bjork ranks among the historians most enthusiastic about the relationship between NAHA and SAHS, and his expressions of this enthusiasm are duly noted in both journals. A moment for collaboration came in 1974 with a project of essays to be presented to Franklin D. Scott called "Scandinavians and America." Included in this collection was a "Plan for the Future" written by Bjork. He focused attention on several dream projects related to Norwegian history but also addressed a broader Nordic audience calling for Danish, Finnish, Swedish, and Norwegian descendants in the United States to "pool their research activities." The common challenges of these communities in funding their respective associations and endeavors could be more easily accomplished through dialogue, he suggested. Having been presented with the question by "well-meaning persons" of whether the occasion of the fiftieth anniversary of NAHA would not be a good opportunity to conclude its work, Bjork replied in his essay that this was most "absurd." He nevertheless saw formidable challenges, which he projected would be more difficult to overcome in the second fifty years than those they had faced in the first.[5]

H. Arnold Barton is another of the scholars who continued this tradition of collaboration. Through his translation efforts on several occasions, Barton diversified the contents of the *Swedish Pioneer Historical Quarterly* by including several Norwegian- and Scandinavian-related articles. Editor Odd Lovoll also frequently crossed back and forth between Norwegian and Swedish circles. His participation in the activities of SAHS is frequent and significant, such as his collaboration at speaking engagements like the society's joint conference with the Swenson Center on "Being Swedish American Today." To mention only some of the people who have been most influential in guiding scholarship in the direction of collaboration is to neglect many. It goes without saying that the current leadership of both societies have continued and intensified this tradition, as is abundantly clear in their coordination of the "Friends and Neighbors" conference at the Swenson Center at Augustana College in 2007. What follows in the remaining sections is a sampling of the contents of the journals that will identify some trends and philosophies present in these comparative studies.[6]

Swedish-Norwegian Comparative Studies

The great migrations of each ethnic group primarily took place during the time in which Sweden and Norway were joined in one united kingdom, so one would expect a natural relationship between Swedish America and Norwegian America and that the union would be a dominant theme in the research of the two historical societies. On a few occasions, the relevance of the union to the immigrant groups has indeed been presented. One is the common record keeping done by the union government, presented by Theodore Blegen in an article from the 1940s, "An Official Report on Norwegian and Swedish Immigration, 1870." Several decades later, Paul A. Varg presented the same report to the readers of the *Swedish-American Historical Quarterly*. These examples demonstrate that the two emigrant groups shared common experiences and were governed by the same administrative bureaucracy; they also establish the degree to which the Swedish government had been aware of the Norwegian emigrants' experiences. The growing Norwegian demands for independence leading up to 1905 also inherently brought into question the relationship of Swedish and Norwegian immigrants to one another. Terje Leiren's article, the "American Press Opinion and Norwegian Independence, 1905," presented the way in which the American press received the event in general. It also explored the degree to which independence strained the opinions of Norwegian Americans regarding their Swedish counterparts. The "emotionalism" described by Leiren was apparently not experienced just by the immigrants but had notable influence throughout the general American public, inspiring commentaries on democratic values and analyses of progressive ideas rather than simply rousing enmity between ethnic groups.[7]

Most of the time, however, the relationships between Swedes and Norwegians have been presented without the framework of the union. This can suggest any number of conclusions, including the possibility that the historians of each group have taken this relationship for granted or even deliberately ignored it. It seems likely, based on the articles contained in the journals, that the union relationship has only been seen as having been important during periods when crucial decisions were made that led to Norway's independence. The rest of the time it was apparently much less relevant. The absence of this theme in the journals would indicate that when Swedish and

Theodore C. Blegen, 1934

Norwegian immigrants interacted, they usually did so based on practical considerations, such as similar languages and cultural practices that allowed them to share newspapers and churches. Shared nationalism based on the union was contentious but not a major factor in interaction.

Furthermore, it has been most common for the comparisons of Norway and Sweden in the journals to be made tacitly. Rarely have scholars in either journal set out to make direct comparisons between Swedes and Norwegians, instead preferring to demonstrate their similarities by including both groups in the same study or by including an article about Norwegians in the journal of SAHS or one about Swedes in NAHA's publication series. With the scope of the journals widened to include articles about the other ethnic group, readers who are familiar with their own group may potentially make comparisons implicitly. An example of this is an essay by Arlow W. Andersen, which presented the connections between Norway and the Norwegian labor movement in the United States for the audience of the Swedish Pioneer Historical Society.

Another example is Ingrid Semmingsen's article on a collection of "America-letters" found in Norway, which she wrote for the *Swedish-American Historical Quarterly*. The large body of work produced by Nils William Olsson also demonstrated an occasional Norwegian turn, particularly with two articles in 1982 that included Norwegian topics. Inclusions like these present an opportunity to see similarities and differences between the ethnic groups and also remind the audience that the experience of one group is often not unique.[8]

The article "The Campaign of the Illinois Central Railroad for Norwegian and Swedish Immigrants" by Paul W. Gates contained more direct comparisons. In it he examined the railroad campaigns to attract Swedish and Norwegian settlers by sending agents to those countries to "induce" emigration in the 1850s and 1860s. The campaigns did apparently result in increased emigration although, at least initially, none of the immigrants purchased land from the railroad. Halvdan Koht also focused on the advertising campaigns targeting both Swedes and Norwegians in his article "When America Called for Immigrants." This study demonstrated the effect that the 1862 Homestead Act had on the migrations, also highlighting the fact that the immigrants were coming from jointly governed countries. Evident in both of these studies is the way in which Swedes and Norwegians were targeted as one demographic by outsiders—such as American consuls and railroad agents—and that they shared some of the same immigrant experiences.[9]

An interesting example of exchange between the fields is a book review by George M. Stephenson that appeared in 1927. The book was *Norwegian American Lutheranism Up to 1872* by J. Magnus Rohne. The practice of having scholars from one field review the work of scholars in the other shows the type of academic integrity reflected in Franklin D. Scott's later praise. The fact that the review was as critical as it was is quite interesting, because Stephenson himself later wrote a definitive work on religious aspects of the Swedish migration, no doubt benefiting from the previous work of Rohne: a clear example of cross-pollination between the fields.[10]

"Scandinavian" as a Synonym for "Norwegian-Swedish"

Studies that have been presented on occasion as "Scandinavian" in actuality have focused only on two of the groups in the region. Thus in many instances *Scandinavian* can really be taken to mean "Norwegian-Swedish." Writers do not seem to have done this deliberately. It does suggest that the term *Scandinavian* can often be used to the exclusion of certain groups. In addition, it might indicate that many times, although an immigrant organization might be called Scandinavian, all groups were not necessarily present or equally represented. A classic example is the use of the term *Scandinavian* by various Lutheran synods, which in reality were often dominated by one or two groups at various periods in their history. This trend is apparent in the article by Paul Benson, "A Cappella Choirs in the Scandinavian-American Lutheran Colleges." In it, he traced the origins of choral tradition in "Scandinavian Lutheran Colleges" while primarily focusing on Norwegian-born choral conductor F. Melius Christiansen and Norwegian American schools such as St. Olaf. The article also highlighted Augustana College in Rock Island, but its focus on Swedish American colleges was relatively small. Danish American institutions were either implied or neglected in Benson's piece.[11]

Another Scandinavian themed-article is an interpretive essay by George M. Stephenson titled "The Mind of the Scandinavian Immigrant." In it he focused only on Norway and Sweden, comparing citizens' motivations for emigration as well as essential aspects of the characteristics and heritage of Scandinavian immigrants: "Of the two countries Norway was the more democratic, but King Democracy reigns just as triumphantly in Swedish-America as in Norwegian-America. Making due allowance for individuals, the Swedish immigrant was bitten by the same germ of democracy as was the Norwegian, although the disease may have run different courses." The absence of Danes in Stephenson's exploration of the Scandinavian mentality is notable but is unlikely an intentional omission. It is perhaps only significant in that it demonstrates a use of terminology and that the comparison here is really being made between Norwegians and Swedes.[12]

While this use of the term *Scandinavian* is perhaps a minor point, it does indicate some problems in presenting comparative studies. Writers commonly use the term *Dano-Norwegian* when specifically addressing those two groups, helped by the fact of their shared written language. The phrase *Swedish and Norwegian* appears less often, and *Swedish-Norwegian* is never used in the titles and articles. Examples of these word choices are the articles by Arlow W. Andersen, "Norwegian-Danish Methodism on the Pacific," and Frederick Hale's "Norwegians, Danes and the Origins of the Evangelical Free Tradition." The reason for this choice is unclear but would seem to indicate that the use of the term *Scandinavian* is not just confined to historians but reveals a preference of the immigrants themselves. That the immigrants frequently chose to use the term *Scandinavian* in the names of their newspapers and churches, even when only one or two of the ethnic groups were present, suggests a considerable desire to be affiliated with a larger group. This is one area where the "special relationship" thesis between Swedes and Norwegians breaks down.[13]

Scandinavian, Nordic, and Multiethnic Studies

While both journals have demonstrated a preference for Swedish and Norwegian comparisons, respectively, this has on the whole been accomplished against the

backdrop of general Scandinavian studies, Nordic studies, and multiethnic studies. The inclusion of the larger context of the immigrant experience has been a
priority of many historians. Again, Kenneth Bjork is an author who frequently
took up truly Scandinavian themes, such as the article he submitted to the
Swedish Pioneer Historical Quarterly divided between three volumes in 1954, the
topic of which was Scandinavian cooperation in San Francisco. In the article,
Bjork explored three joint ventures of Swedes, Danes, and Norwegians: a social
club called the Scandinavian Society, Our Savior's Scandinavian Evangelical
Church, and planned settlements in the San Francisco area. Bjork presented the
thesis that although Scandinavianism may have eventually given way to intensified nationalism toward the end of the nineteenth century, Scandinavians in
North America had initially demonstrated a willingness to cooperate out of
both necessity—the result of small numbers—as well as genuine friendship.
In the areas where Scandinavians were spread out geographically and therefore
prevented from joint action in person, newspapers such as *California Scandinav*
created virtual communities. Such newspapers, furthermore, also attempted to
gather the Scandinavian immigrants physically in common settlements. Much
of the cooperation lasted only through the 1870s, and Bjork's findings demonstrated that it often diminished once the individual groups were able to establish
their own nationally focused organizations.[14]

Such studies seem to have been aimed at placing each nationality into its
broader context and perhaps even to remind the readership of the multifaceted
nature of the immigrant experience. Many other interesting studies have been
done in the common ventures of the Scandinavian groups. The most notable are
the ones that have taken up questions traditionally focused on one ethnic group
and reframed them to include broader Scandinavian interaction. Such is evident
in Frederick Hale's treatment of "Norwegians, Danes and the Origins of the
Evangelical Free Tradition." Hale's article focused on the relatively little research
that had been done on the Dano-Norwegian Free Church tradition in comparison to the Swedish. It had a Scandinavian focus and this time presented the
Norwegians in their relationship with the Danes. Hale not only highlighted the
influence of Swedish evangelists Fredrik Franson and J. G. Princell but also traced
Irish and Anglo-American influences in the evangelists John Nelson Darby and
Dwight L. Moody. Franson's willingness to cooperate with any church, "even
Rome," also demonstrated the ability of immigrants to imagine cross-cultural
interaction and a yearning to step out of ethnic ghettos. Furthermore, it is apparent in reading Hale's article that he was responding to Kenneth Bjork's call for a
more comprehensive study of the Scandinavian American religious experience,
which had been published in the *Swedish Pioneer Historical Quarterly* as a "Plan
for the Future." This article became the concluding chapter in the book Bjork
coauthored with Odd S. Lovoll the following year.[15]

Swedish Pioneer Centennial Association Festival
CHICAGO STADIUM   JUNE 4, 1948

Gathering of Swedish Americans at the Swedish Pioneer Centennial Celebration, Chicago Stadium, June 4, 1948. Speakers included President Harry Truman and Carl Sandburg.

The special relationship thesis between Swedes and Norwegians is, of course, made problematic by the fact that the Norwegians also had a special relationship of sorts with the Danes because of their common written language. This relationship is most apparent in the joint Dano-Norwegian churches and the shared newspapers. But even these papers and churches frequently made connections with Swedes, as indicated by the article "The Danish Language Press in America" by Marion Marzolf. The article demonstrated the high level of cooperation by

Scandinavians in newspaper ventures, especially prior to the Civil War and the establishment of *Den Danske Pioneer* in 1872. Special relationships or not, several people made an effort to present a more inclusive Scandinavian experience, which called for increased attention to Danish America and Finnish America. For instance, in an editor's introduction in 1979, H. Arnold Barton congratulated the Danish community on the recent founding of their own historical society and urged more cooperation with the broader Scandinavian American community rather than the "narrowly-Swedish or Norwegian perspective."[16]

In addition to encouraging a Scandinavian context, both journals have also made some significant attempts to include a Nordic perspective. Janet Rasmussen's article "I met him in Normanna Hall: Ethnic Cohesion and Marital Patterns among Scandinavian Immigrant Women" explored the marriage patterns of eighty-seven immigrant women. Rasmussen included Finnish subjects in these numbers, in addition to Norwegians, Danes, and Swedes. One would expect Finnish and Swedish-Finnish topics to appear in the *Swedish-American Historical Quarterly*; there are few examples of this, however. Anders Myhrman explored the career of the Swedish-Finnish celebrity Selma Josefina Borg in a 1979 article. The close ties between the Swedish and Finnish ethnic groups have been represented by occasional book reviews on Finnish topics in the *Swedish Pioneer Historical Quarterly*. A "Pioneer Tour" of Swedish sites in the Midwest in 1979 included a stop at the John Deere Administrative building and Museum in Moline, which was considered significant as it was the last work of Finnish architect Eero Saarinen. Icelandic immigrants have perhaps been one of the groups least treated by either journal, but it is notable that an article on Icelanders appeared in one of the earliest volumes of *Studies and Records,* "The Icelandic Communities in America: Cultural Backgrounds and Early Settlements," by Thorstina Jackson.[17]

Swedish and Norwegian immigrants naturally interacted with immigrants of many other ethnic origins. Most closely related outside of Scandinavian and Nordic circles are German Americans, a relationship that has been explored in a few articles. For instance, Kenneth Bjork gave mention of the cooperation between Scandinavians and Germans regarding the establishment of churches. Ingrid Semmingsen provided interesting speculation about the influence that German emigrants who were waylaid in Bergen in 1817 may have had on the later departure of the first Norwegian emigrants on the *Restauration.* Despite the historians' preference for Swedish and Norwegian topics, these examples of Scandinavian, Nordic, and multiethnic perspectives demonstrate an attempt by the societies to offset the potential for ethnic tunnel vision and to remind their readership of the broader multicultural environment that the immigrants inhabited.[18]

The Changing Role of Race and Ethnicity in Immigrant Historiography

One of the difficult tasks that both NAHA and SAHS have repeatedly seen the need to address is the complicated and changing ideas concerning race and ethnicity in North America. A scan of the terminology used in articles beginning in 1925 makes apparent that the historians in each society have both reflected the assumptions of their era as well as attempted to present cutting-edge views on ethnicity.

In the first volume of *Studies and Records,* Ristad expressed the hope that the journal would serve the purpose of explaining the contributions of the Norwegian "race" in North America, making frequent use of that term. Certainly at the time many people would have used the word *race* to describe the Norwegian people and other immigrant groups. The word suggests an indelible and even eternal identity, no doubt revealing the hope of some kind of future for the community. While Ristad might have hoped that Norwegian heritage and ethnic communities would continue, he also saw the likelihood that the immigrants would mingle with other groups and be changed by the experience. Ristad appears to have used the word in a flexible sense, as he explained early on in his article: "Where these emigrants have come to settle they have added new energies to the native stock of the races of which they have become a part." This flexible understanding of race causes one to doubt that Ristad understood Norwegian racial identity as people might use that word today. In light of his earlier comments regarding the importance of cooperation with other ethnic elements in publishing the journal, Ristad was not simply using the term *race* in a static way but was also demonstrating some innovation in what that term meant. The Norwegians were at that time already merging with the American or Anglo-American "race," as he explained it, which suggests that what he termed as *race* was not an indelible identity at all but instead quite malleable.[19]

Over the years since his initial statement, Ristad's exhortation to cooperation between NAHA and other groups has been heeded on many occasions, demonstrated in the many articles that have been mentioned thus far. Preferences for Norwegian-Swedish and Scandinavian comparisons may have dominated other multicultural perspectives, but a significant awareness of other populations has been included as well. In the oft-cited interpretive essay "Immigration and Puritanism" (1936) by Marcus L. Hansen, he painted a grand view of the common trends across all immigrant groups, including Irish and African Americans as well as Swedish and Norwegian immigrants. All groups that have migrated to the New World, he proposed, have dealt with similar tendencies toward Puritanism, as their traditional social structures have been broken down by the trauma of relocation and the removal of behavioral restraints. To compensate, they thus became more conservative than their Old World counterparts. He suggested, therefore, that ethnic and racial traits are changed by interaction with new social contexts. Several decades later, Frederick Hale critiqued Hansen's assumptions that the experience of one immigrant group can be so easily applied to others. Referencing J. H. Hexter's theories about "tunnel history," Hale suggested that Norwegian filiopietism had caused historians in the field to take only "rare glances at other groups with whom their forefathers interacted." The exceptions to this negative trend were the many assimilation studies, which inherently took into account interaction with other groups.[20]

Whether Hale's evaluation was overstated or not, by the 1970s an increasing presence of material involved cross-cultural ethnic studies in the journals. This increase has been attributed to the so-called ethnic revival that occurred after the civil rights activity of the 1960s, and in several articles historians highlighted the changes and challenges that this social upheaval brought about in the field of immigration history. Odd Lovoll and Kenneth Bjork explained in their history of NAHA that the renewed interest in European American ethnicities had reminded the academic community of the continued existence and relevance of immigrant heritage, once presumed to have all but disappeared into the dominant Anglo-American population. At the same time, the diversification of the field of history to include sociological and psychological approaches presented the challenge and opportunity to make studies more comparative and multicultural in nature. This approach could complement the earlier "contribution" school of immigration history, which narrowly focused on a single ethnic group with the purpose of explaining its contribution to overall American society.[21]

John Higham's article "Immigrants in Urban America" further widened the perspective of ethnic identity and assimilation trends beyond the Scandinavian context:

> Under the spur of the ethnic revival [of the 1960s and '70s], historians turned inward. Each tended to become a specialist in one particular group . . . All in all, it seems fair to say that during the ethnic revival the scholars who opened to us so much of the inner world of the immigrants left their impact on America largely unexamined. In the 1980s a renewed assessment of how immigration and ethnicity have affected other aspects of American life belongs near the top of the agenda of immigration historians.

His assertion of the value of both the individual group's experience as well as the necessity for cross-cultural comparisons was not an entirely new idea, however, and it would not be accurate to say of either NAHA or SAHS that they had ever truly been "turned inward." The sentiment could be taken as more of a reminder and reformulation of ideas that had been increasing in the two societies since their founding.[22]

Finally, the questions of assimilation, diversity, and homogeneity have been addressed on several notable occasions, a few of which merit inclusion here. The complicated and shifting nature of ethnic identity in North America has long intrigued historians of both societies. Franklin D. Scott, in his address to NAHA in 1950, explained, "American homogeneity is growing slowly out of diversity. What homogeneity now exists is but poorly understood. Why? Perhaps largely because the roots of diversity are not understood." His answer to this problem was that thoughtful scholarship on the part of the two societies could help to answer these questions. It was not satisfactory for historians to assume the complete assimilation of ethnic groups, nor to write history that was narrowly focused on one ethnic group. The "controlled scholarship" that he praised and called for in his speech would necessarily rely on conversations between disciplines and between the ethnic history societies, so that the complete picture of the "cultural interaction and diffusion" of various parts of American society could be more fully understood. Recent journal articles have demonstrated that ethnic identity and diversity are still elusive concepts as they relate to Norwegian and Swedish American history. Chris Susag's article "Retaining Modern Nordic-American Identity amongst Diversity in the United States Today" presented a comparison of how ethnicity is understood and constructed in U.S. Norwegian, Swedish, Finland-Swedish, and Finnish community organizations. His comparison did much to answer questions about the nature of white ethnicity in the United States by looking across specific ethnic lines. This question—how to understand options for ethnic affiliation among white Americans—is a larger issue with much research potential. Susag did well to point out that part of the problem for discussion of these issues is the fact that white ethnic identity has traditionally been discouraged, by both the melting pot model as well as later practices in studies of multiculturalism and diversity, in which it is sometimes identified as a form of racism.[23]

A significant observation to make about NAHA and SAHS is that each has made significant steps to become organizations that are broader than the immigrant enclaves that originally gave them life. Scholars who are involved in the societies are not solely people who personally share the heritage but also include those who have been drawn to the field simply by virtue of its value to overall immigration history and North American history. Personal attachment to ethnic heritage will no doubt continue to play an important role for many who participate in the organizations, but understandings of ethnicity have changed since 1925. The heritage that was once accepted as the property of an ethnic community is now understood as a part of a general American heritage. The land of immigrants has mingled to such a degree that multiculturalism is part of many Americans' personal and complicated ethnic heritage and corresponding identity. Ethnicity is seen not as an indelible racial feature but often as something that crosses strict lines of ancestry. This change in understanding can be attributed in great part to the editors of each journal making early efforts to include both scholars and topics that lay outside the narrow national view of each group. One profound aspect of this exchange has been the relationship between Swedish America and Norwegian America, which has so often been a starting point for historians in exploring the multicultural relationships of the immigrant experience.

A Productive Relationship

If the relationship between NAHA and SAHS is special, which from this study one can conclude that it is, it would be due in great part to the fact that it appears to have been quite productive. Over the years, several participants in each society have taken up themes that integrated the other group into their discussion of immigrant life, cultural preservation, cooperation, assimilation, and diversity. Without wholly separating Norwegian and Swedish Americans from their overall Scandinavian American context, the interaction of Norwegian and Swedish American historians has allowed their research to be fuller than it would have been in isolation. Should the societies pursue similar relationships with other ethnic history communities in the future, one would expect that the nuances of the immigrant experience would be revealed even more clearly.

Norwegian American historian Waldemar Ager famously lamented at the establishment of NAHA in 1925 that the coming of this new society was a sign that Norwegian America was passing away and that the descendants of immigrants would only write history, not make it. In reviewing the relationship between the historians of NAHA and SAHS, however, it is reasonable to conclude that historians also get the occasional opportunity to make history—by changing assumptions about ethnic groups, both past and present, and by producing new understandings of the complicated nature of identity. The Norwegian-American Historical Association and the Swedish-American Historical Society each began as heritage societies that served a limited and easily identifiable population of immigrants and their descendants. Now both organizations have shifted into broader ethnic history societies, which function more as interest groups. Their readership and participants have long ago expanded to include scholars and others who share a general interest in the field. While each serve in the capacity of passing on the ethnic heritages that they represent to future generations of Americans, together they also have come to be respected outside their immediate ethnic groups for their service in transmitting a significant intellectual heritage concerning immigration history and high academic standards for cultural and cross-cultural research. More recent immigrant populations in the United States and Canada will have good role models to look to when the time comes for them to establish new historical associations. Franklin D. Scott seems to have had this in mind when he addressed NAHA members at their fiftieth anniversary luncheon: "Thus the grand theme of cultural interaction and diffusion has been taken up and given life by the Norwegian-American Historical Association; scholarship has been wisely directed, nationalism has been made constructive. Here is a prototype for other groups who would search the past to gain understanding of themselves, and of the America they have helped to build."[24]

Notes

1. Odd S. Lovoll and Kenneth O. Bjork, *The Norwegian-American Historical Association 1925–1975* (Northfield, MN: The Norwegian-American Historical Association, 1975).

2. D. G. Ristad, "The Norwegian-American Historical Association," *Studies and Records* 1 (1926): 151.

3. Franklin D. Scott, "Controlled Scholarship and Productive Nationalism," *Norwegian-American Studies and Records* 17 (1952): 146.

4. Ristad, "The Norwegian-American Historical Association," 148.

5. Kenneth O. Bjork, "A Plan for the Future," in *Scandinavians and America: Essays Presented to Franklin D. Scott*. This *festskrift* was a double issue of the *Swedish Pioneer Historical Quarterly* 25 (1974): 264, 269.

6. Ingrid Semmingsen, "A Shipload of German Emigrants and Their Significance for the Norwegian Emigration of 1825," and Kristian Hvidt, "Scandinavian Discord on Emigration," *Swedish Pioneer Historical Quarterly* 25 (1974). "Conference Report," in *Swedish-American Historical Quarterly* 53 (2002): 69.

7. Theodore Blegen, "An Official Report on Norwegian and Swedish Immigration, 1870," *Norwegian-American Studies and Records* 13 (1943). Paul A. Varg, "Report of Count Carl Lewenhaupt on Swedish-Norwegian Immigration in 1870," *Swedish Pioneer Historical Quarterly* 30 (1979). Terje Leiren, "American Press Opinion and Norwegian Independence, 1905," *Norwegian-American Studies* 27 (1977): 232.

8. Arlow W. Andersen, "American Labor Unrest in Norway's Press: The Haymarket Affair and the Pullman Strike," *Swedish Pioneer Historical Quarterly* 25 (1974). Semmingsen, "A Unique Collection of America-Letters in Norway," *Swedish-American Historical Quarterly* 35 (1984). "Nils William Olsson: A Bibliography of His Work," *Swedish American Historical Quarterly* 35 (1984): 328.

9. Paul W. Gates, "The Campaign of the Illinois Central Railroad for Norwegian and Swedish Immigrants," *Norwegian-American Studies and Records* 6 (1931): 75. Halvdan Koht, "When America Called for Immigrants," *Norwegian-American Studies and Records* 14 (1944).

10. George M. Stephenson, "Norwegian-American Lutheran Church History," *Studies and Records* 2 (1927).

11. Paul Benson, "A Cappella Choirs in the Scandinavian-American Lutheran Colleges," *Norwegian-American Studies* 32 (1989).

12. George M. Stephenson, "The Mind of the Scandinavian Immigrant," *Studies and Records* 4 (1929): 64.

13. Arlow W. Andersen, "Norwegian-Danish Methodism on the Pacific," *Norwegian-American Studies and Records* 19 (1956); Frederick Hale, "Norwegians, Danes and the Origins of the Evangelical Free Tradition," *Norwegian-American Studies* 28 (1979).

14. Kenneth O. Bjork, "Scandinavian Experiment in California," *Swedish Pioneer Historical Quarterly* 5 (1954): 26, 28, 67, 78.

15. Hale, "Norwegians, Danes and the Origins of the Evangelical Free Tradition," 82, 84ff., 96. Bjork, "A Plan for the Future," 105.

16. Marion Marzolf, "The Danish Language Press in America," *Norwegian-American Studies* 28 (1979): 275. H. Arnold Barton, "Editor's Corner," *Swedish Pioneer Historical Quarterly* 30 (1979): 4.

17. Janet Rasmussen, "'I met him in Normanna Hall': Ethnic Cohesion and Marital Patterns among Scandinavian Immigrant Women," *Norwegian-American Studies* 32 (1989). Anders Myhrman, "Selma Josefina Borg: Finland-Swedish Musician, Lecturer, and Champion of Women's Rights," *Swedish Pioneer Historical Quarterly* 30 (1979). "Items," *Swedish Pioneer Historical Quarterly* 30 (1979): 64. Thorstina Jackson, "The Icelandic Communities in America: Cultural Backgrounds and Early Settlements," *Studies and Records* 3 (1928).

18. Bjork, "Scandinavian Experiment in California," 105. Semmingsen, "A Shipload of German Emigrants."

19. Ristad, "The Norwegian-American Historical Association," 147.

20. Marcus L. Hansen, "Immigration and Puritanism," *Norwegian-American Studies and Records* 9 (1936): 6. Frederick Hale, "Marcus Hansen, Puritanism, and Scandinavian Immigrant Temperance Movements," *Norwegian-American Studies* 27 (1977): 40.

21. Lovoll and Bjork, *The Norwegian-American Historical Association*, 6, 7, 8.

22. John Higham, "Immigrants in Urban America," *Norwegian-American Studies* 31 (1986): 12.

23. Scott, "Controlled Scholarship and Productive Nationalism," 130, 148. Chris Susag, "Retaining Modern Nordic-American Identity amongst Diversity in the United States Today," *Swedish-American Historical Quarterly* 53 (2002): 7.

24. Lovoll and Bjork, *The Norwegian-American Historical Association*, 5, 44–45. Scott, "Controlled Scholarship and Productive Nationalism," 148.

Conflict

CHAPTER 8

"We Are Norwegians and Swedes Now, Not Scandinavians"

The Impact of Norwegian Independence on Scandinavian American Politics in the Midwest

JØRN BRØNDAL

In the summer of 1906, about one year after Norway had emerged as an independent nation, Ole A. Buslett, the Norwegian American writer and politician, wrote a letter to *Skandinaven,* the politically most influential Norwegian-language newspaper in the United States. In the letter, he vented his anger at U.S. Senator Robert Marion La Follette, Wisconsin's most powerful politician. Even though James O. Davidson, the incumbent governor of Wisconsin, was a reliable, progressive Norwegian American, La Follette had decided to throw his support behind Irvine L. Lenroot, a Swedish American, in the upcoming gubernatorial race. The fact that a Swedish American was waging battle against a Norwegian American in Wisconsin in 1906, just one year after Norway had gained its independence, led Buslett to reflect on Scandinavian American identity: "Mark this last word: The Scandinavians. That [term] made sense two years ago; now it is different. We are Norwegians, Danes, and Swedes now. If Senator La Follette had not grasped this before, he will soon reach this understanding. Last year's events in the Nordic countries [have] impact on the political life here in the West; whether we are willing to accept it or not, that is how matters stand. We are Norwegians and Swedes now, not Scandinavians; Norwegian and Swedish citizens of Wisconsin."[1]

Was Buslett right? Did the events of 1905 make such a difference in the United States? In this chapter I shall argue that whereas events in Norway and Sweden in 1905 did have a distinct impact on midwestern politics, that impact was limited. Norwegian independence did not lead to any major rupture between Norwegian Americans and Swedish Americans. The fact was that, prior to 1905, within the world of politics the relationship between Norwegian Americans and Swedish Americans had not usually been that close. This chapter will pursue this argument, first, by studying a couple of relationships between Norwegian and Swedish American leaders antedating 1905 and, second, by briefly reviewing two events, one in Wisconsin, the other in Minnesota, that took place shortly after the break between Norway and Sweden. Finally, the chapter will discuss a few long-term factors of importance to the relationship between Norwegian Americans and Swedish Americans.

On March 13, 1889, Peter Hendrickson, the editor of *Skandinaven,* the largest and politically most important Norwegian-language paper in the United States, wrote a letter to his likewise Norwegian American friend Rasmus B. Anderson, describing a recent meeting with a Swedish-born colleague, Johan A. Enander. The latter was editor of *Hemlandet,* then the second-largest Swedish-language newspaper in the United States. Enander had not exactly made a good impression on Hendrickson:

> His education is Swedish and not of the University order. He was 21 years of age when he came here, speaks English very clumsily . . . [H]e is [a] manly and not bad looking man when he has washed his face . . . A man dominated by a more outspoken conceit I never met, and yet I guess he is a pretty good fellow, rarely gets drunk and as far as I can learn is cleaner morally than physically. An agreeable man he can hardly be said to be, and it does look strange to think of such a man as U.S. Minister to the Danish court. They can never there get over the impression that he must be from just over the Sound and not from over the Sea.[2]

Hendrickson's disgust with Enander may well have been politically motivated. Just two days earlier, James G. Blaine, the new U.S. secretary of state, had asked Rasmus B. Anderson, a Democrat, to resign from his position as U.S. minister to Denmark now that Republican Benjamin Harrison had been inaugurated as president following his victory in 1888 over incumbent Democratic president Grover Cleveland. Johan A. Enander was being appointed in Anderson's place. Hendrickson's negative description of Enander may well have been his way of expressing sympathy with Anderson, who now would have to leave Copenhagen and return to the Midwest.[3]

What is striking here is that it seems as if both editor Hendrickson and Rasmus B. Anderson, each of them very prominent Norwegian Americans, hardly knew Johan Enander at all. Hendrickson definitely did not, and he appears to have expected that Anderson did not either, at least not on a personal level. This is rather strange. As noted, Enander was editor of *Hemlandet.* One would have expected that the editor of Norwegian America's politically most powerful newspaper would have known the editor of one of Swedish America's most important newspapers. That, however, was obviously not the case. Hendrickson's statement that Enander's education was "not of the university order" is equally bizarre. It simply does not make sense. After all, already back in 1874 the first part of Enander's three-volume history of the United States had appeared. In itself, that ought to have made Enander look scholarly, yet apparently Hendrickson had no knowledge of this publication. Moreover, Johan Enander, just like Rasmus B. Anderson, believed in, and did his best to propagate, the idea that the Vikings were the first to discover America. Indeed, H. Arnold Barton has suggested that Enander may well have been directly inspired by Anderson to promote this history. Again, Hendrickson apparently had no clue.[4]

This example would seem to indicate that even though many people in the United States subsumed both Norwegian Americans and Swedish Americans under the label of "Scandinavians" or "Scandinavian Americans," not all Norwegian and Swedish American leaders kept in close contact with each other. In all fairness, even though Rasmus B. Anderson may not have known Enander on a personal level, by early 1889 he definitely realized that the latter was his rival for the diplomatic position in Copenhagen. As another Norwegian American editor wrote Anderson in February, "I fear that Mr. Enander has the inside track. The Swedes are clamoring for him of course, his claims being further strengthened by the alliance, defensive and offensive, which exists between him and W. W. Thomas Jr. who is pretty sure of getting the appointment to Stockholm." Obviously, not many feelings were lost between Swedish Americans clamoring for Enander and Norwegian Americans clamoring for Anderson.[5]

Later in life, Anderson found Enander sufficiently important to include him in his autobiography. In this work, Anderson asserted that the reason Enander ultimately decided to decline the position as U.S. minister to Denmark was that he had served a prison term. Whether or not this assertion is true, Enander did at one point admit, at least, to having been expelled from a secondary school in Sweden after having stolen an "article of small value." Enander, on his part, appears not to have nourished particularly warm feelings for Anderson. When the latter came to Rock Island, Illinois, in the late summer of 1890, Enander's Republican paper *Hemlandet* noted pointedly that Anderson—this *Democrat*—did not visit Augustana College.[6]

Another political relationship antedating 1905 involved two Minnesota politicians, Swedish American John Lind and Norwegian American Knute Nelson. In the late 1880s and early 1890s, both men served in the House of Representatives, each of them members of the Republican Party. All in all, their relationship appears not to have been very close during those years; neither was it hostile. Both considered making a run in 1892 for the governorship of Minnesota, and Knute Nelson ended up winning the election. Before that happened, Lind wrote a polite letter to Nelson in which he promised not to stand in the way of Nelson's possible gubernatorial bid, reasoning, "It is the dictate of my judgment and pride as a Scandinavian quite as much as the result of the personal regard I have always entertained for you . . . We cannot afford to stand in each other's way and I don't propose to be in yours." Other observers appreciated John Lind's relative modesty vis-à-vis Nelson in 1892. From Wisconsin, Norwegian American Nils P. Haugen wrote to editor Peter Hendrickson of *Skandinaven,*

> In this connection let me say "inter nos" that, while Lind would like to get the nomination for governor of Minnesota, he has to my certain knowledge left it in the hands of Nelson to say whether his name will be presented to the convention. If Nelson says he is a candidate Lind will support him. It is all left to Nelson's honor. I say this to you in confidence as I think in the interest of harmony between the Norse and the Swedish element you ought to know it.[7]

Judging both by Lind's own words and by Haugen's, each was aware of a need to keep up Scandinavian American harmony, yet both also implied that such accord was not necessarily a natural given. Perhaps indicating some tension between the two politicians already at this point, that same year John Lind informed Knute Nelson that only on one occasion had he felt slighted by the latter, namely when Nelson had acted rather abrasively after being informed by Lind that the Republican William D. Washburn had been nominated for a seat in the U.S. Senate.[8]

The relationship between Lind and Nelson was never particularly warm, but in 1894 the two fell out with each other. At this time, Washburn was incumbent Republican U.S. senator, yet Nelson was planning to run against him. In an effort to thwart Washburn's bid for reelection, Nelson had his allies urge several politicians to run for the seat. Nelson's hope was that if Washburn could not gain a majority in the Minnesota legislature—which in those days chose the state's two U.S. senators—Nelson himself would have a fighting chance. Among the politicians approached by Nelson's allies, with a view to having him act as a stalking horse, was John Lind. The person who approached Lind was a professor at Gustavus Adolphus College. In disgust, Lind resigned from the college's board of trustees. When Nelson in early 1895 did in fact win the election, Lind was angered, as he made clear to a friend: "Knute is King. He won by one of the most corrupt and demoralizing campaigns that I ever witnessed . . . Washburn did not use a cent nor was a penny used in his behalf. We were defeated but it was an honorable defeat."[9]

Thus, years before Norwegian independence in 1905, the relationship between Swedish and Norwegian American politicians, it turns out, was neither necessarily very intimate nor very good. To be sure, there are also instances of cooperation between Norwegian and Swedish American politicians. In the late 1880s and early 1890s, John Lind developed especially close ties in Congress with

Norwegian-born Nils P. Haugen of Wisconsin. Besides cooperating with each other in securing an appropriation for the purchase of Scandinavian literature for the Library of Congress, in 1892 they approached the Republican National Committee with a view to having the Republican Party subscribe to a number of Norwegian- and Swedish-language newspapers, at a time when Democrats and Populists were demonstrating an unsettling ability to lure Scandinavian American voters away from the Republican base. As it turns out, only the Norwegian-language *Skandinaven* ended up being subsidized by the Republican Party that year. In the momentous campaign of 1896, however, there are strong indications that the Republican Party, besides still supporting *Skandinaven,* also showered its funds on the Swedish-language *Hemlandet* and on a number of minor Swedish-language publications. Cooperation between Haugen and Lind also extended, potentially at least, to actual campaigning. In 1894, when Haugen lost the Republican gubernatorial primaries, he received assurances from Lind that the latter would have been "glad to have put in a couple of weeks in your state this fall" had Haugen won. In private, Lind and Haugen also discussed with each other a land speculation scheme in Wyoming and occasionally engaged in family visits.[10]

In the same manner that Swedish American John Lind developed close ties with Norwegian American Nils P. Haugen, Norwegian American Knute Nelson counted some prominent Swedish Americans and Danish Americans among his allies, not least Swedish American colonel Hans Mattson and Danish American Søren Listoe, both of whom had Nelson—at least in part—to thank for their appointments to diplomatic posts in Calcutta and Rotterdam, respectively. Still, political cooperation between Scandinavian American politicians of differing national backgrounds was not a given—and in some cases risked crumbling at a touch.[11]

Norway gained independence from Sweden in the summer of 1905. Following a long crisis over a Norwegian wish to establish its own consular service that dated back to 1892, the bonds between Norway and Sweden snapped. Even though most Norwegian American newspapers were jubilant—whereas the Swedish American press for obvious reasons tended to be a lot more skeptical and critical—the political results in the Midwest were not easily predictable.[12]

In Wisconsin, the Progressive movement under Robert La Follette's leadership experienced a grueling crisis when La Follette decided to back the strongly Progressive Swedish American politician Irvine L. Lenroot for the Republican gubernatorial nomination against the Republican incumbent, Norwegian-born James O. Davidson. He was likewise a Progressive, yet in La Follette's view of a less visionary sort. Conservatives in Wisconsin delighted in the Progressive split. As one conservative commentator noted in mid-June 1905, "The conflict between Norway and Sweden is likely to create quite a political revolution in this state, dividing those nationalities, one of which will not be of Half-breed predilections."[13]

Keyes was right. Norwegian Americans in Wisconsin supported Davidson in large numbers, and the much less numerous Swedish Americans tended to back Lenroot. Many other Wisconsinites, resenting what they viewed as La Follette's bossism and believing that the incumbent governor deserved a term in his own right after having succeeded La Follette when the latter had left for the U.S. Senate in early 1906, supported Davidson in the primaries. Davidson won easily.

One circumstance in connection with the 1906 campaign in Wisconsin seems representative: Swedish American Lenroot, no strong believer in the role of ethnicity in the first place, apparently gave up any pan-Scandinavian appeal to the state's Norwegian American and Swedish American voters. Whereas according to a speech manuscript, Irvine Lenroot intended to address the "Scandinavians" at a midsummer night's celebration in Ashland in 1906, in his actual speech it appears that he made pleas instead to the "Swedes," even if only to urge them to vote as Americans. By August, Lenroot had definitely dropped any idea of addressing the "Scandinavians" collectively. As one observer noted, "What struck me was the Nationality [issue], he said the Republican [party] is divided on Nationality[;] the Germans wants [sic] a German for Governor, the Norwegians wants their own, the Swedes wants their own[;] he said we are Americans and all that ought to be left out." Thus, the political environment in Wisconsin definitely fit into a pattern of Norwegian-Swedish hostility in the aftermath of Norwegian independence, even if the Swedish American candidate—unlike his Norwegian-born rival—never made a very strong case for his ethnic background.[14]

The picture was more complicated in Minnesota. By 1905, Knute Nelson had been U.S. senator of the North Star State for more than a decade. Already during a visit to Norway in 1899, he had created quite a stir when he visited Evanger in Voss in western Norway, where he had lived the first years of his life. During his 1899 visit, he gave a little talk in the Voss dialect on the current tensions between Norway and Sweden: "Where I live there are Swedes and Norwegians in equal numbers, and they live peacefully together. Try to live in peace here at home also! Keep the peace . . . Don't separate with forts along the border!" Nelson's biographers reported that his talk was met by a wall of silence. A similar scene played out in Minnesota in 1905. In a Syttende Mai address, Minnesota's Swedish American governor John A. Johnson had cautiously aired the hope that the border separating Norway from Sweden be eliminated. If the very fact that a Swedish American governor spoke at a Norwegian American celebration was significant, so was the circumstance that twelve days later Knute Nelson, attending a banquet at a Swedish-Norwegian club in Minneapolis, likewise talked about the relationship between Norway and Sweden. He, too, uttered his wish for union, adding that Denmark also ought to join. Norwegian American

The action of the Swedish riksdag seems to show that Sweden has the king, but that Norway holds the ace. — Minneapolis Journal June 22.

"The action of the Swedish riksdag *seems to show that Sweden has the king but that Norway holds the ace," reprinted in* Amerika, *July 7, 1905, from the* Minneapolis Journal

Andreas Ueland was present and later recalled that following Nelson's speech the whole banquet was in an uproar.[15]

Nelson never truly wavered from his standpoint. As his biographers pointed out, he might in fact have used his political leverage with Theodore Roosevelt to influence the president's wait-and-see attitude following Norwegian independence in early June 1905. Instead, Nelson proposed to do nothing, despite the fact that thousands of Norwegian Americans were petitioning Roosevelt for diplomatic recognition of Norway, something that the United States finally granted in November following the Treaty of Karlstad between Sweden and Norway. As it turned out, politically Nelson could afford to remain silent. There was no need to offend Minnesota's large number of Swedish American voters. In 1906, Nelson's Republican colleagues in the Minnesota legislature overwhelmingly elected him to another term in the U.S. Senate.[16]

In analyzing the relationships between a number of prominent Norwegian and Swedish American politicians, a few background factors have to be taken into consideration. Some of those factors revolve around the weakness of pan-Scandinavianism in America. Others reflect the circumstance that the crisis of 1905 did not erupt suddenly.

Scandinavian immigrants did not seem to feel a very strong urge at the grass-roots level to cooperate intensely with each other. In the United States, pan-Scandinavianism was born mainly out of numerical necessity. During the years 1840 to 1890, when the number of immigrants from each of the Scandinavian countries remained low, Scandinavian immigrants of varying national back-grounds sometimes cooperated; at the local level it occasionally continued after that point, depending on the numbers of Scandinavian immigrants present in the immediate vicinity. The reasons for this cooperation were cultural and reli-gious. In this strange new world, fellow immigrants from the other Scandinavian countries tended to appear somewhat less different—and considerably easier to communicate with—than people representing other ethnic groups. With rela-tively few Scandinavians in America, Swedish, Norwegian, and Danish immi-grants tended to work together in religious matters, in the establishment of a Scandinavian-language press, and, in a few cases, also in the creation of social clubs and fraternities. They sometimes settled in close proximity to each other, usually more as a result of parallel timing than of ethnic intent. With the gradual increase in the numbers of immigrants, however, separation along "national" lines took place within these various spheres; Danish-Norwegian cooperation typically outlasted Swedish-Norwegian, in part because of the near-identity between written Danish and the Norwegian *bokmål*.[17]

The reality was that just as the short-lived and weak pan-Scandinavian movement—which had begun to flourish back in the Scandinavian countries in the 1840s—had been an elite project, so was the attempt to establish pan-Scandinavian cooperation among America's immigrants from Norway, Sweden, and Denmark. Ordinary immigrants who by the late nineteenth century had only just begun to awaken to their Old World "national" identities—as opposed to their traditionally stronger parochial or regional identities—usually had little motivation to step beyond ethnic loyalties at the national level and also to iden-tify with fellow Scandinavians from countries other than their own, especially not after 1890.[18]

The waning of pan-Scandinavian feelings in the United States by the close of the nineteenth century is illustrated by the reports of two Danish travel writ-ers touring America in 1870 and the mid-1890s, respectively. Visiting Chicago in 1870, P. Beder commented favorably on Scandinavian American cooperation within the press: "It cannot be denied that you here get a certain practical grip on how to view yourself as a Scandinavian—at least that is what I experienced." Traveling in the United States in the mid-1890s, the Danish journalist and travel writer Henrik Cavling conveyed a completely different impression of the state of U.S. pan-Scandinavianism. Back in 1844, Cavling noted, Skandinavia, the first Scandinavian American association, had been founded in New York City. As a social club bringing together Scandinavian immigrants of varying national backgrounds, it had flourished during the first couple of years, but by the 1890s much had changed. At its fiftieth anniversary in 1894, one member of the association composed a song, the first few stanzas of which declared,

> As times changed, unity frayed,
> And Scandinavianism was forgotten,
> Because Danes, Norwegians and Swedes each wanted to rule,
> Both in America and at home . . .

In Omaha, Nebraska, Cavling further noted that Swedish and Norwegian Americans were not able to agree on who should lead a parade organized by the local Scandinavian club. The result was that the parade disintegrated into violence. Cavling doubted very much whether any pan-Scandinavian association still existed in the United States but ventured that Danish-Norwegian relations were at the time generally much better than Norwegian-Swedish.[19]

Despite the rather sad state of pan-Scandinavianism in the 1890s, two factors did still sometimes gently push immigrants from Norway, Sweden, and Denmark toward Scandinavianism—with very mixed results, to be sure. First, because Americans of non-Scandinavian background usually had difficulty distinguishing between Norwegian Americans, Swedish Americans, and Danish Americans, they tended to subsume all three ethnic groups under the "Scandinavian" or "Scandinavian American" label. P. Beder had noticed this in Chicago in 1870, and so did several other observers of Scandinavian background in the United States.[20]

In no area was this more apparent than in the quintessentially "American" sphere of politics. The competition between the Norwegian American Democrat Rasmus B. Anderson and the Swedish American Republican Johan A. Enander for the diplomatic position in Copenhagen reflected that both the major political parties viewed each candidate first of all as a Scandinavian, without respect to his national attachments. Likewise, in midwestern politics a symbolic slot on the state ticket of each party was often allotted to a Scandinavian. Norwegian American, Swedish American, and Danish American commentators made occasional observations about the Scandinavian members of Congress. In 1890, Danish-born Søren Listoe wrote to Norwegian American Nils P. Haugen, who had survived the Republican debacle of that year, "All *we* have left is John Lind, and we are not a bit proud of the [N]orwegian colle[a]gue you will have in the next house— and don't think you will be." That Norwegian colleague, incidentally, was Kittel

Halvorson of Minnesota, a Populist. By the closing years of the nineteenth century, several Scandinavian Americans had tired of the type of midwestern politics based largely on ethnic symbolism. These people joined the Progressive movement, which in some of its midwestern manifestations attempted to downplay the ethnic factor in politics, if only with limited success.[21]

As the above-quoted letter from Søren Listoe illustrates, a second factor sometimes gently pushed Norwegian, Swedish, and Danish immigrants in a pan-Scandinavian direction: cooperation among the elites of the three ethnic groups. If Swedish American voters felt no particularly strong urge to support a Norwegian American candidate for political office, candidates considered that perhaps some prodding by a few Swedish American editors and politicians would help. To the extent that Scandinavian American leaders saw an advantage in cooperating with each other within the American political system, ethnic networks of voters might follow the elite's lead. As long as the American political system made symbolic room for the Scandinavian Americans precisely as "Scandinavian" ethnics, some cooperation was bound to take place. The point is, however, that even under these circumstances collaboration was not a given, as the relationship between Knute Nelson and John Lind has made especially clear. In the overall picture, the effect of the diplomatic crisis between Norway and Sweden in 1905 was to temporarily diminish further the possibilities of pan-Scandinavian partnership at the elite level.

If the weakness of pan-Scandinavianism helps explain the overall rather limited impact that the break between Norway and Sweden had on midwestern politics, another factor to take into account is that tension between Norwegian American and Swedish American attitudes antedated 1905 by several years. The crisis between Norway and Sweden did not erupt suddenly in 1905 but had been building for more than a decade. Indeed, in the United States the question of establishing a Norwegian consular service was discussed among Scandinavian Americans up through the 1890s. A few reader letters to the Norwegian American press illustrate the tensions. One Norwegian American reader suggested to *Skandinaven* in 1892 that Norwegian Americans sponsor a man-of-war for Norway. Five years later, another reader ridiculed the idea that Norwegian Americans collect money for a gift for Swedish King Oscar II's twenty-five-year jubilee. Yet another Norwegian American observer recommended sarcastically in 1892 that *Svenska Kuriren* be printed in Stockholm rather than Chicago. As early as 1890 another Norwegian American paper referred to the Swedish-language *Svenska Tribunen* as "the Norwegian-eating organ."[22]

Not only did tension between Norway and Sweden antedate 1905: from the 1890s to 1905 the union question was one of a number of factors—which also included the timing of democratic reform in each of the Scandinavian countries—to color ethno-political identity in the United States. Too many historical sources—and too much scholarship—allude to a high level of political activism among Norwegian Americans and to a larger degree of passivity among Swedish Americans to reject such a proposal out of hand. The Danish reporter Henrik Cavling conveyed what he viewed as the differences in political temperament between Danes, Swedes, and Norwegians in the United States by quoting U.S. Senator Knute Nelson:

> When a Dane steps into my office, he bows and says, "Sorry, to disturb you, Mr. Governor!" When a Swede comes in, he stays by the door and out of sheer politeness forgets his mission. A Norwegian, on the other hand, kicks open the door and says, "Hello, Knute!"
> And then, maybe, he spits on the floor and kicks up his feet on the table and speaks to me like the man would talk for whom I must thank for my dignity.[23]

Even though this statement may more reflect Cavling's journalistic hyperbole than Knute Nelson's actual point of view, the statement does convey an image of Norwegian Americans and Swedish Americans that matches more scholarly arguments. In 1935, George M. Stephenson, one of the most important chroniclers of Swedish American history, made a comment on late nineteenth-century Swedish American political culture. In his view, "[t]he Swedes were lacking in political instinct and were not particularly successful in the political arena. Though individual Swedes aspired to public office, their countrymen did not follow the example of the Irish and make politics a profession." Stephenson might have added that in this respect the Swedish Americans were rather unlike the Norwegian Americans. In their level of political activism the Norwegian Americans seemed somewhat to resemble the Irish Americans. Even though the Norwegian Americans and Irish Americans differed on a number of fundamentals—including religious outlook—and tended to view each other with deep suspicion, both groups comprised many individuals who believed that they had a homeland to actively fight for, and both groups boasted above-average levels of political activism.[24]

Adding to the political differences between the Norwegian and Swedish Americans was the circumstance that whereas Norwegian American "nationalism" went hand in hand with the viewpoints of the liberal party in Norway, those Swedish Americans who defended the Swedish-Norwegian Union tended to mirror more conservative arguments. That type of reasoning was frequently of a somewhat subdued nature, as when one Swedish American letter writer in *Svenska Amerikanaren* sulkily queried, "Why in the name of the Lord should Sweden insist on a union with Norway?"[25]

In conclusion, the impact of the events of 1905 in Scandinavia on midwestern politics should not be exaggerated. The events of 1905 did tend to exacerbate

Norwegian American and Swedish American differences in the Midwest and give the "Scandinavian" label a jolt. Even so, pan-Scandinavianism had never been strong in this region in the first place. After 1890 it depended for its survival mainly on the inability of other Americans to distinguish between Norwegian Americans, Swedish Americans, and Danish Americans and on the more than occasional need of members of the three Scandinavian American elites to collaborate with each other to further their own and their groups' ambitions in the American environment. The political stage served as the main arena for those ambitions. Another reason for the limited impact of the events of 1905 was simply that tensions between Norwegian and Swedish Americans had already been building for several years and arguably had already colored Norwegian American and Swedish American political culture.

As it turned out, the Scandinavian label popped up again not long after the events of 1905. In 1906, Ole A. Buslett had stated, "We are Norwegians and Swedes now, not Scandinavians." Even so, four years later, the nationalistic enthusiasm of 1905 having faded somewhat, the same Buslett complained in a letter to *Skandinaven* that his political opponents were doing all within their powers to deprive him of the "Scandinavian" vote. By 1910, even Buslett, who had pronounced pan-Scandinavianism in America dead, was reverting to the tactically convenient practice of employing pan-Scandinavian rhetoric in his run for political office.[26]

Notes

1. Ole A. Buslett to *Skandinaven,* July 28, 1906 (author's translation).

2. In 1889, *Skandinaven* boasted a circulation of 26,400, making it the largest Norwegian American newspaper, whereas *Hemlandet* had a circulation of 26,784, making it the second-largest Swedish American newspaper, only surpassed by *Svenska Tribunen.* To be sure, these figures are open to doubt, since the newspapers had an interest in reporting inflated figures in order to attract more advertising. *N. W. Ayer & Son's American Newspaper Annual* (Philadelphia, PA: N. W. Ayer & Son, 1889), 1001–2. Peter Hendrickson to Rasmus B. Anderson, Mar. 13, 1889, Papers of Rasmus B. Anderson, Wisconsin Historical Society.

3. Lloyd Hustvedt, *Rasmus Bjørn Anderson: Pioneer Scholar* (Northfield, MN: Norwegian-American Historical Association, 1966), 212.

4. H. Arnold Barton, "Partners and Rivals: Norwegian and Swedish Emigration and Immigrants," *Swedish-American Historical Quarterly* 54 (2003): 93–97.

5. Luth Jaeger to Rasmus B. Anderson, Feb. 23, 1889, Anderson Papers.

6. Rasmus B. Anderson, assisted by Albert O. Barton, *Life Story of Rasmus B. Anderson, Written by Himself with the Assistance of Albert O. Barton,* 2nd ed. (Madison, WI: R. B. Anderson, 1917), 547–51; Barton, "Partners and Rivals," 99; Conrad Bergendoff, "A Significant Enander Document," *Swedish Pioneer Historical Quarterly* 21 (1970): 11. See also Hustvedt, *Rasmus Bjørn Anderson,* 212–13. *Hemlandet,* Sept. 4, 1890.

7. George M. Stephenson, *John Lind of Minnesota* (Minneapolis: University of Minnesota Press, 1935), 91, quote 92. Nils P. Haugen to Peter Hendrickson, Mar. 27, 1892, the Papers of Nils P. Haugen, Wisconsin Historical Association.

8. Stephenson, *John Lind of Minnesota*, 95.

9. Millard L. Gieske and Steven J. Keillor, *Norwegian Yankee: Knute Nelson and the Failure of American Politics, 1860–1923* (Northfield, MN: Norwegian-American Historical Association, 1995), 208. John Lind to Nils P. Haugen, Haugen Papers, Jan. 24, 1895

10. Jørn Brøndal, *Ethnic Leadership and Midwestern Politics: Scandinavian Americans and the Progressive Movement in Wisconsin, 1890–1914* (Northfield, MN: Norwegian-American Historical Association, 2004), 167.

11. Gieske and Keillor, *Norwegian Yankee*, 242.

12. On the generally enthusiastic position of most Norwegian American newspapers (with the partial exceptions of *Minneapolis Tidende* and *Sisseton Posten*), see Arlow Andersen, *Rough Road to Glory: The Norwegian-American Press Speaks Out on Public Affairs, 1875 to 1925* (Philadelphia, PA: The Balch Institute Press, 1990), 102–12. For Swedish American attitudes as expressed in four leading Swedish American newspapers, see Olav Tysdal, "The Dissolution of the Union between Norway and Sweden and the Scandinavian Americans," *Scandinavian Studies* 79.2 (2007): 167–96, available: http://findarticles.com/p/articles/mi_hb275/is_2_79/ai_n29422875/. See also *Svenska Amerikanaren*, June 13 and 20, 1905; *Hemlandet*, June 13, 1906, condemning the acts of Norway; *Svenska Amerikanska Tribunen*, on the other hand, urged restraint by Sweden: editorial, June 16, 1905. For American attitudes, see Terje I. Leiren, "American Press Opinion and Norwegian Independence, 1905," *Norwegian-American Studies* 27 (1977): 224–42.

13. For a full review of the 1905 battle in Wisconsin, see Brøndal, *Ethnic Leadership and Midwestern Politics*, 185–203. E. W. Keyes to Marvin Hughitt, in Papers of Elisha W. Keyes, Wisconsin Historical Society, June 11, 1905.

14. See "Mr. Lenroot in Ashland," in "Hon. Irvine Luther Lenroot. Voters' Handbook—1906," 47, and the speech manuscript, "Ashland, June 23, 1906," in Papers of Irvine L. Lenroot, Library of Congress. P. A. Guard to J. O. Davidson, in Papers of James O. Davidson, Wisconsin Historical Society, Aug. 10, 1906.

15. Cf. Gieske and Keillor, *Norwegian Yankee*, 237; and Andersen, *Rough Road to Glory*, 105, 106. According to Gieske and Keillor (*Norwegian Yankee*, 266–67), it was first of all the leader of the Norwegian singers, Dr. Thompson, who expressed his disagreement with Nelson.

16. Gieske and Keillor, *Norwegian Yankee*, 267ff.

17. John R. Jenswold, "The Rise and Fall of Pan-Scandinavianism in Urban America," in *Scandinavians and Other Immigrants in Urban America: The Proceedings of a Research Conference, October 26–27, 1984*, ed. Odd S. Lovoll (Northfield, MN: Norwegian-American Historical Association, 1985), 160; Odd S. Lovoll, "A Scandinavian Melting Pot in Chicago," in *Swedish-American Life in Chicago: Cultural and Urban Aspects of an Immigrant People, 1850–1930*, ed. Philip J. Anderson and Dag Blanck (Stockholm: Almqvist & Wiksell, 1991), 63; John Robert Christianson, "Scandinavian-Americans," in *Multiculturalism in the United States: A Comparative Guide to Acculturation and Ethnicity*, ed. John D. Buenker and Lorman A. Ratner (New York: Greenwood Press, 1992), 112; Harald

Runblom, "A Nordic Melting Pot or 'Unmelting Pot' in North America," in *On Distant Shores: Proceedings of the Marcus Lee Hansen Immigration Conference Aalborg, Denmark June 29–July 1, 1992*, ed. Birgit Flemming Larsen, Henning Bender, and Karen Veien (Aalborg: Danes Worldwide Archives, 1993), 233; B. Lindsay Lowell, "The Scandinavians," in *Encyclopedia of American Social History*, vol. 2, eds. Mary Kupiec Cayton, Elliot J. Gorn, and Peter W. Williams (New York: Charles Scribner's Sons, 1993), 707; and Dag Blanck and Jørn Brøndal, "The Concept of Being Scandinavian-American," *American Studies in Scandinavia* 34.2 (2002): 5–13.

18. Henrik Becker-Christensen, *Skandinaviske drømme og politiske realiteter. Den politiske skandinavisme i Danmark 1830–1850* (Århus: Arusia, 1981), 267; Kristian Hvidt, *Det folkelige gennembrud*, vol. 11 of *Gyldendal og Politikens Danmarkshistorie*, ed. Olaf Olsen (Copenhagen: Gyldendal and Politiken, 1990), 119–20; Hans Try, *To kulturer, en stat*, vol. 11 of *Norges Historie*, ed. Knut Mykland (Oslo: J. W. Cappelens Forlag), 51–52; and Sten Carlsson, "Neutralitetspolitik och unionstvister 1864–1885," in *Industri och folkrörelser 1866–1920*, vol. 9 of *Den svenska historien*, ed. Gunvor Grenholm (Stockholm: Bonnier, 1968), 73. On the original strength of parochial or regional attachments, see for instance Jon Gjerde, "Conflict and Community: A Case Study of the Immigrant Church in America," *Journal of Social History* 19 (1986): 406, and Blanck and Brøndal, "Concept of Being Scandinavian-American," 1–2.

19. P. Beder, *Reiseerindringer fra et Besøg i America* (Copenhagen: Fr. Wøldikes Forlag, 1877), 120 (author's translation). Henrik Cavling, *Fra Amerika* (Copenhagen: Gyldendalske Boghandels Forlag, 1897), 2:142 (author's translation), 143.

20. Beder, *Reiseerindringer*, 120; Blanck and Brøndal, "Concept of Being Scandinavian-American," 1–2.

21. Brøndal, *Ethnic Leadership and Midwestern Politics*, 129–32. Søren Listoe to Nils P. Haugen, the Haugen Papers, Nov. 12, 1890, italics added. On the progressive attack on the politics of symbolism, see Brøndal, *Ethnic Leadership and Midwestern Politics*, 145–203.

22. *Skandinaven*, Aug. 17, 1892. *Skandinaven*, Apr. 14, 1897. *Skandinaven*, Aug. 31, 1892. *Budstikken*, Sept. 10, 1890.

23. For an overview, see Brøndal, *Ethnic Leadership and Midwestern Politics*, 121, esp. fn. 106. Cavling, *Fra Amerika*, 2:66 (author's translation).

24. Stephenson, *John Lind of Minnesota*, 119–20.

25. Dag Blanck, *Becoming Swedish-American: The Construction of an Ethnic Identity in the Augustana Synod, 1860–1917* (Uppsala: Acta Universitatis Upsaliensis, 1997), 21–22. On the use of Norwegian liberal rhetoric on the midwestern stage by various Norwegian American leaders, notably Nicolay Grevstad (who for many years was editor of *Skandinaven*), see Brøndal, *Ethnic Leadership and Midwestern Politics*, 92–95 and 226–35. According to George M. Stephenson, "The Mind of the Scandinavian Immigrant," *Studies and Records* 4 (1929): 71, "Norway in the nineteenth century experienced a renaissance of nationalism dating from the 'Seventeenth of May,' but the Swedish immigrant left his country when national feeling was at a very low ebb." Swedish American letter writer quoted from Tysdal, "Dissolution of the Union between Norway and Sweden."

26. Letter by Ole A. Buslett printed in *Skandinaven*, July 20, 1910.

CHAPTER 9

An End to Brotherhood?

Swedes and Norwegians in America
Discuss the 1905 Union Dissolution

ULF JONAS BJÖRK

In early 1906, a Norwegian immigrant in northern Minnesota wrote to the Norwegian-language weekly *Minneapolis Tidende* to tell its readers a little about life in newly settled Beltrami County. Most of its inhabitants were Scandinavians, according to Gust Pederson, and from their remote location they had "watched the great event which has taken place in Norway in the past year."[1]

The great event that Pederson referred to was the dissolution in 1905 of the ninety-one-year-old union between Norway and Sweden. This chapter will discuss how Swedish and Norwegian immigrants in the United States viewed this faraway event and how their views were expressed in letters in the foreign-language press. Although seemingly remote from the daily lives of Swedes and Norwegians who had chosen a new life in the United States, the union dissolution had implications not only for their relationship to their native lands but also for how the two ethnic communities related to one another.

Past studies have focused on how Norwegian- and Swedish-language newspapers reacted to the 1905 crisis in Scandinavia. Arlow Andersen's two-volume history of the Norwegian American press devotes a chapter to the dissolution and the events leading up to it, and a recent article by Olav Tysdal examines editorial comments and, in passing, reader responses in four Swedish American weeklies. No study, however, has compared the perspectives of Norwegian and Swedish Americans as a starting point for an examination of how the crisis affected the relationship between the two immigrant communities. In a recent study that discusses that relationship over time, historian Arnold Barton suggests that the union dissolution was the source of "growing bitterness between Norwegian and Swedish Americans," but Barton's general perspective does not allow him to elaborate on that observation. Part of the purpose of this study is to ascertain whether such bitterness existed and how immigrants from the two countries expressed it.[2]

In his article, Barton also puts forth the theory that general ethnic rivalries between the two communities were fueled by newspaper editors who were competing with one another and with other leaders of the ethnic community to become champions of their nationality, but he questions whether such senti-ments found resonance among ordinary immigrants. To explore that theory fur-ther and move the focus away from elite community members such as editors, this study looked at letters from readers in four major Scandinavian American newspapers, the Norwegian-language *Skandinaven* (The Scandinavian) and *Minneapolis Tidende* (The Minneapolis Times), and the Swedish-language *Svenska Amerikanaren* (The Swedish American) and *Svenska Amerikanska Posten* (The Swedish-American Post). Of the four, *Skandinaven* and *Amerikanaren* were published in Chicago, while *Tidende* and *Posten* came out of Minneapolis.[3]

Although any determination of the extent to which these letters reflected the opinions of the Swedish American and Norwegian American communities as a whole or even the overall readership of the four papers is impossible, studies of contemporary American newspapers offer some suggestions that seem as valid in 1905 as they are a century later. Such studies have indicated that reader letters do not constitute a scientific sample of the readership or an accurate represen-tation of public opinion. For one thing, newspapers receive more letters than they have space for and are forced to select some contributions over others. Moreover, not every reader is likely to write such letters in the first place: class, gender, writing ability, and attitude toward an issue tend to make some readers more prone to grasp the pen than others. Even with these limitations, reader letters do provide a unique insight into the opinions of at least a portion of a newspaper's audience.[4]

Studies of the immigrant press, however, have paid little attention to contri-butions from the readership. One study that did look at letters from readers is Isaac Metzker's classic collection of letters to the Jewish daily *Forward*. As for the Scandinavian American press, Ulf Jonas Björk has discussed its letters to the editor in two different articles; a 1957 article by Lawrence Carlson and Tysdal's study examined them as well.[5]

The four newspapers selected for this study represented the two main cen-ters of Swedish and Norwegian America, respectively, and although their main circulations were most likely in their home cities and states, all had national aspirations. Judging from the letters examined for this study, they attracted read-ers from across the country.[6]

Circulation figures were notoriously unreliable and subject to exaggera-tion, but *Svenska Amerikanska Posten* and *Svenska Amerikanaren* were probably among the three or four largest papers published in Swedish in North America, as were *Skandinaven* and *Minneapolis Tidende* in the Norwegian immigrant com-munity. *Svenska Amerikanska Posten* reported a circulation of more than 52,000 to the 1906 Rowell's *American Newspaper Directory*, whereas the circulation of *Tidende* was listed as 30,190. Rowell's gave only estimates for *Skandinaven's* cir-culation in 1905 but listed its 1898 circulation as more than 44,000. For *Svenska*

Amerikanaren, Rowell's directory gave an estimated circulation of only 7,500, but the 1906 *Ayer's Directory* listed the Swedish Chicago weekly's print run as 38,500. Histories of the Norwegian-language press routinely list *Skandinaven* and *Minneapolis Tidende* as two of the most influential and successful papers. *Svenska Amerikanaren* was in a similar position in Swedish America, and although *Svenska Amerikanska Posten* was disparaged for its lack of editorial leadership, even its critics admitted it was a very successful and widely read paper.[7]

In content, the four papers were strikingly similar. All offered the basic categories found in most immigrant newspapers in the United States: news and editorials about America, items from the native land, and news stories and notices about fellow countrymen who had immigrated. *Skandinaven, Minneapolis Tidende, Svenska Amerikanaren,* and *Svenska Amerikanska Posten* also shared the practice of devoting special pages to segments of the readership, such as farmers and women.[8]

All four papers also devoted part of their content to letters from readers. In *Amerikanaren* and *Tidende,* that section of each issue seemed to be handled in a rather routine manner, with editors restricting their comments to a warning from the Norwegian Minneapolis paper that anonymous letters would not be published and an admonition by its Chicago Swedish counterpart to readers to write in ink and on only one side of the paper.[9]

In *Skandinaven* and *Svenska Amerikanska Posten,* by contrast, editors took a keen interest in the letters page. In November 1905, *Posten* instituted a limit of four hundred words for each letter, put in place so that "more subscribers may be given an opportunity to speak their piece and more localities may be represented." Two years later the paper's editors expanded the letters department to several pages to accommodate the voluminous influx of reader contributions. *Skandinaven* also expanded its letters department for one issue; on that occasion, in February 1906, it added four pages, all devoted to contributions from "the great throng who rightly may be called *Skandinaven's* co-editors among the readers."[10]

To ascertain what "the great throng" of readers sent to their respective papers about the Union Crisis, I examined issues of the four newspapers between January 1905 and March 1906. The time frame was selected based on three of the most significant events of the crisis, and a brief review of them may serve as an introduction to how the readers of *Svenska Amerikanaren, Svenska Amerikanska Posten, Skandinaven,* and *Minneapolis Tidende* reacted.

By 1905, there had been friction between Sweden and Norway for years, and the union had almost come to an end in the mid-1890s. What set off events in 1905, however, and received attention in the Scandinavian American press, was the breakdown of negotiations over separate consular representation for Norway in late January. The most important date on the path toward dissolution was June 7, when the Norwegian Storting declared that Oscar II was no longer monarch of Norway. The union formally ended on September 23, when delegates from both countries signed an agreement as a result of negotiations in Karlstad, Sweden (although it still remained for the Storting and the Swedish Riksdag to approve the treaty, for the Riksdag to repeal the Act of Union—in mid-October—and, finally, for Oscar II to abdicate the throne of Norway, on October 27).[11]

Both the Swedish American and the Norwegian American press followed the developing crisis and its eventual resolution closely, offering ample fodder for readers to base their opinions on. It first surfaced in the pages that the papers devoted to news from Sweden and Norway, respectively. That part of the content had a counterpart in virtually all immigrant papers, and it offered Scandinavian Americans something unique: even those who had mastered English and were able to read American papers were unlikely to find a great deal of news from Norway or Sweden within them. Although this old country news was broken down to the level of province or city, it was generally introduced by a correspondence from Stockholm for the Swedish weeklies and from Kristiania for their Norwegian counterparts. Those chatty and opinionated pieces took a national perspective and were the first to broadcast the failed negotiations.[12]

Minneapolis Tidende took great pride in its "special correspondent in Kristiania," whose knowledge of Norwegian public affairs and excellent social connections were thought to superbly equip him to report from Norway and file correspondence vastly superior to those of the Minneapolis English-language dailies. *Svenska Amerikanska Posten* also received letters from Sweden, as it began to subscribe in March 1905 to the services of Svenska-Amerikanska Pressbyrån in Stockholm, a news service started by a former Swedish American journalist who supplied a dozen or more Swedish immigrant papers with weekly letters and also acted as a conduit for news from the United States to the press in Sweden.[13]

In the case of *Svenska Amerikanaren*, the source of the Stockholm letters is somewhat unclear. Swedish American journalist Alfred Söderström claimed in a 1910 book that these contributions "always have been and are, with one or two exceptions, produced in the office of the newspaper with the help of scissors and glue." Several facts indicate that Söderström's assertion applied to *Amerikanaren*. First, the standard biographical work on Swedish America's journalists and writers, Ernst Skarstedt's *Pennfäktare,* does not list the author of the letters, C. A. Sachs, either as a "real" person or a pseudonym. Second, a humorous notice in an August 1908 issue of *Svenska Amerikanaren* listed a group of men that editor Oliver Linder had lunch with. All of the men turn out to be his own pseudonyms, and included in this company is Sachs. Finally, the name of *Amerikanaren*'s man in Sweden may well be a play on words and an allusion to the origin of the letters: pronounced properly, it sounds like the Swedish word for scissors *(sax)*.[14]

The letters from Norway in *Skandinaven,* finally, were different in that their main purpose appeared to be to let readers reconnect with the local areas that they had left rather than offer a national perspective. Longer articles contributed the national view, however.

The first reactions from readers to what *Svenska Amerikanaren* called "the Swedish-Norwegian quarrel" and *Minneapolis Tidende* "the crisis in Norway" appeared in the two papers in mid-March and mid-April, respectively. From then until early 1906, *Amerikanaren* published a total of thirty-three letters commenting on the fate of the union. *Tidende,* on the other hand, published only eight. In *Svenska Amerikanska Posten,* the first reader contribution dealing with the union did not appear until June 20, after which an additional thirty-eight letters were published. *Skandinaven* ran its first reader piece about the union in early June and followed up with thirty-three more.

Readers of the two Swedish weeklies were not consumed by the fate of the union—a multitude of letters on other topics appeared during the fifteen months examined in this study—but it clearly concerned them. Moreover, the dissolution remained a topic of discussion long after the issue had been settled politically in Scandinavia and even when the editors seemed to consider it over. Thus a letter published in mid-October in *Svenska Amerikanaren* was appended with an editor's note implying it was time to move on: "It is of no use to bother further about the union, which is already all but dissolved. What is done is done. And we Swedish Americans can do but nothing about the matter."[15]

The Norwegian American readers of *Tidende,* on the other hand, seemed far less engaged. The "Insendelser" page of the Minneapolis paper was heavily dominated by pieces where correspondents described local communities, weather, harvest prospects, and so on (frequently ending with a call to other Norwegians to come to the United States to settle). Letters on topics other than local issues seldom found their way there. For much of the latter half of 1905, moreover, the "Insendelser" department disappeared altogether.

Skandinaven presented a special case. Its editor announced in late March that the paper had received many letters commenting on events in Scandinavia. While commending the "deep and strong love of the motherland" that permeated these pieces, the editorial stated that the frequent calls to fellow Norwegian Americans to prepare for assisting Norway would not "benefit the cause of Norway," as the situation demanded "firmness, calm, and dignity, not frivolous and agitating speech." Consequently, *Skandinaven* announced that it would not publish any of these letters.[16]

By early June, however, the Chicago paper's editors had apparently changed their minds. The change was prompted, perhaps, by an American event that brought the rising tensions in Scandinavia to the immigrant communities across the Atlantic. The year 1905 had started amicably enough between Norwegian and Swedish Americans, with both *Skandinaven* and *Minneapolis Tidende* congratulating their venerable Swedish-language colleague *Hemlandet* in Chicago on its fiftieth anniversary. According to *Skandinaven, Hemlandet's* longtime editor, J. A. Enander, was "one of the best examples of truly Nordic temperament in America."[17]

As May 17, Norwegian Constitution Day, drew close, *Skandinaven's* editors seemed to feel less charitable toward immigrants from its Scandinavian "sister nation." They were particularly concerned about a May 17 celebration in Minneapolis. A Swedish-born attorney, John W. Arctander, had arranged festivities in the Swedish Tabernacle and persuaded Minnesota's governor, Swedish American John A. Johnson, to give the main speech. In addition, Arctander had secured greetings to the celebrants from both President Theodore Roosevelt and Oscar II, the Swedish-Norwegian king. In an editorial with the headline "Abuse of 17 May," *Skandinaven* chided Arctander for his "tactlessness," as he seemed to claim that he and his event represented the Norwegian people. Arctander's hint that Roosevelt might even "put a word in for a resolution of the dispute between Norway and Sweden" made matters worse, as it gave the festivities "a political tone." (In Minneapolis, *Tidende* appeared to see no controversy in Arctander's celebration, reporting on it at length and noting long lines to get in and beautiful decorations.)[18]

The celebration was one of the topics in the first letter about the Union Crisis, published in *Skandinaven* in early June. It was from a reader in Wisconsin, who bluntly referred to Arctander's event as a "humbug" celebration and a "half-mad affair," organized with the sole intent of allowing Sweden to "swallow" Norway. The conclusion of the letter, a greeting to Norway, made clear that *Skandiaven* no longer had any qualms about publishing "agitating speech":

> [I]f bad times would come, if war should strike the country, then a million-and-a-half men and women, who have Norwegian blood in their veins, are ready to help. Some of the younger ones want to return to sacrifice life and blood for their dear old fatherland, and all the others want to offer their pecuniary and moral support. Let them understand at home that we, almost all of us are with them and do not want to forsake our countrymen and our old beloved fatherland in its hour of need.

This early letter was fairly typical of what readers expressing themselves in the two Norwegian-language papers of this study thought as events unfolded in Scandinavia during the summer and fall of 1905. None spoke in favor of preserving the union with Sweden, and many proclaimed their readiness to offer assistance. Support for the actions taken by the Norwegian Storting was also unanimous, as "J. M." in Aberdeen, Washington, expressed: "One thing gladdens me, that the people of Norway are not worried. It completely shows that its Storting and government are united between themselves and are working in complete harmony both outwards and inwards and has the trust of the people."[19]

Clearly, the dissolution of the Swedish-Norwegian Union was an unambiguous and positive event for Norwegian Americans. Their native land gained its independence after centuries of foreign domination, and the separation from Sweden was accomplished without bloodshed. Pride in Norway's course of action carried over to Norwegian immigrants in the United States. What Norway had accomplished in the summer of 1905, wrote a reader from Michigan, "would make us straighten our backs and hold our heads high and proud," causing Norwegian immigrants to "feel doubly glad to be Norwegian-born, to hail from this peaceful, conscientious and politically progressive Norway." Another correspondent agreed, claiming that "we Norwegian Yankees out here in the town of Rockwood, Wadena Co., Minn., felt very warm and proud to be related to the Norwegian Norwegians in Norway, when we read of the great deeds they accomplished on June 7 and later."[20]

The only sources of conflict had to do with what form of government the new nation should have—monarchy or republic—and that a few countrymen did not seem enthusiastic enough about what had happened. The issue of the system of government was a potential disagreement between the Norwegians in the United States and those at home. Establishing a republic would "make things better" for Norway, claimed a reader in Montana, while that may have seemed "American" to many in Scandinavia, "what is good is good also in America, and the republic is, I think, the best that we have." A correspondent in Canton, South Dakota, on the other hand, thought the "home" Norwegians had made the right choice in choosing a monarchy:

> Most Norwegians here dearly wanted Norway to become a republic,
> which is natural enough as we all like it so well here and have learned
> to love the system of government in this country. But Norway's people
> who have managed so well throughout the recent great crisis doubtlessly
> know what is best for them, either a limited monarchy or a republic. If a
> majority thinks that a monarchy is best for Norway at this point in time,
> then that's all well and good. Sometime later, when it is more suitable,
> they can establish a republic.[21]

As to those who had publicly expressed some hesitation about the way the dissolution had taken place, letter writers were unforgiving. The first letter to *Skandinaven* complained darkly about "so-called prominent Norwegians among us, particularly in the large cities, who love to be Swedes," and a subsequent letter to the Chicago paper expressed dismay that some "well-known" Norwegian Americans had "found it opportune to 'deplore the hasty course of the Storting.'" For "Norwegians over here who cannot fully agree with what the government and Storting of Norway are now deciding," the only option was to "remain silent."[22]

For Swedish Americans, the events of 1905 were far more problematic. A few letter writers were sympathetic to Norway's cause, such as "Carl," whose contribution appeared in *Svenska Amerikanska Posten* in September:

> I cannot understand why a large part of the Swedish people is against the dissolution of the Swedish-Norwegian union . . . Norway is one of the most democratic countries of Europe and the people seem to think that they can decide for themselves who should rule over them . . . No, the Swedish people should be grateful that Norway has taken this step and forever ended the controversies and discord that have prevailed among the rulers throughout the time that the union has existed.

Such sentiments were in the minority, however. Far more typical was the belligerent outburst of a reader in Duluth, Minnesota, published in early August in *Amerikanaren:* "Turn Norway into a Swedish province, like Halland, Blekinge and Skåne. Now is the time. It has gone too far, because Norway will never be a good friend, and if they are allowed to carry on, they will become Sweden's enemies for all eternity . . . A year of war would do Norway a great deal of good, and Sweden, too, would gain profit and fortune for all eternity."[23]

As it became increasingly clear toward the end of summer that the Swedish government was determined to preserve the peace, even if that policy meant ending the union, anger welled up within many letter writers against their old homeland. "H. L.," writing from Braddock, Pennsylvania, told *Svenska Amerikanaren's* readers that Sweden had been too indulgent with Norway and that the problem lay in Swedish society itself: "Only the high and mighty has any say in Sweden. But if the little people could speak their mind, things may not turn out better, because a large share of the people probably are more or less lazy and want to have peace no matter what. Sweden has had peace a long time now, and everyone, of course, wants that. But one needs to watch out, so that peace and liberty are not exchanged for worry and captivity."[24]

The reason such hostility toward Norway and bitterness toward Sweden surfaced in letters to the two Swedish American papers can be found by considering the situation in which the immigrants found themselves in the United States. Swedish Americans (and Norwegian Americans, for that matter) were in the process of building a sense of ethnic identity and found themselves jockeying for position with other ethnic groups. As Dag Blanck has shown in his study *Becoming Swedish-American,* part of this identity building in the Swedish American community entailed drawing on Sweden's heroic past; the potency of that appeal is evident from a number of references in the letters to heroes and deeds of yesteryear.[25]

At the time that the majority of the Swedish immigrants arrived in the United States, their old homeland was a small nation on the outskirts of Europe. It had once been a great power, however, and had, as one reader put it in *Svenska Amerikanaren,* "fought for the freedom of both Denmark and Norway and all the world, so that papal darkness would not yet again rule the world." Losing Norway meant that the last vestige of Sweden's great-power past was gone. Moreover, the policy of the Swedish government in 1905—the determination to preserve peace, even if it meant accepting the treatment of King Oscar and acquiescing to ending the union—ran contrary to that heroic past. While the bold declaration of the Storting that Oscar was no longer King of Norway made readers of *Skandinaven* and *Minneapolis Tidende* proud, the conciliatory atti-tude of Sweden toward Norway made "Sweden's descendants on foreign soil blush with shame," according to a letter in *Svenska Amerikanaren,* and it was so "humiliating" and "pitiful" that the author was "downright ashamed of hailing from 'the land of glory and heroes.' "[26]

The possibility of armed conflict in Scandinavia, the exuberant celebrations of the dissolution by U.S. Norwegians, and the rising resentment of Swedish Americans toward both Norway and their own homeland all contributed to increased friction between Swedish and Norwegian immigrants. The letter writer condemning the May 17 festivities in Minneapolis went on to sound the death-knell for any prospect of Scandinavian unity in the United States: "Scandinavianism plays no part among us here except before each election, when a Norwegian or Swede, as the occasion arises, appeals to the sister nation for votes. Next to being American citizens we are Norwegians in this country. We are not Scandinavians; the Swedes are Swedish, and the Norwegians are Norwegian."[27]

What made the ethnic divide clear to Norwegian Americans was that their fellow Scandinavian immigrants, and, above all, the newspapers they subscribed to, seemed incapable of sympathizing with the cause of Norwegian indepen-dence. A *Skandinaven* reader in Montana had looked at the Swedish American press in an attempt to understand its perspective and had found "a great deal of grief about what Norway has done." He could sympathize with that as long as it was "honest grief without vengeance and threats," but he still expressed disbelief that Swedes could not understand how oppressive the union had been for Norway. A farmer in Minnesota likewise told the Chicago paper's readers that he could understand that Swedish American editors were "mightily angry" about the actions of the Storting, but he thought the way they "mocked and scolded" Norway showed a lack of "tact and decency." Such behavior would do "no good" in America, he warned, as it was "not conducive to creating respect for the Swedes" in their new country. Another Minnesota reader agreed, accusing *Svenska Amerikanaren* of sinking to "new lows of ignorance and crudity" and the widely respected *Hemlandet* of following suit.[28]

Swedish American letter writers tended to focus more generally on the Norwegian immigrant community than on its newspapers. Once the dissolution was final, argued "Odd" in Oregon, it was also time to dissolve "intercourse with all that is Norwegian, because we can do without them." One action taken by the Norwegian Americans was particularly galling. In the wake of the June 7 declaration, Norwegian immigrants began circulating a petition asking President Roosevelt to recognize Norway as an independent nation. That step not only amounted to urging an American politician who was broadly popular in Swedish America to side with the Norwegians, it also sought to legitimize the unilateral actions of the Storting. Letter writer Johan Person in Chicago told the readers of *Svenska Amerikanaren* that the petition was an attempt to have Roosevelt "be the first to approve of the insolence of the Norwegians" and noted with satisfaction that "the *Chicago Tribune* writes on its editorial page that the Norwegians better behave until Sweden has declared a divorce." From a small town in South Dakota, a *Svenska Amerikanska Posten* reader noted that the Norwegians there had tried to pass off the effort as Scandinavian in their "truly ridiculous" fliers but that the petition had been signed by only one Swede, one who did not want to suffer "financial loss." In November, another letter to *Posten* claimed that the petition was evidence that "their friendship with us is rather scant" but that their effort had been in vain as it had yielded no result. "Gunter" in North Dakota was equally happy that the president had "not dignified [the petition] with his attention."[29]

Swedish American letter writers made clear that the Norwegians in America would pay a price for their stance during the Union Crisis, particularly in the political arena. In September 1905, a letter published in *Svenska Amerikanska Posten* expressed joy that the union was over: "For us here in America things will also be better, for now Norwegian office-seekers cannot come and remind us that we are a sister nation when we have elections here. One hopes that every Swede eligible to vote here in America then proves himself worthy of his citizenship papers and votes only for the right man, and not just because he has a Norwegian name."[30]

"Gunter" envisioned the same change: "For the Swedish-Americans it is better that Norway was separated from Sweden. Now they do not have to vote for Norwegians or so-called Scandinavians instead of Americans as they previously have done. Now the Swedish-Americans of the United States organize

Unionens upplösning.

Nog Svea länge sågs med Nora vandra;
Med hurtigt mod de gingo raskt framåt,
Men Svea ofta hjälpa fick den andra,
Då hård och ojämn syntes hennes stråt.
Dock tacksamhet från Nora ej man sporde,
Hon missnöjd var med allt hvad systern gjorde;

Och nu hon lämnat har sin goda syster,
Som städse var för henne som en mor,
Och öfvermodig, oförståndig, yster
Hon på sin egen kraft och storhet tror —
Den dagen dock kan ligga ganska nära,
Då systerns hjälp hon åter må begära.

"Svea [the personification of Sweden] generously letting her ungrateful little sister Nora [Norway] leave, with little thanks but predicting she may in the future once again need help from her older sister who has cared for her like a mother," Svenska Amerikanska Posten, *October 3, 1905*

themselves in clubs, and support good Americans for state and county offices. When the Americans learn that the Norwegians are not, as usual, supported by the Swedes, the Norwegian office-seekers will not gain as great a hearing in the state and county conventions the way they did."[31]

Letters to *Skandinaven* suggested that the discord caused by the Union Crisis did, to some extent, reverberate across Scandinavian America. From Dulce, Minnesota, where there were "mainly Swedes," with only "the postmaster and a few others" being Norwegian, Caroline Larson reported that "the Swedes are Swedish-minded and the Norwegians Norwegian-minded, and all of a sudden are at each other's throats and debate the relationship between Norway and Sweden." In Newman Grove, Nebraska, tensions between the two immigrant communities had found an outlet through physical activity in the shape of a tug-of-war between a team of local Norwegians and Swedes. "Those who carried the field would be the victors if there should be a war between the two countries," wrote I. Simonsen, who went on to note, presumably with satisfaction, that "the outcome was that the Norwegians out-pulled the Swedes as if it had been little boys they were dealing with, not just once, but twice."[32]

How deep the animosities resulting from the union dissolution ran is difficult to determine, but there were some signs already in 1905 that they were not permanent. From Chickasha, Indiana Territory (present-day Oklahoma), a letter writer reported that somewhat of a "miracle" had occurred on May 17: Swedes and Danes had decided to take part in the celebration of this "particularly Norwegian holiday," and "the result was a magnificent freedom day that hardly has an equal as far as brotherly feelings are concerned." Similarly, a mass meeting in Bellingham, Washington, during the summer that had declared that any attempt by Sweden to "force Norway back into the union by force of arms will be a crime against civilization and the enlightened spirit of our times" had been supported by both Swedes and Danes. As the year drew to a close, Gust Pederson, quoted in this chapter's introduction, also saw hopeful signs, as he thought that the Scandinavians of Beltrami County "all are now satisfied with the final result" of what had transpired across the ocean in Scandinavia.[33]

As the years passed, it is likely that what had happened in a small Scandinavian community in northern Minnesota became typical of the relationship between Swedes and Norwegians in America.

Notes

1. *Minneapolis Tidende* (hereafter, *MT*), Feb. 23, 1906, 7; Pederson overestimated the Scandinavian dominance in his county: according to the 1910 U.S. Census, Norwegians, Swedes, and Danes, foreign and native born, were only 30 percent of the population. *Thirteenth Census of the United States: 1910*, vol. 4, Population, 996, available: http://www2.census.gov/prod2/decennial/documents/36894832v2ch08.pdf.

2. Olav Tysdal, "The Dissolution of the Union between Norway and Sweden and the Scandinavian Americans," *Scandinavian Studies* 79 (2007): 166–96; Arlow Andersen, *Rough Road to Glory: The Norwegian-American Press Speaks Out on Public Affairs, 1875–1925* (Philadelphia, PA: The Balch Institute Press, 1990), 102–12. H. Arnold Barton, "Partners and Rivals: Norwegian and Swedish Emigration and Immigrants," *Swedish-American Historical Quarterly* (hereafter, *SAHQ*) 54 (2003): 102.

3. Barton, "Partners and Rivals," 102. The two Swedish-language papers were weeklies, while *Minneapolis Tidende* had a daily and a weekly edition and *Skandinaven* had three different editions: daily, twice-weekly and Sunday; for this study, the weekly *Tidende* and the twice-weekly *Skandinaven* were examined, a choice dictated by what was available through interlibrary loan.

4. Brian Thornton, "Published Reaction When Murrow Battled McCarthy," *Journalism History* 29 (2003): 133, accessed through EBSCO Host Research Databases; Emmett Buell, Jr., "Eccentrics or Gladiators? People Who Write about Politics in Letters to the Editor," *Social Science Quarterly* 56 (1975): 440–49; David L. Grey and Trevor R. Brown, "Letters to the Editor: Hazy Reflections of Public Opinion," *Journalism Quarterly* 47 (1970): 450–56, 471; for the gatekeeping function from a Swedish American perspective, see the author's " 'Folkets Röst,' The Pulse of the People: *Svenska Amerikanska Posten* and Reader Letters, 1907–1911," *SAHQ* 50 (1999): 6, 13.

5. Tysdal, 184ff.; Björk, "Folkets Röst"; Ulf Jonas Björk, "Perhaps There Is Someone Who Wants to Know How We Live: 'Public' Immigrant Letters in Swedish-American Newspapers," *SAHQ* 56 (2005): 183–97; Lawrence Carlson, "If Russia Decided to Annex Sweden, How Should We Swedish-Americans Then Conduct Ourselves?" *Swedish Pioneer Historical Quarterly* 8 (1957): 3–18; Isaac Metzker, *A Bintel Brief: Sixty Years of Letters from the Lower East Side to the Jewish Daily* Forward (New York: Schocken Books, 1990).

6. In *Svenska Amerikanaren*, readers in Illinois wrote 38 percent of the letters, with the rest of the Midwest contributing 26 percent, the East Coast 15 percent, and the Far West 12 percent; in *Svenska Amerikanska Posten*, letters from Minnesota accounted for 32 percent, followed by the Dakotas and the Midwest with 16 percent each and the Far West with 13 percent; in *Skandinaven,* writers from Illinois contributed 6 percent, the rest of the Midwest 45 percent, the Great Plains 15 percent, the Far West and the East Coast 6 percent each; in *Minneapolis Tidende*, finally, the percentages were 25 for Minnesota, 12 for the rest of the Midwest, 25 for the Great Plains, 38 for the Far West.

7. *N. W. Ayer & Son's American Newspaper Annual and Directory*, 1906; *Geo. P. Rowell and Co.'s American Newspaper Directory*, 1905; *Posten* publisher Swan Turnblad admitted at one point that he had inflated his paper's circulation figures: see Ulf Jonas Björk, "*Svenska Amerikanska Posten*: An Immigrant Newspaper with American Accents," in Philip J. Anderson and Dag Blanck, eds., *Swedish Life in the Twin Cities: Immigrant Life and Minnesota's Urban Frontier* (St. Paul: Minnesota Historical Society Press, 2001), 213.

For a discussion of *Posten's* reputation, see Björk, "*Svenska Amerikanska Posten*: An Immigrant Newspaper with American Accents"; Jean Skogerboe Hansen, "*Skandinaven* and the John Anderson Publishing Company," *Norwegian-American Studies* [hereafter, *NAS*] 28 (1979): 35–36; Odd Lovoll, "*Washington Posten*: A Window on a Norwegian-American Urban Community," *NAS* 31 (1986): 165–66; Arlow Andersen, "The Norwegian-American

Press," in *The Ethnic Press in the United States,* ed. Sally M. Miller (New York: Greenwood Press, 1987), 266–67.

8. For a general discussion of the content of immigrant newspapers, see Jerzy Zubricki, "The Role of the Foreign-Language Press in Migrant Integration," in *Media Voices: An Historical Perspective,* ed. Jean Folkerts (New York: Macmillan Publishing Company, 1992), 277.

9. "Våra vänners afdelning," *Svenska Amerikanaren* (hereafter, *SA*), Apr. 25, 1905, 9; "Anonyme Insendere," *MT,* Feb. 3, 1905, 4.

10. "Mange 'Breve fra Folket,'" *Skandinaven,* Feb. 2, 1906, 4; "Folkets Röst," SAP, Nov. 14, 1905, 8; "Till våra skribenter," *Svenska Amerikanska Posten* (hereafter, *SAP*), Feb. 12, 1907, 8.

11. Karen Larsen, *A History of Norway* (Princeton, NJ: Princeton University Press, 1950), 488, 492; K. Nordlund, *The Swedish-Norwegian Union Crisis: A History with Documents* (Uppsala: Almqvist & Wicksell Ltd., 1905), 36. A good recent account of the crisis is in H. Arnold Barton, *Sweden and Visions of Norway: Politics and Culture, 1814–1905* (Carbondale: Southern Illinois University Press, 2003), 58–83.

12. See, for instance, the "Konung Oscar sjuk," *SAP,* Feb. 14, 1905, 1; "Transatlantiska notiser," *SA,* Feb. 21, 1905, 2; "Brev fra Norge," *MT,* Feb. 3, 1905, 5.

13. Alfred Söderström, "Nyhetsafdelningen," in Söderström, *Blixtar på tidningshorisonten: samlade och magasinerade af Alfred Söderström* (Warroad, MN: The author, 1910), 170; Efterretninger fra Norge," *MT,* July 21, 1905, 8.

14. *SA,* Aug. 25, 1908, 18. The other pseudonyms appear in Linder's entry in *Pennfäktare.* Söderström, "Nyhetsafdelningen," 168; a Swedish critic made essentially the same assertion, Adrian Molin, *Vanhäfd. Inlägg i emigrationsfrågan* (Stockholm: P. A. Nordstedt & söners förlag, 1911), 77; Skarstedt, *Pennfäktare. Svenskamerikanska författare och tidningsmän* (Stockholm: Åhlén & Åkerlunds förlag, 1930).

15. "En fråga," *SA,* Oct. 17, 1905, 9.

16. "Lad os vise Ro," *Skandinaven,* Mar. 31, 1905, 4.

17. "Hemlandets Jubilæum," *Skandinaven,* Jan. 11, 1905, 4; *MT,* Jan, 20, 1905, 4.

18. "Misbrug af Syttende Mai," *Skandinaven,* May 12, 1905, 4. Arctander was born in Sweden but had grown up in Norway. See Roger McKnight, "The Dinkytown Murder: A Study of Violence, Media Response, and Immigrant Assimilation in Nineteenth-Century Minnesota," *SAHQ* 59 (2008): 57–107. "Frihedsdagen," *MT,* May 26, 1905, 5; *Svenska Amerikanska Posten* ignored the event altogether.

19. "Lad os tone rent Flag!" *Skandinaven,* June 7, 1905, 10; cf. the similar sentiment expressed by P. Langbach, who declared in July that Norwegians in America would support Norway "both spiritually and monetarily and also sacrifice life and blood for her"; "Norge og Unionen," *Skandinaven,* July 19, 1905, 10. "Unions-Striden," *MT,* Sept. 1, 1905, 6.

20. "Indsendelser," *MT,* Feb. 2, 1906, 6; "Syvende Junifest," *Skandinaven,* Nov. 22, 1905, 10.

21. "Foretraekker republiken: En Indsender mener, at Norge nu bør vise Vei for Broderfolkkene," *Skandinaven,* Sept. 20, 1905, 10. "Fra Canton," *Skandinaven,* Nov. 15, 1905, 10.

22. "Næsten alle er allright," *Skandinaven,* July 26, 1905, 10; "Lad os tone rent Flag!"

23. "Montana-bref," *SAP*, Sept. 26, 1905, 15; for a similarly sympathetic viewpoint, see "Nu är det gjordt!" *SA*, June 20, 1905, 9. "Sverige sofver," *SA*, Aug. 8, 1905, 9.

24. "I svensknorska frågan," *SA*, Aug. 15, 1905, 9.

25. "Till Sveas folk," *SA*, Sept. 26, 1905, 9; "Sverige-Norge," *SAP*, Sept. 26, 1905, 15; "Från en norrländing," *SAP*, Oct. 10, 1905, 15; "Sverige-Norge," *SAP*, Sept. 5, 1905, 15; Dag Blanck, *Becoming Swedish-American: The Construction of an Ethnic Identity in the Augustana Synod, 1860–1917* (Uppsala: Acta Universitatis Upsaliensis, 1997), 196–99.

26. "Samtal mellan Hansen och Nielsen," *SA*, Sept. 12, 1905, 9. "Höjden af svenskhet," *SA*, Aug. 8, 1905, 9.

27. "Lad os tone rent Flag."

28. "Taalmodet brister. En Indsender finder at maatte sige lidt i anledning de svenske Skriverier," *Skandinaven*, Sept. 6, 1905, 10; "Breve fra Folket," *Skandinaven*, Oct. 4, 1905, 10; "Foretraekker republiken."

29. "Tycker om Posten, men inte norrmän," *SAP*, Nov. 14, 1905, 15. "Tankar om norrmännen," *SAP*, Feb. 20, 1906, 15; "Från en ung stad," *SAP*, July 11, 1905, 15; "Massemøde," *MT*, June 30, 1905, 7.

30. "Från en norrländing," *SAP*, Sept. 19, 1905, 15.

31. "Tankar om norrmännen."

32. "Breve fra Folket," *Skandinaven*, Aug. 9, 1905, 10; "Breve fra Folket," *Skandinaven*, Aug. 16, 1905, 10.

33. *MT*, Feb. 2, 1906, 7; "Norges Sag," *MT*, July 14, 1905, 6; "Frihedsdagen i Sydvesten," *Skandinaven*, July 26, 1905, 10.

CHAPTER 10

"The Sociological Factor Is Not to Be Underestimated"

Swedes, Norwegians, and American Lutheran Merger Negotiations, 1920–60

MARK GRANQUIST

In working through E. Clifford Nelson's history of Lutherans in North America, the reader comes across an interesting and somewhat enigmatic passage concerning merger negotiations in the early 1940s. A number of midwestern Lutheran denominations, including the Norwegian Lutheran Church in America (NLCA) and the Augustana Synod (Swedish), working under the framework of the American Lutheran Conference, had sponsored Lutheran merger negotiations beginning in the late 1930s, and by 1942 they had come to a watershed point. Having reached a resolution directing Conference officials to negotiate with *all* other American Lutheran groups, the question was how this would be implemented. Commenting on the situation, Nelson reports, "What does not appear in the minutes was the resistance of two Norwegian Lutheran leaders to what they considered Augustana Synod pressure to include the United Lutheran Church in the American Lutheran Conference. Johan A. Aasgaard resented the 'pushiness' of the Swedes (the sociological factor of Norwegian-Swedish tension is not to be underestimated in inter-Lutheran relations)."[1]

From a generally reserved and polite Lutheran historian such as Nelson, these lines are as intriguing as they are enigmatic. On the one hand, the text gives us no specific reference to either the word in quotation, *pushiness,* nor to the parenthetical comment about the Norwegian-Swedish sociological relationships, so the reader does not know exactly where to turn for confirmation. On the other hand, Nelson is a careful historian from the Norwegian Lutheran tradition and an intimate associate of its church leaders and, in its later stages, the process of Lutheran mergers leading up to the formation of the American Lutheran Church (1960–88) and the Lutheran Church in America (1962–88).

Many of the Lutheran leaders present at the negotiations in 1942 had hoped for a larger and more inclusive merger, and the Conference eventually divided— four of the five member denominations formed the ALC, while the Augustana Synod left those negotiations to join with three other denominations to form the LCA. Conference members were divided about how to proceed and whom to invite to the table, and the grand visions of a larger Lutheran merger were not to be fulfilled. One of the key points in this history is the dispute between the Augustana Synod and the NLCA, and the reader is left to ponder whether these dreams of a larger merger really were scuttled by ethnic rivalries and tensions between the Swedes and Norwegians. This chapter will examine this question, not so much to attempt to prove Nelson's claim one way or the other, but to explore the broader and larger questions involved and to find out how the theological and ecclesiastical factors of this matter mesh with the personal and sociological aspects.

Getting at the root of the personal and sociological factors involved in this area, however, is not a simple task. The Lutheran leaders in question, both Norwegian and Swedish, were generally careful individuals and were not likely to make such personal utterances in public forums, such as church newspapers and periodicals, or in official documents. Rather, if this question is to be evaluated, we will primarily have to examine the contemporary private correspondence of the participants; in addition, the later reminiscences of church leaders can also be helpful.

One might be tempted to ask at this point whether such an attempt is, after all, either advisable or salutary—this line of pursuit could become little more than gossip mongering and blame placing. But churches do not always live in the realm of theoretical or theological abstraction; they are embodied and incarnated entities consisting of many individuals, each with his or her strengths and weaknesses. If we are to understand how churches operate, we must see how they function in real time, on the sociological and organizational level as well as the theological or ecclesiastical levels. Further, this particular incident is a key turning point in twentieth-century American Lutheran history—a watershed event that determined much about how Lutherans related to each other in the North American context over the following fifty to sixty years. Properly handled, an inquiry into this subject might illuminate American Lutheran history and instruct the American Lutheran present.

Background to the Merger Process

The first of three waves of twentieth-century merger activity among American Lutherans lasted from 1917 to 1930 and resulted in three new denominations. Most of the Norwegian American groups merged in 1917 to form the Norwegian Lutheran Church in America; a smaller group, the Lutheran Free Church, did not enter this merger. The three groups of eastern-based Lutherans from the colonial Muhlenberg tradition reunited in 1918 to form the United Lutheran Church in America (ULCA). The third merger drew together three midwestern

German groups, the Buffalo Synod, the Ohio Synod, and the Iowa Synod, which formed the American Lutheran Church in 1930. So by 1930, there were roughly a dozen American Lutheran denominations of any particular size, with any number of smaller splinter and independent denominations. These denominations were grouped in two separate cooperative bodies, the National Lutheran Council (1918–66) and the Synodical Conference (1872–1964).[2]

TABLE 10.1
National Lutheran Council and the Synodical Conference Membership, 1940

NATIONAL LUTHERAN COUNCIL	SYNODICAL CONFERENCE
United Lutheran Church, 1.7 million	Missouri Synod, 1.35 million
Norwegian Lutheran, 570,000	Wisconsin Synod, 260,000
American Lutheran, 565,000	Slovak Synod, 23,000
Augustana Synod, 350,000	Norwegian Synod, 9,000
Lutheran Free Church, 50,000	
United Danish, 35,000	
Suomi Synod, 28,000	
Danish Church, 18,000	

Historically, the Missouri Synod had so dominated the other groups within the Synodical Conference that for all intents and purposes we need not concern ourselves with the Synodical Conference. The National Lutheran Council (NLC) was, however, a fairly weak body, charged mainly with coordinating home and foreign mission work, campus ministries, and other cooperative efforts. If one would speak of the "wings" of American Lutheranism at the time, there were three: (1) the United Lutheran Church in America, with about 1.7 million members; (2) the seven remaining members of the NLC, principally the midwestern groups of Scandinavian and German descent, representing about 1.6 million members; and (3) the Missouri Synod and its clients, which represented about 1.65 million members. The three wings were, then, roughly numerically equal; however, the ULCA and Missouri Synod had the advantage of being unified, while the seven ethnic denominations in the middle were anything but together. To rectify this, five of the midwestern denominations formed their own alliance in 1930, the American Lutheran Conference (hereafter "the Conference," 1930–54); the partners in this were the American Lutheran Church, the Norwegian Lutheran Church, the Augustana Synod, the United Danish Church, and the Lutheran Free Church.

Throughout its twenty-four year history, the American Lutheran Conference suffered mainly from an identity crisis. Was it to be the precursor to a merger among the "middle" groups, a defensive alliance against either the ULCA or Missouri Synod, or the catalyst to a larger Lutheran merger involving all the major American Lutheran denominations? At different points in its history and among the minds of its different constituent members, it was all three of these things, but the five denominations never reached a consensus on these issues. The leaders of the American Lutheran Church and the Norwegian Lutheran Church tended to be strongly suspicious of the ULCA and its alleged "liberalism," were more open to the Missouri Synod, and saw the Conference mainly as a defensive alliance or a protomerger of the center. The Augustana Synod, on the other hand, had a long working relationship with parts of the ULCA and was more concerned about Missouri Synod domination. One important part of Augustana tended to view the Conference as a stepping-stone to a larger American Lutheran denomination that would include all three wings of American Lutheranism, although others in Augustana had more limited aims. Obviously, this picture is more complex than these simple characterizations, but on the whole they explain the general leanings of the groups involved.[3]

The Lutheran merger negotiations of the 1930s and 1940s principally involved the five members of the American Lutheran Conference; the key issue was whether the negotiations were to be limited to the Conference membership or open to all American Lutheran denominations. A complicating factor was that the ULCA and the Missouri Synod were on opposite ends of the Lutheran theological spectrum in America, so it was unlikely at this time that a merger would be able to include both of these groups. A merger open to the ULCA would result in the Missouri Synod's noninvolvement in the negotiations. A defensive merger of the five Conference groups, keeping out the ULCA, would be open to cooperation with the Missouri Synod. A merger of the eight National Lutheran Conference groups, however, would mean that the Missouri Synod would not participate. Either one of these two larger scenarios would result in an association of two-thirds of American Lutherans, either a Conference–Missouri Synod alliance or an NLC merger. In either case, the remaining group, either ULCA or Missouri, would be isolated.

As we have seen, the principal tensions within the Conference were between the American Lutheran Church and the Norwegian Lutheran Church, on the one hand, and the Augustana Synod, on the other. We will concentrate on the relations between the Norwegian Lutheran Church and the Swedish-based Augustana Synod as a key to the Conference dynamics and hence to the larger merger negotiations. Norwegian Americans on the whole distrusted the ULCA and wanted a five-way merger within the Conference. Swedish Americans, generally, wanted a larger merger negotiation with all American Lutheran groups, effectively ensuring that though invited, the Missouri Synod would not participate. Hence, we are back to the original question: how much of this key disagreement within the center wing of American Lutheranism was either the result of, or exacerbated by, ethnic tensions among the leaders of Norwegian and Swedish ethnic Lutheranism in North America?

An Appreciation of the Individuals Involved

We have been considering thus far the large-scale aspect of the topic, namely the positioning and attitudes of large Lutheran denominations. But the key element of this chapter concerns individual relationships, especially those between the leaders of the Norwegian Lutheran Church in America and the Augustana Synod. If we are attempting to trace the possible ethnic rivalries and tensions between these two groups, we will need to know something about the key individuals, those whose correspondence we are citing for evidence. Each group had five key leaders.

Norwegian Lutheran Church in America

H. G. (Hans Gerhard) Stub (1849–1931). First president of the NLCA, 1917–25, he came out of the Norwegian Synod tradition and was thus strongly inclined toward the Missouri Synod and a strict Lutheran confessionalism. He authored the "Minneapolis Theses," one approach to Lutheran unity on the basis of absolute theological agreement.

J. A. (Johan Arnd) Aasgaard (1876–1966). Successor to Stub as president of the NLCA, 1925–54, he was in office during the "Americanization" of the NLCA. Aasgaard was intimately involved in the merger negotiations of the 1930s and 1940s and was deeply suspicious of the ULCA. He favored a merger of the Conference.

T. F. (Thaddeus Francke) Gullixson (1882–1969). President of Luther Seminary, 1930–54, he guided the building of Luther as a modern theological seminary. Close associate of both Aasgaard and Lars Boe, he too was very active in the merger process in the Conference. He was close to the Missouri Synod and distrustful of the ULCA.

Lars W. (Wilhelm) Boe (1875–1942). President of St. Olaf College, 1918–42, he was a representative of the "United Church" wing of the NLCA (opposed to the Missouri tendencies of the Norwegian Synod). The leading voice in the NLCA for a broader approach to Lutheran unity, he was close to leaders of the ULCA and the Augustana Synod, especially P. O. Bersell, but was also close to Gullixson and Aasgaard.

F. A. (Frederik Axel) Schiotz (1901–89). Successor to Aasgaard as president of the Evangelical Lutheran Church (subsequent name of the NLCA), 1954–60, he guided the discussions that would lead to the formation of the American Lutheran Church (1960–88).

Augustana Synod

G. A. (Gustaf Albert) Brandelle (1861–1936). President of the Augustana Synod, 1918–35, he presided during the "Americanization" of Augustana. A pastor in Colorado and Illinois, he represented the official "core" of the synod around Augustana College, Rock Island, Illinois. Strong advocate of wider Lutheran union and ecumenism, he argued forcefully, yet unsuccessfully, for the Augustana Synod to enter the ULCA merger in 1918.

P. O. (Petrus Olof) Bersell (1882–1967). Successor to Brandelle as president of the Augustana Synod, 1935–51, he established the synodical headquarters in Minneapolis in 1935. Very active in the American Lutheran Conference, he was well acquainted with the leaders of the NLCA, especially Aasgaard, Gullixson, and Boe. Interested in ecumenical affairs, he set as a priority to establish a federation of the eight National Lutheran Council denominations rather than an organic union.

E. E. (Ernest Edwin) Ryden (1886–1981). Longtime editor of the *Lutheran Companion,* the official periodical of the Augustana Synod, he was also actively involved in the American Lutheran Conference, serving as president, 1938–42. One of the leading voices within the Augustana Synod, he urged merger on the basis of the Conference.

Conrad J. I. (Johan Immanuel) Bergendoff (1895–1997). President of Augustana College and Theological Seminary during the 1930s and 1940s, he was probably the leading theological voice within the Augustana Synod. He advocated a wide-ranging Lutheran merger process open to any Lutheran group that wished to participate. He had strong ties to leaders of the ULCA.

Oscar A. (Algot) Benson (1891–1972). Successor to Bersell as Synod president, 1951–57, he presided over the Augustana Synod during the crucial merger years of 1951–52, which saw the final divide between Augustana and the four other Conference denominations, and the end of the Conference in 1954.

The leadership of the denominations that constituted the American Lutheran Conference was a small fraternity; these men all knew each other well. They had close relations, although they did not always like each other. Boe in particular had a strong relationship with Gullixson and wide-ranging contacts with many of the other leaders; his untimely death in 1942 (a critical moment in the merger negotiations) left a void that was never really filled.

Relations between the NLCA and the Augustana Synod up to 1942

The Norwegian and Swedish Lutherans in North America shared a long common history and occupied much of the same territory on this continent. Norwegian Americans tended to be strongest in the Upper Midwest, from Wisconsin through the Dakotas. While Swedish Americans were also dominant in this region, they had other areas of strength lower in the Midwest, from Illinois to Kansas, and in New England. Both groups were well represented in the Pacific Northwest. On the whole, the Swedish Americans tended more to the urban areas (60 percent), while the Norwegian Americans were more rural (60 percent). Both groups had a long parallel tradition of religious activity in North America, though linguistic differences kept them separate until the 1920s. The Norwegians, or at least a significant portion of them, were drawn into the orbit of the Missouri Synod during the election and predestination controversies of the late nineteenth century. Swedish Americans had some significant connections with one branch of Eastern Lutheranism, the General Council, and shared mission work with that group.[4]

During the 1850s and 1860s, at the very beginning of Lutheranism in the Midwest, the Augustana Synod had both a Swedish and a Norwegian conference, although there were other Norwegian American denominations. The Norwegians withdrew peacefully from the Augustana Synod in 1870, and they remained separate traditions until the formation of the Evangelical Lutheran Church in America in 1988. As long as these two ethnic groups were focused on the maintenance of their respective language traditions, they did not have many contacts with each other. But with the inevitable transition to the use of English, which intensified after World War I, the contacts between Swedish Americans and Norwegian Americans broadened. The center of this cooperation was Minnesota, where both groups were well represented and where they tended to share a common outlook and concerns. Elements of Augustana's Minnesota Conference formed the China Mission Society in 1901, and Augustana missionaries to China worked closely with those from the NLCA. Also in Minnesota, Augustana elements formed the Lutheran Bible Institute in 1919, but this quickly became a common endeavor with the Norwegians. There were eventually four Bible institutes, participation in which tended to be evenly divided between Swedes and Norwegians. Both the NLCA and Augustana lagged behind in English-language home mission work and were challenged in this area on their own turf by the ULCA's Synod of the Northwest, which both Swedes and

Norwegians had reason to resent. Both the ethnic denominations came together in the work of the National Lutheran Council after 1918, especially military chaplaincy, campus ministry, and home missions, the latter an area where they cooperated and clashed in turn. Augustana and NLCA laymen worked together in the formation of the Lutheran Brotherhood; both denominations cooperated in support of Pacific Lutheran College (and later California Lutheran College) and also shared in Lutheran wartime relief and refugee resettlement. The groups shared a long history, especially in the twentieth century.

The Course of Merger Negotiations, 1920–52

The formation of the National Lutheran Council in 1918 came out of necessity, because the eight Lutheran denominations involved needed a cooperative framework for home and foreign missions as well as specialized ministries, such as military chaplaincy. Though it was a rather weak organization, the NLC very quickly became the focus of further merger discussions between the eight groups, with a series of meeting around 1919–20. From these discussions two basic and competing positions on Lutheran unity emerged. One was articulated by H. G. Stub in a document that came to be known as the "Chicago Theses." In it, Stub argued for what E. Clifford Nelson has termed *exclusive confessionalism*—a position that a detailed theological and ecclesiastical settlement of all outstanding issues is required before there can be a settlement between the various Lutheran groups. The other position, developed by ULCA leaders F. H. Knubel and H. E. Jacobs, suggested that closer fellowship and possible merger should be based on agreement about central theological issues and that differences on peripheral matters could be dealt with in time. This position was codified by the ULCA in 1920 as the "Washington Declaration." Nelson termed this approach *ecumenical confessionalism.* The two basic positions would be the foci around which fellowship and merger negotiations revolved from 1920 to the 1950s. The Norwegian Lutheran Church and the American Lutheran Church insisted on the exclusive approach, whereas the ULCA argued for the ecumenical approach; the Augustana Synod was often in the middle, unsure which way to lean.[5]

The formation of the American Lutheran Conference in 1930 was predicated on the general basis of exclusive confessionalism, with the "Minneapolis Theses" of 1930 as the core unifying document. This document was an expansion of Stub's "Chicago Theses" and became the theological key for the new group, which many (especially the NLCA and the ALC) saw as a defensive alignment against the power and influence of the ULCA. The Augustana Synod did enter the Conference but did not share the others' fears about the ULCA; Augustana pushed for larger merger talks open to all American Lutheran groups. This position was shared by the ULCA but vigorously resisted by other members of the Conference.

Through the 1930s, there were a number of bilateral and multilateral discussions on Lutheran fellowship and possible union scenarios, even talks between the ULCA and the ALC, and ULCA and the Missouri Synod. Though these discussions never bore fruit, they led to an air of optimism that progress was being made on many fronts. In 1938, under the leadership of Augustana leaders P. O. Bersell, E. E. Ryden, and Conrad Bergendoff, the Commission on Lutheran Unity of the American Lutheran Conference adopted a resolution calling the Conference unity efforts to "leave the door open, as far as it is concerned, for all Lutheran bodies." Furthermore, the Commission urged all Conference members to establish pulpit and altar fellowship with other Lutheran denominations if they had not done so already. In meetings during 1942 and 1943, the Conference and its executive committee, dominated by NLCA and ALC leaders (Bersell was ill and Boe died in 1942), steered the merger negotiations back to a more exclusivist position with the idea that a new group of theses be written to form the basis of possible fellowship or union. Merger negotiations resumed in 1948 under the auspices of the National Lutheran Council, but these collapsed under the existing differences in 1949. The failure of earlier negotiations led to five-way merger negotiations among the Conference, which began in 1950. The Augustana Synod initially participated in these discussions but still held out for a larger open merger process. After a long debate within Augustana, it decided in convention in 1952 that the synod would await a larger merger process. Failing to convince the other four Conference members of this position, the Augustana delegates walked out of the Conference merger negotiations in November 1952. The four remaining Conference denominations moved forward and formed the American Lutheran Church (1960–88); Augustana and the ULCA, along with a smaller Danish and Finnish group, formed the Lutheran Church in America (1962–88).[6]

Personal and Professional Relationships

Having described the intersection of the NLCA and the Augustana Synod through the first half of the twentieth century—and how they related through the Lutheran merger negotiations—this section will now highlight the personal and professional relationships between the leaders of these two Lutheran denominations. If there is to be evidence of a strong ethnic antipathy between Swedish Americans and Norwegian Americans, it will be found in the correspondence and personal observations of the individuals involved. We shall attempt to trace the interchange of these leaders and tease out the attitudes of these often reticent and "proper" Scandinavians.

Early in the twentieth century, H. G. Stub led the NLCA and G. A. Brandelle headed the Augustana Synod. Both had come into office at the end of the First World War and were involved in the formation of the National Lutheran Council. Stub was the author of the "Chicago Theses" and a proponent of the exclusivist confessional position; he was not positively inclined toward the ULCA. Brandelle was not very visible during the merger negotiations of 1919–20 but was a friend of the ULCA and had unsuccessfully urged Augustana to join its merger in 1918. The available letters between Stub and Brandelle are few and show hints of emotion. In one instance, Stub wrote to Brandelle about developments on the China mission field, where there was a possibility of Augustana cooperating with the missionaries of the Mission Covenant Church (both the Swedish and American branches). Obviously alarmed, Stub openly pressured Brandelle to block any move in this direction: "We, namely The Norwegian Lutheran Church in America, regard the Augustana Synod as our brethren in faith, and could not tolerate a union with Waldenstromians who have been the strongest opponents of the Augustana Synod." On July 20, 1920, Stub wrote to Brandelle seeking Augustana's cooperation in the operation of Pacific Lutheran College, and on November 1, 1920, he wrote with obvious pleasure about his perception that Augustana was on his side of the merger dispute, with the ULCA on the other. Brandelle mentioned Stub in several letters but with only a passing reference: he was alarmed by Norwegian aggressiveness in English-language home missions in Minneapolis and St. Paul but otherwise made little comment.[7]

Another leader in the NLCA at the time, J. A. O. Stub (son of H. G. Stub), displayed a positive attitude toward Swedish Americans. Writing to a ULCA pastor in New York, Stub devoted an entire paragraph to praising the Swedish Lutheran tradition and quoted Archbishop Söderblom approvingly: "The Swedish Church impressed me perhaps most of the European Lutherans. They have piety, poise, and churchly consciousness; they have kept their heritage in churchly customs and usage, brighter than any of us." The younger Stub was also a friend and confidant of Lars Boe, a president of the NLC, and was active in the American Lutheran Conference.[8]

In 1925, J. A. Aasgaard succeeded H. G. Stub as president of the NLCA and overlapped with Brandelle for the next ten years. A series of letters between them in 1926 covers home mission work in Missoula, Montana; the few other letters they wrote to each other are formal and perfunctory. In contrast, very warm and personal letters were exchanged between Brandelle and Lars Boe, president of St. Olaf College and one of the leaders within the NLCA. To Boe in 1931 Brandelle wrote, "I have always appreciated very highly your various points of view and your hearty cooperation. The part of the Lutheran Church allied with the NLC has almost a new outlook on things compared to the situation thirteen years ago."[9]

Brandelle also wrote to Boe at the end of 1932 of his pleasure at reading his "Open Confession" to the American Lutheran Conference. Brandelle, obviously chafing at the exclusivist confessional position of Stub and others, commented to Boe, "Neither am I always satisfied that the so called 'Lutheran Principles' are always related to confessionalism. Often they have a slant which makes me wonder whether after all they are not strictly private property which certain people strive to foist upon others in order to make sure that they are tied to themselves for all time to come." Brandelle openly worried about the unity position of T. E. Gullixson, which he saw as closet "Missourianism." Boe, in return, thanked Brandelle for his "good and long letter" and stated, "One of the reasons I have appreciated you so much during the years we have been associated has been the things you say in your letter." He hoped that their common efforts would have an effect on many of his colleagues, "if only we can wake them up."[10]

Aasgaard's attitude toward the Augustana Synod can be seen in letters to Gullixson and Carl C. Hein, the president of the American Lutheran Church. Hein was often very suspicious of Augustana; he believed that it needed to be "won" to the ALC/NLCA position. When Hein complained to Aasgaard in 1934 about alleged "unionistic" activity by Augustana clergy, Aasgaard urged the best possible interpretation of these actions, namely, that they might not really be unionistic at all. A common complaint by the Missouri Synod and others was that Augustana and ULCA pastors indulged in unionist practices, but Aasgaard was realistic about the possibility of controlling the actions of local pastors. Writing to ALC president Emmanuel Poppen in 1942, Aasgaard confessed that such things happened (though infrequently) in his own denomination and suggested, "I know we all have our shortcomings and need ever to judge ourselves first." In another letter to Poppen, Aasgaard approvingly cited Eric Norelius (pioneer leader of the Augustana Synod) as an example of "sound doctrine and sound practice."[11]

According to some who knew Aasgaard, he had generally good relations with Swedish Americans in the Augustana Synod. Alvin Rogness, who succeeded T. E. Gullixson as president of Luther Seminary in 1954, later recalled that he never "bought" the idea (sometimes cited) that there were personal problems between Aasgaard and P. O. Bersell. About the rumors, Rogness stated, "I never bought that. Because I've seen them together, and temperamentally they were much alike . . . I remember seeing them together in Hannover in 1952 [Lutheran World Federation meeting], Bersell and Aasgaard, and having just a grand time together."[12]

Malvin Lundeen, the last president of the Augustana Synod (1957–62) also commented on this point. About the relationship between Bersell and Aasgaard, he recalled, "They could really clash in debates and that kind of thing, and I think there was a disappointment, although Aasgaard, I think, had a high regard for the Augustana Church. A number of members of the family, the Aasgaard family, were members of the Augustana Church at various places." It has been said that in retirement in Cokato, Minnesota, Aasgaard was a member of a local Augustana congregation because there was no Norwegian congregation in the area.[13]

The other prominent leader in the Norwegian Lutheran Church in America at the time was T. E. Gullixson, president of Luther Seminary. In 1932 he wrote to Lars Boe that he was accepting several young men from the Augustana Synod as students at the seminary, and then reflected to Boe, "I feel that the coming of these Minnesota Conference Swedish boys is a God-send in the development of that fellowship in labor which must be if we are going to handle our job. The Norwegians and Swedes have been too far apart in their work here. Maybe these young men are simply going to trample all the vestiges of that sickening racial antagonism." Commenting to Boe in 1935 about his attendance at P. O. Bersell's presidential inauguration, Gullixson wrote, "Aasgaard and I returned last night . . . I think that the Augustana Synod is going to have a finer leadership than it has recently been supplied with . . . I think the Swedes appreciated our presence." To the fact that the presidents of Conference denominations, and of the ULCA, were all apparently maneuvered into laying their hands on Bersell's head during the ceremony, Boe replied to Gullixson, "It did me a lot of good (to hear it) . . . Not that I am high church, but I rejoice every time I see the 'powers that be' crowded into a corner where they have to practice unionism. It makes me sleep better at nights." If Gullixson and Aasgaard were worried at all that this was practicing unionism with the Swedes, there is no evidence of it.[14]

One of the most interesting leaders in the Norwegian Lutheran Church in America was the president of St. Olaf College, Lars W. Boe. He was a strong advocate of a broad Lutheran merger process and great friends not only with leaders of the NLCA but also with those of Augustana and ULCA. Through the 1930s, Boe was actively involved in the American Lutheran Conference and in discussions with other Lutherans toward closer cooperation and fellowship. Boe often served to "explain" the actions of Augustana to the NLCA leadership and the actions of NLCA to Augustana leaders. Commenting on an editorial by E. E. Ryden in the *Lutheran Companion,* the periodical of the Augustana Synod, Boe wrote to Gullixson in 1939, "I think we should get together, and that very soon, because we Norwegians do have a spirit of realism that that may help overcome the emotionalism of the Swedes." Boe wanted especially to have a closer relationship with the other Conference denominations and saw Augustana as an integral part of that plan.[15]

Around the pivotal merger events of 1942, Boe was particularly active and animated, although illness kept him away from many of the meetings (he died on December 27, 1942). In a letter to Gullixson on October 1, Boe expressed obvious irritation with the Augustana leadership: "I am concerned especially about the attempt on the part of the Swedes to get the U.L.C. into the American Lutheran Conference, which will bring trouble within our own synod." In a long and impassioned letter (six pages, single-spaced) to J. A. Aasgaard on October 29, in advance of the Conference meeting in Rock Island, Boe poured out his frustrations. Boe suggested that Bersell, once a friend, had changed, and not for the better—that Bersell was being driven by "ambition" and "love of power and position" over the insistence that the ULCA be included in the negotiations. Furthermore, Boe wrote, "I feel almost as if Dr. Bersell has permitted us to be 'sold down the river,' and with the disappearance of the American Lutheran Conference goes the vision and the possibility of the contribution of the Scandinavian Lutherans to the ultimate face of Lutheranism in America." Yet a week later, in a letter to Gullixson, who was seriously ill with pneumonia and also unable to attend the meeting, Boe referred to Bersell as "our friend" and deplored the fact that Bersell, too, was ill (with a bleeding ulcer) and would also not be in attendance. One gains the impression that Boe, who was terminally ill at this time, saw the vision of his life's work—a greater Lutheran unity—slipping away from him.[16]

Apparently Boe had copies of his October 29 letter to Aasgaard sent to a number of the leaders of the NLCA; Gullixson received a copy, as did Frederik Schiotz (a younger leader in the NLCA and eventual successor to Aasgaard as president). Schiotz replied to Boe on November 6 and commented on his proposed course of action: "I question whether or not it may receive the enthusiastic acceptance of the Augustana leaders. We have a feeling that they 'sold us down the river' at the meeting last spring. They, on the other hand, have a feeling that the NLCA 'crossed them up' after the Columbus meeting." Late in life, Schiotz suggested that the Augustana Synod was too eager to bring about a large Lutheran union: "Had Augustana had the patience to wait a little longer, the patience that the former American Lutheran Church demonstrated, she might have been a part of the union that came into being." Although significant negotiations and opportunities for a merger took place from 1942 to 1952, ultimately it was not to be; Augustana left the Conference negotiations in 1952 and eventually joined a smaller Danish and Finnish group to form the Lutheran Church in America.[17]

One longtime Norwegian Lutheran leader and head of Augsburg Publishing House, Albert E. Anderson, recalled that Schiotz said that this division was not permanent: "Frederik A. Schiotz always said, 'Finally, we are going to have to merge with, and should, and must for the good of our people, merge with the, the ULCA and Augustana Synod.'" Anderson then added his own opinion on the matter: "Now, when it came to the Augustana Lutheran Church, the ELC [Evangelical Lutheran Church, the subsequent name of the NLCA] people wanted Augustana in this ALC [1960–88] merger. There was very close relationships between Augustana and ELC people. My own marriage is one example of that. And the Augustana Synod was really split on this." There was an air, even then, that the LCA and ALC mergers were not permanent but a step toward the formation of a larger American Lutheran denomination.[18]

Conclusion and Final Thoughts

We are full circle, then, to the initial question, namely, the role of ethnic or socio-logical elements in the American Lutheran merger negotiations during the 1930s and 1940s, specifically the relationships between the leaders of the Swedish Augustana Synod and the Norwegian Lutheran Church in America. How much of the subsequent history of Lutheran merger can be laid at the feet of ethnic tensions? What did these Norwegian and Swedish leaders think of each other, and what were the reasons for the failure to bring the five constituent parts of the American Lutheran Conference together into one unified denomination?

Most certainly tensions cropped up between Swedish Americans and Norwegian Americans, but at the same time these tensions were set within the context of deep and friendly relationships. Both sides dreamed of a uni-fied and strong Lutheran center composed of the midwestern Scandinavian denominations (along with the old ALC), which would be a vital counterweight to the ULCA on the one hand and the Missouri Synod on the other. Swedish American and Norwegian American Lutherans had a long history of living and working together; on the whole they valued and appreciated each other deeply. In this context, then, frustrated comments about "pushy Swedes" or "pushy Norwegians" must be seen as a palpable sense of frustration and loss at the apparent death of a dream of a united Scandinavian American Lutheranism. This is how Boe's long and sometimes bitter letter of October 29, 1942, comes across, for example. It is precisely the depth of their feeling for each other that the occasional angry asides of the participants reveal.

The main chasm between the NLCA and the Augustana Synod was theologi-cal and ecclesiastical rather than ethnic; indeed, their positive ethnic ties and feelings for each other may well have kept them together for a number of years when it was apparent that they were on different courses from each other. The dream, therefore, died hard. Augustana was eventually convinced that it must participate in a merger process that was larger than the American Lutheran Conference, and it endured a painful withdrawal from these negotiations in 1952 to demonstrate its commitment. The Norwegians had a vision of a conservative midwestern center to stand equally with both the ULCA and the Missouri Synod, even if this meant that they would quite literally have to watch the Augustana delegates leave the room. Even after the two denominations went their separate ways, many institutional and spiritual ties still held them together, from the local level to the national.

So what about the sociological and ethnic aspect? It may well have been an issue, but it was not the crucial factor. If one looks at the relationship from another angle, the sociological and ethnic factors may well have been a positive contribution rather than a negative one. E. Clifford Nelson is probably correct: the sociological factor is not to be underestimated. But neither should it be over-estimated, and the positive as well as the negative impact of these factors must be taken into account.

Notes

1. The NLCA changed its name to the Evangelical Lutheran Church in 1946. The Augus-tana Synod changed its name to the Augustana Lutheran Church in 1948. The American Lutheran Conference (1930–54) was a cooperative agency of five midwestern Lutheran groups; besides the NLCA and Augustana, it included the American Lutheran Church (German, 1930–60), the Lutheran Free Church (Norwegian), and the United Evangelical Lutheran Church (Danish). E. Clifford Nelson, ed., *The Lutherans in North America*, rev. ed. (Philadelphia, PA: Fortress Press, 1980), 500.

2. The three groups of eastern-based Lutherans were the General Synod, the General Council, and the United Synod of the South. These traditions had broken apart in the 1860s over the Civil War and because of confessional differences. The American Lutheran Church (1930–30) became a component part of the American Lutheran Church (1960–88), but the two are different entities.

3. The Augustana Synod had been a constituent part of the General Council until 1918; though Augustana did not go into the ULCA merger, parts of Augustana had a long history of cooperation with elements of the ULCA.

4. On the relationship between Norwegian and Swedish Lutherans, see Mark A. Granquist, "Swedish- and Norwegian-American Religious Traditions, 1860–1920," *Lutheran Quarterly* 8 (1994): 299–320.

5. For the basics of the 1919–20 merger negotiations, see E. Clifford Nelson, *Lutheranism in North America, 1914–1970* (Minneapolis, MN: Augsburg Publishing House, 1972).

Exclusive confessionalism has been the position of the Missouri Synod and other conservative midwestern Lutherans, though the discussions on this basis have usually been so ponderous as to rarely achieve anything at all. This was the basis of the formation of the American Lutheran Church (1930–60), although it took years of negotiation to achieve. Missouri itself has never been a part of a successful merger negotiation, although it has absorbed several formerly independent parts of the Synodical Conference, which entered Missouri on Missouri's terms.

"Washington Declaration": this was essentially the way that the ULCA had been formed in 1918; a number of historical and ecclesiastical differences between the three merging groups were deemed to be peripheral, some of which lived on in the ULCA.

6. Nelson, *Lutherans in North America*, 499–500. For details on the November 1952 event, see G. Everett Arden, *Augustana Heritage* (Rock Island, IL: Augustana Press, 1963), 379–96.

7. H. G. Stub to G. A. Brandelle, Feb. 21, 1919, and July 7 and Nov. 1, 1920; G. A. Brandelle to P. A. Mattson, Mar. 8, 1919, all G. A. Brandelle Presidential Papers, Archives of the Evangelical Lutheran Church in America (ELCA Archives), Elk Grove Village, IL.

8. J. A. O. Stub to Rev. A. Wismar, Mar. 7, 1934, ELCA Archives. The positive reference to the Swedish Archbishop Söderblom is especially surprising, because many conservative Lutherans were strongly opposed to his supposed liberalism, even some in the Augustana Synod.

9. G. A. Brandelle to Lars W. Boe, July 4, 1931, Brandelle Papers.

10. G. A. Brandelle to Lars W. Boe, Dec. 31, 1932; Lars W. Boe to G. A. Brandelle, Jan. 5, 1933, both Brandelle Papers.

11. C. C. Hein to J. A. Aasgaard, May 14, 1934, and J. A. Aasgaard to C. C. Hein, May 23, 1934, C. C. Hein Presidential Papers, ELCA Archives. J. A. Aasgaard to Emmanuel Poppen, Mar. 23, 1942, and Jan. 8, 1942, J. A. Aasgaard Papers, ELCA Region 3 Archives, St. Paul, MN.

12. Interview with Alvin Rogness, Dec. 11, 1983, Oral History Collection, Archives of Cooperative Lutheranism, Lutheran Council in the United States of America, transcript pp. 9ff., ELCA Archives.

13. Interviews with Malvin H. Lundeen, Oct. 15, 1977, and July 18, 1978, Oral History Collection, Archives of Cooperative Lutheranism, transcript p. 72, ELCA Archives.

14. T. E. Gullixson to Lars W. Boe, Sept. 26, 1932, and Oct. 4, 1935, T. E. Gullixson Papers, ELCA Region 3 Archives. Lars W. Boe to T. E. Gullixson, Oct. 8, 1935, Lars W. Boe Papers, Archives of St. Olaf College, Northfield, MN.

15. Lars W. Boe to T. E. Gullixson, Mar. 31, 1939, Lars W. Boe Papers.

16. Lars W. Boe to T. E. Gullixson, Oct. 1, 1942, Lars W. Boe Papers. Lars W. Boe to J. A. Aasgaard, Oct. 29, 1942, St. Olaf Archives. Lars W. Boe to T. E. Gullixson, Nov. 6, 1942, T. E. Gullixson Papers.

17. Frederik A. Schiotz to Lars W. Boe, Nov. 6, 1942, St. Olaf Archives. Interview with Frederik A. Schiotz, Nov. 26, 1976, to Feb. 4, 1977, Oral History Collection, Archives of Cooperative Lutheranism, transcript, p. 54.

18. Interview with Albert E. Anderson, July 15 and Aug. 6, 1987, Oral History Collection, Archives of Cooperative Lutheranism, transcript, pp. 9ff.

CHAPTER 11

A Question of Conscience

Minnesota's Norwegian American Lutherans
and the Teaching of Evolution

KURT W. PETERSON

The seven speakers of the World's Christian Fundamentals Association who have touched nearly every considerable center in Minnesota during the last five weeks, bear uniform testimony to the fact that Lutheranism stands solidly for the greater fundamentals of the Christian faith, and with very, very few exceptions favors the anti-evolution bill.[1]

A great majority of the Lutherans in Minnesota, while they accept the fundamental beliefs as taught in the Bible, are opposed to Dr. W. B. Riley's attempt to have the state legislature pass any laws to prohibit the teaching of the evolutionary theory in public schools.[2]

On March 8, 1927, hundreds of Minnesota's concerned citizens packed the Minneapolis State House chamber to hear debate over proposed legislation that would forbid the teaching of evolution in the state's tax-supported primary, secondary, and university institutions. Three hours before the meeting was scheduled to begin the seats were filled, and by the time the hearing got under way the aisles were so crowded that the speakers could barely make their way to the stage. President Lotus Coffman of the University of Minnesota needed a police escort to negotiate the throng. Senator Thwing, Chairman of the Senate Education Committee, warned the audience at the outset that demonstrations would not be permitted. Hardly had the first speaker finished, however, when the audience began to boo and hiss the legislation's backers. Several times Senator Thwing had to gavel the crowd down, and on more than one occasion he threatened to clear the room. The *Minnesota Daily* reported the following day, "sentiment seemed predominately against the bill. Statements of speakers favoring the bill were several times interrupted by prolonged laughter from the galleries, and speeches denouncing the measure were greeted with heavy applause." The morning after the hearing, the Minnesota state senate killed the bill by a vote of 55 to 7. Although the vote was decisive, Minnesota had come closer than any other northern state to passing such legislation.[3]

In the midst of the dozen or so speakers seated on the stage at the senate hearing on the proposed anti-evolution legislation were four Norwegian American Lutheran leaders. Lars W. Boe, president of St. Olaf College in Northfield, Minnesota, and Reverend J. A. O. Stub, pastor of Central Lutheran Church in Minneapolis, spoke in opposition to the bill; and G. T. Rygh, member of the Minnesota Anti-Evolution League and former professor at St. Olaf, and L. A. Vigness, former president of St. Olaf, spoke in support of the legislation. The presence of these four men on stage indicates the importance of ethnic Lutherans in this story as well as how divisive the issue could be. Riley himself gave the Minnesota Lutheran population a prominent role in his grassroots campaign and in his speech at the hearing. He remarked, "nearly one half of the population of Minnesota belongs either directly or indirectly or by family connection to the great Lutheran bodies, and up to date I have not heard of one-half dozen Lutherans who oppose this bill." A month earlier Riley had proclaimed, "Lutheranism stands solidly for the greater fundamentals of the Christian faith, and with very, very few exceptions favors the anti-evolution bill." He naturally thought the state's ethnic Lutheran population would join in his crusade.[4]

Despite his optimistic predictions, however, Riley was unable to garner more than a fraction of the expected Lutheran support. Not only were two of Norwegian American Lutheranism's most prominent leaders speaking against the bill in a public forum, the two Lutheran ministers' conferences of the state refused to support the bill and the presidents of every major Lutheran college also came out against it. Although virtually all ethnic Lutherans thought evolution was a danger to faith and country, most did not agree with Riley's approach to solving the problem.[5]

While several cultural forces were drawing Norwegian American Lutherans into the orbit of fundamentalist social activism, a heritage of ethnic, confessional Lutheranism allowed them to maintain a particular identity in the midst of the politically charged debate over the teaching of evolution in tax-supported schools. On one hand, a high view of scripture, antimodernist theological commitments, accommodation among subsequent immigrant generations, fear of the demise of American civilization, and pragmatic concern for their children enrolled in public schools and universities led many Lutherans to support Riley's crusade. On the other hand, a common confessional tradition, resurgent ethnic nationalism, a heritage of Lutheran ethical teaching, and a commitment to an educational system that was particularly Lutheran provided the resources needed to maintain a particular theological and cultural identity. While Lutherans joined in causes and shared much rhetoric with fundamentalists, they did not surrender a particularly Lutheran perspective. Rather than abandon their Lutheran heritage, each side sought to prove themselves more Lutheran than the other.

The Anti-Evolution Movement in the United States

During the weeks preceding the Minnesota legislature's decision regarding the teaching of evolution in public schools, William Bell Riley and his "Flying Defenders of Fundamentalism" had led a grass roots campaign to drum up support for the bill. One of the most influential figures in American fundamentalism, Riley was pastor of First Baptist Church of Minneapolis, founder and president of Northwestern Bible College (1902), founder of the World's Christian Fundamentals Association (WCFA—1919), and the mind behind the Minnesota Anti-Evolution League (1922). Riley explained that the Anti-Evolution League's purpose was "to force the teaching of the evolutionary hypothesis from the public schools, and to lend all possible aid to the denominations in ridding their schools of the same pseudo-science." He charged secondary teachers and university professors with teaching "science, falsely so-called"—a phrase that became a mantra for the movement.[6]

Riley had drawn up the anti-evolution bill with the assistance of Gerald B. Winrod, fundamentalist leader from Kansas; Winrod read the bill in public for the first time in Riley's First Baptist Church in January 1927. The bill, eventually presented in the state senate on February 25, 1927, by Senator K. K. Solberg, called for the prohibition of the teaching "that mankind either descended or ascended from a lower order of animals, in all public schools, colleges, State Teacher's Colleges, and University of Minnesota, supported in whole or in part by the public education funds of the state of Minnesota."[7]

Between January and March, Riley, Winrod, and fundamentalist activists like Harry Rimmer of California, field secretary for the WCFA, had canvassed the Minnesota countryside, speaking in over two hundred towns. Riley himself spoke more than sixty-five times. These fundamentalist preachers warned the rural masses of the dangers of evolution—that it was a godless, un-American creed that would destroy the faith of their children and the very fabric of American civilization. One of Riley's targets was the University of Minnesota. He thought that most of the students opposed the teaching of evolution but that a modernist faculty and administration were shoving it down their throats. His chief opponent there was President Coffman. Riley and the Minnesota Anti-Evolution League demanded that Coffman personally investigate and purge as necessary all assigned texts in use by the more than eight hundred faculty of the university. Coffman would deliver an eloquent speech at the public hearing arguing for academic freedom and bold scientific inquiry. For him, the battle was one of scientific freedom and creativity versus closed-mindedness and fear; for Riley it was one of God's truth versus the evils of irreligion.[8]

Riley not only was the major figure in Minnesota's battle against the teaching of evolution; as leader of the WCFA he was also responsible for securing William Jennings Bryan for the 1925 Scopes trial in Dayton, Tennessee. Bryan spoke several times in Minnesota between 1922 and his death in 1925 and alongside Riley proposed anti-evolution legislation in many states throughout the country. Between 1921 and 1929, thirty-seven anti-evolution bills were introduced in twenty state legislatures. Although only five states approved such measures (Oklahoma, Florida, Tennessee, Mississippi, and Arkansas), the question of evolution and public education pervaded American religion and politics throughout the 1920s as local newspapers as well as journals and news magazines such as the *Literary Digest* carried regular stories on the subject.[9]

William Bell Riley

Norwegian American Lutheran Concerns

The debate that raged in Minnesota's broader culture also divided Minnesota's Lutheran community. Scholars who have written about Minnesota's anti-evolution legislation often leave ethnic Lutherans out of the story. Those who do recognize their importance tend to treat them as a monolith. In his defining article, "William B. Riley and the Fight against Teaching Evolution in Minnesota," Ferenc Szasz argued that Norwegian American Lutherans "fought this question entirely on the issue of separation of church and state," giving the impression that the vast majority of Lutherans, though theologically conservative and opposed to the teaching of evolution, opposed legislation as a viable option. The truth is that although the issue of church and state was indeed the battleground, Lutherans were split over the issue of evolution legislation. Lutherans did not uniformly reject legislation because of their adherence to a Lutheran two-kingdom theory; rather, they split over how to best adhere to the two-kingdom doctrine as ethnic Americans in a new cultural context.[10]

While the focus of this chapter is on Norwegian American Lutherans, Swedish American Lutherans in Minnesota responded similarly to the question of evolution and its instruction. Most opposed the theory of evolution because it espoused a godless creed, threatened American civilization, and put young people's faith in jeopardy; but most also opposed cobelligerency with the fundamentalists. In the early decades of the twentieth century, Lutherans of all stripes discussed how to address Darwinism, with a diversity of response within and among various synods. For example, Swedish Americans in the Augustana Synod often maintained a more open stance regarding evolution, with some prominent authors emphasizing the harmony of faith and science. Others, following the teachings of the prominent Swedish American pastor Byron Nelson, argued that evolution was not just a scientific theory but a complete worldview that denied the core of orthodox Christianity. Mark Granquist has noted other differences of opinion regarding evolution among the Augustana Synod, the Norwegian Evangelical Lutheran Church, and the United Lutheran Church. In the final analysis, while there was diversity among ethnic Lutherans, most would have assumed that humans were specially created by God and therefore would have remained generally conservative on the question of evolution through the era between the two world wars.[11]

No Lutheran wanted to abandon what he or she saw as a particularly "Lutheran" identity. At one basic level, that meant simply that Lutherans were not Reformed or, even less to their liking, fundamentalist. In fact, even many conservative Lutherans who favored legislation against the teaching of evolution in Minnesota's tax-supported schools made sure to distance themselves from North American fundamentalism. In addressing Riley and evolution legislation, one Lutheran pastor wrote,

> For the safety and future of our Lutheran Church, we shall have to fight largely without embracing every individual and organization that terms itself "Fundamentalist." Without minimizing in the least the splendid qualities of Dr. Riley, and many other Reformed Fundamentalist leaders, we must never forget the difference between Lutheranism—which is true Fundamentalism, and "Reformed Fundamentalism." Knowing what we do of the teaching of these Reformed leaders on many of the fundamental doctrines of our Christian religion, we can hardly grasp their hand and address them as "my brother," except it should be as . . . "my sick brother."[12]

While Riley's fundamentalist cause would not lead ethnic Lutherans to abandon their theological identity, many factors drew Norwegian American Lutherans toward the mainstream of American religious culture, leading them to share doctrinal and political positions with evangelicals. The longer they lived in the United States, the more they were interested in the social issues that confronted the American people. As religious conservatives they were antimodernists, and their opposition to Protestant Liberalism began to take an American form. They opposed evolution, affirmed the verbal inspiration of scripture as a bulwark against liberalism, and feared for the future of their country that was being jeopardized by an atheistic menace. In addition, the majority of Norwegian Americans were at the lower end of the middle class; as a result, they were ripe for the revivalist and empowering message of American fundamentalism.

Similar to the fundamentalists, as far as Norwegian Americans were concerned, evolution was not just a scientific theory. It had become a symbol for everything that was wrong with modernism and everything that was wrong with America. G. T. Rygh, Lutheran educator and proponent of anti-evolution legislation, thought that the theory of evolution was symbolic of all theories that

> inculcate a cosmic philosophy in direct contradiction of the Bible. The doctrines that men are of brute ancestry and have brute blood in their veins; that the Bible is an unreliable book made up largely of myths and traditions; that sin is not sin, but rather the phenomena of evolutionary development, for which men are not accountable to God; that Christ Himself is but a product of evolution—these and similar teachings promulgated in the schools, are an offense to Christian believers and a grievous wounding of their conscience. Children and young people are shaken in their confidence in the Bible. Their faith is undermined, causing them and their parents unspeakable anguish and woe.

Evolution threatened to destroy not only the Christian faith but the moral underpinnings of American civilization as well. A certain R. Sletten wrote a letter to the *Lutheran Church Herald* arguing, "Our civilization is not based on atheistic theory nor [*sic*] on evolution theory as modified before; but it is based on the fundamentals of Christianity. If the latter should be destroyed, the very fabric of our civilization would be gone."[13]

In making this claim, Norwegian American Lutherans echoed the sentiments of American fundamentalists who, after World War I, had rallied around evolution as their primary cause. In 1921–22 the evolution issue rose to the forefront and promptly absorbed most of the conservatives' energy. Thereafter, their main effort was directed toward the passage of state laws to halt the teaching of evolution in tax-supported schools. The shift in focus can largely be attributed to William Jennings Bryan. The outbreak of World War I led many conservatives to renewed interest in evolution. The aggressiveness of the Germans was seen as a practical application of the Darwinian concept of survival of the fittest. Conservatives had long been suspicious of German theology, and this stance was conveniently subsumed in the rise of the evolution issue. Bryan wrote, "I found that Darwinism was undermining the Christian faith, and then I found he had become the basis of the world's most brutal war, I then found . . . that he is the basis of the discord in industry." Evolution linked everything together: German theology (higher criticism), the decline of religious commitment, moral decay, and the challenge of democracy. If fundamentalists could destroy evolution, they could save their faith and America by restoring its status as a Christian nation.[14]

In the contest between modernists and fundamentalists, there was no mistaking which direction most Lutherans gravitated. They were "profoundly in sympathy" with the fundamentalist cause. Lutherans became quite concerned when the pronouncements of modernists attacked their conservative beliefs. As a consequence, Lutherans began to move off the sidelines, increasingly taking interest in issues that threatened conservative Protestantism. An article in the *Lutheran Church Herald* expressed regret that the fundamentalist faction within the Northern Baptist Convention had failed in its move to have the New Hampshire Confession of Faith, which laid particular emphasis on the divine authorship and inerrant nature of scripture, be adopted by the whole church. The article went on to say,

> Our own Lutheran Church has not suffered from higher criticism or modern theology in bygone days. The Lutheran church of many European countries has. The clergy of our Church and the professors at our theological seminaries are standing on Biblical grounds. But who knows what changes may take place. Therefore, let us watch and work for the fundamentals. As to our laymen, we have heard a few who are of the modern type.

During the early decades of the twentieth century, ethnic Lutherans were on guard against liberal Protestantism.[15]

The history of American Lutheranism provides clues as to why Lutherans combated liberalism but in a way different from Reformed fundamentalists. In the early years of the nineteenth century, Lutherans faced a crisis of the threat of rationalism and the seduction of Americanization through the effects of Reformed revivalism, which was dominating American evangelicalism. Lutherans generally added their weight to the Great Awakening and the Great Revival of the West, thereby minimizing the distinctly Lutheran confessional principle and embracing the emphases of American evangelicalism. This attitude was clearly advocated by Samuel S. Schmucker, president of the Lutheran seminary at Gettysburg and the most influential American Lutheran theologian of the era. He is generally known as the leader of "American Lutheranism," which was judged to be non-Lutheran by some who considered it too Americanized and untrue to its Old World confessional heritage.[16]

The American Lutheranism prominent in the early nineteenth century was overcome eventually by a growing interest in more conservative and traditional neoconfessionalism. This new thought arrived in the United States in three ways: German theological literature, the mass migration of German and Scandinavian immigrants, and a revival of interest in the Lutheran liturgical tradition. The neoconfessionalism that came to America in these ways became a movement to combat religious indifference, not via the methods of American "evangelicalism" but by a repristination of the scholasticism of the seventeenth-century Lutheran dogmaticians and through a continuing emphasis on pietistic orthodoxy, the latter especially among Scandinavians. As Norwegian American Lutherans entered the twentieth century, they were armed with a conservative repristination theology that emphasized the inspiration of the Bible and traditional orthodoxy in the face of the liberal onslaught.[17]

Fundamentalist-type rhetoric also began to characterize Lutheran doctrinal statements. In 1925 a group of Norwegian American Lutherans drafted the "Minneapolis Theses" as a bulwark against liberal Protestantism. The theses stated that "the synods accept without exception the canonical books of the Old and New Testaments as a whole, and in all their parts, as the divinely inspired, revealed, and inerrant Word of God, and submit to this as the only infallible authority in all matters of life." The language of "inerrancy" supplemented the language of the 1917 constitution of the Norwegian Lutheran Church of America, which stated only that "the Holy Scriptures, the canonical books of the Old and New Testament, are the revealed Word of God and therefore the only source and rule of faith, doctrine, and life." Thus, Norwegian Lutherans, like fundamentalists in the older American denominations, reaffirmed the traditional values of evangelical Christianity.[18]

While Norwegian American Lutherans began to use fundamentalist rhetoric in their public and doctrinal statements, few if any ethnic Lutherans would have thought of themselves as "fundamentalist." Historian Mark Noll has asked the question, "Why is it that the original Protestant 'evangelicals,' the Lutherans, seem to have so little in common with the large, amorphous group of American Protestants who also call themselves 'evangelicals'?" There has been a historical disengagement between Lutheran and Calvinistic elements in American history. Noll pointed to five constituting experiences within American Reformed evangelicalism in which Lutherans did not participate: affirmation of the American Revolution; evangelization of the Enlightenment; commitment to revivalism; experience of cultural domination; and controversy with modernism. Although, as shown earlier, Lutherans did wrestle with modernity, they did not exhibit the anti-intellectual flair that fundamentalists did. During the 1920s several Lutheran colleges matured into first-rate liberal arts colleges. Although Lutherans toyed with fundamentalism, they never pursued adoption into the family.[19]

Norwegian American Ethnic Identity

It was not just a commitment to being distinctly Lutheran that allowed Norwegian American Lutherans to maintain a unique religious and cultural identity. Resurgent ethnic nationalism also allowed ethnic Lutherans to uphold a distinct identity vis-à-vis North American coreligionists, alongside whom they battled the teaching of evolution. By the second decade of the twentieth century, Norwegian Americans chose to look past their theological differences and form a denomination based on ethnic Norwegian identity. As the fundamentalist versus modernist controversy was ripping American Reformed denominations in two, ethnic denominations were joining together, uniting disparate theological camps under a common ethnic umbrella.[20]

When Norwegians landed on U.S. shores, the theological divisions that existed in Norway splintered them into several different denominations. Old country groupings included Haugean pietists and strict confessionalists, anticlericalists and champions of the clergy, revivalists and rationalists, ritual formalists and those who dismissed traditional liturgies—all held together under the authority of the state church. As long as the church was subordinated to the civil government, these disparate elements coexisted in one big, if not necessarily happy, family. In the free religious climate of the United States, however, individual churches developed without formal civil ecclesiastical authority to bind them together. What were *factions* in Norway became *denominations* in the United States. Throughout the second half of the nineteenth century these groups were defining themselves, forming churches and educational institutions.

In 1890 the Hauge Synod, the Norwegian Augustana Synod, the Conference for the Norwegian-Danish Evangelical Lutheran Church, and the Anti-Missourian Brotherhood merged to form the United Norwegian Lutheran Church. That denomination, in turn, joined with the Norwegian Synod in 1917 to form the Norwegian Lutheran Church of America (NLCA), which encompassed most immigrants from Norway who elected to affiliate with congregations of their ethnic Lutheran heritage. Some ethnic Norwegian denominations did not join the NLCA in 1917 (namely the Lutheran Free Church and the Church of the Lutheran Brethren). Although these mergers were never all encompassing, however, the NLCA represented the majority of Norwegian Lutherans in America. Haugean pietists and high church formalists, as well as every ecclesiastical persuasion in between, joined together in an expression of Lutheran and ethnic unity.[21]

As second- and third-generation Norwegian Americans were increasingly accommodating to American culture, the immigrant community gathered to celebrate the centennial anniversary of Norwegian emigration to North America. The organizers emphasized the Americanness of Norwegian immigrants, choosing symbols that portrayed them as good citizens committed to democracy. President Coolidge addressed the crowd and called them "good Americans." But, tension divided the community regarding how they should relate to American culture. Some decried the murderous effects of American commercialism on the human spirit and Norwegian ethnic identity, while others sought to dispel the notion that Norway and its people were primitive and lacking in culture.

The organizers sought to prove themselves to be *both* American and Norwegian. National romantic impulses brought on by Norway's recent full political autonomy provided a sense of ongoing ethnic identity. After the country's nearly five-hundred-year union with Denmark ended in 1814, and after its subsequent separation from Sweden, which finally resulted in full autonomy in 1905, Norway's patriotic leaders had worked to develop a sense of national identity free from foreign domination by celebrating and restoring ethnic characteristics and cultural values embedded in the country's peasant traditions. It was these nationalistic elements that found their way into the centennial celebration and undermined the dominance of Americanization ideology by making Norway—not the United States—the sacred space of the narrative. A pageant performed during the centennial event celebrated the Viking heritage—a heritage that extended far beyond pioneer settlement in the United States. By rooting themselves in a significant history before their arrival in America, these immigrants saw themselves as superior to Yankees, asserting that it was their ancestors who arrived in North America first, that Norwegians had established the values of democracy and fairness.[22]

As the Norwegian American community at large wrestled with its identity, the Lutheran Church reflected the same tensions in its debate over the language question. By the early twentieth century it had become clear that if Norwegian American Lutherans wanted to maintain influence over the American born, they would have to adapt to English. By the 1920s, most Norwegian immigrant children attended American common and public schools, where they learned English as the language of culture and commerce. The 1920s, however, was a period of language transition. Many feared the loss of identity that would accompany the loss of language, and ethnic conservatives continued to advocate for the use of the Norwegian language. Instruction at Luther Seminary was conducted in English and Norwegian well into the 1930s, and it was not until the end of the 1920s that English eclipsed Norwegian in classroom use. In the late twenties, almost half of Norwegian American churches still conducted services in Norwegian, though by 1941 that number was less than 12 percent. Although the Norwegian language was dying, it was not dead. Significant numbers of Norwegians still clung to their native tongue as an expression of ethnic identity and pride.[23]

Another means by which Norwegian Americans maintained a uniquely Lutheran identity was education. In the late nineteenth and early twentieth centuries, Norwegian Americans gladly sent their children to common schools to learn English, the language of commerce and politics. But they also founded many academies and colleges for religious education, with an emphasis on preserving Norwegian as the language of the heart, church, and home. Most immigrants had learned to read in Norway's public schools and in confirmation in the Norwegian state church, so literacy was very high. Many members of the Norwegian and other national Lutheran groups formed voluntary associations and established their own schools. By doing so, they followed the example of other American church bodies since the beginning of settlement in North America. Lutherans also participated in the college-building fever that accompanied westward expansion.[24]

Beginning in the early 1870s, Norwegian Lutherans launched an academy movement that resulted in the formation of more than seventy-five secondary and normal schools in the United States and Canada. Supplementing the publicly supported common schools, academies offered young Norwegian immigrants the opportunity to equip themselves for productive involvement in the society and economy of their new country. These schools occupied a middle ground; they both provided an excellent education so that students could matriculate into American culture and preserved students' Norwegian heritage. In the twentieth century, the number of public high schools grew and the number of academies decreased; by the Great Depression almost no Lutheran academies remained. The most durable and enterprising among them developed into colleges. St. Olaf and Concordia both became colleges in the 1890s. By the 1920s, then, most Norwegian American children were being educated in local American public schools and the Norwegian academies had largely faded into the past. The issues that Norwegian American parents faced were American ones. Most could not afford private education; in addition, the options for private education had dwindled. They were out on the frontier with the American public school as the only educational option for their children and they would fight to save it from corruption.[25]

The Spectrum of Norwegian American Attitudes about Evolution

Because most Norwegian American Lutheran children attended Minnesota's public schools in the 1920s, Lutherans in general were concerned about the content of the curriculum as well as the values teachers conveyed to their youth. In addition to their interest in primary and secondary schools, Lutherans also turned their eye to the University of Minnesota, where fifteen hundred Lutheran young people were pursuing a college education. While all agreed that evolution was immoral and therefore should not be taught in the younger grades, Lutherans disagreed as to its place in the college curriculum. Many thought it should not be taught in college classes; however, most Lutheran educators had no problem teaching evolution, as long as it was not taught as fact. Professors at St. Olaf and Concordia taught evolution as a theory, and President Boe of St. Olaf stated clearly, "The students at St. Olaf are made familiar with the evolutionary theories. I do not think [however] that any of the professors are teaching them as fact." Boe reasoned that college students could discern theory from fact and believed they must be made aware of the advances in modern science.[26]

Lars W. Boe, president of St. Olaf College in Northfield, Minnesota

A growing divide developed among Norwegian American Lutherans. Some felt that evolution should not be taught under any circumstances and were willing to do anything to ensure it would be excised from all public school curricula; others approached the issue less tendentiously, being careful not to employ detrimental means to achieve a desirable end. Intellectuals who rejected the bill argued on theological grounds, seeking to preserve the integrity of historic Lutheran teaching. Those who supported anti-evolution legislation tended to argue on pragmatic grounds; legislation was simply the best solution to the problem.

The editors of the *Lutheran Church Herald* and most Lutheran intellectuals came out strongly against anti-evolution legislation. They reacted to the many advocates who were arguing that this issue was not necessarily a religious one but a constitutional one. By supporting the legislation, proponents claimed they were not acting as Lutheran Christians but as individual citizens who saw the state violating the constitution by establishing atheism as the religion to be taught in the classroom. In an article in the *Lutheran Church Herald*, editor G. T. Lee wrote, "You cannot make the people of Minnesota believe that Dr. Riley is a mere private citizen who introduces laws merely to enforce the constitution of the state . . . Dr. Riley is known throughout the state as a militant Baptist and crusader against evolution and his expressed purpose and intention is to protect the Bible story of creation by introducing a law which shall eliminate a false science which is diametrically opposed to the truth of the Word of God." Clearly this was not merely a constitutional issue; principles of true religion were at stake as Lutheran leaders sought to protect their faith from corrosive infiltration by the state.[27]

Lee further contended, "We fully agree with Dr. Riley in his attitude to evolution, and furthermore agree with him that the men teaching evolution in such a manner as to oppose the creation story of Genesis are violating the Constitution of the State of Minnesota. But we do not agree with Dr. Riley when he proposes to drive this demon out of the schools by legislation." Instead of turning to the state for muscle in solving this problem, Lutheran intellectuals argued that new laws would be ineffectual. Laws would not change attitudes. Lee communicated his perspective on legislation by writing, "There is a legal maxim which says: *De minimis non curat lex*—law does not concern itself with very small things. To us Christians it is not a small thing, but the state in its functions is limited, and cannot enter far into the field of morality and religion by its legislative enactments and punishments." Furthermore, Lee wrote, "The church cannot further its cause by distrusting its own spiritual weapons, and grabbing the sword of the state. It has been tried and always proved disastrous."[28]

The editors of the *Lutheran Church Herald* laid down in plain language their perspective on legislation just weeks before the bill came up for a vote. They agreed that "teachers who promulgate and teach this pagan theory of man's descent from animals is violating the compact formed by the people of the State of Minnesota when they adopted the Constitution." "Nevertheless," they continued,

we do not believe that this situation can be remedied by legislation. Nothing will be accomplished except to create animosity and bitterness which will simply aggravate the situation and be a challenge which will make the atheistic element more aggressive, and give some a chance to pose as martyrs of religious persecution. The Church of God never depended on force, or violence, or on the arm of the law for its propagation. By the power of truth it has even prospered under persecution. *Vestigia terrent* (the footsteps frighten me). If we begin with religious legislation, we may be led on a step further and overstep the boundary line between church and state which statesmen like Gladstone, supreme court judges, and churchmen have never been able to define definitely. Whenever the Church has controlled the state, as it did in the Middle Ages, it has abused its power and become corrupt. It does not have to depend on carnal weapons, but upon the power of truth and the Spirit of God, whereby it is able to destroy the strongholds of Satan. We have a mania for passing laws and neglect to enforce them.[29]

Reverend J. A. O. Stub also recognized the double-edged sword of legislation when he wrote, "If we can properly legislate against the teaching of evolution, what is to prevent legislation in favor of evolution? And again, such attempted legislation will add fuel to the position of rationalists and materialists wherever they are found."[30]

When they read the words of Lutheran theologians in the *Lutheran Church Herald,* many lay people interpreted the response as intellectual rationalization that, in the end, supported the teaching of evolution. In March 1927, a certain A. G. Nelson wrote a postcard to L. W. Boe, president of St. Olaf, which read, "I have twelve grandchildren and I have promised each of them tuition at St. Olaf if they want to go there when they get old enough. But today I feel tempted to recall my promise. What do you think would have been the result if you had taken your stand on the evolution question before the late [capital] drive?" As far as Mr. Nelson was concerned, Boe's support of professors who taught evolution and his stand against anti-evolution legislation were tantamount to modernism. Boe clarified his position and that of other Lutheran leaders in his response: "I am against legislation, not because I am an evolutionist, but because inviting the State to legislate on matters of this kind is contrary first of all to the teachings of Jesus; in the second place, it is contrary to the whole position of the Lutheran church on the question; and in the third place, contrary to the words and spirit of our Constitution. I am not an evolutionist in any sense. I stand on the Lutheran position throughout, both on the question of the Word of God and Justification by Faith."[31]

Boe also argued that those who were true to Lutheranism agreed with him. Although Riley had succeeded in getting many Lutherans "off track," Boe replied to Nelson, "I am sure that you will find, if you write the Lutheran theologians and leaders in our day, that they take the same stand as I do." Boe's

Reverend J. A. O. Stub, pastor of Central Lutheran Church in Minneapolis

response illustrated the tendency of these two groups to talk past one another. Conveying the same message, Boe wrote to President Coffman of the University of Minnesota, "With very few exceptions, the teachers in colleges, theological professors, and church leaders, are against any legislation on this matter." A town versus gown distinction separated Lutherans on the issue of evolution legislation. Boe contended that Lutheran theologians and educators represented true Lutheranism on the matter and that Riley had enticed many lay people to sacrifice their faith convictions.[32]

In rejecting legislation as an option, Norwegian American church leaders sought to stay true to their Lutheran heritage by dismissing anything that appeared to be Reformed. L. W. Boe wrote, "The tendency to use the state for religious purposes is either Catholic or it comes from the Reformed Church. We shall have to solve this question some other way as Lutherans." In making this statement Boe divorced American Lutheranism from fundamentalism altogether. For him, the desire to dominate culture was fully inconsistent with Lutheranism. The editors of the *Lutheran Church Herald* agreed, writing, "While the Reformed churches following in the footsteps of Calvin, who burned Servetus for heretical teachings, have persisted in religious legislation both in England and in the American colonies, using ducking stools, jails, penitentiaries, fines, boring of the tongue, lopping off the ears, burning at the stake and hanging . . . to protect the pure religion, the Lutheran Church through 400 years of history is practically free from the taint of religious persecution." Many Lutherans wanted nothing to do with Riley and legislation because they wanted nothing to do with the Reformed tradition. Their fight was not simply over the teaching of evolution; for them, the heart of their Lutheran theological heritage was at stake.[33]

While some leading Lutheran educators doggedly fought the anti-evolution bill on theological grounds, many Lutherans passionately confronted the issue pragmatically as concerned parents. Lay people were more interested in their children's education than in preserving orthodoxy. Many individual churches wrote resolutions protesting the teaching of evolution in public schools, some actively encouraging legislation as the solution. For example, a committee at Bethel Norwegian Lutheran Church in Minneapolis drafted the following resolution in 1927:

To the Members of Our Legislature: Inasmuch as under our Constitution, religious instruction in our tax-supported schools is unlawful, we believe it to be equally unlawful to teach or instruct pupils attending such schools, evolution or other theoretical doctrines tending to destroy, undermine, or question the teachings of the Bible in any particular, especially as to the origin of man.

Wherefore, we, the 1,100 members of Bethel Norwegian Lutheran Congregation, Minneapolis, Minn., through our authorized committee, petition your Honorable Body to take such measures *by law or otherwise,* as is necessary to stop such instruction in our tax-supported schools.

This individual committee requested that state representatives use any means possible, including legislation, to remove evolution from the public schools. Earlier in the decade, two Norwegian Lutheran ministers were among a group of pastors who convened in 1922 to draft a resolution demanding the cessation of the teaching of evolutionary theory as a science in tax-supported schools. They included in their resolution the open threat of an appeal to the legislature for laws to eliminate such teaching. The two Lutheran ministers who signed this 1922 resolution, B. E. Bergesen (NLCA) and O. H. Sletten (LFC), had both taught at Riley's Northwestern Bible and Missionary Training School.[34]

Regarding the charge that supporters of the bill were violating the Lutheran and American principle of the separation of church and state, Reverend G. T. Rygh responded, "These citizens are doing nothing of the kind. They are making use of their constitutional right to petition the Legislature for redress of a sore grievance. Their grievance is that the public schools are being used for the destruction of faith in the Bible as the Word of God and the inculcation of a false religion." He shifted the burden of proof, arguing that it was not defenders of the bill but "defenders of this false religion—evolution—in the common schools of the State" who were mixing the functions of church and state. Rygh claimed, "They use the common schools as the medium through which to promulgate their anti-Christian religion." Because public educators were violating the constitutional provision that the state cannot establish religion or prohibit the free exercise thereof, Rygh reasoned that those who taught evolution should be legally prohibited from doing so.[35]

L. A. Vigness, former president of

G. T. Rygh, member of the Minnesota Anti-Evolution League and professor at St. Olaf College

L. A. Vigness, president of St. Olaf College

St. Olaf, concurred: "The design of the proposed Anti-Evolution Bill is to put a brake on the progress now being made with increasing speed year by year toward a state religion." Vigness saw the state taking an active role in eliminating the Christian faith and the Kingdom of God on earth. In order to further the kingdom of Christ, Vigness supported legislation to control an apostate faith that was destroying a Christian culture. He wrote, "To say that I am against the doctrine of evolution, but at the same time to say that I oppose the movement toward forbidding the use of my civic influence and my money as means to aid in its promulgation, is an utterly untenable position." To remain passive was to surrender American culture and Norwegian American children to the wiles of modernism.[36]

Although some Lutheran educators such as Rygh and Vigness argued in support of legislation, most Lutheran support of the anti-evolution bill came from local pastors and lay people who experienced the crisis more poignantly than intellectuals. C. K. Solberg, pastor of St. Paul's Lutheran Church in Minneapolis, wrote a letter to the editor of the *Lutheran Herald* in April 1927 in which he summarized the position of prolegislation Lutherans who feared for the future of their children in a modern society whose schools would lead them into godlessness. He responded to the public claim that Lutherans were opposed to legislation, calling it "erroneous and misleading." He wrote, "I venture to say from what I have observed during the present agitation of this issue, that there are by far more of our Lutheran citizens of Minnesota favoring this legislation in the matter than opposing it. It goes without saying that all Lutherans are anti-evolutionists." He chided G. T. Lee for dismissing the possibility of legislation and therefore "doing nothing" about the problem.

For Solberg, there was a trade-off between evolution and Christianity, period. He preached, "Evolution is taught as the origin of man instead of creation by an Almighty God. Many a youth has been shipwrecked in his Christian faith by this pernicious teaching. In many cases it leads to infidelity and atheism, merely a logical consequence. Have we not a right as taxpaying citizens and parents to demand that this glaring violation of religious liberty be stopped?" He reasoned more from a pragmatic social starting point than a theological one. Solberg was not interested in high-minded theology that could not engage current problems—he feared for his children and those of his flock. He pleaded, "Let the evolutionists hold their anti-Biblical views as to the origin of man and present them wherever they can receive a hearing, but not in the public schools where my children and the children of a very large constituency of the citizenry of our state are daily exposed to this faith destroying influence."[37]

Other Lutherans rejected Lutheran intellectuals and their refusal to support the anti-evolution bill more vociferously. A certain J. Torval Norby wrote to the editor of the *Lutheran Church Herald*, "Mr. Editor, there are thousands of us within our own Church that fail to see the soundness of your arguments on this particular point. Mr. Vigness, editor of *Lutheraneren*, I am convinced, is right when he says your position is untenable in this matter." He chided the high-minded for not making an effort to walk in his shoes. He charged, "This matter of evolution being taught at our higher institutions of learning does not, I am inclined to believe, bother those of you who happen to live near enough to our church schools to be benefited by them. But how about us who live out on the frontiers and cannot afford to send our sons and daughters to our own schools, even though we are required to support them? Yea, how about us?" Norby continued, crying, "[Are we to] stay at home and let those who favor the teaching of the humbug called evolution go to the polls and there solemnly perpetuate the foisting of this infidelity upon our children?!" Norby concluded that as citizens of the United States Lutherans had something to say regarding the laws that governed their land and under which the Church had to work. To reject evolution and then tie the hands of Lutherans by preventing them from pursuing preventative legislation was inconceivable. For many Lutherans, America was not going to hell in a handbasket on their watch.[38]

Conclusion

Many immigrant Lutherans had no option but to send their children to America's public schools. They could not afford private education, and even if they could, by the 1920s few Lutheran parochial academies remained. As a result, most Lutherans fought this battle on pragmatic grounds, arguing that something had to be done to protect their children from the scourges of atheistic modernism. For many, legislation was the only realistic option. High-minded theology was convenient only for the wealthy and the highly educated. They sought to remove evolution from public education entirely. Lutheran educators, however, saw this popular response as shortsighted and a departure from historic Lutheran orthodoxy. If church history had taught Lutherans anything, they reasoned, it had warned them of the dangers of mixing church and state. Lutheran intellectuals argued that by supporting anti-evolution legislation, Lutherans were capitulating to a corrupting Reformed tradition that was at odds with Luther's two-kingdom theory. Lutherans should think as Lutherans.

The camps that formed among Lutherans regarding anti-evolution legislation reflected larger tensions present in the Norwegian American Lutheran community. As they fought over the appropriate Lutheran response to the bill they also battled over the proper relationship between church and society—between Christ and culture. Many argued for legislation on pragmatic grounds but did not surrender their Lutheran identity while doing it. For them, mandating modernism was tantamount to mixing church and state, and thus violating the conscience of Christians who exist within it. While many Lutherans were cobelligerents with fundamentalists on the question of teaching evolution, they argued for the cause on different grounds. Theirs was not an effort to regain cultural authority lost by World War I or an effort to control American culture; rather, their goal, as Lutherans, was to prevent the state from violating their consciences and those of their children thorough the establishment of religious modernism. The evolution question of 1927 reveals that while institutional American fundamentalism had a profound effect upon ethnic Lutherans, drawing them further into typically American forms of cultural and political discourse, Norwegian American Lutherans relied on a robust Lutheran heritage to maintain a unique confessional identity.

Notes

1. From a pamphlet entitled *Lutheranism and Anti-Evolution Legislation: Church and Convention Resolutions and Articles by Leading Lutheran Educators,* which included editorial comments and the writings of two prominent pastors of the Norwegian Lutheran Church in America, G. T. Rygh and L. A. Vigness, Feb. 1927.

2. Rev. J. A. O. Stub, pastor of Central Lutheran Church in Minneapolis, quoted in *Minneapolis Sunday Tribune,* Jan. 2, 1927, 1. The article was on the opinions of Stub and Dr. Joseph Stump, President of Northwestern Lutheran Theological Seminary, who were in agreement on this matter.

3. *Minneapolis Daily,* Mar. 10, 1927. On this date, virtually every newspaper in Minnesota ran stories on the hearing, and all agreed that sentiment was almost universally opposed to the bill. Between 1921 and 1929, thirty-seven anti-evolution bills were introduced to twenty state legislatures. Five were passed, in Oklahoma, Florida, Tennessee, Mississippi, and Arkansas. See Philip J. Anderson, "David F. Swenson, Evolution, and Public Education in Minnesota," in *Swedes in the Twin Cities: Immigrant Life and Minnesota's Urban Frontier,* ed. Philip J. Anderson and Dag Blanck (St. Paul: Minnesota Historical Society Press, 2001), 313n2 for a full bibliography of anti-evolution legislation.

4. *Minneapolis Tribune,* Mar. 10, 1927, 1. In January of 1923, the *Literary Digest* published "Shall Moses or Darwin Rule Minnesota Schools," an article based on a poll of Protestant ministers around the state. One hundred fifteen clergy came out strongly against the teaching of evolution, while only seventy-seven supported it. See Anderson, "David F. Swenson, Evolution, and Public Education in Minnesota," 309–10.

5. See Ferenc M. Szasz, "Three Fundamentalist Leaders: The Roles of William Bell Riley, John Roach Straton, and William Jennings Bryan in the Fundamentalist-Modernist Controversy" (PhD diss., University of Rochester, 1969), 279; and Ferenc M. Szasz, "William B. Riley and the Fight against Teaching of Evolution in Minnesota," *Minnesota History* 41 (1969): 215–16. This award-winning article is an excellent summary of the major issues and actors involved in the Minnesota anti-evolution campaign. Szasz explains clearly Riley's role, why evolution was such an important issue for fundamentalists, and why Riley's dreams of populist support never materialized.

6. Quoted by Ferenc M. Szasz, "William B. Riley and the Fight against Teaching Evolution in Minnesota," 205, as cited by Anderson, "David F. Swenson, Evolution, and Public Education in Minnesota," 309.

7. Cited in Ferenc M. Szasz, "William B. Riley and the Fight against Teaching Evolution in Minnesota," 211–12.

8. The complete text of Coffman's speech can be found in "The President's Report for the Year 1926–1927," in *Bulletin of the University of Minnesota* 30:11–16. It was also published in the *Minneapolis Tribune,* Mar. 10, 1927, 7; and the *Minnesota Daily,* Mar. 10, 1927, 3.

Riley claimed to be fighting this battle for the students and he thought he had their support. The students, however, did not agree. The March 8 *Minnesota Daily* (The University of Minnesota student daily) was given entirely to a protest against the bill. The *Daily* called for a mass demonstration the next day to "express true student opinion." On March 8, classes were dismissed at noon—a half hour early—so the entire student body could attend the rally. Students packed the University Armory to capacity—more than 5,000 of the 9,600 students—and hundreds more were unable to get in. The meeting roared its unanimous condemnation of the Riley bill and passed a resolution disapproving the measure and urging the state legislature to defeat it. At the hearing on March 8, Howard Haycraft, managing editor of the *Daily,* presented the petitions. While he was speaking, Riley interrupted the proceedings with a demand to question Haycraft. The motion was denied but later granted. "Will you swear that the vote in that mass meeting was unanimous?" he asked Haycraft. "No," replied the editor. "To be strictly accurate, I should have said that the vote was 4,999 to 1." Upon this, the galleries burst into cheers and laughs and the judge had to gavel the room to order, threatening to empty the room unless people maintained decorum. (Virginia Walker, "Minnesota's Anti-Evolutionists," *Ivory Tower,* Sept. 28, 1959, 8.)

9. For a discussion of William Bell Riley and William Jennings Bryan and their roles as fundamentalist leaders and advocates for anti-evolution legislation, see Szasz, "Three Fundamentalist Leaders," and C. Allyn Russell, *Voices of American Fundamentalism: Seven Biographical Studies* (Philadelphia, PA: Westminster Press, 1976). For a discussion of the evolution crisis of the 1920s more broadly, see William B. Gatewood, Jr.,

Controversy in the Twenties: Fundamentalism, Modernism, and Evolution (Nashville, TN: Vanderbilt University Press, 1969), introduction; and Ferenc M. Szasz, *The Divided Mind of Protestant America, 1880–1930* (Tuscaloosa: University of Alabama Press, 1982), introduction and conclusion. Gatewood quotes many primary sources at length to provide contemporary context, and Szasz provides a discussion of the role evolution played in dividing fundamentalists from liberals during the initial decades of the twentieth century. Gatewood's *Preachers, Pedagogues and Politicians: The Evolution Controversy in North Carolina, 1920–1927* (Chapel Hill: University of North Carolina Press, 1966) is the best case study of a state evolutionary conflict. On William Jennings Bryan, see Lawrence W. Levine, *Defender of the Faith, William Jennings Bryan: The Last Decade, 1915–1925* (New York: Oxford University Press, 1965); and J. C. Long, *Bryan: The Great Commoner* (New York: D. Appleton & Co., 1928); for primary sources on Bryan, see Joel Carpenter, ed. *William Jennings Bryan on Orthodoxy, Modernism, and Evolution* (New York: Garland, 1988). On the Scopes trial, see L. Sprague de Camp, *The Great Monkey Trial* (Garden City, NY: Doubleday, 1968); Ray Ginger, *Six Days or Forever? Tennessee v. John Thomas Scopes* (New York: Oxford University Press, 1974); and Jerry R., Tomkins, ed., *D-Days at Dayton: Reflections on the Scopes Trial* (Baton Rouge: Louisiana State University Press, 1965).

In recent years Garland Publishing Company has brought out several edited volumes of primary sources on fundamentalism and evolution. The following are some examples of these excellent resources: Joel Carpenter, ed., *The Fundamentalist-Modernist Conflict: Opposing Views on Three Major Issues* (New York: Garland, 1988); Ronald L. Numbers, ed., *Antievolutionism before World War I* (New York: Garland, 1995); Ronald L. Numbers, ed., *Creation-Evolution Debates* (New York: Garland, 1995); Ronald L. Numbers, ed., *Early Creationist Journals* (New York: Garland, 1995); Ronald L. Numbers, ed., *Selected Works of George McGready Price* (New York: Garland, 1995); William Bell Riley, *The Finality of Higher Criticism, or, the Theory of Evolution and False Theology* (New York: Garland, 1988); William Bell Riley, *Conservative Call to Arms,* ed. Joel Carpenter (New York: Garland, 1988); and William Vance Trollinger, Jr., *The Anti-Evolutionary Pamphlets of William Bell Riley* (New York: Garland, 1995).

10. Szasz, "William B. Riley and the Fight Against Teaching Evolution in Minnesota," 215–16. See also Ronald L. Numbers, *The Creationists: The Evolution of Scientific Creationism* (New York: Knopf, 1992), 46. He argued, "Lutherans, . . . despite their overwhelming rejection of evolution, generally preferred education to legislation and tended to view legal action against evolution as a dangerous mingling of church and state." On the whole, scholars of American fundamentalism read Lutheran intellectuals on these questions and not popular literature; thus they miss out on a rich cache of writing that argues that Lutherans should have backed the anti-evolution legislation. For a thorough discussion of Lutherans involved in the evolution crisis, the roles they played, and the positions they took, see Bruce E. Eldevik, "Lutherans and Evolution in Minnesota: An Examination of Lutheran Attitudes and Responses to the Proposed Anti-Evolution Legislation of 1927" (master's thesis, Luther Northwestern Theological Seminary, 1989).

11. See Maria Erling and Mark Granquist, *The Augustana Story: Shaping Lutheran Identity in North America* (Minneapolis, MN: Augsburg Fortress, Publishers, 2008),

217–24; and Mark Granquist, "Byron Nelson and American Lutheran Attitudes toward Evolution," in *Lutherans in America—A Twentieth Century Retrospective: Essays and Reports of the 20th Biennial Meeting of the Lutheran Historical Conference* 19 (St. Louis, MO: Lutheran Historical Conference, 2005):146–65.

12. T. H. Megorden, *Lutheran Church Herald* (hereafter, *LCH*) 11.14 (Apr. 5, 1927): 430.

13. Rygh, *Lutheranism and Anti-Evolution Legislation*, 7. R. Sletten, *LCH* 11.13 (Mar. 29, 1927): 396.

14. Bryan's speech before a Chicago audience, printed in *Moody Bible Institute Monthly* 23 (Apr. 1923). See Szasz, *The Divided Mind of Protestant America*, ch. 9: "Bryan and the Controversy over Evolution," 107–16.

15. Todd Nichol, "The American Lutheran Church: An Historical Study of its Confession of Faith according to its Constituting Documents" (ThD diss., Graduate Theological Union, 1988), 181, 182. Paul Carter, *The Spiritual Crisis of the Gilded Age* (DeKalb: Northern Illinois University Press, 1971), ix; William R. Hutchison, *The Modernist Impulse in American Protestantism* (Cambridge, MA: Harvard University Press, 1976), 195. O. Qualen, "Fundamentalists Defeated," *LCH* 6 (July 25, 1922). Riley led the move to impose this doctrinal statement upon the Northern Baptist Convention. See C. Allyn Russell, *Voices of American Fundamentalism: Seven Biographical Studies* (Philadelphia, PA: Westminster Press, 1976), 96. For a good discussion of the Lutheran tendency to lean toward fundamentalist doctrines, see Eldevik, "Lutherans and Evolution in Minnesota," 48–49.

16. Among these critics were Charles Porterfield Krauth (Schmucker's colleague at the seminary) and the Reformed theologians of Mercersberg, John Nevin and Philip Schaff. See James H. Nichols, *Romanticism in American Theology: Nevin and Schaff at Mercersburg* (Chicago: University of Chicago Press, 1961), 92–93.

17. For a brief summary of American Lutheran history, see E. Clifford Nelson, *Lutheranism in North America, 1914–1970* (Minneapolis, MN: Augsburg Publishing House, 1972), introduction.

18. Quoted material found in E. Clifford Nelson and Eugene L. Fevold, *The Lutheran Church among Norwegian-Americans: A History of the Evangelical Lutheran Church* (Minneapolis, MN: Augsburg Publishing House, 1960), 285n5.

19. Mark A. Noll, "Children of the Reformation in a Brave New World: Why 'American Evangelicals' differ from 'Lutheran Evangelicals,'" *Dialog* 24.3 (Summer 1985): 176–80. See also David Valleskey, "Evangelical Lutheranism and Today's Evangelicals and Fundamentalists," *Wisconsin Lutheran Quarterly* 80.3 (Summer 1983): 180–220.

20. A similar pattern can be seen among Swedish Baptists. When faced with the fundamentalist/modernist controversy of the 1920s, they opted not to join either side but to separate themselves from the Northern Baptist Convention altogether and function as an independent denomination. Since their birth in the United States the Swedish Baptists had been receiving funds from the American Baptists. When those funds began to have strings attached, they refused funding and developed their own missions programs, Sunday school programs, and home missions societies. Although they gravitated toward fundamentalist theological convictions, their ethnic unity presided over their conservative theological identity as they chose ethnic identity over the fundamentalist/

modernist options. For a thorough discussion of the relationship between Swedish Baptists and American Baptists, see the "Colloquy on the Historical Connections between the Baptist General Conference and the American Baptist Churches, USA," *American Baptist Quarterly* 6.3 (Sept. 1987).

21. For a brief history of Lutheran division and unity, see Frederick Hale, *Norwegian Religious Pluralism: A Trans-Atlantic Comparison,* Text and Studies in Religion 59 (Lewiston, NY: Edwin Mellen Press, 1992), 13–14. The number of Lutheran denominations is staggering, and trying to understand when they separated and when they joined together is quite difficult. For a complete discussion of the various Lutheran groups in America, see Nelson, *Lutheranism in North America, 1914–1970.* His book contains a chart of Lutheran groups that graphically displays which groups separated and merged throughout a very complex history. See also Martin E. Marty, "Lutheran Churches in America," in *Dictionary of Christianity in America,* ed. Daniel G. Reid, Robert D. Linder, Bruce Shelley, and Harry Stout (Downers Grove, IL: InterVarsity Press, 1990), 670–74. Marty also provides a chart that makes sense of the many Lutheran groups in America.

22. April R. Schultz, *Ethnicity on Parade: Inventing the Norwegian-American through Celebration* (Amherst: University of Massachusetts Press, 1994).

23. See Nelson, *The Lutheran Church among Norwegian-Americans,* 247, 251.

24. See Carroll Engelhardt, *On Firm Foundation Grounded: The First Century of Concordia College, 1891–1991* (Moorhead, MN: Concordia College, 1991), 11. There were nine colleges when the American Revolution began. At the time of the Civil War there were 250, of which 180 still survive. Approximately another 700 were attempted and failed by 1900. Several religious groups built educational institutions immediately upon arriving in a new area.

25. See Richard W. Solberg, *Lutheran Higher Education in North America* (Minneapolis, MN: Augsburg Publishing House, 1985), 226–29. For a discussion of the founding and early development of private colleges and universities in Minnesota, see Merrill E. Jarchow, *Private Liberal Arts Colleges in Minnesota: Their History and Contributions* (St. Paul: Minnesota Historical Society Press, 1973). For histories of Lutheran colleges, see Carroll Engelhard, *On Firm Foundation Grounded,* and Joseph M. Shaw, *History of St. Olaf College, 1874–1974* (Northfield, MN: St. Olaf College Press, 1974).

26. University of Minnesota estimate provided in *LCH* 6 (Oct. 17, 1922): 1315. The editorialist called upon Lutheran students at the University of Minnesota to attend William Jennings Bryan's upcoming lecture on Sunday, October 22, 1922. He thought it would be an opportunity "to hear the other side of the evolution question." He claimed that the university's regular practice was to bring in self-avowed modernists like Harry Emerson Fosdick to address the students. L. W. Boe to M. Michelson, May 3, 1927, Lars W. Boe Papers, Archives of St. Olaf College, Northfield, MN. See Shaw, *History of St. Olaf College,* 285, and Engelhardt, *On Firm Foundation Grounded,* 77, for a discussion of the teaching of evolution as a scientific theory in Lutheran colleges.

27. *LCH* 11.7 (Feb. 15, 1927): 196. The *LCH* was the English organ of the Norwegian American Lutherans and began to be published in English in 1905. Its editors generally argued against legislation. The *Lutheraneren,* the Norwegian Lutheran paper published in Norwegian, was headed up by L. A. Vigness and from 1922 to 1927 published several

articles in favor of legislation. For the dispute between the *LCH* and the *Lutheraneren,* see Eldevik, "Lutherans and Evolution in Minnesota," 75–85.

28. *LCH* 11.7 (Feb. 15, 1927): 196. G. T. Lee to L. W. Boe, Aug. 22, 1927, Boe Papers. Lee summarized his opinions on the anti-evolution legislation as it pertained to matters of church and state in a pamphlet entitled "Church and State," published in Feb. 1927. L. W. Boe summarized the argument in this pamphlet in *LCH* 11.11 (Mar. 15, 1927). Boe wrote, "The main thesis of the pamphlet is that it is contrary to Scripture, contrary to the historical Lutheran position, and essentially wrong policy to invite the state to legislate on matters belonging to the sphere of religion."

29. *LCH* 11.3 (Jan. 18, 1927): 68.

30. J. A. O. Stub to L. W. Boe, Jan. 7, 1927, Boe Papers.

31. A. G. Nelson to L. W. Boe, Mar. 11, 1927, Boe Papers.

32. L. W. Boe to A. G. Nelson, Mar. 11, 1927; L. W. Boe to Lotus Coffman, Mar. 8, 1927, both Boe Papers.

33. L. W. Boe to A. G. Nelson, Mar. 16, 1927, Boe Papers. *LCH* 11.3 (Mar. 29, 1927): 388.

34. Bethel quotation cited in the pamphlet *Lutheranism and Anti-Evolution Legislation,* 4, emphasis mine. *LCH* 6 (Nov. 7, 1922): 1413.

35. Rygh, *Lutheranism and Anti-Evolution Legislation,* 6.

36. L. A. Vigness, *Lutheranism and Anti-Evolution Legislation,* 12, 15.

37. *LCH* 11.14 (Apr. 5, 1927): 429.

38. J. Torval Norby, Letter to the Editor, *LCH* 11.14 (Apr. 5, 1927): 428.

Community

CHAPTER 12

Journeymen or Traditional Emigrants?

Norwegian and Swedish Engineers and Architects in North America, 1880–1930

PER-OLOF GRÖNBERG

Unlike a large portion of those whom left the country districts of Norway to take up land in the Middle West, the engineers burned no bridges behind them; in fact a majority had every intention of returning to the homeland after acquiring experience, perhaps a fortune, and possibly, too, a great reputation. They had no farms to sell and no families to care for. A ticket for the voyage to America, a few dollars to keep them going until they found a job, some articles of clothing—these with exceptions were all that they carried with them. In a short time they would return to visit parents and friends in Europe; a few years more and they would return to take over engineering posts in Norway. This fact—the tendency of many to regard America as a place of temporary residence only—colored their life in the New World and gave it an orientation that was different from that of the main body of Norwegian Americans. Thus in a social as well as purely economic sense the story of the engineers is a distinct and in many ways a separate chapter in American urban life.[1]

Norwegian American historian Kenneth O. Bjork describes engineers as a specific group of transatlantic migrants differing considerably from immigrants settling as farmers in the midwestern prairie. At a 1901 meeting of returned engineers and architects, one participant claimed that Swedish technicians rarely migrated in order to settle permanently but rather to acquire knowledge and experience and return to use them back home. The destination pattern in North America usually diverged from that of the main body of immigrants. Bjork describes the engineer as someone who "made his way to the large metropolitan centers—New York City, Philadelphia, Pittsburgh, Chicago, the Twin Cities, and later to the cities of the west coast; but smaller industrial centers such as Butler, Pennsylvania, and Schenectady, New York, often exerted an equally great attraction."[2]

Bjork's observations connect to a European tradition of journeyman migration with medieval roots; for centuries Scandinavian artisans rarely could become masters without having spent time abroad. Journeymen acquired knowledge and skills that contributed to a continuous development of artisan technology. In the nineteenth century, technically educated people largely took over the role. Innovations such as Atlantic steamships extended the tradition beyond Europe. There was a lot to see and learn in the New World. Visitors to the World's Columbian Exposition in Chicago in 1893 returned impressed. Lecturers told Scandinavians about the marvels of electricity in Thomas Edison's country, a Swedish engineer reported in enthusiastic terms about the modern tools, and the Norwegian commissioner stated that no other country was as technologically advanced as the United States. Nine years later, a returned engineer claimed in a lecture in Kristiania (Oslo) that the United States was technologically superior to Europe in an astounding way.[3]

Swedish historian Lars O. Olsson credited this view of U.S. technology as the most important factor encouraging engineers to cross the Atlantic. Nevertheless, it is a misconception to separate it completely from general emigration. Naval architect Hugo Hammar described how as a child he had heard about many in the province who left for America and became successful. Third to Ireland and Iceland, Norway was the European country that lost the highest share of its population to North America, and Sweden was fourth. Every technology graduate who crossed the Atlantic was, of course, not a "journeyman." Some intended to settle permanently in the United States and others simply remained.[4]

In this chapter, we will discuss differences in migration strategies and patterns among Norwegian technical school graduates and their Swedish colleagues in the light of the two traditions and differences in terms of industrialization and technical development.

Industrialization and Technical Education in Norway and Sweden

Although Norway and Sweden were very similar, they diverged as regards industrialization. To mark the hundred-year anniversary of the dissolution of the union, Swedish historian Bo Stråth wrote a comparative book about the countries in the nineteenth century; his Norwegian colleague Francis Sejersted wrote on the twentieth. Agrarian interests in Sweden were weakly organized and could easily be marginalized. Conservatives, liberals, and social democrats formed a vague modernization and industrialization alliance. Capital and labor clashed but also agreed that large-scale industrialization offered a solution to the country's problems and supported development. Higher technical education was an important cornerstone. Already in the early nineteenth century some Swedish institutions were forerunners of technical universities: the Technological Institute in Stockholm and Chalmers in Gothenburg. The former's change of name to the

Royal Institute of Technology in 1877 implied a higher status. Positive experiences from the late nineteenth century spurred an early-twentieth-century view that Sweden was able to reach a higher level of industrial development. Industrialists based their authority on structures from the traditional iron industry, where owner power was perceived as natural. Their skills in creating a modern industry meant legitimacy and societal power, and Swedish industrialists reached a position of influence on more or less equal terms with politicians and public institutions.[5]

Norwegian industrialists were subordinate in a greater degree to political and democratic institutions. Norway had developed a sustainable small industry and was slightly more urbanized and somewhat richer than Sweden in 1870 but did not manage to bring about a large-scale industrialization. Modernization was primarily directed toward small industry and agriculture. Norway's highest technical education was offered by the vocational schools in Kristiania, Bergen, and Trondheim. Before a university of technology opened in Trondheim in 1910, graduates primarily sought higher education in Germany and Switzerland. Norway lacked, in addition, the large nationwide banking system—one that often invests and develops strategies to establish modern large-scale industries. According to Sejersted, Norwegians wanted industries and banks but were skeptical of large-scale ones. Storting passed a modern joint-stock company law only in 1910. Many of the institutions that had been present in Sweden for several decades were still absent in early twentieth-century Norway; they were established quickly after 1905. The period from 1905 up to 1920 can be characterized as an industrial breakthrough. The view of Sweden as distinguished by greater large-scale industry has survived into the present day. Mass-producing Swedish companies did not, of course, resemble American ones, but the gap was somewhat narrower compared to Norway.[6]

Hypothesis

This chapter hypothesizes that the differences between industrialization and engineering in Sweden and Norway influenced the transatlantic migration patterns from both countries. The classical "push and pull factors," used in migration research for almost a century, may have worked differently for engineers and architects. The large-scale Swedish companies imply a larger domestic labor market and a stronger demand for engineers, even if we must keep in mind that Sweden also educated a significantly higher number. Nevertheless, we are assuming that it was more difficult for Norwegian engineers to find employment at home and that transatlantic migration was more prevalent among Norwegian graduates than among Swedish. A domestic labor market that was more of a "push factor" in Norway than in Sweden also implies that Norwegian engineers who already were in the United States also had weaker incentives to return than their Swedish colleagues.[7]

The propensity to return was probably also influenced by possibilities to use knowledge acquired in North America. Sweden had a more advanced industrial sector than Norway, so it was likely easier for Swedish engineers to apply the know-how they had accrued in the United States. This contributed to a stronger return incentive for the Swedes. The Swedes to a larger extent than the Norwegians tended to follow the journeyman pattern and therefore returned more frequently than did the Norwegians. Norwegian engineers may have been more likely to view themselves as ordinary emigrants when they departed. This implies that the ones who returned did so after a comparably longer duration in North America as well as at an older age. Their return was perhaps more often connected to nostalgia, but this is not to say that they could not act innovatively upon return.

Another possible aspect of Norwegian engineers viewing themselves more as ordinary emigrants is that they tended to follow general patterns of emigration to the United States to settle in the Midwest, which more or less constituted the heart of both Norwegian and Swedish America. The Swedish journeyman theory implies that Swedish engineers more often found their way to technological and organizational spearhead companies applying, for instance, mass production methods and organizations in line with the Taylorist or Fordist spirit.

The hypothesis of this chapter is that Bjork's observations on the differences between Norwegian engineers and the main body of Norwegian Americans are even more relevant when comparing their Swedish colleagues with the typical immigrants from Sweden. This chapter assumes that, compared to their Norwegian colleagues, Swedish engineers and architects (a) migrated to North America to a lesser extent and returned to a higher, (b) were younger and stayed for a shorter duration, and (c) settled to a lesser extent in what are perceived as Scandinavian areas of the United States, such as rural or small-town districts in the Midwest.

Dutch sociologist Frank Bovenkerk has divided migrants into four categories based on intentions and outcome: (1) intended temporary migrants who do in fact return; (2) intended temporary migration without return; (3) intended permanent migration followed by a return; and (4) intended permanent migration without return. We assume that technical school graduates from both countries primarily were preparing themselves for a career back home, i.e., located in the first category, but also that this pattern was more marked among the Swedes. A higher percentage of their Norwegian colleagues were hypothetically ordinary emigrants seeking a lifelong future in North America. This study, of course, is based on biographical notes; we cannot access qualitative sources revealing the true intention of all graduates. Our interpretations cannot therefore be fully precise.[8]

Source Material and Cohorts

This study includes engineers and architects who completed at least three years of education at technical schools in Norway and Sweden between 1880 and 1919. Technology and engineering fields make up the majority; architects were also educated at academies of arts and the like, but they are not included in the study. Education received by architects from technical schools was more similar to an engineer's compared to architects educated at art schools. Especially in Norway, the distinction between an architect and a constructional engineer was unclear; the two groups often performed similar types of work.

This study's database is comprised of 94 percent (2,924 of 3,099) of the Norwegian and 71 percent (5,531 of 7,836) of the Swedish graduates. Norway is better covered, but the Swedish number is higher because it had more than twice as many graduates. The Norwegians in the database graduated between 1880 and 1914 at the vocational schools in Kristiania (952 of 1,100), Trondheim (891 of 894), and Bergen (483 of 497). Mining engineers also graduated at Norway's only university at the time (80 of 89). All of these institutes gave three- and four-year courses up until 1915 and two-year courses after that date. Engineers and architects examined at the Norwegian Institute of Technology (518 of 519) between 1915 and 1919 are also included. The Swedish engineers and architects in the database graduated from the Royal Institute of Technology (2,697 of 2,993), Chalmers (1,567 of 1,623), and the upper secondary schools in Malmö (688 of 696) and Örebro (578 of 1,141). Nearly 1,400 graduates left the technical upper secondary schools in Norrköping, Borås, and Härnösand, but they are not included in the database due to shortcomings in the source material.

Both the Norwegian and Swedish source material consist of biographical notes in directories issued by the technical schools and technical associations as well as obituaries in newspapers. Qualitatively good Norwegian directories exist from the schools in Bergen and Trondheim as well as the Norwegian Institute of Technology; the school in Kristiania did not issue its own biographical directory. Information about the engineers from Kristiania is mostly collected from Bjarne Bassøe's biographies of Norwegian engineers from 1961 and from the press cutting archive at the National Library. Bassøe's biographies have shortcomings and do not cover graduates before 1900. More or less all the missing cases from Norway are from before 1900. Bassøe's biographies are written long after the subjects' careers have ended. He bases some of the notes on earlier biographies, but a comparison of his information to data from the school in Trondheim and the Norwegian Institute of Technology reveals that some information is left out, such as visits at universities abroad. Information only based on Bassøe, then, underscores migration.[9]

In Sweden, Örebro's directory covers just under half of the graduates because it focused on the ones alive in 1925 who sent notes to the editors. Yearly lists are available from 1926 and have been used in order to follow the candidates up to 1930; the same has been done for the last year (1930) as regards Chalmers. Malmö graduates have only been followed until 1928 because this was the biographies' publishing year. With the above mentioned reservations, the Swedish institutes have issued qualitatively good directories. Historian Sten Carlsson used the directories for a study of Swedish engineers in Chicago and claimed that the ones covering the Royal Institute of Technology and Chalmers are excellent, while the ones from Malmö and Örebro have shortcomings. There are, however, deficiencies also in the directories of the large institutes, especially in the one from Chalmers. The notes in the upper secondary schools' directories can be regarded as almost equally good in quality. The three technical upper secondary schools in Borås, Norrköping, and Härnösand do not have relevant source material.[10]

Technical School Graduates' Transatlantic Migration and Return, 1880–1930

In figure 12.1 we can see that the hypothesis of a stronger transatlantic migration among graduates from Norway holds true. Every fourth Norwegian technical school graduate from 1880 to 1919 went to North America before 1930, compared to a little less than every fifth Swedish graduate. The connection between a domestic labor market that functioned more as a push factor in Norway and Norway's relatively stronger transatlantic emigration seems to be relevant. Both rates were higher than for engineers and architects from "low emigration countries" like Denmark and Finland, from which less than every sixth graduate crossed the Atlantic.

Figure 12.1 shows, however, also that Norwegian engineers and architects generally were more prone to go abroad than their Swedish colleagues; this is relevant for all international destinations and not only North America. The reason is the already indicated educational migration to primarily the German-speaking countries prior to the establishment of the Norwegian Institute of Technology.

Eskil Berg was a Swedish engineering student who emigrated after he had read the following words in a letter he received in 1895: "Now the matter is this: come over at once, without waiting any more time in Europe. There is nothing to be got there, everything here. You better start with the idea that you will never go back except for a visit. I never saw a sensible man, who had lived a few years in the United States, willing to go back to Europe to stay." Its sender was the German-born engineer Charles P. Steinmetz at General Electric. Berg, who also had a brother in General Electric's hometown of Schenectady in upstate New York, crossed the Atlantic without even finishing his education. He settled for

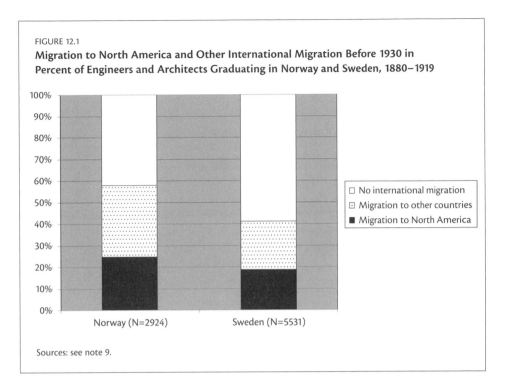

FIGURE 12.1

Migration to North America and Other International Migration Before 1930 in Percent of Engineers and Architects Graduating in Norway and Sweden, 1880–1919

- □ No international migration
- ⊡ Migration to other countries
- ■ Migration to North America

Norway (N=2924)   Sweden (N=5531)

Sources: see note 9.

good. Hypothetically, however, the more attractive Swedish labor market made Berg's countrymen less inclined to follow advice like Steinmetz's compared to their Norwegian colleagues.[11]

Table 12.1 shows the migration pattern of the Scandinavian technical school graduates who went to North America. The table pays no attention to international migration patterns prior to the arrival in the United States or Canada; i.e., it includes both graduates who had North America as their very first international destination and graduates who had resided in one or more other countries before they came to North America: 24 percent of the Norwegian and 20 percent of the Swedish graduates arrived after a temporary residence in another foreign country. These stopovers were primarily to German-speaking countries, especially for the Norwegians.

The hypothesis holds true. Every second Norwegian engineer and architect either remained in North America after the first immigration or settled there after back-and-forth migration to the native country or temporary migration to other countries. The corresponding share for the Swedes was nearly 10 percent lower. The share of returnees was also higher for Sweden. The domestic labor market enticed more Swedes than Norwegians to move back home. We should keep in mind, however, the considerably higher Swedish number of technical school graduates.

TABLE 12.1

Pre-1930 Settlement and Migration Patterns after Arrival in North America (United States and Canada) among Engineers and Architects Graduating in Norway and Sweden, 1880–1919

Country	Norway		Sweden	
SETTLEMENT	N	%	N	%
1. Permanent settlement in North America (1)	**363**	**49.3**	**420**	**40.3**
1a. Upon first immigration	315	42.8	384	36.8
1b. Upon 1 or more temporary returns (2)	36	4.9	24	2.3
1c. Upon 1 or more temporary stays in other countries	12	1.6	12	1.2
2. Permanent settlement the rest of the world (1)	**29**	**3.9**	**53**	**5.1**
2a. Upon immigration from North America	21	2.9	33	3.2
2b. Upon 1 or more temporary returns home (2)	8	1.1	20	1.9
3. Permanent settlement in the home country	**344**	**46.7**	**570**	**54.7**
3a. Upon 2 or more stays in North America (2)	16	2.2	16	1.6
3b. Upon 1 stay in North America, 1 or more stays in the rest of the world	61	8.3	109	10.5
3c. Upon first return	267	36.3	445	42.7
Total	**736**	**100.0**	**1,043**	**100.0**
Ever returned (3)	388	52.7	614	58.9
Never returned	348	47.3	429	41.1
Total	**736**	**100.0**	**1,043**	**100.0**

(1) Died in area or lived there in 1930;
(2) May also include residence in the rest of the world;
(3) Categories 1b, 2b, 3a, 3b, 3c. Sources: see note 9.

Historian Gudmund Stang used the basic immaturity of the Norwegian industrial economy to explain the engineers' proneness to international migration. Stang also identified a Scandinavian tendency of oversupply of qualified engineers that was clearer in Norway than in Sweden and Denmark. The small-scale and petite-bourgeoisie colored industrialization in Norway offered not only fewer employment possibilities than the more large-scale Swedish one but perhaps also lower wages. When Bjork in 1940 asked engineers why they left for America, one stated, "I was not born in my father's office." Another argued that it was "next to impossible to secure technical employment in Norway." A third claimed that the native country offered "prevailing salaries and particularly slow schedules of advancement." Some Norwegian industries seemed to prefer foreign engineers in leading positions. In 1885, an engineer wrote an indignant letter to the editor of the technical association's journal after he had read an advertisement for a technical director at a cellulose factory in a German technical journal but had been unable to find the same notice in Norwegian counterparts. The often-expressed patriotism, he claimed, was never evident in practical life, and he called the action a tragic lack of confidence in Norwegian ability. He continued, "we might as well emigrate immediately." The factory owner responded that the German journal was read also in Norway and that countrymen with requested qualifications were welcome, but he believed that there were not any. Eighteen years later, the limited possibilities were still discussed. First-year students had problems finding employment even in minor positions, whereas experienced engineers lost both public and private employment because of the shortage of work. A Norwegian society for engineers and architects, functioning as a kind of employment clearinghouse, was formed in New York as a response to the increasing number of technical school graduates that had arrived. As one of Bjork's respondents claimed, North America appeared to be "the only way out."[12]

These conditions imply also that Norwegian technical school graduates in North America had fewer chances of finding work back home than their Swedish colleagues. A larger share of the Norwegians, therefore, settled permanently in North America. Stang noted that an oversupply of technicians was present in all Scandinavia. The Swedish technical association's journal stated in 1910 that this was the reason so many engineers sought their livelihood in North America. Complaints about the increasing number of engineering graduates were raised.[13]

Migrating abroad was sometimes viewed as a necessity also among engineers in Sweden, especially at times when low-paid employment was the only domestic option for those entering the profession. Nevertheless, statistics indicate that the Swedish labor market could absorb graduates to a somewhat higher extent. We interpret the stronger Norwegian tendency to remain in North America as a sign of more traditional emigration, although it is really too simple to equate uncritically the latter with permanent settlement. This is especially true after around 1890, when many Scandinavians also followed a general tendency of migrants from all over Europe intending to return to take over a farm or start a smaller business after a few years of work across the Atlantic. Most immigrants did after all settle permanently, and Norwegian and Swedish general return rates rarely exceeded 20 percent on a yearly basis before 1930. The lower return rate of Norwegian technical school graduates is closer to the general one than their Swedish counterparts.[14]

Age and Duration of Stay among the Returnees, 1880–1930

As we have indicated, all transatlantic migration of technical school graduates did not follow the target migration patterns. We have seen that Swedish graduates returned to a higher extent, but 47 percent of their Norwegian colleagues did settle permanently in Norway after one or more temporary stays in

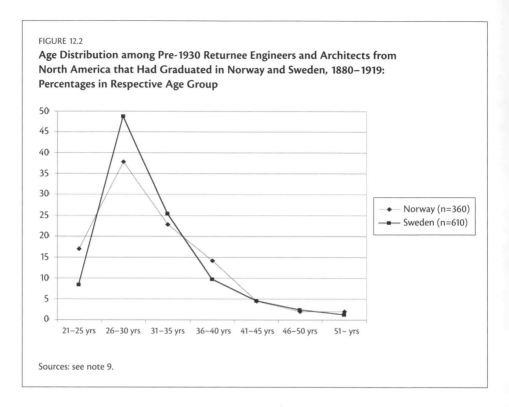

FIGURE 12.2

Age Distribution among Pre-1930 Returnee Engineers and Architects from North America that Had Graduated in Norway and Sweden, 1880–1919: Percentages in Respective Age Group

Sources: see note 9.

North America. Also among the returnees, however, we assume that a higher share of the Swedes had crossed the Atlantic with an initial return aim in mind. Hypothetically, relatively more Norwegian graduates had migrated with the initial purpose to settle permanently but changed their mind along the way. Alternatively, they had planned to return but closer to retirement age. This implies that returning Norwegian graduates were often older and had spent a longer period in North America. Figure 12.2 shows the age pattern.

Figure 12.2 shows that higher shares of the returning Swedish graduates were between ages thirty-one and thirty-five years and especially between ages twenty-six and thirty years. However, a larger share of the Norwegian returnee graduates was in the youngest group—twenty-one to twenty-five years—which partly can be explained by the fact that graduation often occurred at a somewhat earlier age in Norway. The group of ages thirty-six to forty years was relatively larger among the Norwegians, whereas there were hardly noticeable differences among returnee graduates over forty. The average Norwegian graduate returnee age was 31.3 years, the Swedish, 31.1 (not a significant difference), but if we consider the older Swedish graduate age structure, our assumption makes more sense. More or less every engineer and architect was working age upon return, but—with the youngest group as an exception—the Swedes generally had more working years left. This conclusion is further strengthened by looking at the duration of stay in figure 12.3.[15]

Swedish returnee engineers and architects had generally been away for a shorter period; we interpret this as an indication of them being target migrants, i.e., in Bovenkerk's first category to a higher extent. The average duration of stay was 5.6 years for the Swedes and 6.4 years for the Norwegians. The median duration of stay was four years for Sweden and five for Norway. As we can see, higher shares of Norwegian graduates had been away for more than ten years, and especially between eleven and fifteen years.

It is difficult to define the optimal duration of stay for a target migration. The Italian historian Cerase has made a typology of return migrants. The length of stay abroad does have significant implications on their impact on the home society when immigrants return. This has been observed by the British geographer Russell King:

> If this is very short, the returning migrant may have little power to be a modernizing or developmental influence on the home region: Cerase's return of failure. If too long, returnees may be so old, or alienated from

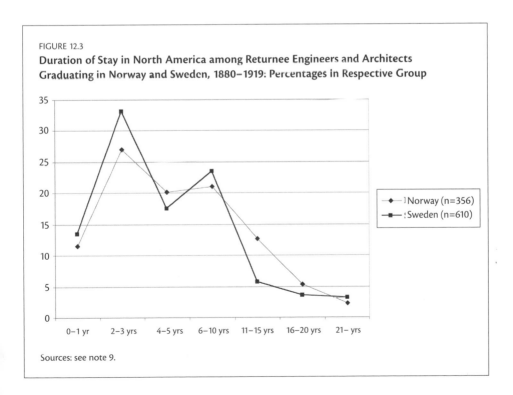

FIGURE 12.3

Duration of Stay in North America among Returnee Engineers and Architects Graduating in Norway and Sweden, 1880–1919: Percentages in Respective Group

Sources: see note 9.

their "home society" that again the influence they can exert will be small—Cerase's return of retirement. Somewhere in between, the potential exists for Cerase's return of innovation, whereby migrants have the right combination of accumulated skills, attitudes and energies to bring about real change in the places to which they return.

If we generally interpret two to three years' duration of stay in North America as "somewhere in between" and assume that the duration of stay within such an interval implies more target migration, we can conclude that the Swedish engineers and architects show more indications of this pattern than their Norwegian colleagues. The higher Norwegian shares in the groups that had been away for eleven years or longer also point in this direction. As we are discussing target migration, which may imply a shorter temporary period of studies at a university or practice at a workshop or the like, it is difficult to use Cerase's argument that a shorter duration—in this context, less than a year—implies less power to bring about change on the technical school graduates. Therefore, we look upon this group as target migrants in this context and note a small Swedish majority here, as well.[16]

Patterns of Settlement in North America

So far, it appears that Norwegian technical school graduates possessed more traits in common with ordinary emigrants than did their Swedish colleagues. Might this also be reflected in a settlement pattern more in line with the general Norwegian emigration to North America? Canada is left out of table 12.2 since counters made no differentiation between the Scandinavian nationalities in the censuses before 1921. Nevertheless, if we add Canada's Norwegian- and Swedish-born in 1921 to the ones in the 1920 Census for the United States, we get an indication that around 16 percent of North America's Norwegians lived in Canada compared to 9 percent of the Swedes. This relatively stronger Norwegian representation is reflected among the graduates in this study: every tenth Norwegian graduate employed in North America had at some point worked north of the border compared to every fourteenth Swedish graduate. Almost all of them also worked in the United States. The settlement patterns within Canada diverged, however, from the general one. Graduates from both countries were often employed in Ontario and Quebec, while Norwegian and Swedish immigrants generally settled in the western provinces of British Columbia, Saskatchewan, Alberta, and Manitoba.[17]

In table 12.2, we can study the average Norwegian and Swedish population from 1880 to 1920 in the different American states as well as the share of technical school graduates that worked in each state between 1880 and 1930.

Table 12.2 shows that engineers and architects from both countries first and foremost went to industrial regions and areas of interest from a technological point of departure, not simply to the Scandinavian destination states. Virginia is one example: a total of around 1,150 Norwegian and Swedes lived there in 1920. Around 4 percent of the technical school graduates in the United States worked in Virginia; the principal reason was the shipyard at Newport News. Torbjørn Hermanrud stated the motivation for his migration: "In this time, when so many Norwegian shipyards are extended and several new ones are planned, it could be interesting to see how one of the largest American shipyards is arranged." He was impressed with the organization of the shipyard. He also admired the advanced technology and the working conditions at Newport News. The shipyard had automatic cranes, oxygen and acetylene materials for welding, a connected iron foundry, as well as good bath and toilet facilities. The yard could also be warmed up during winter and chilled in the summer. Other important Scandinavian engineers visited Newport News, such as Wilhelm Swensen, later manager for the Norwegian navy shipyard in Horten, and Hugo Hammar, managing director of Sweden's largest and most modern shipyard, Götaverken, in Gothenburg. Swensen and Hammar introduced American-inspired methods at their shipyards.[18]

New York and Pennsylvania were the most important destinations for both Swedish and Norwegian technical school graduates. Illinois was the third most important destination for the Norwegians and fourth for their Swedish colleagues, whose third most important state was Massachusetts. The Norwegian graduates' fourth state was New Jersey. Scandinavian technical school graduates therefore migrated primarily to America's industrial heartland. The North American manufacturing belt had Boston as its northeast corner, Washington, DC, the southeast, St. Louis the southwest, and Milwaukee the northwest. The belt stretched into Canada and included the southernmost tip of Ontario. One of the important destinations, especially for Swedish engineers, was Schenectady in New York, General Electric's home base. The company offered immigrant engineers the opportunity to learn cutting-edge technology. One of these immigrants was Carl Silvander. He worked at General Electric when the company developed and produced generators for the power plant at Niagara Falls. Silvander returned to Sweden where he headed ASEA's construction of so-called giant generators to power stations in Sweden and in Norway.[19]

The North American manufacturing belt was also a prime destination for ordinary Swedish emigration, containing a relatively large group of industrial workers. A rough average of 45 percent of the Swedish immigrants in the United States lived within the manufacturing belt compared to 19 percent of the Norwegians. From this perspective it was the Swedish rather than the Norwegian technical school graduates who followed their countrymen's general settlement patterns.[20]

TABLE 12.2

Average Norwegian and Swedish Population (based on the population every tenth year) in States of United States, 1880–1920. Percent of Engineers and Architects (from technical schools) Graduating in Norway and Sweden, 1880–1919 that Worked in Each State at Any Point, 1880–1930

Country	Norwegians				Swedes			
STATE	AVERAGE POPULATION % (N=321718)	RANK	ENGINEERS, ARCHITECTS % (N=551)	RANK	AVERAGE POPULATION % (N=506653)	RANK	ENGINEERS, ARCHITECTS % (N=872)	RANK
Alabama	0.04	37	0.55	30	0.09	33	0.57	23
Alaska	—	—	1.27	19	—	—	0.34	30
Arizona	0.05	35	0.18	39	0.09	34	0.11	37
Arkansas	0.02	44	0.36	36	0.06	39	0.23	34
California	1.74	11	6.91	6	3.32	11	5.39	8
Colorado	0.6	17	1.09	20	1.93	14	1.38	17
Connecticut	0.25	23	1.45	17	2.53	13	3.33	11
Delaware	0.01	48	1.64	16	0.05	42	0.92	20
District of Columbia	0.03	39	1.09	20	0.05	43	1.38	17
Florida	0.09	32	0.00	43	0.13	31	0.46	26
Georgia	0.03	40	0.36	36	0.04	44	0.23	34
Hawaii	—	—	0.00	43	—	—	0.11	37
Idaho	0.45	20	0.36	36	0.58	26	0.11	37
Illinois	8.58	5	23.09	3	17.73	2	15.60	4
Indiana	0.12	28	2.73	13	0.88	23	1.49	15
Iowa	7.06	6	1.09	20	5.01	5	0.46	26
Kansas	0.43	22	0.91	25	2.65	12	0.34	30
Kentucky	0.02	46	0.91	25	0.04	46	0.00	45
Louisiana	0.08	33	0.73	28	0.07	38	0.57	23
Maine	0.13	26	0.55	30	0.35	27	1.49	15
Maryland	0.09	31	1.45	17	0.07	37	2.98	12
Massachusetts	1.08	14	6.55	7	5.23	4	15.94	3
Michigan	2.08	10	3.27	12	4.53	6	4.36	9
Minnesota	28.85	1	7.64	5	19.31	1	2.06	13
Mississippi	0.02	41	0.00	43	0.06	41	0.00	45
Missouri	0.17	25	2.73	13	0.98	20	1.15	19
Montana	1.41	12	2.36	15	0.91	22	0.57	23
Nebraska	0.84	16	0.73	28	4.16	7	0.11	37

Large cities and metropolitan areas like New York, Boston, Philadelphia, and Pittsburgh hosted quite a number of Swedish (and in some cases also Norwegian) immigrants. Bjork stated that immigrant engineers could "step right into a well-organized Norwegian life in any of the major northern cities." This was also the case for their Swedish colleagues, but in other areas Norwegians and Swedes comprised major shares of the total population.[21]

Country	Norwegians				Swedes			
STATE	AVERAGE POPULATION % (N=321718)	RANK	ENGINEERS, ARCHITECTS % (N=551)	RANK	AVERAGE POPULATION % (N=506653)	RANK	ENGINEERS, ARCHITECTS % (N=872)	RANK
New Hampshire	0.10	30	0.55	30	0.29	29	0.34	30
New Jersey	0.90	15	8.73	4	1.36	17	12.39	5
New Mexico	0.02	42	0.00	43	0.04	45	0.00	45
New York	4.73	9	38.55	1	7.46	3	42.09	1
Nevada	0.04	38	0.00	43	0.09	35	0.11	37
North Carolina	0.01	49	0.18	39	0.02	48	0.46	26
North Dakota (1)	9.53	4	0.18	39	1.57	15	0.11	37
Ohio	0.24	24	5.64	8	0.82	24	8.83	6
Oklahoma	0.05	36	0.00	43	0.11	32	0.00	45
Oregon	1.21	13	1.09	20	1.18	19	0.69	22
Pennsylvania	0.55	19	25.45	2	3.66	9	30.16	2
Rhode Island	0.11	29	0.00	43	0.95	21	0.92	20
South Carolina	0.02	47	0.00	43	0.02	49	0.00	45
South Dakota (1)	4.77	8	0.55	30	1.38	16	0.00	45
Tennessee	0.02	43	0.55	30	0.08	36	0.00	45
Texas	0.44	21	0.91	25	0.70	25	0.46	26
Utah	0.6	18	1.09	20	1.19	18	0.34	30
Washington	4.82	7	5.27	9	3.58	10	1.72	14
Vermont	0.02	45	0.18	39	0.17	30	0.11	37
Virginia	0.07	34	3.82	11	0.06	40	4.24	10
West Virginia	0.01	50	0.55	30	0.03	47	0.23	34
Wisconsin	17.35	2	5.27	9	4.07	8	5.62	7
Wyoming	0.13	27	0.00	43	0.31	28	0.11	37

(1) based on the numbers for Dakota Territory in 1880
Sources: Torben Grøngaard Jeppesen, Danske i USA 1850-2000 – en demografisk, social og kulturgeografisk undersøgelse af de danske immigranter og deres efterkommere (Odense, 2005), 196, 198, 199, 277–80; see note 9.

Norwegian-born people constituted 8 percent and Swedish-born 5 percent of Minnesota's total population in 1880. Clearly Minnesota was in this respect both a "Swedish" and a "Norwegian" state. In 1920, Swedes represented 4.6 percent of Minnesota's total population and Norwegians 3.7 percent. Bjork argues that the attraction spilled over onto the Norwegian engineers: "The Twin City area has a heavy Scandinavian population. It is therefore not surprising that many

Norwegian engineers should have been attracted to this metropolis center, which after the dull 1870s experienced a rapid growth. They were employed both by the many railroads that serve the Northwest and by engineering departments in the two cities." Minnesota was the fifth most common American state for Norwegian engineers and architects to be employed. The engineering departments of Minneapolis and St. Paul, as well as the Northern Pacific Railway Company, were workplaces where—to use Bjork's words—"Norwegian could not fairly have been considered a foreign language."[22]

Minnesota attracted four times as many Norwegian as Swedish technical school graduates. In fact, more Swedish technical school graduates moved to Ontario and Quebec than Minnesota. Norway educated a significantly higher percentage of civil and constructional engineers than did Sweden. The Twin Cities often offered employment within the building of their infrastructures. Some of the area's Norwegian engineers were important for this development. Carl Illstrup is viewed as crucial for the design of Minneapolis's modern sewer system, and Kristoffer Olsen Oustad played, together with Norwegian colleagues, a major role as a bridge builder.[23]

Chicago was another area where Scandinavians were relatively well represented. It attracted more Scandinavian engineers and architects than Minnesota. This is hardly surprising: Chicago was America's second city and one of its most important industrial centers. Every fifth Norwegian technical school graduate in North America was employed in Chicago, and every seventh Swedish. Technicians remaining in the city after the 1893 exposition formed a Swedish Engineers' Society, whereas the first purely Norwegian association for technicians came into being only in 1923. The Norwegian Club of Chicago was a longstanding meeting place for old friends from the technical schools and a place where technicians could establish necessary contacts for their professional and social lives. The engineers' society played this role for the Swedes. This can indicate a difference between graduates from the two countries: a stronger willingness among the Norwegians to interact with the main body of the immigrants versus a stronger draw to professional affiliations for the Swedes. This is not to say, however, that Swedish engineers and architects did not do the same. Many members of the engineer society were, for instance, also members of organizations like the Swedish Cultural Association of America and Chicago's numerous Swedish provincial societies.[24]

Engineers and architects of both nationalities became well known in Chicago. Isak Rasmusen Faleide and Alfred Alsaker, both from Bergen, constitute Norwegian examples. Faleide started a construction company and developed a jack that was used until the 1970s. Alsaker published, according to Bjork, a unique study of unemployment based on mathematical equations. John Ericson, namesake of the countryman who constructed the *Monitor*, was appointed city engineer in 1897, modernized Chicago's water-supply systems, and constructed bridges. Albin Witting, Illinois Steel Company's leading engineer, was also well known in Chicago's Swedish community. He wrote in Swedish newspapers about the lack of Swedish American patriotism and was referred to in the 1911 appendix to the Swedish Royal Commission on Emigration.[25]

Returning to our hypotheses, the observations regarding settlement patterns diverge. Swedish technical school graduates to a larger extent followed in the footsteps of the main body of emigrants. This can be explained by the fact that the Swedes who crossed the Atlantic more often had occupations connected to industry and consequently to a greater extent went to the same industrial areas as the technicians. Even if high absolute numbers of Swedes and Scandinavians settled in, for instance, New York and Massachusetts, their percentage of the overall population was still rather modest. In areas like Minnesota and Chicago, people of Scandinavian descent constituted major shares of the total population. These areas had a strong attraction for Norwegian engineers and architects.

Summary and Conclusion

Were Norwegian and Swedish technical school graduates going to North America as journeymen or traditional emigrants? First and foremost, there are reasons to state that the main body of engineers and architects educated at technical schools from both countries followed the journeyman pattern rather than the patterns of traditional emigration. The return rates for the graduates were significantly higher than for general emigration to North America from these two high-emigration countries. Swedish industrialization was faster and included modern large-scale industries. The Norwegian industry was primarily small scale. We assumed, therefore, that the Norwegian labor market functioned more as a push factor and consequently less as a pull factor, once the graduates were in North America. This held true. Norwegian technical school graduates migrated across the Atlantic and once there were more likely to settle permanently than were their Swedish colleagues.

A majority of all graduates followed a pattern that can be called target migration; as they departed for America, they aimed at returning home. They were in the Dutch sociologist Frank Bovenkerk's first category of migration—an intended temporary one that, in fact, ended in a return. This category applied especially to the Swedes. The Norwegians were more strongly represented in Bovenkerk's fourth category—migrants intending to settle permanently and who never returned.

We have also assumed that the Norwegians who returned to a larger extent belonged to Bovenkerk's category of migrants who had intended to settle permanently but changed their minds and returned. This implies that the returning

Norwegian graduates were older and had spent longer periods in North America than their Swedish colleagues before coming home. The main lines of this assumption were also correct, although the results were less unambiguous. The differences were relatively small.

The results connected to our final assumption, that the Norwegian graduates followed in the footsteps of general emigration to North America, are also somewhat ambiguous. Graduates from both countries primarily went to the manufacturing centers in New York, New Jersey, Massachusetts, Pennsylvania, and Illinois, places that offered the best employment opportunities. Many ordinary Swedish immigrants also lived in these areas. From this perspective, it was rather the Swedish graduates who moved more to places where countrymen in general resided, as nearly every second Swedish American lived within the manufacturing belt compared to every fifth person of Norwegian origin. In areas like Minnesota, and to a certain extent Chicago, Scandinavians constituted major shares of the total population and could make a more significant impression in local and regional communities. These regions seem to have held a stronger attraction for Norwegian engineers and architects.

Notes

1. Kenneth O. Bjork, *Saga in Steel and Concrete: Norwegian Engineers in America* (Northfield, MN: Norwegian-American Historical Association, 1947), 35–36.

2. "Svensk-amerikanska ingeniörers och arkitekters möte i Gefle," in *Teknisk Tidskrift. Allmänna afdelningen* 30 (1901): 209. Bjork, *Saga in Steel and Concrete,* 38.

3. Thomas Parke Hughes, *American Genesis: A Century of Invention and Technological Enthusiasm, 1870–1970* (New York: Viking, 1989), 15; Sigmund Skard, *USA i norsk historie: 1000–1776–1976* (Oslo: Det norske samlaget, 1976), 180; Ole Hyldtoft, *Teknologiske forandringer i dansk industri 1896–1972,* 7:15; Per-Olof Grönberg, *Learning and Returning: Return Migration of Swedish Engineers from the United States, 1880–1940* (Umeå: Umeå University, 2003), 227, available: http://urn.kb.se/resolve?urn=urn:nbn:se:umu :diva-119.

4. Lars O. Olsson, *Technology Carriers: The Role of Engineers in the Expanding Swedish Shipbuilding System,* Doktorsavhandlingar vid Chalmers tekniska högskola. Ny serie 1628 (Göteborg: Chalmers tekniska högsk., 2000), 50–51; Hugo Hammar, *Minnen. 1, Från Ölands Alvar till livets* (Stockholm: Geber, 1937), 253–55, 271; Hugo Hammar, *Minnen. 2, Som emigrant i U.S.A.* (Stockholm: Geber, 1938), 11. Harald Runblom and Hans Norman, *From Sweden to America: A History of the Migration,* Studia historica Upsaliensia 74 (Uppsala: Acta University Upsaliensis, 1976), 129.

5. Francis Sejersted, Lars Andersson, and Per Lennart Månsson, *Socialdemokratins tidsålder: Sverige och Norge under 1900-talet,* Sverige och Norge under 200 år (Nora: Nya Doxa, 2005), 26–28; Bo Stråth, *Union och demokrati: de förenade rikena Sverige och Norge 1814–1905,* Sverige och Norge under 200 år (Nora: Nya Doxa, 2005), 527–28.

6. Sejersted, Andersson, and Månsson, *Socialdemokratins tidsålder*, 28–30; Stråth, *Union och demokrati*, 527–28; Francis Sejersted, *Demokratisk kapitalisme* (Oslo: Universitetsforlaget, 1993). Stråth emphasizes regional policy behind the decision to locate the Norwegian Institute in Trondheim, but one can also argue that Trondheim had built the foundations for the technical university by developing the qualitatively best technical vocational school in Norway.

7. Harry Jerome, *Migration and Business Cycles* (New York: National Bureau of Economic Research, 1926); Brinley Thomas, *Migration and Economic Growth: A Study of Great Britain and the Atlantic Economy* (Cambridge: Cambridge University Press, 1973).

8. Frank Bovenkerk, *The Sociology of Return Migration: A Bibliographic Essay*, Publications of the Research group for European migration problems 20 (The Hague: Martinus Nijhoff, 1974), 10–18.

9. Norwegian National Library, Oslo: Press cutting archives; *Ingeniørmatrikkelen. norske sivilingeniører 1901–55 med tillegg* (Oslo: Teknisk ukeblad, 1961); *Vi fra NTH: de første ti kull: 1910–1919* (Stavanger: Dreyer, 1934); Leif Eskedal, *BTS-matrikkelen. ingeniører uteksaminert ved Bergen tekniske skole 1875–1975* (Bergen: Skolen, 1975); *Norske ingeniører og arkitekter: kort oversigt over Den norske ingeniørforenings og Norskearkitekters landsforbunds historie, samt biografiske oplysninger om de to organisationers nulevende medlemmer med portrætter* (Kristiania: Abel, 1916); Einar Jansen, *Norsk biografisk leksikon*, 1927; Trondhjems tekniske læreanstalt, *Trondhjemsteknikernes matrikel: biografiske meddelelser om samtlige faste og hospiterendeelever av Trondhjems tekniske læreanstalt 1870–1915: med ca.1300 ungdomsportrætter* (Trondhjem: F. Bruns boghandel, 1916); *Ingeniører fra 1896 fra Kristiania Tekniske Skole: biografiske Oplysninger samlet til 25 Aars Jubileet 1921* (Kristiania: [Bokkomiteen], 1921); *KTS: 50 årsberetning om Ingeniørkullet fra Kristiania tekniskeskole 1896* (Oslo, 1946); *Ingeniørene fra K.T.S 1897–1947* (Oslo, 1947); *Tillegg til Trondhjemsteknikernes matrikel*, 1932; *Hvem er hvem? Biografisk leksikon: Utgit i anledning av Norsk bokhandlermedhjælper-forenings 25 aars jubilæum* (Kristiania: Festkomiteen, 1911); Kristiania tekniske skole, *Festskrift i anledning af Kristiania tekniske skoles 25-aars jubilæum i juni 1898* (Kristiania: J. Chr. Gundersens bogtrykkeri, 1898); "Tidsskrift for kjemi, bergvesen og metallurgi"; Kristiania tekniske skole, "Beretning om Kristiania tekniske skoles virksomhet i skoleaaret . . ."

Gösta Bodman, *Chalmers tekniska institut: Matrikel 1829–1929* (Göteborg: [s.n.], 1929); Emil Forsberg and Emil Adlers, *Tekniska föreningen i Örebro 1875–1925: Minnesskrift utgiven med anledning av föreningens femtioåriga verksamhet* (Stockholm: Red., 1925); Govert Indebetou and Erik Hylander, *Svenska teknologföreningen 1861–1936: biografier* (Stockholm: Svenska teknologföreningen [distributör], 1937); *Malmö teknologförbund: Minnesalbum utg. i anledning av Malmö tekniska läroverks 75-åriga verksamhet: 1853–1928* (Malmö: [Rektor Montén, Tekn. lärov.], 1928); "Civilingenjörer och arkitekter utexaminerade från Chalmers tekniska högskola: jämte redogörelse för Chalmersska ingenjörsföreningens och Chalmersska forskningsfondens verksamhet" (Chalmerska ingenjörsföreningen, 1957), unAPI.

The reason details were omitted is probably that Bassøe covers a large number, around ten thousand, Norwegian engineers (all graduates between 1901 and 1955) and thereby deliberately left out some information on the elderly graduates to give space to the more recent ones.

10. Sten Carlsson, "Swedish Engineers in Chicago," in *Swedish-American Life in Chicago: Cultural and Urban Aspects of an Immigrant People, 1850–1930,* eds. Philip J. Anderson and Dag Blanck (Urbana: University of Illinois Press, 1992), 182. Landsarkivet i Härnösand; Härnösands Tekniska Skolas arkiv; A. G. J. Eurenius, *Matrikel öfver eleverna i Tekniska elementarskolan i Norrköping från skolans början år 1857 till och m. v. till 1912* (Norrköping: Norrk. tidn:s, 1912); *1862–1912. Minnesskrift utg. vid Teknologföreningens 50-jubileum af deras ombudsnämnd: Porträttkatalogens redaktör: Sigurd Köhler [Teckningar: J.Hedaeus]* (Borås, 1912); *Matrikel över ingenjörer, utexaminerade från Högre tekniska läroverket i Norrköping, förutvarande Tekniska gymnasiet resp. Tekniska elementarskolan, från skolans början år 1857 t.o.m. vårterminen 1961* (Norrköping, 1962).

11. Cf. Grönberg, *Learning and Returning,* 69.

12. Gudmund Stang, "A Measure of Relative Development? A Note on the Education and Dispersion of Scandinavian Engineers 1870–1930," in *I det lange løp,* eds. Bjørn L. Basberg, Helge W. Nordvik, and Gudmund Stang (Bergen-Sandviken: Fagbokförlaget, 1997), 94, 96. X, "Patriotisme," in *Teknisk Ugeblad,* 9 (1885): 43; Laur. Jensen, "Patriotisme," in *Teknisk Ugeblad* 14 (1885): 67; Dixi X, "Patriotisme," in *Teknisk Ugeblad* 17 (1885): 85. "N. I. A. F. i New York," in *Teknisk Ugeblad* 20 (1903): 208–9.

13. G. W., "Teknikerna och utvandringen," in *Teknisk Tidskrift. Veckoupplagan* 51 (1910): 415.

14. Sten Carlsson, *Swedes in North America: 1638–1988: Technical, Cultural and Political Achievements* (Stockholm: Streiffert, 1988), 58. On return migration, see Mark Wyman, *Round-Trip to America: The Immigrants Return to Europe, 1880–1930* (Ithaca, NY: Cornell University Press, 1993). Ingrid Semmingsen, *Veien mot vest. 2, Utvandringen fra Norge 1865–1915* (Oslo: H . Aschehoug & Co. [W. Nygaard], 1950), 460; Lars-Göran Tedebrand, "Remigration from America to Sweden," in *Historia och demografi: Valda texter,* vol. 1 (Umeå: Historia och demografi, 1999).

15. Average graduation age was 22.9 years for the Swedes and 22.1 for the Norwegians. The distribution of graduates on age in percent was: Norway (n = 2923), 16–19 years 10.6; 20–21 33.9; 22–23 31.7; 24–25 15.7; 26–27 4.9; 28–29 1.8, 30 years or older 1.3; Sweden (n = 5529), 16–19 7.3; 20–21 19.8; 22–23 37.6; 24–25 23.3; 26–27 8.0; 28–29 2.3; 30 years or older 1.7. Sources, see note 9.

16. Bimal Ghosh, *Return Migration: Journey of Hope or Despair?* (Geneva: United Nations, 2000), 12, 24. King's interpretation of Cerase's typology, however, places target migrants in a group called *return of conservatism,* whose entire stay abroad is colored by the fact that they aim to return to the home country. This may be true in one sense, but it does not imply that target migrants cannot be innovative.

17. Helge Nelson, *The Swedes and the Swedish Settlement in North America,* republished as *Scandinavians in America* (Lund: C.W.K. Gleerup, 1943), 354; Gulbrand Loken, *From Fjord to Frontier: A History of the Norwegians in Canada* (Toronto: McClelland and Stewart, 1980).

18. Torben Grøngaard Jeppesen, *Danske i USA 1850–2000: En demografisk, social og kulturgeografisk undersøgelse af de danske immigranter og deres efterkommere* (Odense:

Odense Bys Museer, 2005), 196, 198–99, 278, 280. Torbj. Hermanrud, "Newport News Shipbuilding and Dry Dock Co," in *Teknisk Ukeblad* 47 (1915): 581, 582–84. Original in Norwegian: I denne tid da saa mange norske skibsbyggerier utvides og flere nye er planlagt, kunde det være av intresse at se hvorledes et av de største amerikanske skibsbyggerier er arrangert. R. F. R., "Planmæssig Arbeidsordning. Frederik Winslow Taylor. Kortfattet referat av advokat Ludvig Meyers foredrag i Polyteknisk forening den 14de november 1916," in *Teknisk Ukeblad* 47 (1916), 527.

19. Harm J. De Blij and Peter O. Muller, *Geography: Regions and Concepts* (New York: Wiley, 1991), 196–97. Grönberg, *Learning and Returning*, 128–29; Leonard S. Reich, *The Making of American Industrial Research: Science and Business at GE and Bell, 1876–1926,* Studies in Economic History and Policy (Cambridge: Cambridge University Press, 1985); George Wise, *Willis R. Whitney, General Electric and the Origins of U.S. Industrial Research* (New York: Columbia University Press, 1985).

20. We have added the states Massachusetts, Connecticut, Rhode Island, New York, New Jersey, Maryland, Delaware, District of Columbia, Pennsylvania, Ohio, Indiana, and Illinois to the belt. However, the American manufacturing belt includes only parts of several of them and, in addition, minor parts of Missouri and Wisconsin and the populous part of Ontario, Canada. Adding Missouri and Wisconsin levels out the differences and gives 36 percent of the Norwegians inside the belt compared to 50 percent of the Swedes. Wisconsin makes the difference. Some of the Norwegians in Wisconsin lived, of course, in Milwaukee, but a majority probably in the areas of the state located outside the manufacturing belt.

21. Bjork, *Saga in Steel and Concrete*, 432.

22. Bjork, *Saga in Steel and Concrete*, 53, 140

23. This pattern of movement to Canada has earlier been noted by Carlsson, who however assumes that there were many second- and third-generation Swedish Americans among the engineers in Minneapolis–St. Paul: see Carlsson, "Swedish Engineers in Chicago," 185. Bjork, *Saga in Steel and Concrete*, 52, 140–41.

24. The first society was difficult to sustain as the Swedish exposition visitors began leaving Chicago in the years that followed. A Scandinavian society seems to have existed between 1903 and 1908 but was impossible to hold together in light of the tensions in the aftermath of the 1905 dissolution of the union between Sweden and Norway. In 1908, a number of Swedish engineers decided instead to form the Swedish Engineers' Society of Chicago, which existed until the late 1980s: see Per-Olof Grönberg, "'My Kind of Town'? Ethnicity and Class as Determining Factors for Return Migration or Permanent Settlement among Swedish Engineers in Chicago 1910–1930," in *Swedishness Reconsidered,* ed. Daniel Lindmark, vol. 121 (Umeå: Institutionen för nordiska språk, University of Umeå, 1999), 121–42; and Byron J. Nordstrom, "*Trasdockan:* The Yearbook of the Swedish Engineers' Society of Chicago," in eds. Anderson and Blanck, *Swedish-American Life in Chicago,* 193–212. Grönberg, *Learning and Returning*, 78; Per Nordahl, "Lost and Found—A Place to Be: The Organization of Provincial Societies in Chicago from the 1890s to 1933," in *Swedishness Reconsidered,* vol. 65.

25. Bjork, *Saga in Steel and Concrete*, 441–42, 478–81; Odd S. Lovoll, *A Century of*

Urban Life: The Norwegians in Chicago before 1930 (Northfield, MN: The Norwegian-American Historical Association, 1988), 284. Carlsson, "Swedish Engineers in Chicago," 187; Allan Kastrup, *The Swedish Heritage in America: The Swedish Element in America and American-Swedish Relations in Their Historical Perspective* (Minneapolis, MN: Swedish Council of America, 1975), 384.

CHAPTER 13

Corncobs to Classmates

Swedish Americans at a Norwegian American College

JOY K. LINTELMAN

The nickname for students, alumni, and athletic teams at Concordia College in Moorhead, Minnesota, is "Cobbers," a shortened version of the earlier nickname "Corncobs." An unusual appellation for students at a Christian liberal arts institution, the name developed from a rivalry that existed between students at two different Moorhead schools. One, Hope Academy, was founded by Swedish Lutherans, and the other, Concordia College, was established by Norwegian Lutherans. According to early Concordia faculty member Rasmus Bogstad, after Concordia had opened in the early 1890s, young men from Hope interrupted Concordia literary programs with the chant:

Corncobs! Corncobs!	(Corncobs! Corncobs!
Hva' ska' Ni Ha?	What will you have?
Lutefisk and lefse—	Lutefisk and lefse—
Yah! Yah! Yah!	Yah! Yah! Yah!)

While Concordia students soon gained revenge against the Hope students with "pugilistic fist-fights," the nickname of Corncobs stuck, ultimately shortened to Cobs and then Cobbers in the 1920s, and remains as a label held dear by generations of Concordia College students and alumni into the twenty-first century.[1]

The name-calling incident indicates late nineteenth-century divisions between Swedish and Norwegian Americans in the Red River Valley of Minnesota and North Dakota. Also representative of this split was the founding of Concordia College, which was initially established as a Norwegian alternative to the Swedish Hope Academy. When Swedish-Lutheran Hope opened in 1888, Norwegian-Lutheran congregations were invited to send their sons and daughters to the school. Norwegian-Lutheran pastors in the region were not eager to promote the offer, however. Their decision was likely based in part on the facts that Norwegians greatly outnumbered Swedes in most of the Valley and that Hope had achieved full enrollment already in its second term. Recognizing that Hope could never accommodate all of the Norwegian students in the region, the Norwegians might have considered joining with the Swedes to expand the facility. Instead, in 1889 a group comprised mostly of Norwegian-Lutheran pastors began discussing the creation of a separate Norwegian-Lutheran school in Moorhead. These plans came to fruition in 1891 when Concordia College (though really only an academy at that point) opened its doors for students.[2]

While the establishment of the two Moorhead Lutheran schools, as well as the Corncob taunting incident, suggests at least competitive if not negative inter-relations between Norwegians and Swedes on the northern plains, an examina-tion of interaction between the two ethnic groups at Concordia College over time reveals that relations between Norwegian and Swedish immigrants and their descendants were more friendly than not. While Norwegian Americans have comprised the majority of Concordia students throughout its history, small minorities of Swedish American students have consistently chosen to attend the college. The closure of Hope Academy in 1896, the ease with which Norwegian and Swedish immigrants could communicate with each other, and the shared history and traditions (particularly with regard to the Lutheran faith) of Swedish and Norwegian Americans in the region all encouraged positive interactions between the two groups. These reasons also help explain the continued presence of Swedish Americans at this Norwegian American school.

Hope Academy's inability to weather the economic downturn of the 1890s as compared with Concordia's survival during that decade was probably tied to the relatively smaller Swedish population in the region. When Hope's doors shut in 1896, no other comparable Swedish-Lutheran school existed in the area. Hope Academy's closing contributed to Concordia's developing reputation as a school that could meet not only the educational needs of Norwegian-Lutheran fami-lies in North Dakota and northern Minnesota but those of Swedish-Lutheran families as well.[3]

The cooperation between Norwegian- and Swedish-Lutheran immigrants in the early years of Scandinavian emigration to the United States probably also made it easier both for Swedish Lutherans to consider attending Concordia and for Norwegian Lutherans to accept and welcome them. The roots of the United [Lutheran] Synod (whose clergy and congregants were the initial supporters of Concordia) included collaboration between Norwegians and Swedes. The Scandinavian Evangelical Lutheran Augustana Synod was established in 1860 and consisted of both Swedish and Norwegian congregations. This collabora-tion lasted until 1870, when the Norwegians amicably left the Augustana Synod to establish the Norwegian-Danish Augustana Synod and the Conference of the Norwegian-Danish Evangelical Lutheran Church in America. These two groups, along with anti–Missouri Synod members of the Norwegian Synod (established 1853), merged in 1890 to form the Norwegian United Church synod, some of whose members were instrumental in the creation of Concordia College.[4]

While Concordia was established as a Norwegian alternative to the Swedish

Hope Academy, the college early on developed an emphasis on its religious rather than its ethnic heritage and identity. For example, though the college's first principal, Ingebrikt F. Grose, was a Minnesota-born Lutheran of Norwegian and German parentage, additional faculty included an Ohio-born Lutheran and a Pennsylvania-born Lutheran, neither of whom possessed Norwegian ancestry. According to college historian Carroll Engelhardt, only six of nine faculty members teaching in the college's first year had Norwegian ancestry.[5]

Emphasis on religion rather than ethnicity was also evident in Concordia publications in the college's first decades. Historical accounts of the college's founding and purpose in its early catalogs did not mention Norwegian heritage. For example, the 1909–10 catalog stated as Concordia's aim the "Christian education of young men and women," with no reference to ethnic (or even Lutheran) roots. A description of the communities where Concordia was located and programs it offered reveals more clearly the college's open attitude toward Swedish Lutherans and other non-Norwegian Lutherans. In a section entitled "Churches," the catalog listed eight different Lutheran congregations in Fargo and Moorhead, only half of which were Norwegian Lutheran. The list was followed by a statement declaring: "Norwegian, Swedish, English, and German Lutheran students will find, in the two cities, churches in which the services are conducted in their own language." Also suggesting that the college viewed its constituency as broader than only Norwegians were the "Special Courses" for "those who lately have come from Norway, Sweden, or Germany" and who needed instruction in English or other subjects "of which the American citizen cannot afford to be ignorant."[6]

Local businesses advertising in Concordia publications in the early twentieth century suggest that outside opinions of the college's student body were varied. Some suggest a view of the college as a Norwegian institution, such as the Caspary Fur Company, whose advertisement in the college newspaper, though written mostly in English, included the line, "Vi er norske og ønsker vore landsmend som Kunder" (We are Norwegian and wish to have our countrymen as customers). A Fargo drug store advertised "the following line of goods not usually kept in Drug Stores: . . . Norwegian School books, Norwegian Hymn Books." But other community members exhibited a broader conception of the college. The newspaper also carried advertisements for businesses owned by Swedes, including a tailor shop, a confectionary, and a dentist. A clothing store advertisement in the college catalog included the following in Norwegian: "Skandinaviske Studenter er Særskilt indbudne til at besøge os" (Scandinavian students are especially invited to visit us).[7]

An editorial from the college newspaper written in 1916 as Concordia was shifting from academy to college envisaged it as a "Lutheran University of the Red River Valley." The college's negotiations with its supporting bodies also

Advertisement for Caspary Fur Company

suggest this vision. When three Norwegian-Lutheran synods merged in 1917 to form the Norwegian Lutheran Church in America, church officials of the new synod determined it impractical to provide financial support for two colleges in the same region: Concordia in Moorhead and Park Region Lutheran College (established in 1892) in Fergus Falls. According to Engelhardt, when then college president J. A. Aasgaard made a pitch for Concordia's continued existence as a college (graduating its first baccalaureate class in 1917), he "presented population charts based on the 1910 Census which showed that several thousand more *Scandinavians* lived within fifty and one hundred miles of Moorhead than lived within a similar radius of Fergus Falls [emphasis mine]." The presentation suggests a conviction that Scandinavian Lutherans, not only Norwegian Lutherans, were part of the college's constituency. Since church officials ultimately assigned the college program to Concordia and the academy program to Park Region, they likely also supported Aasgaard's vision.[8]

Concordia fundraising publicity in the 1920s also emphasized a Lutheran rather than a Norwegian identity. A 1926 yearbook advertisement referred to Concordia as "The Lutheran College of the Great Northwest," and in the 1925–26 college catalog, the Fargo-Moorhead church listing no longer referred to Lutheran churches by ethnic group but instead stated, "The location of the College in the midst of a large Lutheran population served by nine pastors in the two cities is of particular social and religious advantage for those who attend a Lutheran college." Similarly, an article in the college newspaper in 1926 noted that "the nearest Lutheran college is three hundred miles away" and that Concordia was "the only four year Lutheran College in the territory extending north from the Twin Cities and west to the Rocky Mountains."[9]

Concordia's desire to attract more than just Norwegian American Lutheran students was evident in the 1930s, as well, when the college's administration saw

Advertisement for the Hub

the increasing cooperation between Scandinavian Lutheran synods that was then taking place as a way to enhance its pool of potential students. The American Lutheran Conference, a cooperative federation of several Lutheran Synods, was established in October 1930. The Conference contained Norwegian, Swedish, and Danish Lutherans (including the Norwegian Lutheran Church of America, the American Lutheran Church, the Augustana Synod, the United Danish Evangelical Lutheran Church, and the Lutheran Free Church). Since none of the other member synods of the American Lutheran Conference had established a four-year college in North Dakota, Montana, or northern Minnesota, Concordia's President Brown hoped that synods outside the Norwegian Lutheran Church of America who participated in the Conference would encourage young men and women in their congregations to attend Concordia.[10]

This attitude is also reflected in a portion of the college catalog entitled "The Ideals of Concordia College" that ran from the late 1930s through the early 1950s. A subsection entitled "Aims of the Founders" read, "The Lutheran pioneers who peopled the great agricultural empire of the Near Northwest envisioned an insti-tution that would transmit to posterity the rich cultural heritage of their racial

Advertisement for Concordia College

group. But their primary concern was the preservation and dissemination of their religious faith. Our fathers labored and sacrificed to establish a *Christian* liberal arts college." Though the reference to "racial group" is vague, a section entitled "Territory and Constituency" a few pages later described the college's constituency as not only Norwegian Lutherans but also "Lutheran people of other synodical affiliations."[11]

Concordia's program offerings contributed to its attraction for non-Norwegians. While some of the colleges established by Norwegian American Lutherans, such as Luther College in Decorah, Iowa, had as their initial purpose preparing young men for the ministry (or parochial school teaching), Concordia's curriculum cast a broader net. Unlike Luther, Concordia was a coeducational institution from the start. And while religion classes were a part of Concordia's curriculum, courses of study were developed early on that, according to Engelhardt, "emphasized practical training in pedagogy and business." The college from its inception appealed to a broader constituency than young men desiring to serve as pastors in Norwegian immigrant congregations. For example, second-generation Swedish immigrant Oscar Euren completed business classes at Concordia over the course of three years near the turn of the century, and Emilia Johnson and Julia Johnson, young first- and second-generation Swedish American women, attended classes at Concordia in 1905. Their attendance also suggests that though the Norwegian language might be heard on Concordia's campus through World War II (more frequently in hallways or dormitories than in classrooms), this fact did not prevent Swedish American students from enrolling. The Norwegian language would have been comprehensible to students who spoke the Swedish language.[12]

A focus on a Scandinavian-Lutheran constituency did not mean that Concordia ignored its Norwegian American roots, though the college's attention to and celebration of its Norwegian American ancestry waxed and waned over time. Engelhardt found Concordia's sense of Norwegian heritage to be strongest in the years just before World War I. It was at this time that monuments honoring Norwegian historical figures Ivar Aaasen and Hans Nilsen Hauge were erected on the campus and a college Norwegian literary society called *Norden* donated both a portrait of writer Bjørnstjerne Bjørnson and a bust of playwright Henrik Ibsen to the campus library. Norway's independence from Sweden in 1905 likely contributed to a sense of loyalty to the homeland among Norwegian Americans at the college, although surviving college documents indicate little direct response to the event. Norway's celebration of the centennial anniversary of its 1814 Eidsvoll Constitution may also have encouraged ancestral pride on the campus.[13]

Another resurgence of pride in Norwegian heritage occurred in connection with the one hundredth anniversary of Norwegian emigration to America in

1925, when Concordia administrators and faculty helped plan and orchestrate a celebration at the Minnesota State Fairgrounds. At this time professor of Norwegian (Norse) J. A. Holvik also sponsored a spectacular pageant entitled "Norsemen in America." The pageant highlighted Norwegian American history and the contributions of Norwegians to the United States, from Viking journeys to North America to historic Norwegian American figures such as Civil War Union officer Hans Christian Heg and midwestern politician Knute Nelson. Once these mid-1920s festivities had passed, public displays of Norwegian pride waned for several decades. Immigration restriction and economic changes in Norway and the United States by the late 1920s resulted in a significant decrease in Norwegian emigration to America. Increasing numbers of Concordia students were second- and third-generation immigrants unfamiliar with Norwegian language or history, their decisions to attend the college probably driven more by proximity and religious affiliation than by ethnic heritage. College leaders also focused on economic survival of the institution during the years of the Great Depression.[14]

Focused attention to Norwegian ethnic heritage did not reemerge at the college until the 1970s, when the interests of Concordia students and faculty paralleled developments occurring in the broader society at large. The celebration of the U.S. bicentennial, the publication (and later television miniseries) of Alex Haley's investigation of African American heritage, *Roots,* and a new recognition and acceptance of the continued ethnic diversity of the United States resulted in increased curiosity about and pride in immigrant and ethnic heritage. Concordia honored its "Norwegianness" in these years through such activities as events surrounding the sesquicentennial of Norwegian immigration to America in 1975 and visits by Norwegian dignitaries and royalty. Increased academic interest in ethnic heritage was evident in the establishment of a Scandinavian studies program in 1977, which, as its name implies, did not exclude study of other Scandinavian nations. While the language component of the program usually only included Norwegian, Scandinavian studies courses in literature and history not only focused on Norway but provided broader course content encompassing Scandinavia and Norden.[15]

Pride in Norwegian heritage was also evident in changes in the college catalog at this time. A section of the 1978–80 catalog entitled "History of the College" declared, "The history of Concordia College is really that of the Norwegian Lutheran immigrants to the Red River Valley," who "were not yet adjusted to the language and customs of America and felt more secure sending their children to a school where Norwegian was spoken and traditional values were taught." It was also noted, however, that the college had "always maintained a strong relationship with the Lutheran congregations of the Upper Plains area." Perhaps to counter an exclusionary tone, the catalog for 1979–81 included an additional section entitled "Concordia Today," which noted, "Of course Concordia's student body today is not limited to Norwegian Lutherans. In fact, students come from many backgrounds and many places—from over 40 states and 15 countries representing about 30 different religions and denominations."[16]

The resurgence of interest in ethnic heritage in the 1970s likely also contributed to the short-lived existence of both a Swedish Club and a Swedish Folk Ensemble on Concordia's campus. Few records from the organizations have survived, but the college newspaper included notices of their activities beginning in the fall semester of 1977. The 1978 college yearbook entry for the club described its social function and also revealed a spirit of friendly competition with campus Norwegians: "The Swedish Club is open to all students that are Swedish. They were a social group that went to shows, held two potluck suppers, and challenged the overwhelming [probably a reference to number of members] Norwegian club for donations for the Lenten Project." The 1979–80 Swedish Club activities included social events celebrating Swedish heritage as well as a victorious volleyball tournament against campus student clubs representing East Asians, French, Germans, Norwegians, and Spanish-speaking peoples. The Swedish Folk Ensemble performed at various venues both on and off campus. According to college newspaper notices, the Swedish Club did not exist after spring 1980. And in the fall of 1980 the Swedish Folk Ensemble changed its name to "Scandinavisk [Scandinavian] Folk Ensemble." Swedish-only groups were difficult to sustain. A focus on Scandinavia encouraged participation from students of both Swedish and Norwegian heritage. A short-lived Scandinavian Sauna Society also existed in the early 1980s.[17]

Emphasis on Scandinavia rather than separate Nordic nations was evident in other areas of the campus in the 1980s as well. In 1987 the Scandinavian studies program sponsored a Scandinavian May Seminar travel abroad course. A newspaper story about the opportunity explained that the program was "initiated to help students understand their culture and family heritage," noting "nearly 80 percent of Concordia students either have Scandinavian heritage or come directly from one of the Scandinavian countries." The course included travel in the Nordic nations of Norway, Sweden, Finland, and Denmark and ultimately enrolled nine students.[18]

In addition to considering how Concordia's history, recruitment, and programming affected relations between Swedish Americans and Norwegian Americans, another important question remains: how many young men and women of Swedish American heritage actually chose to attend Concordia? Unfortunately the college did not keep careful records of students' ethnic heritage. Still, as illustrated by the references to Oscar Euren and Emilia and Julia Johnson above, it is clear that some Swedish immigrants and their descendants enrolled at Concordia. Evidence from early decades is sketchy and is based on scattered references in various college publications. For example, among the seniors listed on the Concordia basketball team in 1916 was a young man named Hilding Wallin, with the nicknames of "Wallin" or "Swede." The college paper noted jokingly, "his greatest ambition is to emulate Gustavus Adolphus." Questionnaires completed by Concordia students serving in World War I included one by Eugene Trygve Halaas indicating his father was Norwegian and mother Swedish. A 1923 yearbook included among the senior class a photograph of Jeanette Westberg, a young Cobber from Moorhead whose photo was accompanied by the caption, "Of course I'm 'Svensk' [Swedish]." Sophomore Ferdinand Anderson was listed in the 1929 yearbook with the nickname "Swede."[19]

More detailed information about numbers of Swedish Americans attending Concordia can be gleaned from surviving records of students' church affiliation. From 1940 through 1980 the college not only kept track of how many Lutherans and non-Lutherans were attending Concordia but also noted the different Lutheran synodical affiliations of its Lutheran students. Using membership in the Lutheran Augustana Synod (LAS) [for 1940–61] and Lutheran Church of America (LCA) [for 1962–80] as a proxy for Swedish American heritage and membership in the Evangelical Lutheran Church (ELC) [for 1940–59] and American Lutheran Church (ALC) [for 1960–80] as an indicator of Norwegian American heritage provides a good representation of the number of Swedish and Norwegian Americans attending Concordia for approximately forty years. The data indicate that Swedish American students never exceeded 10 percent of the student body from 1940 through 1980 (see figure 13.1). On average, Swedish-Lutheran students represented 5.6 percent of Concordia's student body during these decades. In comparison, Norwegian-Lutheran students averaged 73.4 percent of Concordia students in these years. These figures should also be viewed in the broader context of the number of students of Swedish and Norwegian ancestry living in North Dakota and northern Minnesota, the regions from which Concordia has historically drawn (and continues to draw) most of it students. A comparison of the number of confirmed members in the Red River Valley Conference of the LAS/LCA with confirmed members from the North Dakota and Northern Minnesota Districts of the ELC/ALC shows that the number of Lutherans of Norwegian heritage within Concordia's territory greatly exceeded the number of Lutherans with Swedish heritage. From 1940 through 1970 approximately nine times more confirmed members of the ELC/ALC lived in the area than did LAS/LCA Synod confirmed members. In 1980 when growth of ALC membership slowed slightly, there were still approximately 6.5 times more ALC members than LCA members. Despite their smaller presence in the region, from 1940 through 1980 students of Swedish American heritage attended Concordia in small but relatively steady numbers.[20]

In terms of how the small minority of Swedish Americans attending Concordia

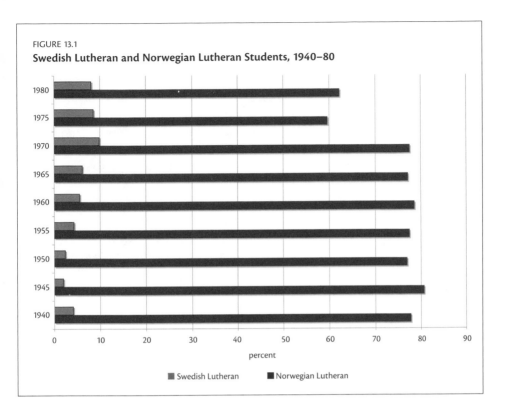

FIGURE 13.1

Swedish Lutheran and Norwegian Lutheran Students, 1940–80

percent

■ Swedish Lutheran ■ Norwegian Lutheran

fared among a sea of Norwegian Americans, a careful examination of the college newspaper suggests that students of Swedish ancestry found Concordia to be a friendly and comfortable place. For example, Swedish American students might have recognized the pastors from local Swedish-Lutheran churches who spoke periodically at college chapel services. Extracurricular activities, such as the student literary societies popular in the early twentieth century, included Swedish authors among their topics for discussion. Films by Swedish director Ingmar Bergman were periodically shown on campus, and the college even hosted a premiere of his film *Magic Flute* in 1978. Swedish American students may also have been reassured by the presence of Swedish Americans on Concordia's faculty. The college newspaper reported in 1940 about Swedish American G. L. Schoberg, a Concordia faculty member who had also attended Concordia as a student. The story described how Schoberg, when offered a position at the Swedish-Lutheran Augustana College in Rock Island, Illinois, had turned it down. He explained to the reporter that he had "watched Concordia since 1921" and felt "confident in her future." A 1962 article about Concordia religion faculty member and Swedish-Lutheran Gustavus Adolphus College alumnus Gene Lund noted that he "claimed no problem of divided loyalty," though he admitted a preference for the Cobbers in sporting events. The college even chose for its centennial commencement speaker in 1992 Swedish American Nils Hasselmo, who was then president of the University of Minnesota.[21]

Positive relationships between Swedes and Norwegians at Concordia are also evident from such items as the college newspaper's marriage announcement of Swedish American Dorothy Jenson and Norwegian Leiv Hansen in 1947. And a 1948 *Concordian* included an article about a Swedish immigrant woman newly employed at the college cafeteria, illustrating friendly interaction between Swedish and Norwegian Americans and opening with the lines, "Have you overheard a lively Scandinavian chattering lately while deciding between carrots and celery in the caf [cafeteria] line? Anna, the genial Swedish newcomer to the cafeteria force, may have been conversing with one of her many friends behind the counter." In the 1950s one of the female student societies, Kappa Beta Kappa, celebrated Swedish Christmas customs and even crowned their own "Lucia Bride."[22]

Friendly rivalry was the norm for athletic contests between Norwegian-Lutheran Concordia College and Swedish-Lutheran Gustavus Adolphus College. For example, an article describing a 1926 Concordia loss to Gustavus commented on the Concordia team's "tough assignment" with the "flag-chasing Swedes" and referred to two of the Gustavus players as "Swedish 'Big Berthas' " who sank "field goals with reckless abandon." Apparently in reference to the well-known size of their athletes, a 1929 article about a Concordia-Gustavus basketball game referred to the "huge Swedes from Gustavus" and the "giants from the Swedish institution." A student even suggested in 1938 that the Cobber/Gustie football and basketball games should have "some type of trophy or symbol of triumph" in competitions with their "natural rival" and suggested an "old Scandinavian war ax or hatchet" as an appropriate prize.[23]

Good-natured joking about Swedish and Norwegian rivalry occurred on the occasion of a visit by Norwegian King Olav V in 1982 and also provides evidence that Concordia students maintained some awareness of the ethnic heritage of the college and its students. A spoof in the college newspaper accused the campus Swedes of reacting negatively to the king's visit, unveiling a plan to "build a huge Viking warship" and take over the campus pond, providing a venue from which "thousands of overcooked Swedish meatballs" could be launched at Norwegians as they passed by. The writer also described a "newly formed radical feminist nationalist group, Daughters of Sweden," who intended to protest during the king's royal procession, as well as a plan to place lutefisk and "unpickled herring" in the auditorium where a royal convocation was to be held.[24]

Satire was not only aimed at campus Swedes. A 1997 April Fools' issue of the college newspaper poked fun at both Swedes and Norwegians. The writer described Concordia as founded by "nomadic Norse goofballs" and upholding "traditional values, like looting and plundering." An imagined professor in the

AGLOW are Kappa Beta Kappa members Marilyn Prosser, 'Lucia Bride' Marilee Thompson and Marcia Norstad at Tuesday's meeting.

"Aglow—Lucia Bride"

"Norwegian Department" was described as annoyed by "pesky Swedes." The fictitious faculty member had developed a plan to help students "get back to their roots." Among the steps included in the plan were: "1. Students would be required to show at least 80% Norwegian stock (see rule #2). Those who fail to do so will be forced to row in the galleys. 2. All students of Swedish heritage will be permitted to attend [Concordia], but only after being spayed or neutered."[25]

Swedish Americans were never a large presence on Concordia's campus, though some students of Swedish heritage chose to attend Concordia throughout its history. Their relatively small number seems more the result of factors of demography and early settlement history than of animosity between the two ethnic groups. Significantly fewer Swedish Americans lived in the region from which the college drew its students than did Norwegian Americans. This examination of Swedes and Norwegians at Concordia College also illustrates that ties of common religious belief among Scandinavian Lutherans in the Upper Midwest encouraged young Swedish Americans to attend Concordia, and that the Norwegian American heritage of the college and the Norwegian ancestry of the bulk of its students did not preclude Swedish Americans from attending. The young Swedish American men whose gibes resulted in Concordia students' unusual agricultural moniker might be surprised at the number of Swedish American Cobbers the college has produced.

Notes

1. The author extends her thanks to Richard Chapman, Carroll Engelhardt, and Lisa Sjoberg for their comments on a draft of this work, and to the Concordia College archival staff for their helpful research assistance.

Rasmus Bogstad, *The Early History of Concordia College: A Record of the School from 1891 to 1910* (s.l: n.p., 1932), 177–78.

2. "Swedish-American Organizational Records," *Swenson Center News* 1 (1986): 6; Carroll L. Engelhardt, *On Firm Foundation Grounded: The First Century of Concordia College (1891–1991)* (Moorhead, MN: Concordia College, 1991), 21, and Carroll L. Engelhardt, *Gateway to the Northern Plains: Railroads and the Birth of Fargo and Moorhead* (Minneapolis: University of Minnesota Press, 2007), 140.

3. Swedish Lutherans established a two-year school, Northwestern College, in Fergus Falls in 1901 (it closed in 1932) and a similar school, North Star College, in Warren, Minnesota in 1908 (which survived through 1936). Augustana Evangelical Lutheran Church, *The Augustana Synod A Brief Review of Its History, 1860–1910* (Rock Island, IL: Augustana Book Concern, 1910), 128–29, 134–35.

4. Richard W. Solberg, *Lutheran Higher Education in North America* (Minneapolis, MN: Augsburg Publishing House, 1985), 212. Todd Nichol, "Family Trees: Norwegian-American Lutheranism, 1846–1917," Luther Seminary, available: http://www.luthersem.edu/archives/familytrees.asp; see also Mark A. Granquist. "Swedish- and Norwegian-American Religious Traditions, 1860–1920," *Lutheran Quarterly* 8.3 (1994): 299–320.

5. Ethnic heritage for early faculty members was determined by examining manuscript U.S. Federal Census data. Grose was located on the 1910 Federal Census, Elmer D. Busby on the 1920 Federal Census, and George H. Gerberding on the 1880 Federal Census. Engelhardt, *On Firm Foundation*, 26, 32.

6. *The Concordia College Record and Catalog of Concordia College 1909–1910* (Moorhead, MN: Moorhead Independent, n.d.), 7, 14, 27. In the 1914–15 catalog, reference was made to courses for those newly arrived "from Germany or the Scandinavian countries" (16). The "Special Courses" were no longer offered in the 1917–18 catalog, the point at which Concordia had established its college baccalaureate curriculum.

7. [Advertisement], *[Concordia College] Crescent* 3.1 (Nov. 1911): n.p. [Advertisement], *[Concordia College] Crescent* 1.3 (Jan. 1910): 21. [Advertisement], *[Concordia College] Crescent* 6.1 (Oct. 1914): n.p. [advertisement for O. P. Edlund, Merchant Tailor, who is listed as born in Sweden on the 1920 Federal Census, and Chas. Hagelin, Confectionery, who is listed as born in Sweden on the 1910 Federal Census]; and [Advertisement], *[Concordia College] Crescent* 6.3 (Dec. 1914), n.p. [advertisement for Dr. Paul Verne, Dentist, who is listed of Swedish parentage on the 1920 Federal Census]; [Advertisement], *Concordia College Record* 7.2 (1903): 48.

8. "A Greater Concordia," *[Concordia College] Crescent* 8.1 (Oct. 1916): 10–11. Engelhardt, *On Firm Foundation*, 61.

9. Engelhardt, *On Firm Foundation*, 74; Concordia College (Moorhead, MN), *The Scout* 3 (Moorhead, MN: Junior Class, Concordia College, 1926), 216, and *Concordia College Record, Concordia College Catalog 1925–1926* 30.11 (Apr. 1, 1926): 13. *Concordian*, Apr. 19, 1926. Using modern interstate highways not available in the 1920s, the distance to other Lutheran colleges would be approximately 240 miles to Augsburg in Minneapolis and 245 miles to Augustana in Sioux Falls.

10. E. Clifford Nelson, *The Lutheran Church among Norwegian-Americans, Vol. 2, 1890–1959* (Minneapolis, MN: Augsburg Publishing House, 1960), 305. The Conference existed from 1930 through 1954. Engelhardt, *On Firm Foundation*, 109.

11. *Concordia College Record, Concordia College Catalog 1937* 41.1 (Feb. 1937): 12, 15, emphasis in original.

12. Odd S. Lovoll, *The Promise Fulfilled: A Portrait of Norwegian America Today* (Minneapolis: University of Minnesota Press, 1998), 102–3; Luther College Faculty, *Luther College through Sixty Years, 1861–1921* (Minneapolis, MN: Augsburg Publishing House, 1922), especially chs. 2 and 13; Engelhardt, *On Firm Foundation*, 32, 38; Oscar E. Euren interview, July 4 and 8, 1971, Northwest Minnesota Historical Center, Moorhead, MN; *Concordia College Record* (Sept. 1905): 50; and the 1905 Minnesota Census (Emilia is spelled *Emelia* on the 1905 Census).

13. The Bjørnson portrait is engraved with a notation about its donation from the Norden Society in 1911 and is currently held in Concordia College Library storage. The Ibsen bust is referenced in the "Resolutions committee report on Ness and Shurson's reports, 1911," Concordia College Archives, Moorhead, MN. Erling Nicolai Rolfsrud, *Cobber Chronicle: An Informal History of Concordia College* (Moorhead, MN: Concordia College, 1966), 162; Engelhardt, *On Firm Foundation*, 57. Thanks to Katie Rotvold, Concordia College archival staff, for tracking down dates for the Ibsen bust and Bjørnson portrait.

14. Engelhardt, *On Firm Foundation*, 96; and "Norsemen in America," *The Scout* (Moorhead, MN: Junior Class, Concordia College, 1926), 3, 135.

15. *Norden* includes the Nordic countries of Norway, Sweden, Denmark, Finland, and Iceland. Engelhardt, *On Firm Foundation*, 301. On Scandinavian studies courses, see, e.g., *Concordia College Record* 81.8 (Dec. 1977): 51, 85–86.

16. *Concordia College Record* 81.8 (Dec 1977): 5–6; *Concordia College Record* 83.7 (Oct. 1979): 11.

17. *Concordian*, Oct. 11, 1977; *1979 Cobber [Yearbook]* (Moorhead, MN: Concordia

College, 1979), 267; *1980 Cobber [Yearbook]* (Moorhead, MN: Concordia College, 1980), 149; and *Concordian,* Nov. 7, 1980. Regarding Folk Ensemble performances, see, e.g., *Concordian,* Jan. 24, 1980. On the Sauna Society, see *1981 Cobber [Yearbook]* (Moorhead, MN: Concordia College, 1981), 204.

18. *Concordian,* Feb. 6, 1987. Enrollment data for the course obtained from Concordia Registrar's Office.

19. *Crescent,* Mar. 1916; Eugene Trygve Halaas, "Questionnaire," World War I Collection, RG 20 Military, Subseries 2 Questionnaires, FF 31, Concordia College Archives, Moorhead, MN; *The Scout* (Moorhead, MN: Junior Class, Concordia College, 1923), 40; and *The Scout* 4, 73. The 1920 Federal Census for Moorhead confirmed Westberg's Swedish heritage, the 1930 Federal Census Anderson's. I was unable to verify Hilding Wallin's ethnic heritage from census data.

20. Evangelical Lutheran Augustana Synod of North America, and N. J. W. Nelson, *Report of the Eighty-First Annual Convention, June 10–15, 1941* (Rock Island, IL: Augustana Book Concern, 1940), n.p.; Augustana Evangelical Lutheran Church, *Report of the Ninety-Second Annual Convention, June 12–17, 1951* (Rock Island, IL: Augustana Book Concern, 1951), 630–35; Augustana Evangelical Lutheran Church, *Report of the One-Hundred-Second Synod, June 12–18, 1961* (Rock Island, IL: Augustana Book Concern, 1961), 764–70; Lutheran Church in America, *1972 Yearbook* (Philadelphia, PA: Board of Publications of the Lutheran Church in America, 1971), 342–45, 386; Lutheran Church in America, *1982 Yearbook* (Philadelphia, PA: Board of Publication of the Lutheran Church in America, 1981), 67, 378–81; Norwegian Lutheran Church of America, *Annual Report District Conventions 1941* (Minneapolis, MN: Augsburg Publishing House, 1941), 340–53; Evangelical Lutheran Church, *Lutheran Year Book of the Evangelical Lutheran Church 1952* (Minneapolis, MN: Augsburg Publishing House, 1951), 21–23; American Lutheran Church of America, *1962 Year Book* (Minneapolis, MN: Augsburg Publishing House, 1961), 209; American Lutheran Church of America, *1972 Yearbook of the American Lutheran Church* (Minneapolis, MN: Augsburg Publishing House, 1972), 267; American Lutheran Church of America, *1981 Yearbook of the American Lutheran Church* (Minneapolis, MN: Augsburg Publishing House, 1981), 327. The Red River Valley Conference consisted of the entire state of North Dakota plus the Minnesota counties located in the Red River Valley. The North Dakota District represented the entire state of North Dakota, and the Northern Minnesota District encompassed a region beginning north of Minneapolis and St. Paul up to the Canadian border. For maps of the various districts, see Oscar N. Olson and George W. Wickstrom, *A Century of Life and Growth: Augustana, 1848–1948* (Rock Island, IL: Augustana Book Concern, 1948), and Evangelical Lutheran Church, *Lutheran Yearbook of the Evangelical Lutheran Church* (Minneapolis, MN: Augsburg Publishing House, 1950), 20. Thanks to Mark Granquist of Luther Seminary in St. Paul, Minnesota, and Joel Thoreson of Evangelical Lutheran Church in America Archives for assistance in obtaining these statistics.

21. On Swedish-Lutheran pastors, see, e.g., *The Concordian* for Feb. 9, 1921; Sept. 22, 1926; Jan. 19, 1928; and Jan. 13, 1938. On Swedish authors, see, e.g., the Mondamin Literary Society heard a presentation on Selma Lagerlöf at its May 1923 meeting ("Mondamin," *Concordian,* May 18, 1923). *Concordian,* Jan. 20, 1978. Bergman's "The Magician"

was screened in 1965 (*Concordian,* Jan. 15, 1965), and "Smiles of a Summer Night" played in fall semester 1972 (*Concordian,* Oct. 13, 1972). *Concordian,* Apr. 25, 1940; Oct. 5, 1962; and Apr. 3, 1992.

22. *Concordian,* Oct. 10, 1947; Sept. 24, 1948; and 12 and 19 Dec. 1958.

23. "Gusties" is the nickname for Gustavus students. *Concordian,* Mar. 9, 1926; Feb. 1, 1929; and Mar. 3, 1938.

24. *Concordian,* Oct. 1, 1982.

25. *Concordian,* Apr. 1, 1997.

CHAPTER 14

A Scandinavian Enclave on Lake Superior's North Shore

Settlement Patterns and Community Building among Norwegians, Swedes, and Swede Finns in Hovland, Minnesota, 1888–1932

PHILIP J. ANDERSON

Human life has always aspired to a personal and collective sense of place and being rooted in belonging, even in the complex patterns of migration where the old and the new become negotiated over time in transformed identities. It has been said that homemaking is the endless, unfinished business of humanity. The Scandinavian notion of *landskap* has come to refer to a "lived territory" that combines in a dialectical manner a group's sense of place (e.g., home, town, county, state, nation, folk) with its physical features (e.g., landscape, scenery, climate, flora, fauna). Scholars have noted that "collective socialization" is not accidental but forged in the midst of these realities.[1]

The Scandinavian immigrants who arrived in Hovland in northeastern Minnesota at the end of the nineteenth century may not have conceived of their lives in this way, but they possessed an innate sense of *landskap*, which in time created a community identity that was conscious of "the Big Lake" and "the North Shore" (where Hovland would soon be dubbed the Lake Trout Capitol); the "Arrowhead Country" and "Canoe Country," with its lakes, rivers, and forest rich in resources and nonhuman inhabitants; and the old history and culture of its first homemakers, their American Indian neighbors, and the legendary voyageurs. Such a landscape also attracted visitors, artists, and writers in great numbers.

My personal interest in the general topic of this chapter perhaps began with little awareness at the age of two when I first came to a rustic cabin on the rocky shore of Lake Superior six miles east of the village of Grand Marais, in the "tip of the Arrowhead" of northeastern Minnesota. The land was homesteaded in 1896 by Ole E. Erickson, my aunt's grandfather (by marriage to my father's oldest brother). I stayed at this awe-inspiring place with its view westward down the shore to the Sawtooth Mountains on many occasions, often in conjunction with numerous trips into the canoe country of its backyard—the Boundary Waters Canoe Area Wilderness.

My appetite for the region became whetted not only by its isolation and beauty, including the largest inland sea in the world, with 10 percent of its fresh surface water, but also by the history of its native peoples (first the Dakota and then the Ojibwe), followed by French-Canadian voyageurs and the fur-trade empires from Grand Portage on Lake Superior to the inland posts at Lake Athabaska of the English Hudson's Bay Company, the Scottish North West Company, the XY Company, and John Jacob Astor's American Fur Company. Following the fur companies' collapse by the early nineteenth century, the Treaty of La Pointe opened the north shore of Lake Superior to white settlement in 1854, principally Scandinavian in the immediate decades following the 1880s. I was not yet aware that Ole Erickson was one of the first Swedes to settle in the area, or that his half mile of lakeshore and 146 acres of woods was at that time the western boundary of Hovland Township.

My scholarly interest began in the mid-1980s when we set about preserving an old house, a further ten miles east along the shore near the center of Hovland. It was built in 1915 by another immigrant homesteader, Anders Haagensen Solgaard ("Andrew Solgard" in the United States), a Norwegian commercial fisherman. He built the house at age fifty-nine and as a widower. From a family of sea captains, he had emigrated from Langesund in Telemark in 1880. Solgard developed his homestead, fished for five years, contracted breast cancer, and died penniless in 1921 at the county infirmary in Chicago, where he had joined his daughter Jacobine Peterson (married to a Swede) and her family during the last weeks of his illness. After much searching, I finally found him buried about ten minutes from our home on the northwest side of Chicago in a grave marked only with the number "662" in the largely Scandinavian Mount Olive Cemetery. Because Solgard died intestate, his homestead—his only asset—went to Jacobine. She sold the property in 1923 to Norwegian immigrant brothers Nels and Jacob Norman and their half-brother, Edwin Nilson. Both Nels and Jacob married the first year, and eventually five adults lived together in the small house.[2]

The 24-by-16-foot two-story balloon-framed structure that Solgard built with the help of his inland Swede Finn neighbor-farmer Andrew Westerlund had been shipped down the lake from Duluth on a package steamer, possibly the *America*, to the Hovland dock in Chicago Bay a couple miles to the east, since there was as yet no developed road along the lake. Resisting the suggestion of the local volunteer fire department to burn it for practice, we gutted the building to determine its soundness, since it had been left unchanged since the late 1920s. Inside the walls, serving as insulation, we found Norwegian- and English-language periodicals, magazines, catalogs, food packages, and advertisements (including "Tubbs Bilious Man's Friend Removing Sick Headache" with a photograph of the "Chandtedah-Kinnickinnic Campfire Girls, River Falls, Wis. 1915"); remnants of Andrew's wool trousers, shirts, and socks; cloth Union Leader tobacco pouches—draw strings and tax stamps intact; and abundant gill net stuffed in around the six windows and one door. Outside, we are still finding buried floats for herring nets and bottles of all shapes and sizes, ranging from People's Root Beer in Duluth to what were obviously stronger beverages of choice.[3]

Thus began nearly twenty years of rebuilding a piece of the material immigrant fishing culture that has mostly disappeared from the 145 miles of bays, coves, and inhospitable stretches from Duluth to Hat Point at Grand Portage, where in 1920 there were 276 commercial fishermen and families, 80 to 90 percent of whom were Norwegian American. Consequently, I have been studying the Hovland community in general for some time but have progressively become more deeply immersed in the historical sources with an eye toward a larger research project—inspired in part by books like Odd Lovoll's *Norwegians on the Prairie* and its look at rural community life in small western Minnesota towns.[4]

What kind of rural is Hovland? The project that seeks in part to answer that question has gradually evolved with layers of questions and new leads to explore. I have analyzed census data and read reels of microfilmed newspapers in the Grand Marais Public Library and Minnesota Historical Society. In hours spent examining warranty and patent deeds at the county courthouse I have attempted to reconstruct the highly unusual and crazy patchwork quilt of homesteading, speculating, trading, accommodating or being used by aggressive timber companies, extensive tax delinquencies, and loan defaults. I have also explored the abundant photographs, oral histories, official records, and other sometimes hidden resources at the Cook County Historical Society. In addition to conducting oral interviews (including topics like backwoods stills and occasional bootlegging during Prohibition and beyond), I have been photographing what survives of the material culture in the eight different settlements that comprised early Hovland.[5]

There is a special, if not unique, story to tell about the Norwegians, Swedes, and Swede Finns (as well as others, of course) who settled in Hovland beginning in 1888; its settlement patterns and community building through the generations; the growth of wilderness tourism and presence of some notable seasonal residents (such as Olle i Skratthult during the 1920s); and the manner in which expressions of symbolic ethnicity still thrive today, whether among the descendants of pioneer families or the most recent arrivals. In all, the evidence suggests extensive cooperation among these ethnic neighbors forging a community that has had a strong Scandinavian character, though the Norwegians were by far the dominant group. What follows are the main outlines of a work in progress with some preliminary findings and areas of further exploration and analysis. I have chosen 1932 to be a somewhat arbitrary terminus for this chapter, primarily because it is the year of completion for the major highway that more directly penetrated this isolated community, whose dependence on Lake Superior and primitive roads and bridges for travel had maintained a pioneer way of life well into the twentieth century.

Settlement Patterns

The government of Minnesota's most northeasterly county was established in 1882, twenty-four years after statehood. Stretching the final eighty-one miles of Lake Superior shoreline to Canada, with over fifty miles due north on its western boundary to the border, triangular Cook County combines considerable wilderness lands with a sparse population (over 90 percent of it today is protected federal and state land). In 1880, its population of white residents was only sixty-five, one of whom was Norwegian; by the turn of the century that figure would rise to 810. In 1905, the Minnesota Census listed among the foreign born and their children 408 Norwegians and 421 Swedes in Cook County. During this time approximately 300 Anishinaabe (also known as Ojibwe and Chippewa) lived along Lake Superior, having resided there since the latter seventeenth century, divided somewhat equally between the Grand Portage Reservation and the village of Chippewa City, settled on the eastern edge of Grand Marais in 1882 when workers were recruited to help construct the rock breakwater in the harbor. Because of the large number of Scandinavians in Duluth (e.g., 7,564 Norwegians in 1900), the port city at the head of Lake Superior became a natural conduit for exploring the riches of minerals, fish, and timber to the northeast for Scandinavian immigrants who had usually settled in various midwestern states prior to a secondary or even subsequent migration to the North Shore.[6]

Hovland was first settled in 1888 by two Norwegian immigrant families along either side of the Flutereed River, which flows into the somewhat sheltered and picturesque Chicago Bay, eighteen miles east of Grand Marais and twenty-two miles from the Canadian border. It has the distinction of being the first organized township in Cook County, which occurred in 1894. White settlement had begun in Grand Marais in 1871 with the arrival of the Yankee Mayhew brothers from Massachusetts; despite concerted planning, the county seat did not become a town until 1899, and then a village in 1903.[7]

Norwegians and Swedes, however, had begun trickling into the county during the 1880s. The Norwegian fisherman Henry Redmyer settled in about 1880 at the Cross River, in what is now Schroeder (named after a timber company), thirty miles west of Grand Marais. Charles A. A. Nelson emigrated from Norrköping in Sweden and settled on the Poplar River, ten miles east of Redmyer, in 1886. He christened the place Lutsen in honor of the fallen king Gustaf Adolf, who was killed at Lützen in 1632 during the Thirty Years' War. In addition to fishing, logging, and trapping, "C–double A" (as he was known) expanded his home in 1893 to accommodate travelers; he became "the father of the tourist industry" in Minnesota, and his home became today's well-known Lutsen Resort. Adolph Carlson (known as "Little Adolph" because he was only 5 foot 2) arrived in the county in 1887—having emigrated from Sweden in 1880—and figured prominently in the history of Hovland from its inception. Listed in the 1900 U.S. Census as a "Land Explorer," he was an untiring mining prospector who roamed the entire wooded and lake-studded county for decades, owning and trading numerous tracts of land.[8]

Swedes began to arrive on Maple Hill, an inland settlement five miles north of Grand Marais, in 1893; principally farmers and loggers, they built a school, a Swedish Lutheran church and cemetery, and a town hall. Maple Hill quickly became the largest Swedish community in Cook County and organized as a town in 1899. Also in the spring of 1893, three young Norwegian boat builders and fishermen—John Tofte, Hans O. Engelsen, and his brother Torger—settled along the shore near the Temperance River (its name reputedly derived from the fact that it has no bar at its mouth) between Redmyer's homestead and Nelson's spot at Lutsen. It became the town of Tofte in 1896, named after their home community in Norway, Toftevaag, on the island of Halsnoy south of Bergen. Twenty-six adults and children from that community eventually joined them in 1902. Along with Hovland, Tofte was the primary Norwegian fishing community along the North Shore. Swedes and Norwegians, therefore, were mixing freely as neighbors from the beginning of white settlement in Cook County, with the sources showing no readily apparent trace of ethnic competition or strife. Within this broader pattern of settlement, Hovland is arguably the most interesting case study of interethnic cooperation because of the mixture of Norwegians, Swedes, and Swedish-speaking Finns in eight definable settlements, with the center of transportation as well as communal and commercial life in Chicago Bay.[9]

The most notable fact of these settlements along the North Shore, and especially in Hovland given its distance down the lake, was the absence of a railroad beyond Two Harbors, only twenty-five miles northeast of Duluth with an additional 102 miles to Hovland. Large docks were built there to accommodate the booming ore industry from the Iron Range north and west of Lake Superior. The dreams of a railroad that would extend all the way to Fort William and Port Arthur in Ontario, which in fact had lured Ole Erickson (a grocer on Washington Avenue in Minneapolis) as a yet-to-be-established railroad speculator to the North Shore, were kept alive for decades but never realized.[10]

This meant that the lake was the primary means of transportation from April to February when free of ice; during the late winter and spring primitive trails, roads, and bridges, requiring continual maintenance because of deadfalls and washouts, had to suffice. The early settlers in Hovland became accustomed to walking great distances, perhaps up to ten miles to reach the center of the community at Chicago Bay to secure basic staples, share in town life, or board one of the ships that departed for Duluth. It was not uncommon to walk on one's own "shank's horses," usually in winter, the eighteen miles of the John Beargrease sled-dog trail to the county seat of Grand Marais to conduct business and enjoy some extended social interaction. The absence of a railroad helped keep the community relatively isolated until the expanding auto industry of the 1920s brought inevitable road improvements. Even today, this sense of isolation is key to the character of the region, one that has never established an urban or industrial network.[11]

Ole Brunes and Nels Ludwig Eliasen, two Norwegian cabinetmakers in Duluth, built a twenty-six-foot sailboat and in the late spring of 1888 began to look for potential fishing grounds. So taken with the beauty and prospects of Chicago Bay, they each homesteaded on either side of the Flutereed River. Together they built a 16-by-18-foot hewn-log cabin for Brunes. When their families joined them (each had a wife and four children), all twelve lived in this small structure for several months until Eliasen completed his home on the east side of the river. The following year, John Jacobsen and his son Bernt arrived, joined in 1890 by his wife and six remaining children along with his brother Olaus, all traveling from Norway. Nels Ludwig Eliasen was also joined that year by his younger bachelor brothers, John (his fiancée came from Norway in 1891) and Emil.[12]

The small community was growing, and residents proposed the name Hamar in 1889 when applying for a post office. Uncle Sam rejected it, and the families settled on Hovland; legend has it that Anna Brunes, Ole's wife, suggested it as the name of her grandfather's home in Norway. Bert Fesler, who conducted a North Shore fisheries census in August 1890, described "a nice settlement of about 20 Norwegians in Chicago Bay (Hovland P.O.). They gave us a 10 pound trout, along with four speckled beauties." Though these were largely fishing families, moose hunters and sport fishermen began arriving in 1893, so Brunes expanded his little log cabin into a boarding house that could sleep six guests. Eliasen then built what is reputed to be the first tourist cabin on the North Shore on his side of the Flutereed River. The 1895 Minnesota Census listed forty-three people in Hovland, which it uniquely labeled "Norland Township"—its only apparent occurrence in the sources: twenty-four Norwegian born (twelve were children); six American-born children of at least one Norwegian parent; four Swedish bachelors (only Adolph Carlson would appear in later censuses). Seventy percent were Norwegian and 9 percent were Swedish; 79 percent of Hovland, therefore, was Scandinavian.[13]

By the turn of the century, Hovland had come to comprise four settlements: the burgeoning Chicago Bay community, the heart of it all; Horseshoe Bay, a mile to the east, which had three families of Norwegians; Big Bay, three miles to

Community gathering at the new bridge over the Brule River, 1910

the east, which had three homes—including that of the Swede, "Little Adolph" Carlson ("bachelor, community barber, politician, and obsessive prospector"); and finally what was becoming known as Flutereed Valley—the Eliasens, Jacobsens, and other Norwegians homesteading up to a few miles north and west of Chicago Bay, often called farmer-fishermen as they entered into a kind of subsistence farming. An 1899 town census printed in the *Cook County Herald* listed twelve families, six bachelors, eighteen male and ten female voters (the latter a noteworthy fact, more than twenty years before suffrage), eleven married women, six girls and eight boys of school age, ten children under age five, and ten men of marriageable age. Apparently, the six bachelors were considered to be confirmed in their status.[14]

The 1900 U.S. Census listed only one other Swede besides "Little Adolph," namely, my *släkt till släkt* (kin of kin) relative Ole Erickson, now described as a "Farmer." Though he was a dozen miles to the west, this was Hovland Township in 1900 (thirty-four miles from Ole's homestead—the western boundary—to the Canadian border at the Pigeon River). The census listed seventy-two individuals in twenty-three households, thirty-five of whom were Norwegian (twenty-five Norwegian born). This census is an anomaly in that it included individuals working for the F. C. Fuller Logging Company of Minneapolis, of which seven were local Anishinaabe (Ojibwe), thus making up 48 percent, while the Norwegians comprised only 49 percent and the two Swedes the remaining 3 percent (52 percent Scandinavian). All but two were listed as speaking English.[15]

During the first decade of the twentieth century, an additional four communities were settled in Hovland, thus making a total of eight. First was the Lake Shore Road (sometimes called the Dog Trail Road), where a half dozen Norwegian fishermen (known as "herring chokers" all along the North Shore), mostly unmarried (including Andrew Solgard eventually in 1915), claimed homesteads along a four-mile stretch west from Chicago Bay to the Brule River. The second was known as Poplar Hill, about three and a half miles west but a mile inland from Lake Superior, where three Swede Finn families arrived in 1906 from the iron ore mines in Eveleth (the Westerlunds, Sundquists, and Soderlunds) and cleared the largest farming acreage. Andrew Westerlund's brother, Alex Englund, arrived in 1911 and homesteaded on adjacent land; he soon married and began raising a family. The third was simply called the North Road and extended into a very remote area about ten miles north toward Lost Lake, where two Norwegian families, the Hansens and Thoresons, began farming, logging, and trapping in 1907. The final settlement of Moose Valley, about two miles east of Chicago Bay and inland to the north and east for another six miles—bordered on the north by an impressive ridge—was settled by Swedish immigrant farmers in 1910, the Johnsons and Ellquists. All eight Hovland communities would continue to develop slowly in the years ahead, and their isolation from each other would slowly decrease as roads and transportation improved.[16]

A summary of census data between 1910 and 1930 demonstrates a steady, if not growing, Scandinavian enclave, even as Hovland continued to expand its population. In 1910, Hovland (now enumerated between the Brule River and Canada) had nearly doubled in a decade to 130 individuals in forty-one households: 50.7 percent Norwegian (thirty-three Norwegian born and thirty-three American born); 13 percent Swedish (ten and seven); and 12.3 percent Swede Finn (ten and six)—a total of more than 75 percent Scandinavian. In this census, however, Anishinaabe individuals and families were listed as part of Grand Portage; the congressional Dawes Act of 1887 had prescribed allotments of eighty acres on reservations (thus introducing the alien concept of private land ownership to American Indians) and also allowed for non-natives to acquire and own land. Tribal government in Grand Portage had been removed by Congress in 1889 but would be restored in 1934.[17]

The 1920 Census indicates Hovland had grown to 175 persons in fifty-three households: 58.3 percent Norwegian (fifty-five foreign born and forty-seven American born), the growth being largely young fishermen; 8.6 percent Swedish

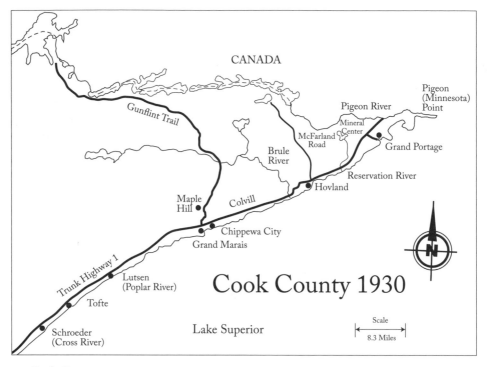

Cook County, 1930

(ten and five), Moose Valley and Adolph Carlson; and 14.3 percent Swede Finn (seven and eighteen), Poplar Hill—a total of 81 percent Scandinavian. And finally in the 1930 Census Hovland grew further to 193 individuals in fifty-one households: 52.8 percent Norwegian (fifty and fifty-two); 9.8 percent Swedish (ten and nine); and 8.3 percent Swede Finn (four and twelve—several parents and children had died of influenza or tuberculosis)—a total of 71 percent Scandinavian. This census fixed the present-day boundaries from the Brule River on the west to the Reservation River on the east (113,488 acres—about half in private ownership, unusually high for Cook County), a distance now of only ten miles along Lake Superior rather than the original thirty-five in 1900 or twenty-five in 1910. It also included for the first time the new community of Mineral Center, six miles northwest of the historic site of the Grand Portage trading post. This was the midpoint on the newly developed road from the Reservation River inland to the "Outlaw Bridge" (so named because in defiance of the law it was constructed clandestinely by automobile clubs in Duluth and Port Arthur) crossing the Pigeon River into Canada. According to the most recent 2000 U.S. Census, 272 persons in 122 households live in Hovland, swelled considerably in the summer by seasonal residents and retired snowbirds.[18]

Flutereed Valley School patriotic program. Teacher Newton Bray with Norwegian, Swedish, and Swede Finn children

Community Building

A closer look at the various components of Hovland life illustrates active, committed individuals and families as well as a Scandinavian community by all appearances living in ethnic harmony with a clear American identity. This chapter explores several areas of community life that could be greatly expanded in a more detailed, comprehensive history. The county newspaper, typical of the day in that much of the news was national and international from syndicated sources, nevertheless provides a very full description and "feel" of Hovland's social and political life. Its local correspondents on a weekly basis were comparatively more detailed and creative in their journalistic assignment than others reporting from elsewhere in the county. Unfortunately, the names of these scribes went unrecorded, though it is likely that most of the content during the first third of the century was penned by schoolteacher and county commissioner Newton Bray, who had moved to Hovland from Massachusetts, where he was a descendant of an old colonial family.[19]

Chicago Bay was definitely the hub of Hovland, primarily because between 1902 and 1905 the Eliasen brothers with the help of neighbors built a long rock-cribbed dock with a warehouse that could accommodate the large steamships—such as the *Dixon, Easton, Bon Ami, Argo,* and *America*—that plied the North Shore beginning in Duluth, circumnavigating Isle Royale (which had a thriving seasonal resort and Scandinavian commercial fishing population between 1890

The steamer Easton *at the Hovland dock unloading oats for the nearly two hundred horses working in the logging camps on the Pigeon River, 1909*

and 1940), and returning to Duluth. Thus, there were frequent stops in Chicago Bay, which became the commercial center at stores begun by Louis Ellingsen, who had bought the small hotel from the Brunes in 1904 (greatly expanding it), and Martin Jacobsen, who also operated the post office and eventually in 1929 Hovland's first telephone exchange. These amenities became important not only to Hovland locals scattered throughout the settlements but to loggers working in the woods as far as the Pigeon River on the border, the American Indians who walked the thirty-five miles between Chippewa City and Grand Portage (often camping behind Ellingsen's hotel and store, the halfway point), and the growing number of tourists, sport fishermen, and hunters.[20]

In addition to gaining a post office in 1889, Hovland residents built a log town hall in 1893 at the mouth of the Flutereed River on Eliasen's property, which became the center of town government and its school board, the first school (with a library assembled by Adolph Carlson in 1901), and the site for weddings, dances, and musical performances. In the 1890s, a non-Scandinavian editor of the newspaper in Grand Marais, A. DeLacy Wood, often walked the eighteen miles to Hovland to enjoy its hospitality and warm community spirit; he soon purchased property in Big Bay. In the July 15, 1893, issue of the *Cook County Herald,* he wrote at length about the supper and dance at the town hall with the Hovland string band (John Eliasen was known countywide for his fiddling), jig dancing, songs in Norwegian, and harmonica solos. This event celebrated the first wedding in Hovland—a pioneer logger and commercial fisherman, Fred

Eliasen family musicians: Louis, Edwin, Ludwig, John, Emil

Jackson (who emigrated from England in 1879 and came to Cook County in 1883), and seventeen year-old Norwegian Annie Jacobsen. Since there would not be a Norwegian church (or one of any kind) organized in Hovland until 1907, they were married at her parents' home. Moreover, dances and community gatherings were frequent, especially during the long winter months. Fourth of July celebrations were notable, with boat races, dancing, supper followed by more dancing, and finally fireworks. A new and larger town hall was built in 1915; one of the first community events was a "moving picture exhibition" of the spy film *Lieutenant Rose and the Sealed Orders*.[21]

Because of the remoteness of the outlying settlements and the poor and unreliable roads and trails, shortly after the Swede Finns had arrived in 1906, they cooperated with Norwegian families to found an additional school in Flutereed Valley. Soon after the Swedes settled in Moose Valley in 1910, they formed a school at the end of the road, some eight miles from Chicago Bay. For almost three decades, the most pressing need of Hovland and its town government (formed in 1894) was roads and bridges to connect the settlements. All of the able-bodied men in Hovland were expected to devote time and labor (at two dollars a day, or four to five dollars if they supplied their team of horses and driver) to building and maintaining these vital links within the community.[22]

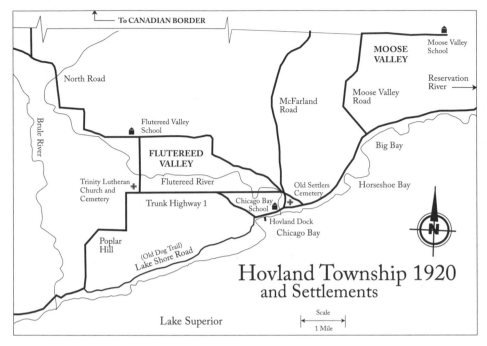

Hovland Township, 1920

The church has often been said to be the first child of a Norwegian or Swedish immigrant community, and Hovland initially presents something of a puzzle in this regard. It would be nineteen years before a congregation was formed. Because of the township's remote location, families had been dependent on itinerant Norwegian-Lutheran ministers (referred to by some locals as *sky pilots*), who would visit infrequently and conduct services in homes and provide baptism and communion. Shortly after settlement, community women arranged for a sewing circle as well as an aid society: benevolent functions usually associated with organized churches. Eventually, Zion Lutheran Church was established during 1907 in Chicago Bay, a central location. Because Chicago Bay's four-mile distance was too far to walk regularly to attend services, the Swede Finns on Poplar Hill, along with several Norwegian families in Flutereed Valley and on the North Road, organized a Hauge Synod congregation in 1909 and called it Trinity. The Zion congregation dissolved and merged with Trinity in 1912. Though comprised of Norwegians, Swede Finns, and Swedes, Trinity retained the Norwegian language and ecclesial affiliation of the majority of its members, relying on pastoral services by the Norwegian pastor in Grand Marais who also served congregations in Lutsen and Tofte. By the end of 1913, Trinity had put up a church building at the intersection of the main east-west road from

Poplar Hill, thus establishing until the 1930s a second, small commercial center in Hovland. This main road into Chicago Bay was improved during the 1920s and became part of Trunk Highway 1, the automobile road pushed up the North Shore after World War I. The church also had a cemetery, which supplemented the so-called Old Settlers cemetery in Chicago Bay.[23]

By the First World War (in which several young Hovland immigrants fought), the scattered communities that made up Hovland had collectively achieved their own version of institutional completeness, sufficient within its isolation yet linked to the outside world by Lake Superior. The expansion of improved roads during the 1920s brought additional dimensions significant to a fuller study of Hovland, only hinted at here. The first was the considerable expansion of the tourist industry, which had been present from the very beginning with the Brunes/Ellingsen Hotel. The highway eventually brought seasonal cabin owners. The earliest was John Spelman, an Oak Park, Illinois, businessman, sportsman, and artist who in 1905 bought property at Thorson's Harbor, the fishing site two miles west of Chicago Bay homesteaded by Norwegian immigrant Adoph Thorson. Other early sites included a community of seven log cabins just west of Thorson Harbor and [Anton] Grande Bay named Pal's Cove, designed and built during the 1920s by the Minneapolis architect Chilson "Stooge" Aldrich for himself and his friends; Naniboujou Lodge on the Brule River in 1929 (an exclusive sportsman's club with Babe Ruth, Jack Dempsey, and Ring Lardner as charter members—only to collapse in the aftermath of Black Friday); and the small housekeeping cabins developed by Scandinavian fishing families to accommodate the explosion of automobile family tourism, especially as fishing began to decline after the Great Depression until its heyday in the 1950 and early '60s.[24]

Another development, which has enriched Hovland to the present day, is the wide variety of people attracted there in a seasonal, and sometimes professional, way. Many were Scandinavian Americans, and three Swedes who were there in the 1920s and early '30s merit considerable attention. First, a young Swedish American artist, Dewey Albinson, first passed through in March 1922 and until the 1940s spent most summers in Grand Portage painting and recording nature and Ojibwe culture. Second, Hjalmar Peterson (Olle i Skratthult) purchased a homestead from John and Alma Eliasen in 1922. Having played the Princess (later Wigwam) Theater in Grand Marais and the Hovland Town Hall many times (well publicized in the newspaper), sometimes joined by groups like the Swedish National Dancers from Chicago, and always followed by a big dance, he considered his expanded cabin (for his troupe and groupies) a favorite getaway until, deeply in debt, he lost it in 1931 to Charlie Johnson, an acquaintance in Duluth who had lent him a thousand dollars in a failed attempt to revive his traveling act during the Depression. Olle's accordion player, Werner Noreen,

Lake Superior Fish Houses, *engraving by Dewey Albinson, c. 1925*

returned to Hovland in 1932, where he remained until his death in 1967. His wife Olga's nephew, Gust Berglund, came from Sweden in 1928 to join Olle's troupe, and he also would remain in the area. Many local Hovlanders played with the group for area concert dates, which, during Prohibition, sometimes included late-night parties across the border in Canada. And third, the well-known wilderness adventurer and writer Calvin Rutstrum arrived in Hovland in 1923 and lived alone in the woods along the Flutereed River for nine years. He had much to say in his writings about the Scandinavians in Hovland at that time.[25]

A Scandinavian *Landskap* in Minnesota

In its relatively brief history and in its present—after the decline of commercial fishing and the tourist cabin phenomenon, which had culminated in the heyday of the community during the 1950s (replete with several gas stations, cafes, and general stores)—Hovland has retained a distinct pan-Scandinavian character, worn lightly without many of the overt symbols found in some other North American towns and neighborhoods. Only mailboxes, occasional signage, and place-names at the entry to cabins and homes indicate a visual symbolic ethnicity. The descendants of the original families generally seem to eschew such visible identifying ethnic markers. It is a place where the Norwegian, Swedish, and Swede Finn heritage is elicited especially when meeting and getting to know people.

These contacts might be at Trinity Lutheran Church (the present building, designed by Arnold Flaten in a style that combines the Scandinavian with the North Woods), constructed by its members with assistance from three summer work camps of St. Olaf College students in the late 1940s (led by professors Flaten and Howard Hong), when its location finally moved down to the highway by the lake. Its current pastor is a granddaughter of Ole Rølvaag, Norwegian immigrant author of the classic novel *Giants in the Earth*. Acquaintances may also be made at frequent gatherings of the Hovland Community Club or fundraisers for the Hovland Volunteer Fire Department at the town hall next to the church (where, in addition to dances and regional art fairs, neighbors meet to discuss local issues), or at its adjacent thriving general store, bakery, and café. The highway is now mainly a thoroughfare for Americans and Canadians speeding on their way to someplace else, required only for a short stretch to slow down to forty miles per hour. A stroll through Hovland's two cemeteries, reading headstones in Norwegian, Swedish, and English, awakens a curiosity about who these people were: for example, "Här hvilar min kära maka" (here lies my beloved husband) or "Our Darling Baby. Här hvilar August Lennart" or "Lost on Lake Superior" or "Home from the Cruel Sea and Now in a Peaceful Harbor" or "Together Forever" or "He Should Have Hauled One More Load." What led them to emigrate, what did they do here to survive, and what kind of special rural place did Hovland prove and continue to be?

What may account for the relative absence of ethnic tension and competition within this largely Scandinavian community? Perhaps a humorous incident serves as an example: Claus Monker, with his family one of the first Swedish American settlers on Maple Hill, became a prominent leader of Cook County and, in time, a practicing attorney. On one occasion he had Billy Drouillard (son of Hovland's first chair of town supervision, John) on the witness stand, and others had been asked about their nationalities. "He says to Billy, 'I suppose you're Norwegian too?' 'No, no, no, Mr. Monker, I'm Swede!'" Billy was part Anishinaabe and Monker Swedish. Half-a-dozen possible responses to the question of unified community are summarized below.[26]

First, though the township comprised eight settlements, Hovland had a commercial and transportation center at Chicago Bay. Second, virtually all the Scandinavian immigrants had lived elsewhere in the United States prior to migrating to Hovland and spoke English as well as their native tongues, mutually understood and a unifying link to homeland culture. Third, the relative isolation of the scattered settlements in Hovland, which persisted at least into the 1920s, necessarily fostered community building. Fourth, settlers often had shared pre-migration experiences in fishing, farming, and logging, and the overlapping of multiple wilderness vocations and skills naturally led to degrees of cooperation and dependence—sometimes in life-or-death settings. Fifth, during the first three generations, interethnic marriage was not uncommon among those raised in local families. And finally, the combination of a single church and a vital town hall life, with schools to educate children, provided social networks and regular opportunities to be together—intensified during long, cold winters. One must recognize as well that the somewhat stereotypical bachelors were scattered along the shore and throughout the woods, sometimes preferring to be left alone but more often craving social interaction among permanent and seasonal residents. These Norwegians, Swedes, and Swede Finns were neighbors who cooperated both out of necessity and friendship, with themselves and with non-Scandinavians, in building as Americans their new lives and the community of Hovland. This was part of the larger *landskap* they received, shared, helped forge, and came to love as home.

Notes

1. Homemaking as unfinished business is a recurrent theme in the writings of Wendell Berry. For a discussion, see Norman Wirzba, ed., *The Art of the Commonplace: The Agrarian Essays of Wendell Berry* (Washington, DC: Shoemaker & Hoard, 2002), vii–xx. See also Orm Øverland, *Immigrant Minds, American Identities: Making the United States Home, 1870–1930* (Urbana: University of Illinois Press, 2000); and Jon A. Gjerde, *The Minds of the West: Ethnocultural Evolution in the Rural Middle West, 1813–1917* (Chapel Hill: University of North Carolina Press, 1997).

The concept of *landskap* employed in this manner is expanded beyond a narrow historical definition of "province" to include the land itself, its features and inhabitants through time. According to Gabriel Bladh, commenting on Dalecarlia in Sweden, "a kind of cultural regionalism was developed where the unit of *landskap* had a central position as both an arena of practices and a symbolic territory" (in Michael Jones and Kenneth R. Olwig, eds., *Nordic Landscapes: Region and Belonging on the Northern Edge of Europe* [Minneapolis: University of Minnesota Press, 2008], 222). See also Michael P. Conzen, ed., *The Making of the American Landscape* (Boston: Unwin Hyman, 1990); Eric Hirsch and Michael O'Hanlon, ed., *The Anthropology of Landscape: Perspectives on Place and Space* (Oxford: Clarendon Press, 1995); and Arnold R. Alanen, *Pines, Lakes, & Mines: A Fieldguide to the Cultural Landscapes and Architecture of Northeastern Minnesota* (Madison, WI: Vernacular Architecture Forum, 2000), a study that extends along Lake Superior but not as far as Cook County.

2. *Cook County News-Herald*, Sept. 16, 1915, and Oct. 28, 1915, described briefly Solgard's progress in building "his new frame house" on his homestead, a quarter mile of lakeshore and fifty-six acres.

Nels and his new bride, Gudrun, who came directly from Norway to Duluth to marry in 1923, lost their first two babies at the homestead in 1925 (Fred at seven months, the other stillborn and unnamed). The homestead was sold in 1927, and they moved four miles east to establish a fishery at Big Bay. Nels was an immigrant from the Lofoten Islands, like so many fishermen along the North Shore, and had arrived in 1911. He was also a veteran of World War I.

3. "Down the lake": in the days before the advent of the automobile highway along the North Shore, the twin ports of Duluth and Superior were at the "head" of the Great Lakes; thus, one traveled "up" to Duluth and "down" in return. This nomenclature is now popularly reversed. Local residents also speak of traveling east and west, not north and south, along the lakeshore.

4. For background, see June Drenning Holmquist, "Commercial Fishing on Lake Superior in the 1890s," *Minnesota History* 34 (1955): 243–49; Matti Kaups, "Norwegian Immigrants and the Development of Commercial Fisheries along the North Shore of Lake Superior: 1870–1895," in *Norwegian Influence on the Upper Midwest,* ed. Harald S. Naess (Duluth: University of Minnesota, Duluth, 1976), 21–34; and Kaups, "North Shore Commercial Fishing, 1849–1870," *Minnesota History* 46 (1978): 42–58. Odd S. Lovoll, *Norwegians on the Prairie: Ethnicity and the Development of the Country Town* (St. Paul: Minnesota Historical Society Press, 2006).

5. For example, the number of acres delinquent in taxes was 88,360 in 1926, declined to 15,840 in 1929, and soared to 203,680 in 1931. Land speculators took advantage of this and over time did quite well, since so much land was lakeshore and eventually part of the Boundary Waters Canoe Area Wilderness.

6. For the early history of Cook County to 1900, see Willis H. Raff, *Pioneers in the Wilderness: Minnesota's Cook County, Grand Marais and the Gunflint in the 19th Century* (Grand Marais, MN: Cook County Historical Society, 1981). On census figures, see Carlton C. Qualey and Jon A. Gjerde, "The Norwegians," in *They Chose Minnesota: A Survey of the State's Ethnic Groups,* ed. June Drenning Holmquist (St. Paul: Minnesota Historical Society Press, 1981), 223; and John G. Rice, "The Swedes," in Holmquist, ed., *They Chose Minnesota,* 251. See Stacie L. Drouillard, "The Village of Chippewa City and the Grand Marais Chippewa, 1850–1950," MLS thesis, University of Minnesota, Duluth, 2005, 2.

7. Raff, *Pioneers in the Wilderness,* 13–76, and Raff, *Law and Order in the Wilderness: The First 100 Years of Local Government in Minnesota's Cook County* (Grand Marais, MN: Cook County Historical Society, 1982), 20ff. Early sources usually rendered Flutereed a single word (Flutereed River and Flutereed Valley) with some exceptions, and longtime residents generally continue that usage, as I do in this chapter. More recently, official maps, signage, and websites have adopted Flute Reed River.

8. Raff, *Pioneers in the Wilderness,* 77–92.

9. Raff, *Pioneers in the Wilderness,* 107–14, 219–89.

10. The "Grand Marais and North Shore Railroad Company" was incorporated by Edward E. Lewis of Grand Marais on Mar. 25, 1895, capitalized at $500,000. All other officers lived in Minneapolis, including its vice president, Ole E. Erickson. The railroad was to follow the shoreline from Duluth to the Canadian border at the Pigeon River, with branch lines from Horseshoe Bay in Hovland (the natural shipping point for logging), from Grand Marais, and from the Poplar River (Lutsen), all to the west end of

254 ❖ PHILIP J. ANDERSON

Gunflint Lake, and from there further west to Ely. Lewis's promise to have three hundred men clearing and laying track within weeks never materialized. Though a failed ambition, the plan nevertheless brought Ole ("Cuckoo" to his friends) Erickson to his homestead six miles east of Grand Marais in 1896. He no doubt thought this would be a natural station and community along the line, and indeed he was one of the founders of Colvill in 1906, named after his neighboring homesteader, Colonel William Colvill, the Civil War hero at Gettysburg, politician, lawyer (attorney general of Minnesota, 1866–68), and newspaper man from Red Wing. Raff, *Pioneers in the Wilderness*, 198–99; and Raff, *Law and Order in the Wilderness*, 15–16.

11. Many went to Grand Marias around Christmas "for a week or two . . . celebration you know . . . 'cause in those older days everybody knew each other and wherever you came to a house that's where you stayed as long as you wanted to . . . no questions asked . . . and they treated you royally . . . (chuckle) . . . yeah (chuckle)." August Brunes interviewed by his son James, 1970 (transcript OH-0028 Cook County Historical Society, Grand Marais, MN). John Beargrease (1862–1910) was the son of an Anishinaabe leader in Beaver Bay, about halfway between Duluth and Grand Marais. For twenty years he carried mail along the North Shore by boat until freeze-up and then by primitive dog trail. See Daniel Lancaster, *John Beargrease: Legend of Minnesota's North Shore* (Duluth, MN: Holy Cow Press, 2009). In 1901, the men of Hovland began to improve the Dog Trail for winter travel. The editor of the newspaper noted that in clearing Chicago Bay Boulevard of deadfall, many "Indian relics" were discovered in the ditches along the way (*Cook County Herald*, Aug. 24, 1901).

12. It took some time for the accepted place names Chicago Bay (sometimes called Sickle Bay) and Flutereed River (sometimes called Red Fruit Creek) to become fixed. For the early settlement of Hovland to 1900, see Raff, *Pioneers in the Wilderness*, 93–107.

13. For a personal account of the earliest years in Hovland, see August Brunes (son of Ole and Anna), "My Memories" (manuscript, Cook County Historical Society, Grand Marais, MN). Bert Fesler, "The North Shore in 1890," a paper presented at an assembly in Grand Portage, Aug. 23, 1930, and printed in the *Cook County News-Herald*, Nov. 3 and 10, 1955. 1895 Minnesota Census, microfilm, Minnesota Historical Society, St. Paul, MN.

14. *Twelfth Census of the United States: 1900*, microfilm, Grand Marais (MN) Public Library.

15. For many years, prior to his death at his homestead in 1920, Erickson would bring his produce to the Minnesota State Fair, winning several prizes. Those who farmed the unproductive acreage of Hovland also managed to produce an amazing array of crops and vegetables. *Twelfth Census of the United States: 1900*, microfilm, Grand Marais Public Library.

16. See Timo Riippa, "The Finns and Swede-Finns," in Holmquist, ed., *They Chose Minnesota*, 314–22. For an inventory of Swede Finns, compiled from the 1920 U.S. Census, death records, and newspaper obituaries, see Patricia Zankman, "Swede-Finns in Cook County, Minnesota," available: http://www.genealogia.fi/emi/emi3d6e.htm. It is estimated that 20 to 25 percent of all Finnish immigrants in Minnesota were Swede Finns. Finland was not a country prior to 1917, so Swede Finns had no ethnic association to Finnishness. Before that they were Swedish-speaking subjects of Russia. Immigrants

referred to themselves as Swedes and because of language naturally joined Swedish churches and clubs (though the Order of Runeberg was a Swede Finn association), finding no common identity with Finnish immigrants since Old World attitudes of tension and mutual perception were sometimes present among the first generation (Mika Roinila to the author, Oct. 22, 2007).

See "Memories of Moose Valley, Hovland, MN., as told by Mildred (Millie) Johnson Mainella," manuscript, Cook County Historical Society, Grand Marais, MN. Born in 1908, Millie died in 2011 at age 103. David P. Holmes, *Salt of the Earth: A History of Hovland, Minnesota, and Its People* (St. Cloud, MN: North Star Press, 2010). The expansive title of this small book is somewhat misleading in that it is primarily the story of two early families—the Johnsons and the Sundquists—and subsequent generations in the Hovland community.

17. *Thirteenth Census of the United States: 1910,* microfilm, Grand Marais Public Library. Carolyn Gilman, *The Grand Portage Story* (St. Paul: Minnesota Historical Society Press, 1992). *A Guide to Understanding Chippewa Treaty Rights* (Odana, WI: Great Lakes Indian Fish & Wildlife Commission, 1991).

18. *Fourteenth Census of the United States: 1920,* and *Fifteenth Census of the United States: 1930,* both microfilm, Grand Marais Public Library. *Twenty-second Census of the United States: 2000.* The results of the 2010 U.S. Census were not yet available at the time of writing.

19. Particularly in the years from 1901 to 1915, the *Cook County Herald* and the *Cook County News-Herald* occasionally included a column drawn from other sources titled variously "Tid-bits of News from Scandinavia" or "Scandinavian News—Items from the Old Home." This covered mostly selected news, sometimes folksy, from Norway and Sweden with a few passing references to Denmark and the Nordic countries of Finland and Iceland. Only one column in 1905 reported briefly on the dissolution of the union in Norway and Sweden three months earlier (*Cook County Herald*, Sept. 16). It did report, however, on "Prominent Swedish Americans Get Together in Chicago," the founding of the Swedish Historical Society of America (*Cook County Herald*, July, 15, 1905). When it disbanded in 1934, the society's library and records went to the Minnesota Historical Society.

20. The Hovland dock, which still exists in a partially damaged condition on its original log and rock cribs, contributed greatly to increased traffic of commerce and people. For the thriving, mostly Scandinavian, culture of fisher families on Isle Royale, see, for example, Howard Sivertson, *Once Upon an Isle: The Story of Fishing Families on Isle Royale* (Mount Horeb, WI: Wisconsin Folk Museum, 1992). These families had extensive interaction with North Shore communities, and some fishermen in Hovland had also fished Isle Royale. August Brunes, interviewed by his son James, 1970, 8.

21. *Cook County Herald*, July 15, 1893.

22. For more than thirty years, John McFarland worked to carve out a trail, and then a road, from Chicago Bay northward for eighteen miles to what later became known as McFarland Lake; he was a major figure in Hovland during his spare time, having become the schoolteacher in Grand Portage in 1888. Said to be the first prospector in the county beginning in 1866, within a decade he was concentrating his efforts in the area around

Pine Lake in a partnership with Adolph Carlson and John Gustafson. He died in April 1900, "ill and tired and discouraged." The McFarland Road is now known as the Arrowhead Trail. Cf. Raff, *Pioneers in the Wilderness*, 141ff.

23. For a survey of the congregation's early history, see Elsie Palmer, *The Seventy-fifth Anniversary Celebration of Trinity Lutheran Church*, a booklet published by the congregation in 1984. Palmer was a fine local historian, born to the Swede Finn Soderlund family on Poplar Hill in 1909, and longtime columnist of the "East End News," rich in historical recollections, for the *Cook County News-Herald*.

24. "The Spruce Point Saga by Ellen Spelman Eliasen, 1988," in Barbara Spelman Allen, comp., "History of Property Ownership in the Hovland, Minnesota, Area," manuscript, Cook County Historical Society, Grand Marais, MN.

See Chilson D. Aldrich, *The Real Log Cabin* (New York: Macmillan Company, 1928). Chilson was a Minneapolis architect who acquired a half mile of lakeshore in 1920 and began building log cabins for himself and his friends. The book reveals that while he was not the best builder or stonemason, he romanticized the north-woods experience in masculine ways typical of the genre at the time. His wife Darragh, for whom he built a small, perched writing cabin called the "Crow's Nest," was a reputable novelist, poet, playwright, journalist, and early WCCO radio announcer.

25. Ernest Dewey Albinson (1898–1971) was a Minneapolis-born Swedish American who became one of Minnesota's most distinguished artists. He appealed for the protection of the northern Lake Superior region and an appreciative understanding of its native culture by painting landscapes and portraits and later by writing, saying that "my works are part of the rugged nature that I have depicted and that now is a thing of the past." See Dewey Albinson, "A Grand Portage Story and Some Other Tales from the North Country," 1963 manuscript, P2386, MHS Notebooks, Minnesota Historical Society, St. Paul; Mary T. Swanson, "Dewey Albinson: The Artist as Chronicler," *Minnesota History* 52 (1991): 264–78; and Gilman, *Grand Portage Story*, 122ff.

Hjalmar Peterson (Olle i Skratthult—Olle from Laughtersville), arrived in Minneapolis in 1906 (permanently in 1911) from Värmland, Sweden (where he was born in 1886) and became the best-known *bondkomiker* (vaudeville peasant comic) regionally and nationally. His career flourished during the late teens and twenties—the waning heyday of Swedish America—the same years he spent considerable time at his retreat in Hovland. He died in 1960. See, for example, Anne-Charlotte Harvey, "Performing Ethnicity: The Role of Swedish Theatre in the Twin Cities," in Philip J. Anderson and Dag Blanck, eds., *Swedes in the Twin Cities: Immigrant Life and Minnesota's Urban Frontier* (St. Paul: Minnesota Historical Society Press, 2001), 149–172. See also Gust Bergland interviewed by Adolph Toftey, Mar. 19, 1974, transcript OH-0024, Cook County Historical Society, Grand Marais, MN. Bergland commented on their performances in the Wigwam Theater, which many Ojibwe attended: "And as soon as Olle would come up on stage, they would laugh and they'd clap their hands and they had such a good time! I couldn't understand how they could understand him and he was talkin' everything in Swedish!" 2.

Calvin Rutstrum (1895–1982), born in Indiana to Swedish immigrants and raised in Minneapolis, arrived in Hovland on the *America* in 1923 and soon acquired inland acreage along the Flutereed River, where he mainly lived until 1931, heading deeper into the wilderness on Seagull Lake to escape changes brought about by roads and automobiles. The author of fifteen books about wilderness and how to live and survive off the land, Rutstrum (a contemporary of another Swedish American, Sigurd Olson) became a well-known author of the North Country extending into the far reaches of Canada. He wrote about his Hovland life and adventures in *Challenge of the Wilderness* (Minneapolis, MN: T. S. Dennison & Co., 1970). See also Jim Dale Vickery, *Wilderness Visionaries* (Merrillville, IN: ICS Books, Inc., 1986), 160–87.

26. J. Henry Eliasen, interviewed by M. J. Humphrey, Jan. 8, 1979, transcript OH-0039, Cook County Historical Society, Grand Marais, MN, 16. For the significant contribution of John Drouillard to Hovland and surrounding areas, see *Cook County News-Herald,* Dec. 10, 1925. Of French descent, he married Isabelle Anaquete (also known as Elisebeth Anakwad) in 1876. Together they had twelve children.

CHAPTER 15

Norwegians and Swedes in Willmar, Minnesota, in the Early Twentieth Century

Neighbors, Friends, Schoolmates, and Lovers

BYRON J. NORDSTROM

The setting for this chapter is the town of Willmar, Minnesota. Located about ninety miles west of Minneapolis, it is the county seat for Kandiyohi County. It is named after Leon Willmar, a Belgian who worked as an agent for the St. Paul and Pacific Railroad (later the Great Northern Railroad), and its real growth only came when that railroad reached the community in 1869. In 1875, Willmar's population was 1,004. Fifteen years later it had risen to 1,825, and by 1900 it was 3,409. Today this figure is just over 18,000.[1]

Little has been written about the ethnic history of Willmar, and what follows is a somewhat eclectic introduction to the place and the possibilities that present themselves for further research based largely on four sources: Victor Lawson's *Illustrated History and Descriptive and Biographical Review of Kandiyohi County, Minnesota*; the *1910 United States Census Population Schedules*; the *Willmar Tribune* from 1905; and my own family's history. The chapter has three parts. The first looks at residential and commercial Willmar and examines where some of the Norwegians and Swedes lived, what places they occupied in the town's economic life, and who some of the more successful among them were. The second examines how the Norwegian-Swedish Union Crisis of 1905 was covered in the town's English-language, weekly newspaper. The third personalizes the story and looks at my own family—Norwegian on my mother's side and Swedish on my father's side.

Where They Lived, Who They Were

In the later decades of the nineteenth century, Willmar and the county that surrounded it were important ethnic settlement magnets for Belgians, Dutch, Germans, Irish, Norwegians, Swedes, so-called Yankees (residents born in the United States of U.S.–born parents), and others. Scattered across the neighboring countryside were tightly knit ethnic enclaves, often built around churches and frequently peopled by immigrants from relatively small emigration regions in the home lands. Ethnic patterns established in these years carried over into the early decades of the twentieth century.[2]

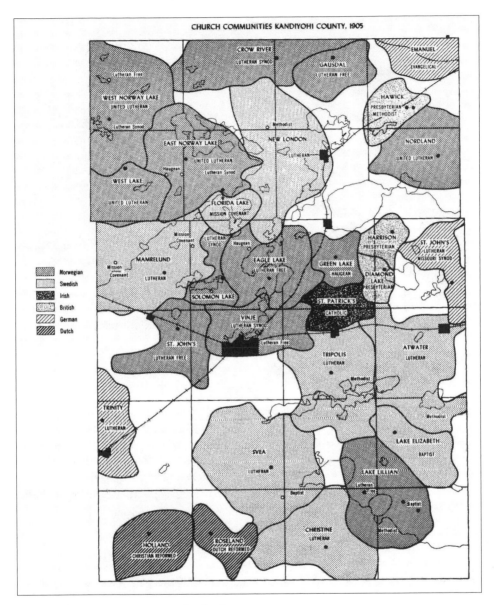

CHURCH COMMUNITIES KANDIYOHI COUNTY, 1905

Church communities in Kandiyohi County, 1905

When I began this study, I expected the settlement patterns for Willmar's ethnic populations to echo closely those I had discovered many years ago in my work on the Sixth Ward of Minneapolis in the late nineteenth and early twentieth centuries. Maps picturing the distribution of a random sample of Norwegians and Swedes in Minneapolis's Sixth Ward in 1910 show they are grouped in

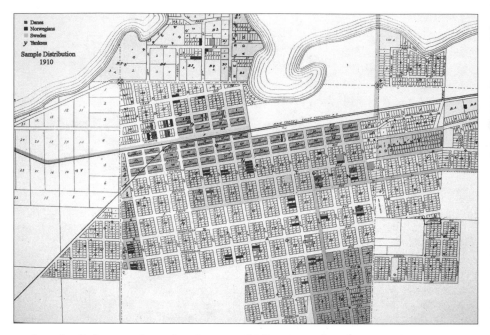

Sample of ethnic residence distribution in Willmar, 1910, based on U.S. Census Population Schedules

relatively distinct ethnic enclaves, usually clustered together close to churches, employment opportunities, or cost-based housing options. As the map above indicates, however, no such clear pattern emerged from a random sampling of where Danes, Norwegians, Swedes, and Yankees lived in Willmar in 1910. Still, there appear to have been some definable ethnic neighborhoods, as in the case of the clusters of Norwegians on Seventh Street and Fifteenth Street or of the one of Swedes along Fourth Street. A number of boarding houses were exclusively Norwegian or Swedish, and Norwegians and Swedes (and others) frequently lived in relatively close proximity as neighbors.

Why the variety in residential distribution? The answer to this question probably lies in a number of factors that determined where people took up residence in Willmar. Certainly, ethnicity was important. So too were economic status; proximity to a specific church, school, or job; intentional settling in development projects initiated by ethnically specific builders; what housing was available when specific individuals arrived; and the simple fact that there was less room to spread out and establish ethnic enclaves. The settlement map of Willmar is a mixture of accident, intent, and circumstances. In some cases, individuals could actually choose to live on a block or in a new tract of houses in a decision made with some measure of ethnic concern. In other instances—perhaps most—individuals simply settled where they could.

Another way of looking at the Norwegians and Swedes in Willmar is through an economic lens. What jobs did they hold or what businesses did they own or operate? (See table 15.1.) The occupation or employment information available in the census population schedules reveals that the adult male Norwegians and Swedes in Willmar represented a broad and complex cross-section of this aspect of their lives. At the same time, a relatively predictable range of employment or occupational needs and opportunities was available in a very typical railroad, farm-service, and county government town of the period. Among these were openings for unskilled laborers with the railroad, road building and repair, or construction. One notch up the socioeconomic ladder were jobs for skilled tradespeople—carpenters, cabinetmakers, blacksmiths, tailors, plumbers, and so on. A few of these tradespeople owned and operated their own businesses. Other opportunities lay in the service sector—groceries, food, banking, government, and education. A handful of citizens were professionals such as doctors, dentists, and lawyers; however, not surprisingly, this niche tended to be dominated by the supposed Yankee establishment and some second-generation ethnic Americans. Adult Norwegian American and Swedish American women also fit a relatively predictable pattern in terms of their work or occupation distribution. The overwhelming majority were spouses working at home. Among those who worked outside the home were domestics, seamstresses or milliners, and schoolteachers.

Unquestionably, Norwegians and Swedes were heavily involved in the commercial life of the town. Of 153 businesses listed in the 1905 county history, at least seventy-nine were Scandinavian owned or operated. The owner of each was not tracked in the census sources, but thirteen were run by Swedes who paid to have their biographies included in the county history, and an equal number were run by Norwegians who did the same.

An interesting, but largely unanswerable, question is: did Swedish Americans frequent only the Swedish-owned business and Norwegian Americans frequent only the Norwegian-owned businesses? On this question the sources are silent, but my best guess is that to some extent such ethnic preferences were the case but not exclusively. Products, brand, price, availability, proximity, and reputation were probably just a few of the considerations that shaped the consumers' decisions. If one were to risk any overarching generalizations on this topic, it is likely that cafés, morticians, and photographers drew the most loyal ethnic customers.

My third sample for insight into who the Norwegians and Swedes in Willmar were was the 1905 Kandiyohi County History. Residents could elect to purchase a biography to be printed in this publication. Here financial means and, possibly, inclination or personal vanity played determining roles. Forty-four first- and second-generation Norwegian or Swedish Americans made up this cohort. They are listed and briefly described in the figure on page 264.

FIGURE 15.1
Scandinavian Businesses in Willmar, c. 1905

Norwegian- and Swedish-operated businesses are identified by an N or S. From: Victor E. Lawson, *Illustrated History and Descriptive and Biographical Review of Kandiyohi County, Minnesota*

NAME	BUSINESS	FOUNDED	NATIONALITY *
Chris Ackerman	Meat Market	1889	
Anderson Brothers	Jewelers	1892	
Anderson Land Company	Developers	1903	N
Backlund & Jansrud	Photography	1889	
Benson Plumbing & Heating	Plumbing	1905	N
Julia Berg	Dressmaker		
P. J. Berg	Tailor	1891	
A. P. Bergeson Construction	Cement & Sidewalks	1900	
Berkness and Peterson Co.	General Merchandise	1900	
Bjornberg, Blomquist & Wahlstrand	Grocers	1905	
A. Bjorsell Building	Construction	1895	S
J. P. Carlson	Shoemaker	1880	
Carlson Brothers & Frost	Druggists		S
C&E Christenson	Machinists	1880	
A. J. Ekander	Blacksmith	1881	
J. J. Ekander	Tailor		
A. F. Elfstrum & Co.	Druggist	1891	
D. Elmquist	Jeweler	1902	
Erickson Company	Milling, Feed & Groceries	1900	
Martin Forsberg & Co.	Builder	1891	S
Ole Forstrom	Merchant & Tailor	1870	
C. E. Gerretson	Dentist	1899	
O. B. Glarum	Glarum Hotel	1876	
S. S. Glarum	Grocer	1878	
H. A. Hanson	Dentist		
Hedin & Co.	Butcher	1900	S
Emil Hegstrom	Music Director	1905	S
Iverson Sisters	Millinery	1888	
O. A. Jacobson	Painting & Wallpaper	1891	
A. C. Johnson	Clothing	1904	
John Johnson	General Merchandise		
Matilde Johnson	Dressmaker	1900	
Johnson, Friedland & Norman Co.	Dry Goods & Clothing	1904	
Jorgenson & Swenson	Harness Makers	1900	N/S
Kalbeck & Renstrom	Restaurant	1905	
J. I. Lindner	Cigar Maker	1893	
Lundquist Brothers	Hardware	1890	S
Markhus & Crosby	Theater/Opera House	1878	
Melin Brothers	Farm Implements	1903	
A. Moss	Shoemaker	1870s	
A. E. Mossberg	Druggist	1878/1891	S
A. L. Nelson	Musical Instruments	1882	S
E. A Nelson & Co.	Cement blocks	1905	
Erick Nelson	Builder	1887	S

NAME	BUSINESS	FOUNDED	NATIONALITY *
N. O. Nelson	Farm Elevator	1889	S
Ole J. Nickelson	Hotel	1898	
A. F. Nordin	Lawyer	1888	
Anna Nybakke	Dressmaker	1903	
Ohsberg, Selvig & Co.	Hardware	1892	
H. T. Olson	Marble Works	1898	
I. C. Olson	Undertaker	1879	
M. Olson	Restaurant	1902	
Olson & Skoolheim	Builders	1899	
Olson & Soderling	Tailors	1903	
Samuel Osmundson	Musical Instruments, Bicycles.	1880s	S
B.T. Otos	Metropolitan Barber Shop	1902	N
J.T. Otos	Insurance & Real Estate	1893	N
K.T. Otos	Broom Manufacturer	1904	N
G. H. Otterness	Lawyer	1901	N
Person & Johnson	Cigar Makers	1898	
Algot Peterson	Harness Maker	1893	
Andrew Peterson	Furniture, Musical Instruments & Undertaking	1889	S
J. R. Peterson	Physician	1901	
Peterson & Qvale	Lumber	1901	N
Peterson & Wellin	General Merchandise	1897	S
Peter Rasmuson	Barber	1877	
S. A. Rasmuson	Blacksmith	1891	
P. H. Roise	Clothing & Dry Goods	1904	N
O. E. Ruble	Loans & Real Estate	1892	N
K Samuelson	General Merchandise	1904	
G. O. Sand	Clothing	1902	S
E. T. Sandbo	Restaurant	1893	
Olof Sandbo	Candy and Cigars		
F. W. Segerstrom & Co.	Musical Instruments, Furniture & Undertaking	1903	
Skoog & Anderson	Meats	1892	
Sletten & Strand	Flour, Feed, and Groceries	1904	
S. E. Stansberry	Farm Implements	1903	
William Swenson	Restaurant	1902	
Ralph Telstad	Grocer	1903	
Nels Thompson & Co.	General Merchandise		
Wennerlund & Nelson	Jewelers	1883	
L. A. Wold	Photography	1888	
Ellen Youngberg	Millinery	1900	
** I lum Bang (Chinese)	Laundry	1898	

* NOTE: N(orwegian) and S(wedish) in the right column indicates ethnicity is actually known from information in Lawson.
** Inserted out of curiosity.

Biography Summaries

Andrew A. Anderson. **N**. Land-developer

Peter Bonde. **DA** Blacksmith & land developer

Andrew Bjorsell. **S**. Builder and contractor

Charles B. Carlson. **S**. Druggist and alderman

Ludvig Dale. **N**. Journalist

August O. Forsberg. **S**. Populist journalist

Martin Forsberg.**S**. Builder, contractor, sash and door company owner

Lewis Fridland. **S**. Co-owner of "Johnson, Fridland & Norman" and 3rd ward alderman

Erick Glad. **S**. Builder of grain elevators

O. B. Glarum. **N**. Shoe maker and hotel keeper

S. S. Glarum. **N**. Grocer, school board member, alderman, temperance advocate

Hans S. Hilleboe. **NA** Teacher, temperance advocate, editor of *The Hammer*, temperance candidate for governor in 1894, principal of Willmar Seminary

Emil Hegstrom. **SA** Music instructor and organizer of an orchestra in Willmar

Erick Holt. **N**. Creamery operator and 3rd ward alderman

Christian Johnson. **D**. Physician. Established *The Willmar Tribune*.

Lewis Johnson. **SA** Journalist, grocer, creamery operator, brick maker, general merchandiser

George E. Johnson. **NA** Printer

Martin Jorgenson. **N**. Harness maker

Ole Lundquist. **SA** Tinner, hardware merchant, county sheriff

Victor E. Lawson. **SA** Teacher, printer, journalist, editor of *The Willmar Tribune*, chair of The People's Party

Lars Molin.**S**. Farmer, brick maker, entrepreneur

Lewis Molin.**S** Dry goods merchant and city alderman

A. E. Mossberg. **S**. Pharmacist

Erich Nelson. **S**. Furniture merchant and contractor

J. Emil Nelson. **SA** Teacher, compositor, printer, reporter, joint owner of *The Willmar Tribune*, insurance agent, and temperance advocate

Nels O. Nelson. **S**. Grain elevator operator, township clerk-supervisor-treasurer, state legislator, and alderman

Samuel Nelson. **SA** Teacher

Swan Nelson. **S**. Farmer, grain elevator operator

Andrew Nordloff. **S**. Farmhand and land agent

George H. Otterness. **NA** Attorney, and speculator, Presbyterian

John T. Otos. **N**. Real-estate agent, musician, and Presbyterian.

Andrew Peterson. **S**. Farmer, carpenter, furniture businessman

Peter Martin Peterson. **NA** Carpenter

Solomon Porter. **S**. Real estate agent and county treasurer

Sigurdt Berger Qvale. **N**. Lumber merchant, chair of the county Republican party, alderman, and mayor

P. H. Roise. **N**. Golden Rule Store owner

Severin Rasmussen. **N**. Blacksmith

Ole E. Ruble. **NA** Real-estate agent

Albert E. Rice. **N**. Politician, former Lt. Governor, newspaper owner, banker

Gilbert O. Sand **N**. Clothing store owner

George H. Stephens **S**. "Night Marshall"

Lars Olson Thorpe **N**. Former Register of Deeds, bank teller

Mikkel Olson Thorpe **N**. Trustee of Willmar Seminary, boarding house operator, real estate agent

Martin E. Tew **N**. cattle herder, farmhand, rr worker, newspaper salesman, book dealer, threshing crew worker, teacher, newspaper man, Populist, soldier in the Spanish American War, lawyer, lecturer, author

Norwegian and Swedish Biographies, from Victor E. Lawson, Illustrated History and Descriptive and Biographical Review of Kandiyohi County, Minnesota

What is common to these biographies? Each describes the origins—birthplace, parents' birthplace(s), upbringing, and time of immigration if of the first generation—of the individual. This cluster of information always came first. Then, the focus of each biography shifted. Ethnicity vanished almost entirely. Where these people had lived before they came to Willmar (often the list of places was long and reflected considerable mobility) was almost always described. These details were followed by information on schooling, jobs, participation in local governmental units, political party attachments, and successes. Usually, brief mention was made of spouses and children. None mentioned nonchurch organization memberships. Only three included church affiliation details. Some included a personal photograph, and all of these showed neat, well-kept, serious-looking men in dark, three-piece suits. A few even paid to include a photograph of their home—all pleasant two-story frame houses on well-shaded lots. What seems clear is that these men (and their spouses when they are mentioned) had ethnic origins that were worth noting, but they were also consciously *American* in what they did, how they lived their lives, and how they chose to present themselves—or how author Victor Lawson chose to present them.

1905 and the *Willmar Tribune*

An issue that must have captured the attention of every Norwegian and Swede in Willmar (and across the nation) was the Union Crisis that developed in the early months of 1905 and was played out until late fall that year.

Norway entered into a largely involuntary, dynastic union with Sweden in 1814. Perhaps acceptable or endurable at the outset, this arrangement became less and less so, especially in the closing decades of the nineteenth century. Issues of constitutional difference, separate histories, differing economic development, national symbols (flags), and national identities drove the two peoples apart, especially in the nationalistically charged atmosphere of the period. One crisis in the mid-1890s nearly led to war.

In early 1905, a new government in Christiania (present-day Oslo) with strong popular support consciously created a constitutional crisis over the question of Norway's right to establish an independent consular service. (Norway shared Sweden's consular service at the time and had no independent foreign policy or foreign service.) A law, passed by Norway's parliament (Storting), was sent to the Union king, Oskar II, in late May. According to the Norwegian constitution, Oskar II could veto this measure, and that is precisely what he did. Now, strictly speaking, if the letter of the constitution was followed, a sequence of elections and resubmissions of the law should have ensued. Instead, the Norwegian government resigned in response to Oskar's veto, no new government could be formed, the king was declared unable to fulfill his constitutional obligations, and, therefore, the political union was severed. A crisis was the intent, and a crisis is what the Norwegians got. Tensions ran high during the summer of 1905. War was a possibility, although probably not a very serious one. The aging king was deeply hurt, as were some Swedes, particularly political conservatives. In the end, however, peace prevailed and the Union was dissolved formally through the Karlstad Conventions, signed on September 23, 1905, and quickly approved by the two country's parliaments.

No doubt many of Willmar's Norwegians and Swedes followed the year's events with great interest. Certainly, some subscribed to one or more of the many weekly, biweekly, or monthly Norwegian- or Swedish-language newspapers that gave great attention to the crisis. Most probably read or listened to reports about the crisis from those who did read the town's weekly English-language paper, the *Willmar Tribune*—a paper whose publisher-editor was Victor E. Lawson (1871–1960). Born in Paxton, Illinois, he came to Willmar in 1880. He served as a member of the board of trustees of Gustavus Adolphus College and as a member of the Minnesota state senate from 1927 to 1938. Lawson was a Swedish American, but the staff of the newspaper was multiethnic.

The *Willmar Tribune* gave considerable attention to the Union Crisis, but it did not make it a central element of any weekly edition. The front page was always devoted to local news—farm accidents, parties, weddings, local elections, the weather, and the like—all the things Minnesotans are known, typically, to talk about. The second page covered international and national news. There, the main focus of attention was on the Russo-Japanese War for most of the year. Subsequent pages included how-to information (e.g., how to build a bookcase or rocking chair), fashion news, recipes, rural congregational activities, county account records, and many advertisements for local businesses. What one might loosely call the editorial page was generally the work of one person, probably Lawson, and common themes there included the Russo-Japanese War, corruption in American industry or politics, farm prices, and temperance. (Local option made Willmar a "dry" town.) Unfortunately, no letters to the editor were printed in the paper.

Scandinavian news was covered in a regular column called "Gossip from Scandinavia: Events That Have Occurred in the Old Countries." The contents were gleaned mainly from other newspapers—some of them probably ethnic weeklies—and wire services. Some important news might receive freestanding space in the column, but generally news from each Nordic country fell under a separate national heading. Often, the Union Crisis took center stage in the column, but it shared space with news of murders, business developments, the weather, and the like. To some extent the news in this column resembled what often appeared in the ethnic papers, news from homeland provinces. There were only a few articles about the Union question on the world news page.

The first mention of the brewing crisis appeared in the January 5, 1905, issue of the paper, when note was made that "there is evidently a bad hitch in the negotiations between the cabinets of Norway and Sweden for the establishment of a separate consular service for Norway." Two months later, in the March 3 issue, a prominent (but unidentified) local Norwegian American reportedly said, "Norway wants separate consuls to look after her commercial welfare. I can see no way by which a clash can be avoided unless Sweden grants Norway's request. Whether Sweden will resist the attempt of Norway to withdraw, if Norway decided to break the bonds of the union, is a question I cannot answer. If she does, then there will be war." To illustrate the often rather odd blending of news items in this part of the paper, the lead item under the subheading "Sweden" was a paragraph about one J. Anderson who had invented a "superior" bottle stopper.[3]

In the last week of March, the paper reported that Christian Michelsen had taken over as prime minister in Norway and that his government was committed to asserting Norway's "constitutional right . . . to a separate consular service and to preserv[ing] Norway's sovereignty as a free and independent kingdom." He was also reported to have said that the Norwegians were united in these goals and wanted to remain friends with the Swedes. These remarks were echoed the following week, when Michelsen was reported to have said that Norwegians "wanted to live in peace and good understanding with all, especially with our Swedish neighbors" and added that "Norwegians are entitled, both historically and constitutionally, to live our own national life."[4]

As the crisis heated up in Scandinavia, several leading figures in Norwegian and Swedish cultural life took up the cause. Bjørnstjerne Bjørnson and Fritjof Nansen (Norwegians) and Sven Hedin (a Swede) were often cited in the "Gossip from Scandinavia" column. For example, on April 26, Hedin was reported to have called for a quick settlement of the crisis in order to avoid Great Power meddling, and Bjørnson was said to have published "political treatises" in Christiania and Stockholm in which he proposed a national referendum in Norway to settle the question.[5]

Appropriately, on May 17, 1905, an article began with the words, "An attempt ought to be made in these columns to give a clear account of the present friction between" the two countries, followed by exactly that, a description of the consular and union questions, assessments of the two peoples, which called the Norwegians "adamant" and the Swedes "stubborn," and the conclusion that the "Norwegians are confronted with a very difficult and delicate task."[6]

Coverage of the issue in June, as the Norwegians went ahead with a formal break in the Union, included mention of a huge May 17 celebration in Christiania at which Nansen was reported to have said, "the Norwegians would not permit themselves to be trampled upon." This was followed by reports of the constitutional crisis that followed King Oskar's veto of the Norwegian consular bill. On June 14, readers learned that the union flag had been "hauled down" in Christiania, to be replaced by the pure Norwegian tricolor, and a headline read "Final Act Taken to Break from Sweden." Two weeks later, focus was on the Swedish government's efforts to reach a peaceful solution, the Swedish Conservatives' calls for war, the Swedish Social Democrats' calls for peace and "unconditional acceptance of accomplished fact in Norway," the hero's welcome Bjørnson received in Copenhagen, mention of how Norwegians were stockpiling food and mining bridges along the border with Sweden, the story of a citizens' meeting at Dals-Ed on the border that resulted in a declaration of brotherhood and peace, and the report of a Scandinavian Historical Conference at Lund that the Norwegians did not attend and "would have been more pleasant if they had been there."[7]

Matters remained charged throughout the summer; and the paper continued to report regularly on Swedish government and parliamentary positions, King Oskar's hurt pride and his opposition to a successor from the Swedish royal family in Norway, preparations for war, comparison of the Norwegian and Swedish military forces, peace rallies, and the utterances of great men on both sides of "the keel." One humorous episode was reported to have taken place between Prime Minister Michelsen and Bjørnson. In an exchange of telegrams, Bjørnson reportedly wrote, "Now it is time to stick together," and Michelsen replied, "Now it is time to keep the mouth shut." Appeals to both Norwegian Americans and Swedish Americans for financial support were also mentioned but in no way endorsed by the paper, while at the same time note was made of the apparently booming "tourist" traffic of Norwegian Americans to Norway— "It is so interesting, you know, from a political viewpoint."[8]

Related to the tourism theme, the newspaper reported about a tour of Scandinavia taken by Willmar's Danish American physician, Dr. Christian Johnson. It appeared on August 18: "In regard to the crisis in Norway and Sweden, the doctor says he entertains not the slightest doubt but that the differences between the two sister nations will be settled in a peaceful and amicable manner. This is the impression he received while sojourning there and observing the attitudes and expressions both of the public and the press."[9]

Formal resolution of the crisis came in the fall of 1905. On September 27, the *Willmar Tribune* reported that "the Swedish-Norwegian difficulty has at last been adjusted to the satisfaction of both nations, and all that now remains is the drafting of a treaty providing for the submission of future disputes to arbitration." While not entirely accurate, this statement was correct in principle, and there was genuine optimism about the negotiations going on at Karlstad. On October 4 the paper reported that issues such as how to deal with cross-border reindeer migrations had been resolved and then quoted the Norwegian newspaper *Verdens Gang*'s announcement of the formal conclusion of the agreements at Karlstad: "The message which has been awaited with the highest tension has at last arrived. The negotiations at Karlstad will result in peace."[10]

The formal ratification of Karlstad Conventions by the two parliaments occurred soon after and was reported on October 18 in Willmar. The Swedish parliament was said to have been unanimous; the Norwegian Storting's vote was reported to have been 101 to 16 in favor. Subsequently, "Gossip from Scandinavia" included mention of the formal signing of the agreements ending the Union, the appearance of Sweden's pure flag, the succession of a Danish prince as Haakon VII, and discussions of a republican movement in Norway. The editor of the newspaper apparently felt that not enough was being said about the news from Norway, and he issued an apology to Norwegian American readers on November 8, saying that the "The [U.S. and state] political discussion is still crowding out much important news from the Norwegian press. This is our reason why Norway has received less space than usual in this paper."[11]

By the end of the year, the crisis had virtually vanished from the pages of the *Willmar Tribune*. In the December 27 issue, the "Gossip from Scandinavia" was that a new telephone line was being installed between Norway and Sweden,

"Ibsen is said to be doing well," and Haakon and Maud were being feted lavishly in Norway.[12]

What the above shows is that Willmar's one regular newspaper was, first and foremost, an American paper that dealt with world, American, and state news, local affairs, and public interest information. It did have a clear political stance—against trusts, exploitation of farmers, liquor, government corruption, and so on. In addressing the most sensitive issue to confront a very large segment of the town's population, the Union Crisis, the newspaper's editor worked to present a consistently unbiased and balanced picture. One never senses that he favored one side or one outcome in the conflict. He never seemed to take a stand and did not devote a single column to the crisis on the editor's page.

Victor Lawson was a Swedish American. So why did he clearly avoid taking sides? We do not really know. He does not tell us. We can venture a few guesses, however. Perhaps it was because the crisis was one taking place at a distance and affected neither him nor the Norwegian and Swedish Americans in Willmar directly. Perhaps it was because he was an assimilationist, whose main concerns were American and not those of immigrant groups or ethnicities. Perhaps it was because he was genuinely neutral or was being careful not to fan potential ill feelings within the Norwegian and Swedish communities of Willmar. He may also have been dedicated to keeping things calm by being balanced. The truth likely lies in a mixture of these.

In general, I believe one may also conclude from this look at the *Willmar Tribune*'s coverage of the Union Crisis that it was not seen to be the most important event or topic of the year for people in Willmar—even to a Swedish American editor who worked with a staff of both Norwegian Americans and Swedish Americans. The validity of this generalization is reflected by what was taking place in Willmar that year. The Union Crisis does not seem to have triggered much of a response in the town. There were no articles about local demonstrations for one side or the other; no reports of fights, brawls, or assaults; no calls for contributions to Norwegian or Swedish national defense funds. Town news was dominated by local and state politics, social events including celebrations of American holidays, congregational happenings, and the like. Of course, none of this means there were no incidents, no heated discussions at local restaurants, no violent exchanges. It is just that this one source does not reveal them.[13]

The Bensons and the Nordstroms

Finally, I want to turn briefly to my own family history because it embodies the Norwegian-Swedish theme of the larger study of this book. I am half Norwegian American and half Swedish American—third generation in both cases. I am a long-suffering ethnic schizophrenic. I also have a special connection to Willmar. My parents were born (father in 1899 and mother in 1903) and raised there. They lived within a few city blocks of each other. They met, dated, and wed there. Then in the 1920s they moved away, as did most of their siblings, to establish a new and almost entirely nonethnic life in Minneapolis. My recollections are that the two families had little to do with each other. They never assembled together. When we visited, we visited each separately; and my mother did not seem to like my father's family, while my father was silent (as usual) about most of his in-laws.

My mother's father, Ben Benson, was a Norwegian-born immigrant who came to Willmar via New York. He was a plumber by trade, and in the early twentieth century owned and operated Benson Plumbing. His wife, Ida, was also Norwegian born. The family of four children lived in a typical Willmar white frame house at 715 A Street. Ben was successful and his business prospered. Under his son Morris's leadership, the company moved to Minneapolis and morphed into a plumbing and heating supply dealership, which in time was transplanted to Pittsburgh, Pennsylvania.

How Norwegian were Ben and the family? It is hard to say. I never knew him; he died on Pearl Harbor Day in 1941, so I can only venture some guesses based on family lore. By reputation, he was a serious, taciturn man. His business was apparently first in importance. It was the core of his success and identity. He served Willmar and not just the Norwegians of Willmar. Whatever religious affiliation he brought with him, he seems to have abandoned. He and the family attended the local Methodist church. I do not know if he belonged to the Masons or the Elks or the Odd Fellows. He could have. His wife Ida seems to have been the maintainer of Norwegian-ness in the family. She never spoke English well and her daughters used Norwegian at least until they went to school. Then the language apparently was quickly lost by the new generation. She prepared what many would consider traditional Norwegian foods, especially at Christmastime. Once grown, all but one of the children married outside of Norwegian America.

Sumner m Lilian Cutter (Yankee)
Bernice m Alvin Nordstrom (Swedish American)
Maurice (Morris) m Mary Krago (English American)
Gladys m Cyrus Hansen (Norwegian American)
[Mary and Lilian were the longest lived. Each passed away in 2008.]

My father's father, Isaac Nordstrom, was born in Ransäter, in Värmland, Sweden. The son of a miller, he emigrated in 1880 and worked as a laborer on farms west of Willmar. His wife was Augusta Forsberg, whose parents owned a farm near Pennoch. The couple settled in Willmar, where Isaac worked as

Isaac Nordstrom and family, c. 1915

a carpenter and the custodian of the county courthouse. The family home, another typical clapboard-sided frame house, was at 421 South Fourth Street.

I dimly remember "Gran'pa Ike." He was a gruff, silent old man—frozen in a seedy wingback chair, constantly gnawing on an unlit pipe and demanding attention from his youngest daughter, Laila. He did not seem to like children very much. But family lore paints him as a clever, hardworking, skilled-with-his-hands man, devoted to his family, possessor of a good sense of humor, and politically conservative. Much like Ben Benson, it seems, he was engaged in his community not as a Swedish American but as an American and as a Willmarite. He was a member of a local Odd Fellows lodge. Because of this, the family left the Swedish-Lutheran fold and migrated to the Episcopal Church. He subscribed to, and apparently regularly read, *Svenska Amerikanska Posten* from Minneapolis, spoke Swedish with his wife (whom I never knew), and never lost his accent. I see him, in some ways, as Karl Oskar Nilsson in Moberg's novels—at least in his later years. He died at age ninety-eight.

His children were not particularly ethnic. I knew most of them. They were all successful professionals and rather typically second-generation Swedish Americans. Cookies, table prayers, and some family traditions defined their ethnic identities. In terms of marriage partners, the list below shows what happened with this side of my family:

Morris [Mauritz] m Carrie Elfstrom (Swedish American)
Leonard m Olive Blankenship (English American)
Albert m Mable Magnuson (Swedish American)
Alvin m Bernice Benson (Norwegian American)
Edna m Fred de Ruyter (Dutch American)
Laila m Ed Bedney (possibly East European)

I do have cousins on both sides of this family. Some of them are interested in their ethnic backgrounds, mostly in a kind of passing fashion.

Conclusions

What does all of this say about Norwegians and Swedes as immigrants in a relatively small but growing town in Minnesota? People who know me know that often I take a kind of gadfly position on ethnicity and its importance in the United States. Perhaps I believe what I am saying; perhaps I am just trying to get others to rethink some things. I do believe that ethnicity can be overemphasized and people can be oversimplified in our attempts to understand the past and the present. Identity is an immensely complex thing. None of us are mono-dimensional. None of us are just Norwegian Americans or Swedish Americans or any hyphenated Americans or, for that matter, simply Americans. We define and redefine ourselves constantly—by our preferences, ideas, politics, religion, jobs, careers, organizational affiliations, interests, passions, hobbies, and the like. And these definitions are constantly influenced by context—by time and place.

Willmar was an ethnic town. No question about it. It had half a dozen Norwegian and Swedish churches. It had some distinctly ethnic blocks or neighborhoods. It certainly had businesses that catered to Norwegians or Swedes or Scandinavians or other ethnic groups. Many of the town's celebrations (Syttende Mai) or cultural events (a visit by Olle i Skratthult and his Peasant Comic Orchestra) had some ethnic component, and many of the first- and second-generation Norwegians and Swedes in the town included ethnic elements in their identities. At the same time, Willmar was a dynamic, growing place in small-town America. The worlds of the Swedes, Norwegians, and every other ethnic group overlapped, and interactions were unavoidable. Of course, there may have been animosities. Bad jokes may have been told. Insults flung. Kids may have picked on each other on school playgrounds with the inevitable ethnic taunts. But passions do not seem to have been intense. Battles do not appear in the printed sources. As was the case with my own family, families merged and ethnicities were diluted. The worlds of these people intersected at home, work, school, and church. The shops they frequented, their friendships, their shared participation in county, town, and school government and in congregations and secular organizations brought them together. The town newspaper was for everyone. It was American, not ethnic. If it had a bias, it was political.

This brief survey and look at one family's history suggests that the Norwegian Americans and Swedish Americans of Willmar, Minnesota, behaved in familiar ways when considered against the larger backdrop of immigration history. To use a familiar cliché, Willmar was a relatively small melting pot in which a number of ethnic groups lived and worked together. The Norwegians and Swedes (as well as the Belgians, Dutch, Germans, and others) were occasionally able to build small but ethnically cohesive neighborhoods, establish ethnic congregations, and enjoy social lives that often bore ethnic elements. The first-generation immigrants remained closest to their roots, reflected in church membership, language retention, newspaper preferences, and choice of spouses. They made clear efforts to become American, however, especially the men. They learned English, joined nonethnic organizations, and accepted the choices and the diverging life paths taken by their children. Typically, the second-generation children were less interested in their backgrounds. They forgot the immigrant languages (if they ever learned them), left the immigrant churches, moved out of the old neighborhoods, and chose spouses with little or no regard for ethnicity. What remained of old country customs was often limited to a few special foods and an occasional table prayer. If there was bitter rivalry between the Norwegians and Swedes of Willmar, especially around the time of the dissolution of the Union between the two countries, it is not evident in the sources. Of course, Willmar is just one of many small towns where Norwegian and Swedish immigrants found new homes, and my family's history is but one among thousands. Many more people and places could be studied. I suspect, however, one would find similar patterns, patterns that would repeat themselves over and over again—in place *and* in time.[14]

Notes

1. *Thirteenth Census of the United States: 1910. Abstract.* Washington, DC.: U.S. Government Printing Office, 1913, 70; Victor E. Lawson. *Illustrated History and Descriptive and Biographical Review of Kandiyohi County, Minnesota.* (St. Paul, MN: The Pioneer Press Manufacturing Departments, 1905), and http://www.city-data.com/city/Willmar-Minnesota.html.

2. John G. Rice, *Patterns of Ethnicity in a Minnesota County, 1880–1905,* Geographical Reports (Umeå: Department of Geography, University of Umeå, 1973).

3. *Willmar Tribune* (hereafter, *WT),* Jan. 5 and Mar. 3, 1905.

4. *WT,* Mar. 29 and Apr. 5, 1905.

5. *WT,* Apr. 26, 1905.

6. *WT,* May 17, 1905.

7. *WT,* June 7, 14, 28, 1905.

8. *WT,* July 12, 1905.

9. *WT,* Aug. 18, 1905.

10. *WT,* Sept. 27 and Oct. 4, 1905.

11. *WT,* Oct. 18 and Nov. 8, 1905.

12. *WT,* Dec. 27, 1905.

13. I am reminded of how the Swedish novelist Marianne Fredriksson treated the crisis in *Hannah's Daughters.* Ordinary people who lived along the border between Sweden and Norway, who had friendships and family ties across that border and whose lives were intertwined, hoped for a peaceful solution to a crisis created by politicians. Their relationships showed none of the animosity toward each other that one might expect.

14. Today, Willmar is again a town of new immigrants. This time they are principally Hispanic. They make up nearly 16 percent of the current population and have had important impacts on a number of aspects of life (including organizational, religious, economic, and cultural) in the community. See http://www.city-data.com/city/Willmar-Minnesota.html.

CHAPTER 16

The Basis for Pan-Scandinavian Cooperation in Minneapolis–St. Paul

Nordic Involvement in American Politics Prior to 1930

DAVID C. MAUK

The first two voluntary organizations among Nordic immigrants in St. Paul and Minneapolis, Minnesota—a Lutheran church in each city—conform to the conventional view of pan-Scandinavian institutions. Swedes and Norwegians joined forces early in community development to form a congregation made up of both nationalities because each group alone held too few individuals to establish a separate organization. In the conventional view, pan-Scandinavianism is as a whole a relatively short-lived phenomenon—a kind of institutional "marriage of convenience" that ends in more or less amicable divorce as soon as one partner in the alliance feels secure enough in its numbers to go its separate way. The concept applies to the leisure-time associational life of immigrants, focusing on institutions founded by the foreign-born generation and its children. This chapter first examines how well the traditional model of pan-Scandinavianism explains the experience of Swedish and Norwegian Americans in the Twin Cities. Then it presents the demographic foundation for a more broadly conceived notion of inter-Nordic cooperation in American politics based on the groups' significant population size. Finally, it details their involvement in local politics during the historical period prior to 1930.[1]

Conventional Pan-Scandinavianism in Minneapolis–St. Paul

In the Twin Cities, the generic features of pan-Scandinavianism were evident as soon as two or more of the nationalities became present in the 1850s. Their interrelated northern European histories, mutually understandable languages, and similar cultures including Lutheranism and a common base of values, as Odd Lovoll says, "tied them to each other, even when [they were] disagreeing." From the beginning, he continues, "fragmentation and confrontation . . . held sway among Swedish, Danish, and Norwegian brethren and sisters" in the United States, where they "had at best a love-hate relationship." The intramural groups confronting each other in the 1800s and early 1900s were often, for example, representative of subcultures in the Nordic homelands rather than "Swedes" or "Norwegians."[2]

The first institutional evidence of Swedish-Norwegian immigrant cooperation is instructive in both the circumstances of its origin and the causes of its
demise. In 1848 Swedish immigrants and a smaller contingent of Norwegians
formed the Scandinavian Methodist Episcopal Church on the Near East Side
of St. Paul, the first Protestant congregation in the territorial capital. Despite its
pan-Nordic name, the church membership included only a minority of Norwegians and even fewer Danes. Like the majority of members, the leadership
was Swedish. They worshipped together until 1873, when the Norwegians left to
form a separate congregation in the newly organized Norwegian Methodist District of Minnesota. In the Cedar-Riverside neighborhood of Minneapolis, five
Swedish and three Norwegian men voted in 1866 to bring their families together
in the Evangelical Lutheran Augustana Church, a congregation in the pan-
Scandinavian Augustana Synod. In its first two years this church was served by
both Swedish and Norwegian immigrant preachers who came in from surrounding rural settlements. At the end of this short period, however, the growth of the
Norwegian element as well as disputes over the administration of the Sunday
school and plans for a building led the congregation to split along ethnic lines.[3]

John Jenswold provides a persuasive portrait of the conventional model of inter-
Nordic institutional association in "The Rise and Fall of Pan-Scandinavianism
in Urban America," noting that "the full flowering of organizational pan-
Scandinavianism produced a plethora of institutions covering a variety of immigrant interests in Minneapolis in the 1870s and 1880s. Norwegians united with
Swedes in Scandinavian temperance societies, brass bands, singing societies, rifle
companies, athletic clubs, and drama groups." Jenswold emphasizes that the city's
business and educated Scandinavian elites created exclusive clubs. Class and
occupational interests also provided the central motivation for the early union
locals that Scandinavian laboring men and women formed to protect their interests. In accordance with the social attitudes of the time, some leisure associations
were also limited to one gender—women's clubs, both religious and secular or
job related, as well as men's business and workingmen's groupings. Even the celebration of "national days," such as Syttende Mai and Svenskarnas Dag, became
Scandinavian events in the Twin Cities during those decades.[4]

By 1890, asserts Jenswold, "the era of interethnic good feelings began to
wane." He sees nationalist feelings growing forcefully among Norwegian
Americans through the fifteen years between the start of the 1890s and the dissolution of the union with Sweden in 1905. However, according to Carl G. O.
Hansen, later the long-serving editor of *Minneapolis Tidende*, the Twin Cities'
largest Norwegian-language newspaper, the golden age of patriotic "norskdom"
began in the early 1880s, a decade earlier than Jenswold suggests, when Hansen
witnessed some of the early activities of the Minneapolis chapter of Norway's
Liberal Party (*Venstre parti*), which stood for full Norwegian independence.

Thus, the classic period of pan-Scandinavianism in the Cities might be viewed as lasting only a decade and a half—from 1865 through the 1870s. This assessment is perhaps not surprising when one remembers the timing of Norwegian mass emigration, which occurred simultaneously with the flowering of national romanticism and the idealization of Norwegian peasant culture in the homeland after the American Civil War. One crucial way leaders in the Norwegian diaspora could at once show support for nationalists in Norway and celebrate American liberties, Jenswold asserts, was to construct an ethnic identity with a strong element of anti-Swedish feeling. An aristocratic arrogance, oppressively bureaucratic manner, and economic exploitation of neighbors—alleged flaws in Swedish society, judging by the comments in the Norwegian American press and immigrant leaders' speeches—were a noticeable element in the baggage of Swedish immigrants that led to inter-Nordic conflicts on both sides of the Atlantic. The Norwegian American elite claimed a more democratic, egalitarian spirit, in line with American ideals.[5]

A developing ethnic ideology on the one hand and sufficient numbers to support its own constellation of community institutions on the other led Norwegian Americans out of the early period of conventional pan-Scandinavianism. Even though the two groups continued to share residence in the same core area in Minneapolis, the Cedar-Riverside district, most of the old voluntary congregations and societies split up, according to Jenswold, and "more ethnically exclusive" Swedish or Norwegian residential clusters grew up in their secondary settlement areas in the city. In fact, as we shall see, Swedish and Norwegian Americans continued to share Nordic American associations of some sort and in Minneapolis–St. Paul formed such a large demographic segment of the population that group size itself had crucial consequences for pan-Scandinavian cooperation.[6]

Demographic Dominance and the End of Conventional Pan-Scandinavianism

In St. Paul, the pan-Scandinavian Methodist church was in practice always a congregation in which, despite its Scandinavian name, Swedish immigrants dominated. In Minneapolis, a Norwegian dominance grew in the Augustana congregation even though Norwegian leaders of the church complained that it was in reality a *Swedish* institution. Both of these variations reveal common strains in pan-Scandinavian institutional cooperation—situations in which one Nordic nationality group dominates and the other leaves when its group offers sufficient support. In addition, organizations among these closely related nationality groups sometimes bore the name of one of them but in reality were genuinely Scandinavian, that is, had a mixed membership in which none of the groups dominated. The nature of individual organizations was dynamic, and associational life among the Nordic immigrant groups evolved over time. Because of the large numbers of each nationality, both the Norwegian and Swedish communities grew to be largely self-sufficient and institutionally complete in both Minneapolis and St. Paul by 1890. A full set of separate nationality organizations welcomed newcomers in 1900–1914 and 1920–29. Yet the new waves of immigrants, representing later stages of the homeland societies, to a noticeable degree established their own associational life and founded some new pan-Scandinavian groups. Complicating this dynamic picture further were surviving kinds of pan-Scandinavianism, including the political organizations and activities that are the main focus of this study.

Indistinguishable from each other to most old-stock Americans in the early years of their settlement, the individual Nordic nationalities were usually lumped together and called "Scandinavians," "Swedes" because they were most numerous, or "Yon Yonson" because of their apparently identical accents. As Jenswold notes, the ignorance of old-stock Americans strengthened Scandinavian immigrants' pan-Nordic solidarity when they faced mainstream culture in the United States. Conditions there drove Scandinavians to seek comfort and mutual support in each other's company. In practice, they both strenuously articulated differences in nationality background and cultivated their common Nordic cultural legacy. In each other's company, each group felt its unique national characteristics keenly. In Minneapolis's Augustana church, for example, A. H. Edsten, recently arrived from Norway, became so offended on learning that the congregation's Sunday school was taught in Swedish that he led a separate school himself rather than have the congregation's four Norwegian children learn their catechism in Swedish. As historian Odd S. Lovoll asserts, "Non-Nordics" were by Scandinavian Americans "regarded as different—the *real* foreigners."[7]

In Minneapolis, the unique reality from the 1880s onward has been that when Swedish and Norwegian Americans could stand together, they have had an unmatched potential for influence on the community as a whole. As the outsider and muckraker Lincoln Steffens put it while on his tour to uncover corruption in American cities in 1902, Minneapolis was "the metropolis of the Northwest . . . the metropolis also of Norway and Sweden in America . . . the second largest Scandinavian city in the world," where the New England Yankee predominates and "the 'Roundhead' takes the 'Squarehead' out into the woods, and they cut lumber by forests, or they go out on the prairie and raise wheat and mill it into fleet-cargoes of flour." The city, Steffens, said, had a "round Puritan head . . . and a great, big Scandinavian body." His purple prose captures well the vivid impression the local Scandinavian population's size and energy made and immortalizes the ethnic slur that had already caught on.[8]

The demographic realities recorded by the census bureau confirm the cor-

rectness of Steffens's journalistic thrust, at least in terms of the population dominance of the two Nordic American groups. In 1900, slightly over 44 percent
of the entire population of Minneapolis consisted of foreign-born Swedish and
Norwegian Americans and their children, a decline from 1890, when they made
up just over 46 percent of the city's residents (see table 16.1). In St. Paul, the two
Nordic groups represented a little under a quarter of the capital's population in
1900 and a little over a quarter in 1890—still a very significant demographic reality there, if considerably less so than in Minneapolis. As late as 1930, the first two
generations of Swedish and Norwegian Americans contributed over a quarter
of Minneapolis's population and 14 percent of the people in St. Paul. The census
data does not include third and later generations of Scandinavian Americans, a
group that increased exponentially during these decades and made up for the
decreasing size of the first generation that came before 1900. The residential,
social, cultural, and political ramifications of these demographic foundations
have been enormous in the history of the Twin Cities.

Residential Concentration and Neighborhood Expansion in St. Paul

The first Swedish residents of St. Paul, poverty-stricken rural peasants, built
cheap wooden houses in the Phalen Creek gorge on the city's Near East Side
in the late 1850s and worked in nearby brewing and milling establishments.
For more than fifty years, some Swedes and their families got their start in the
gorge squatter town, which in popular parlance has kept the name Swede Hollow even 150 years later. As their fortunes improved, they left the narrow valley
for healthier parts of the neighborhood and, with the arrival of later, better-
situated contingents of Swedish-born newcomers, the city's Swedish American
core expanded north along Payne Avenue to Arlington Hills, Lake Phalen, the
city limits, and suburban Maplewood. Between the 1890s and 1910 in the East
Side (Ward 1), the Swedish born alone composed between a quarter and a fifth
of the population; along with their children, their total presence very likely
approached half of the local residents. Even in 1930, the Swedish born alone still
composed 12 percent of the population, and a decade later, the geographer John
G. Rice asserts, the district remained the "Swedish heart of the city."[9]

Real estate values and residents' prosperity rose with the height of the land
and the distance north from downtown. Swedish Americans shared this east
side expansion with Norwegian Americans but were by far the larger group in
what in reality was the primary Scandinavian core section of the city. Norwegian
Americans first clustered in this area on streets south of Lake Phalen in Ward 1,
where in 1900 their first two generations comprised from nearly 6 percent up
to a fifth of the population in some census enumeration districts. Together with
the large population of Swedish Americans, the Norwegian American element

TABLE 16.1

Norwegian and Swedish Immigrants and Their Children in Minneapolis–St. Paul

	1880	1890	1900	1910	1920	1930
Minneapolis	46,887	164,738	202,718	301,408	380,582	464,356
(% of city population)						
Norwegian born	(5.6%)	(7.7%)	(5.7%)	(5.4%)	(4.3%)	(3.3%)
Second generation	?	(10.8%)	(10.9%)	(5.9%)	(6.5%)	(7.3%)
Total % of city		**18.5%**	**16.6%**	**11.3%**	**10.8%**	**10.6%**
Swedish born	(6.8%)	(11.8%)	(9.9%)	(8.8%)	(8.1%)	(5.4%)
Second generation	?	(15.9%)	(17.6%)	(9.0%)	(9.2%)	(9.8%)
Total % of city		**27.7%**	**27.5%**	**17.8%**	**17.3%**	**15.2%**
Grand total	**12.4%**	**46.2%**	**44.1%**	**29.1%**	**28.1%**	**25.8%**
St. Paul	41,473	133,156	163,065	214,744	234,698	271,606
Norwegian born	(1.6%)	(2.6%)	(1.8%)	(1.9%)	(1.6%)	(1.3%)
Second generation	?	(3.8%)	(3.8%)	(2.5%)	(2.9%)	(3.3%)
Total % of city		**6.4%**	**5.6%**	**4.4%**	**4.5%**	**4.6%**
Swedish born	?	(8.9%)	(6.0%)	(5.3%)	(4.2%)	(3.1%)
Second generation	?	(11.7%)	(11.5%)	(6.2%)	(6.1%)	(6.3%)
Total % of city		**20.6%**	**17.5%**	**11.5%**	**10.3%**	**9.4%**
Grand total		**27.0%**	**23.1%**	**15.9%**	**14.8%**	**14.0%**

Source: U.S. Federal Censuses, 1880–1930. "?" indicates that the 1880 Census did not count the parentage of those enumerated.

and a much smaller group of Danes (around 3 percent) made up a Scandinavian American majority on the East Side. As Rice explains, the area became a "self-contained neighborhood," with jobs, reasonable housing, and a full range of Scandinavian American churches, societies, businesses, shops, cafés, restaurants, bars, and entertainments. The Scandinavian languages functioned for daily communication in homes, in the business district, and in books, magazines, and newspapers. Between the 1890s and the 1930s, the East Side Scandinavian district stretched from the bluff above the Mississippi River to the northern suburbs. Here civic life focused on Scandinavian and Scandinavian American viewpoints, whether the issues involved were secular or religious or revolved around local politics.[10]

From the end of the 1870s into the twentieth century, Norwegian immigrants and their children also maintained separate neighborhoods on streets nearer downtown than Swede Hollow and in the Mount Airy section of the city. Norwegian Americans made up 10 and 15 percent of the residents in these

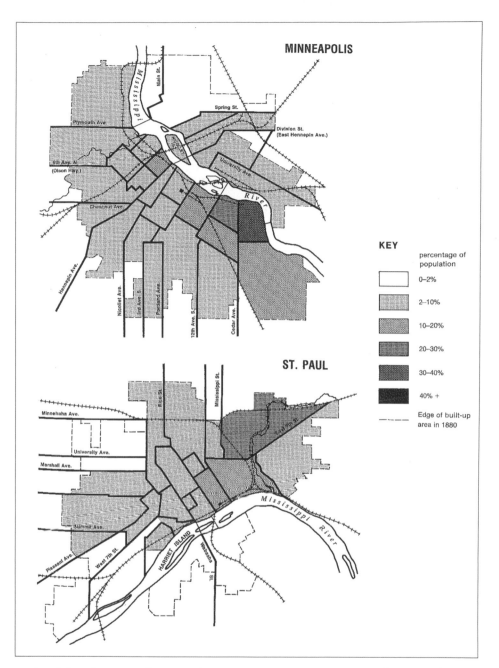

MINNEAPOLIS

ST. PAUL

KEY

percentage of
population

0–2%

2–10%

10–20%

20–30%

30–40%

40% +

Edge of built-up
area in 1880

Swedish settlement in the Twin Cities, 1880. From June Drenning Holmquist, ed.,
They Chose Minnesota: A Survey of the State's Ethnic Groups (*St. Paul:*
Minnesota Historical Society Press, 1981)

parts of town in 1900. But the highest concentration of Norwegian Americans at the century's start—a quarter of the population—appeared in enumeration districts on both sides of the north-south axis of Oakland Cemetery and around the downtown end of the graveyard. In these "Norwegian" areas there were a few of the group's ethnic churches, shops, bars, and rooming and boardinghouses, but the number and range of institutions was not nearly as complete as in the Scandinavian district along Payne Avenue. After 1900, Swedish and Norwegian Americans created both smaller pan-Scandinavian areas and more ethnically exclusive Norwegian or Swedish districts on St. Paul's West Side, some of them close to the Midway between the Twin Cities.[11]

Swedish-Norwegian Neighborhood Cores and Expansion in Minneapolis

As sociologist Calvin F. Schmid concisely expressed his demographic findings about foreign nativity in Minneapolis in 1930, Swedish American residents "dominated most wards" and their Norwegian American cousins comprised the next largest part of the population. The exceptions to this rule were the Near North Side (Ward 3), where Russian Jews figured as a large majority, and the city's Northeast neighborhood (Ward 1), where Polish Catholics were by far the largest group. The general Swedish-Norwegian preponderance dated to the 1880s and 1890s, but significant shifts in the Nordic concentrations took place over the decades to 1930. In the mid-1890s, 40 percent of the Cedar-Riverside (Ward 6) district had been born in one or the other of those two countries, and with their children and the area's Danish residents they then comprised an overwhelming majority.[12]

This population provided the foundation for a strengthened version of the same kind of self-contained community and pan–Scandinavian American civic culture as existed on St. Paul's East Side. Primarily a working-class stronghold but home to Augsburg Seminary as well as to several Scandinavian churches whose faculty and clergy early became leading public figures in Minneapolis, the ward's population represented diverse views and segments of opinion. Through the period, some Swedish and Norwegian immigrants lived with other poor people in Bohemian Flats, a squatters' community on the floodplain at the river's edge. In 1930 only roughly half as large a part of Cedar-Riverside was Scandinavian born, but some 1,600 Nordic Americans still lived there.[13]

The Franklin Avenue or Seward neighborhood (Ward 11), directly south and west (today the eastern half of the Phillips neighborhood between Franklin Avenue, Twenty-fourth Street, Tenth Avenue South, and the river), became the city' second-largest Scandinavian center as some Swedes and Norwegians moved to better housing there and new waves of immigrants exceeded Cedar-Riverside's capacity to hold more newcomers. In 1895, nearly a quarter of this ward was Scandinavian born and, with continued in-migration as well as second- and third-generation residents, by the 1900 Census in some enumeration districts the population was close to two-fifths or one-half Swedish or Norwegian American. As was the case further north, this ward too was soon marked by the building and activities of these groups' immigrant churches, meeting halls, businesses, and social organizations of all kinds. In 1930, the area remained solidly Scandinavian: over a fifth of the ward was still Scandinavian born at that point, and they and numbers of their children and grandchildren maintained the area's Nordic character.

Scandinavian Americans expanded their south-side residential concentration beyond Twenty-fourth Street into Ward 7 and on through the Powderhorn and Nokomis neighborhoods to the city limits. The portion of Nordic-born residents declined little between 1895 and 1930 (from 18 percent to 15.5 percent) because of continued immigration through the 1920s, from later generations' movement south, and despite the passing of portions of the first generation. As they succeeded materially, working- and lower-middle-class Scandinavian Americans moved into new modest housing developments there. The demographic and economic processes in Ward 12, parallel on the east to the Mississippi, were quite similar: this district was home to slightly more Swedish and Norwegian immigrants in 1895; in 1930 its residents remained 12 percent Scandinavian born. As elsewhere in South Minneapolis, later generations and newcomers swelled the Nordic population as their economic situation improved.

Generally speaking, in South Minneapolis just inland from a street of impressive homes with river views on the extreme east, the cost of real estate and fortunes of residents rose from the most modest working class on the far east to the most costly around the row of lakes in Wards 4, 8, and 13 on the far west. In 1895, Nordic Americans made up just over 10 percent of the area directly west of downtown around Loring Park and west of Hennepin Avenue past Cedar Lake to the city limits (Ward 4), and by 1930 their presence there had declined to only 3.5 percent. In the next west-side ward, number eight, though slightly smaller, the Nordic proportion of the population declined about as much. In the southernmost district of the city, Ward 13, the proportion and decline was identical with that in Ward 4. These prosperous districts were home to the small pan-Scandinavian elite who shared the wards with people of the same socioeconomic class. People such as Judge Andreas Ueland and his family lived on the shore of a lake in a western ward but went to ethnic events and institutions in the core areas. If Calvin Schmid's statistical charts had included members of the second and third generations of these groups for 1930, the decline his demographic bar charts show for their presence in the western wards would be much less. His overall commentary on Swedish and Norwegian Americans' migration within the city in fact is indicative of an increase in their numbers in its more southern

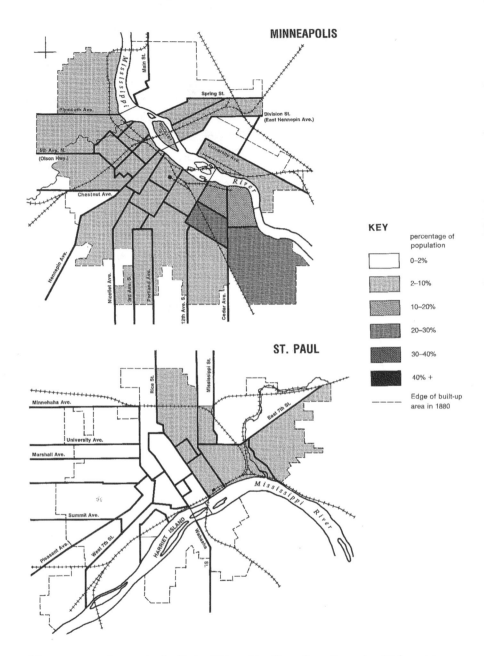

MINNEAPOLIS

ST. PAUL

KEY

percentage of
population

0–2%

2–10%

10–20%

20–30%

30–40%

40% +

Edge of built-up
area in 1880

*Norwegian settlement in the Twin Cities, 1880. From June Drenning Holmquist,
ed., They Chose Minnesota: A Survey of the State's Ethnic Groups (St. Paul:
Minnesota Historical Society Press, 1981).*

and far northern wards. He notes the general population decrease in central city wards and then asserts that "there has been a definite tendency for the Swedish [and Norwegian] population to move away from Wards 6 and 11 southward into Wards 7, 8, and 12 and northward into Ward 10." The greatest population increase south of downtown among Swedish and Norwegian Americans in the period occurred, he then specifies, in the city's southwest corner in Ward 13.[14]

On the north side of the city, very large Swedish Norwegian centers also appeared. Between the Civil War and the 1890s, immigrants established "Swede-town" clusters in northeast Minneapolis, first near downtown St. Anthony by the Mississippi River in the sawmilling areas of Ward 1 and later in the spreading industrial areas further inland in Ward 9. Norwegian workers joined in providing the work force in these areas, making it more Scandinavian. More than a fifth of Ward 9 was Swedish- or Norwegian born in 1895, and 12 percent remained so in 1930. Along the east side of the river in the lumbering areas of Ward 1, 6 percent of residents belonged to these Scandinavian groups in 1895. Five years later in some enumeration districts—for example, east of Fifth Street to Broadway—28 percent of residents were Norwegian born and the Swedish born comprised an addition to that working-class Nordic population. In 1930, however, only a little over 3 percent were still Scandinavian born in areas near downtown on the east side of the river.[15]

Both groups, but especially Norwegian immigrants, were early concentrated in the city's Near North section directly beyond downtown's warehouse district west of the river as well. Here a colony of lumberyard and sawmill workers from Selbu in the middle northern county of Trøndelag developed a community that grew in size and complexity to the end of the century. Some of its residents founded the Sons of Norway in 1895 and Daughters of Norway in 1897, which together grew into the nationality group's largest organizations in North America by the 1920s. Through the twentieth century these organizations' membership base was working class, like the communities in which they originated. In 1895, more than 13 percent of Ward 3 had been born in Scandinavia. Three decades into the twentieth century, 3.5 percent of the people in the ward, some 1,900 residents, still had their family origins in Sweden or Norway.[16]

The Camden section (Ward 10), a huge area nearly rural in its northern reaches in 1895, attracted many Scandinavians in both the Near North and Northeast to relocate in the ward's new housing as their material fortunes improved. According to Schmid, one-fourth of the people living there were Scandinavian immigrants in the mid-1890s. Their ability to show political influence was evident in the 1894 local elections when a Norwegian immigrant, Fred A. Schwartz, won a city council seat. As housing developments marched north, the area drew working- and middle-class Scandinavian Americans from South Minneapolis as well. In 1930, when nearly 10 percent of Ward 10's residents continued to be

Nordic born, many more members of the Scandinavian American community's later generations strengthened local support for public figures such as Swedish-Norwegian politician Floyd Bjerstjerne Olson. Camden, like the far south and southwest sections of the city, represented for many the first step toward leaving the city for the suburbs.[17]

According to people interviewed for the Twin Cities History Project, by the late 1940s and 1950s the whole of South Minneapolis and large swaths of the city's northern districts had become home to so many people of Swedish and Norwegian American ancestry that their religious forms, holidays, and foodways became well known in community life and accepted in public schools, where the Swedish and Norwegian languages were taught and ethnic clubs with faculty advisors and student newspapers helped maintain their countries' history and cultural heritage from 1910 into the postwar period.[18]

An Enduring Category of Pan-Scandinavian Voluntary Associations: Local Political Organization and Cooperation

Politics opened fertile grounds for pan-Scandinavian cooperation in St. Paul and Minneapolis. In both cities, Swedish and Norwegian immigrants were present in such large numbers that they could provide the major parties with the margin of victory in local elections from the 1880s onward. They saw their political potential in the wards of their greatest concentration and became voting citizens. They formed Scandinavian Republican and Democratic clubs in those sections of each city, with little regard to the traditional reputation of the state capital as a Democratic stronghold and Minneapolis as primarily Republican. The major parties' organizations assisted them in establishing partisan clubs as part of courting them as a voting bloc and promoting their leading political activists. Men from the clubs won places as delegates to city and county party meetings. In this role they mediated between their voting group and the party's levels from precinct and ward to city, state, and the nation as a whole, depending on the election year. When they functioned successfully, they often became candidates first for local primaries within the party and then for general elections between the parties, usually for alderman or assemblyman from their neighborhood.

For example, O. H. Oace, born in Norway in 1848, first worked as a carpenter on the Scandinavian East Side of St. Paul. He later moved farther west to Ward 9, where he became a general building contractor and employed Scandinavian workers to construct fixtures for churches and stores. These connections positioned him well to run for and win election as the president of the Ninth Ward Scandinavian Republican Club from 1884 to 1900. The Republicans nominated him as Ramsey County commissioner in 1900 and proposed him as representative from the thirty-third district of Minnesota to the state assembly the same year. Men like Oace, and the Scandinavian immigrant voters who supported them, not only shared common cause in finding a political voice and representation but, working alongside native-born Americans, became more integrated in local civic life. Eventually, pan-Scandinavian cooperation would help put men in the state senate, governor's chair, and Congress from Minneapolis, the more heavily Scandinavian of the two cities.[19]

In St. Paul, John Blom, a Swedish American, became the city's first Scandinavian alderman when he won election to the common council from Ward 1 in 1888. His delegation of ten men from the ward to the Ramsey County Republican convention that selected him as the party's candidate included seven with Scandinavian surnames. Blom was reelected the next year but lost in 1890. Two years later, pan-Scandinavian cooperation successfully supported the election of Norwegian American Republican Hans P. Jensen from Ward 9, north-central St. Paul, in the area around Oakland Cemetery. Jensen won support through his nomination by the Prohibition as well as the Republican Party.[20]

From the mid-1880s, St. Paul newspapers announced Democratic Party events aimed at local Scandinavian voters. The party helped Nordic Democrats organize a club in 1886 and assisted the club with public events to mobilize the city's large Scandinavian working-class vote on its side in upcoming partisan battles with the Republicans. In late October 1886, the St. Paul Scandinavian Democratic Club held a mass meeting in Arlington Hall on Payne Avenue in the midst of predominantly Scandinavian Ward 1. The program included speeches in English, Swedish, and Norwegian, the last being delivered by the Minneapolis Norwegian-language newspaper editor and Democratic candidate for Minnesota secretary of state, Luth. Jaeger. A week later the club reserved the city's Exposition rink so that "hundreds of Scandinavian laborers for whom the meeting was especially intended" might choose to swell the party's ranks. The city's mayor, after apologizing for not being able to address "his hearers in their own language," praised great men of Sweden and Norway and said he chose to speak to them as citizens of Minnesota. Then the club's chairman introduced "one of the best Swedish orators in the country," who emphasized the importance of being politically active. The next speaker, Democratic officeholder W. P. Murray, gave a partisan speech that portrayed the Republican candidate for the U.S. Senate, William Windom, as a tool of the "wheat interest" who had "never paid so much [in] taxes as the poor laborer of Swede Hollow." He then contrasted such a man with the thrifty, hardworking Scandinavian immigrant, saying that he remembered when the first Scandinavians arrived in the state. Noting that he came from a community "where fully two-thirds of the population were of that nationality," he claimed that "there was no nationality that more easily affiliated with the American people."[21]

The new demographic realities that appeared in just a few decades encouraged old-stock Americans to show more knowledge of and respect for Scandinavian cultures and nationalities than they had in the past. In the process of working to win the votes of Swedish and Norwegian Americans, they inadvertently revealed the limits of their knowledge and the qualities they most valued in a local immigrant working class. The years from the peak of Swedish and Norwegian mass immigration to the Twin Cities in the 1880s through the large wave of Nordic newcomers from 1900 to 1914 created a local political culture typical of American urban life in the industrial age. The large majority of foreign-born voters lived in high-population-density, working-class quarters close to their places of employment. The majority of them still spoke, or more fluently spoke, their native languages rather than English and worked as the kinds of unskilled or semiskilled laborers that much of the general public associated with immigrant working men and women. Out of such circumstances arose the style and content of the political meetings described above.

In 1892, the delegates to the Democratic Party Ramsey County convention from Wards 1 and 3 also included men with Scandinavian family names, and the Swedish American Democrat J. P. Peterson ran unsuccessfully for alderman from Ward 1. Most successful Nordic candidates in St. Paul's municipal elections, however, continued to be Republicans until 1914. From the mid-1890s to World War I, no Scandinavian Democrats won election as an alderman, while the Swedish Americans John Lindahl, John Blomquist, and Andrew Dahlquist and the Norwegian Americans John Larsen, O. H. Oace, and John E. Holt served Wards 1, 3, or 9 as Republican aldermen—the result of pan–Scandinavian American political cooperation within the Republican party. Norwegian immigrant grocer John Larson, St. Paul's storekeeper in charge of maintaining all outdoor municipal equipment from 1900 into the 1920s, launched his career from the district just south of Oakland Cemetery in Ward 9, where Norwegian and Swedish immigrants clustered around 1900. Winning support from both Nordic groups, he served as Republican alderman for two terms in the late 1890s.[22]

In Minneapolis, the earliest political representation Scandinavian Americans won on the municipal level came a decade earlier than in St. Paul, and from the end of the 1880s onward it was a constant of the political life of more sections of the mill city than of the state capital. The difference resulted from the much greater number of jobs available for immigrant workers in the industrial district powered by the falls of the Mississippi. The political influence of Scandinavian Americans in Minneapolis was roughly commensurate with the fact that they comprised just under twice as big a portion of the city's population as they did in St. Paul. In the Cedar-Riverside district (Ward 6) of the near south side, Nordic representation on the city council began when A. H. Edsten, a Norwegian immigrant, became the first Scandinavian American alderman in 1874. From 1878 to 1882, John W. Anderson, a Swede, represented the Near North (Ward 3) and made it the second section of the city to elect a local Scandinavian American resident to the city council.

By the 1890s, after considerable numbers of both Swedish and Norwegian immigrants had moved to Wards 3, 6, 7, 10, 11, and 12, the Scandinavian American population centers on both sides of downtown were repeatedly represented on the city council by aldermen from the Nordic countries. Two examples on the south side will make the situation clear. After Edsten's term, two prominent Norwegian Americans, Dr. Karl Bendeke and A. C. Haugan, both Democrats, held a Cedar-Riverside seat from 1878 to 1888. Then the Republicans, Swedish American Clarence Johnson and Norwegian American Chris Ellingsen, won election as Ward 6 aldermen through the end of the 1880s. After that, the Swedish Republican John A. Swenson and Norwegian Democrat Lars M. Rand became its representatives. Throughout the 1890s, the Seward neighborhood (Ward 11) elected a Nordic alderman. An informal sharing of aldermanic seats between the two large Nordic immigrant groups in both of these wards, regardless of party, reflected demographic realities and allegiances. In the twenty-four years leading up to World War I, Swedish and Norwegian Americans appeared to alternate in aldermanic positions from these sections of the city, which might suggest that a plurality of voters wanted to elect a Scandinavian and cared less about the candidate's nationality group.[23]

Minneapolis had major party clubs for Nordic groups in different parts of the city beginning in the 1880s. A Scandinavian Republican Club of North Minneapolis, for example, formed in 1888, but by that time the city's south-side Scandinavian Democratic Club sent delegates to the national gathering of the party's clubs, where delegates met President Grover Cleveland and the following exchange took place: "John Landberg, secretary of the Scandinavian Democratic Club of Minneapolis, confronted the president. He had a showy badge on announcing his club, his race, and his residence. He said: 'Mr. President, you have won the respect and confidence of the Scandinavians of Minnesota, and we are going to carry the state for you.' 'I hope so,' replied the president. 'We look to your state with a considerable degree of hopefulness and with a little uneasiness, but our hope is greater than our fear.'" Valued by the president and confident of Nordic voters' importance in his home state, this local activist not only makes clear his intention to make sure they act effectively as a voting bloc but also reveals a strong belief in pan-Scandinavian political cooperation and increasing integration into the American political system.[24]

During the fifty years from the mid-1870s to 1914, the same sharing of offices between Swedish and Norwegian immigrant politicians took place in the city as a whole and in Hennepin County, where Minneapolis is located. Men from both groups served in municipal offices such as the park board, the courthouse commission, the municipal bench, and city engineering positions. Members of both Nordic groups won election as county sheriff, treasurer, and commissioner. Swedes or Norwegians also held a broad range of other elective city and county offices. If a man from one of the groups ran against a man from the other, Nordic voters would have to choose. This reality would seem to favor Swedish American candidates, whose nationality group was much the larger of the two from 1890 onward, but in this period more Norwegian than Swedish Americans won election victories in the city and county. Perhaps, as the Swedish American newspaper editor and local historian Alfred Söderström asserted, it was Norwegian Americans' greater "national feeling" that made them stand for and win local elective office with the support of their compatriots. But the voting power enjoyed by candidates from both groups likely more often came from the greater support they derived from occasions for a degree of Scandinavian solidarity at the polls.[25]

The political historian Carl H. Chrislock labeled the best-known Scandinavian American politician in this period, Lars Rand, a "ward boss" who functioned as a charismatic working-class leader. Rand used his heavily Norwegian-accented English to great effect with the Scandinavian American laboring majority in the district when it counted, arguing forcibly for the eight-hour day and equal rights for immigrants in the competition for city jobs during campaigns. He was reelected from Ward 6 between 1890 and 1910, and during his tenure the police constables, firemen, and public maintenance crews of Cedar-Riverside became thoroughly Scandinavian American. His long-standing success in municipal politics also stemmed from his cooperation with a German American alderman from another immigrant quarter, Ward 3 in the Near North, to protect the local liquor interest, whose saloons lined the main commercial streets of both wards. The two men negotiated the rule that became known as the "Rand Ordinance," which made enforcing Sunday closing laws for city saloons difficult at best. In this they supported not only the businessmen in the liquor trade but the many immigrant workers, largely but far from exclusively Scandinavian and German in Cedar-Riverside and the Near North, who found solace, social relaxation, and sites for debates as well as roughhousing in saloons.[26]

Conclusion

Swedish and Norwegian Americans were so numerous in the core Scandinavian districts of Minneapolis and St. Paul that from the 1890s these areas were home to pan-Scandinavian groups like the major party political clubs as well as to a broad separate set of nationality-based institutions. Within the Twin Cities' large Nordic communities there was room for Scandinavian third-party voters, pro-saloon and temperance or prohibition forces, varieties of Lutherans as well as Methodists, Baptists, and Covenanters, woman suffrage associations, and a spectrum of social welfare institutions and associations, many of them led by women. Until causes had run their course, Scandinavian groupings for or against them often remained vital. The conflicts involving Nordic groups on each side of the temperance issue, for example, continued until the Volstead Act was passed in 1919, and Minneapolis's Scandinavian Woman Suffrage Association remained active for its cause until the Nineteenth Amendment granted women the right to vote in 1920. A Swedish-Norwegian women's organization in the Scandinavian Augustana Church started social welfare activities for the poor in Cedar-Riverside in the 1860s, and when the congregation split along national lines, so did the women's social work. In times of acute need, however, such as during the economic hard times that lasted through much of the 1890s, pan-Scandinavian relief associations reappeared.[27]

The common thread is a perception of requirements that cannot be met by one Nordic nationality group alone, whether these needs are based on religious, social, ideological, or economic circumstances of the historical period. This study has focused on the pan-Scandinavian political clubs for the major parties in the Twin Cities. They lasted longer than Jenswold predicted because they filled needs for the foreign-language-speaking immigrant generation at least until World War I, and the voting power of that generation attracted the major parties until then, after which the protests against "hyphenated" Americans and the electoral reforms of Progressives weakened ethnic urban machine politics of the sort that Lars Rand represented. The Scandinavian Americans who were active in political clubs or who ran for one of the multitude of local offices constituted, of course, only a small minority compared to the ethnic electorate they and the major parties hoped to mobilize to vote for one party or the other.

The uniquely large portion of the Twin Cities' population in the combined first and second generations of Swedish and Norwegian Americans gave pan-Scandinavianism the potential to decide elections if its vote was swung decisively to one of the major parties or to a third party. Political scientist Michael Barone found that during the 1890s and first years of the twentieth century, when the major parties suffered significant defections to more radical third-party groups, such as the Farmers' Alliance and Populists, the largest movement away from them at the polls was among the body of working-class Scandinavian Americans. As he summarizes his findings, "The Scandinavians were the most volatile element; during periods of economic distress they were often willing to switch from Republicans to the Alliance or Populists. And it was primarily among Scandinavians that the Populists' appeals for working class support found any reward at all." When the major parties won the Scandinavian workers back at the local and state-level elections, asserts Barone, they did so by nominating Scandinavian American candidates. Thus, he says that Minneapolis and St. Paul were the largest cities where the Populists made an exceptional showing because in the Twin Cities that vote was not a "labor vote but a Scandinavian vote." The immigrant generation and their children in the Cities, he speculates, seem not to have become "as firmly attached" to the "old parties" as other voters.[28]

That conclusion, however, is not convincing because it could easily have been the case with German Americans, another large immigrant group in the Cities. The causes for sustained pan-Scandinavian political behavior in Minneapolis–St. Paul seem more clearly related to the host society's sense that they were a single group, their own awareness of combined group size, their cultural similarity, and the urban conditions shared by their large working-class majority. An expanded study focused on the reasons the Twin Cities' Scandinavian Americans were drawn to the Farmers' Alliance and the Populists would investigate the political importance of these urbanites' own or familial background in rural districts of the Upper Midwest.

Notes

1. John R. Jenswold, "The Rise and Fall of Pan-Scandinavianism in Urban America," in *Scandinavians and Other Immigrants in Urban America: The Proceedings of a Research Conference, October 26–27, 1984*, ed. Odd S. Lovoll (Northfield, MN: Norwegian-American Historical Association, 1985), 159–70; see especially 162–53.

2. Odd S. Lovoll, *The Promise Fulfilled: A Portrait of Norwegian Americans Today* (Minneapolis: University of Minnesota Press, 1998), 58.

3. Arlow W. Andersen, *The Salt of the Earth: A History of Norwegian-Danish Methodism in America* (Nashville, TN: Norwegian-Danish Methodist Historical Society, 1962), 54–55, 76–77; James S. Hamre, *From Immigrant Parish to Inner City Ministry: Trinity Lutheran Congregation, 1868–1998* (Minneapolis, MN: The author, 1998), 9–10; Alfred Söderström, *Minneapolis Minnen. Kulturhistorisk Axplockning från Qvarnstaden vid Mississippi* (Minneapolis, MN: The author, 1899; facsimile by Nabu Public Domain Reprints, n.d.), 217–19.

4. Jenswold, "Rise and Fall of Pan-Scandinavianism," 160–61.

5. Jenswold, "Rise and Fall of Pan-Scandinavianism," 162–67; Carl G. O. Hansen, *My Minneapolis: A Chronicle of What Has Been Learned and Observed About the Norwegians in Minneapolis Through One Hundred Years* (Minneapolis, MN: The author, 1956), 57–62, 75–77.

6. Jenswold, "Rise and Fall of Pan-Scandinavianism," 162.

7. Jenswold, "Rise and Fall of Pan-Scandinavianism," 160; Hamre, *From Immigrant Parish*, 10; Lovoll, *The Promise Fulfilled*, 58, emphasis added.

8. Lincoln Steffens, *The Shame of the Cities* (New York: S. S. McClure, 1902), 43.

9. Calvin F. Schmid, *Social Saga of Two Cities: An Ecological and Statistical Study of Social Trends in Minneapolis and St. Paul* (Minneapolis, MN: Minneapolis Bureau of Social Research/Minneapolis Council of Social Agencies, 1937), charts 77 and 84; John G. Rice, "The Swedes," in *They Chose Minnesota: A Survey of the State's Ethnic Groups*, ed. June Drenning Holmquist (St. Paul: Minnesota Historical Society Press, 1981), 262.

10. Rice, "The Swedes," 262–63.

11. Rice, "The Swedes," 262; Schmid, *Social Saga of Two Cities,* 157. The commentary on Norwegian American neighborhoods comes from analysis of the systematic samples of residential patterns among Norwegian immigrants and their children in the Twin Cities at the 1880, 1900, and 1920 manuscript censuses. The North American Population Project's William Block of the University of Minnesota played a crucial role in the sampling and analysis of this work done for the Twin City History Project (TCHP hereafter), which has been sponsored by the Norwegian-American Historical Association, the Minnesota Historical Society, the Minnesota Endowment for the Humanities, and the Norwegian University of Science and Technology. The main goal of the TCHP is to produce a social history of Norwegian immigrants and their descendants in Minneapolis–St. Paul from 1849 to 2000. The Norwegian-American Historical Association plans to publish that volume, tentatively entitled *The Heart of the Heartland,* in 2013. A major effort to collect data systematically through public sources such as census and archival collections, as well as over one hundred in-depth interviews with community members and occasionally their neighbors, has made it possible to trace the development of the Norwegian American community and the relations of Norwegian Americans with other population groups in the Twin Cities in the nineteenth and twentieth centuries.

12. Schmid, *Social Saga of Two Cities,* 156–57, charts 76 and 82; Rice, "The Swedes," 262. See table 16.1.

13. Hansen, *My Minneapolis,* 142; Schmid, *Social Saga of Two Cities,* 156–57, chart 76; TCHP samples for Wards 6, 11, 12, 13.

14. Schmid, *Social Saga of Two Cities,* 157; TCHP samples.

15. Schmid, *Social Saga of Two Cities,* chart 76; TCHP samples.

16. Hansen, *My Minneapolis,* 19–20, 156–58; Schmid, *Social Saga of Two Cities,* 157.

17. Hansen, *My Minneapolis,* 134; Schmid, *Social Saga of Two Cities,* charts 83 and 85; George H. Mayer, *The Political Career of Floyd B. Olson* (St. Paul: Minnesota Historical Society Press, 1987), 7–11.

18. Hansen, *My Minneapolis,* 310–15. TCHP interviews with Sam Bergaas (Apr. 20, 1999), Ruth Crane (Oct. 8, 1998), Hoover Grimsby (Dec. 16, 1998), Mary Ann Olson (May 11, 1999), and Marilyn Sorensen (Mar. 4, 1999).

19. Rufus J. Baldwin, "Municipal History," in *History of the City of Minneapolis,* ed. Isaac Atwater (New York, Munsell & Company, 1893), 1:97. The capsule biography of O. H. Oace comes from *The Appeal: A National Afro-American Newspaper,* Nov. 3, 1900, 4.

20. *St. Paul Daily Globe,* Apr. 8, 1888, 1; Apr. 22, 1892, 1.

21. *St. Paul Daily Globe,* Oct 23, 1886, 4; Oct. 29, 1886, 4.

22. TCHP, 10 percent sample from the 1900 Census; interview with John Larson's granddaughter, Eunice Baker, June 1, 2000; *St. Paul Daily Globe,* Apr. 8, 1888, 1; Apr. 22, 1892, 1; *The Appeal: A National Afro-American Newspaper,* Nov 3, 1900, 4; *R. L. Polk & Co.'s St. Paul City Directory 1894–1914* (St. Paul, MN: R.L. Polk & Co., 1915).

23. Hansen, *My Minneapolis,* 132–33. Hansen notes that in 1874 Cedar-Riverside was in Ward 10, but later in the decade it became Ward 6. Alfred Söderström, *Minneapolis Minnen,* 214–15; *St. Paul Daily Globe,* May 24, 1888, 3; May 26, 1888, 3. The first Nordic

alderman elected from Ward 9 on the city's northeast side, a Swedish American, did not take office until the end of the 1880s and was not followed by other Scandinavian Americans until around the turn of the twentieth century.

24. Quoted from the *Baltimore Herald* in the *St. Paul Daily Globe,* July 15, 1888, 11.

25. Söderström, *Minneapolis Minnen,* 213–14.

26. Carl H. Chrislock, "Profile of a Ward Boss: The Political Career of Lars M. Rand," in *Scandinavians and Other Immigrants in Urban America,* ed. Lovoll, 93–107; James Gray, "Aldermen Come and Go but Lars Rand Goes on Forever," *Minneapolis Journal,* Dec. 30, 1906; Hansen, *My Minneapolis,* 133–37.

27. The work of the two best-known local immigrant Scandinavian historians includes many examples of longer-lasting inter-Nordic cooperation between the two nationality groups. See Carl G. O. Hansen, *My Minneapolis,* 22–27, 53–55, 62–63, 84–86, 92–97, 122, 130, 153–54, 229, 249, 310–14, and Alfred Söderström, *Minneapolis Minnen,* 141–46, 217, 234–35, 242, 263–66, 270–76. On the breadth of Scandinavian religious activity, see in addition Söderström, *Minneapolis Minnen,* 216–57, and Hansen, *My Minneapolis,* 178–84. Anja Bakken, "Our Country Gives Us the Vote—America Refuses It" (unpublished master's thesis, Norwegian University of Science and Technology, 1998), 104–12, offers an interesting analysis of pan-Scandinavian women's groups that worked for voting rights for women in Minneapolis. For an example of longer-lasting Nordic relief organizations, see "Scandinavian Union Relief Home, Circ 1925," an anniversary pamphlet donated by the Minneapolis United Fund (1925) to the collection of Minnesota Historical Society research librarian Debbie Miller, who in turn allowed the author to make a copy.

28. Michael Barone, "The Social Basis of Urban Politics: Minneapolis and St. Paul, 1895–1905" (unpublished graduate student essay, Harvard University, n.d.), 9, 22–23, copy in author's collection.

CHAPTER 17

Scandinavianism in the Rocky Mountain West

Pragmatic and Programmatic

JENNIFER EASTMAN ATTEBERY

In May 1893 the Norwegian-language newspaper *Montana Posten* reported enthusiastically that the May 17 (Norwegian Constitution Day) celebration in Helena was a success, attended by Norwegians, Swedes, and "other nationalities." But the *Posten* editor also complained about a misinformed announcement that had appeared in the English-language *Helena Independent* that the Scandia association would be giving a ball "in celebration of the union between Norway and Sweden." Members of the panethnic group Scandia included some of the most intelligent of Helena's Norwegians, the editor protested; was it possible that none of them knew the significance of May 17? In an 1892 local news column, editors of the Swedish-language *Utah Korrespondenten* noted that there would be a May 17 celebration that year in Calder Park. All Scandinavians in the Salt Lake City area were cordially invited to attend and hear speeches and songs from the *fosterland* (motherland). This was one of the many spring and summer celebrations dotting the calendar between the first of May and Pioneer Day, the Latter-day Saint (LDS, Mormon) celebration of their entry into Wasatch Valley, on July 24. In the newspaper advertisements and reporting of the 1890s, the Scandinavian Utahans maintained a careful parity among these Norwegian, Danish, Swedish, American, and LDS holidays.[1]

In western settlements such as those in Montana and LDS Utah, historical circumstances provided an opportunity for Scandinavianism, that is, explicit or implicit promotion of a panethnicity that elided the national divisions among Norwegians, Swedes, Danes, Icelanders, and sometimes Finns, lumping these groups into a general rubric based on perceived language or cultural similarities and common social, religious, and political interests. How and why this lumping occurred and whether it was successful are well illustrated in two Rocky Mountain regions, the Mormon culture area centered in Utah and the western Montana mining and smelting and, later, agricultural region.

In Utah, Scandinavianism was actively promoted through programmatic means, intentionally encouraged both by the structures of the LDS church and by secular committees and organizations that were often auxiliaries of the LDS church. (Of course, a small non-LDS Scandinavian community also existed in nineteenth-century Utah, a subject beyond the scope of this chapter.) In Montana, Scandinavianism was more pragmatic than programmatic; while institutions played a role, informal social patterns were important in creating and sustaining Scandinavianism. The differing historical and social contexts of Scandinavianism in these two regions during the period 1890 through the 1920s produced differing Scandinavianisms reflecting different cultural strategies. These strategies included both symbolic but empty ethnic claims "free from affiliation with ethnic groups" and intentional selection and intensification of essential parts of Scandinavian custom serving "to preserve cultural values" even when the specifics of cultural practice were inexactly replicated or even replaced.[2]

A degree of Scandinavianism can be found throughout North America during the nineteenth and early twentieth centuries. For example, Kenneth Bjork and Ernst Ekman point to Scandinavianism in 1860s San Francisco, where a group of immigrants, half Swedish and the remainder Norwegian and Danish, banded together in 1859 as the Scandinavian Society, a group that like many of the era pooled the members' dues for benefits to those among them who fell ill or were injured. The society also maintained a library of Scandinavian-language books and newspapers and organized an annual children's Christmas party. With the number of founding members relatively small—seventy-four according to Ekman—and the distribution across groups rather even, a panethnic group would have made sense in 1860s California, especially when one of the motivations was garnering enough members to support the society's protective function. Bjork and Thomas Benson trace Scandinavianism, too, in California's midcentury Swedish and Norwegian religious groups, land developments, and the "Scandinavian Navy," as the coastal fishermen came to be called. As numbers of immigrants from the Scandinavian countries grew, though, Scandinavianism was in trouble; Bjork sees its dissolution in California beginning in 1875 when the Swedish Society of San Francisco was formed.[3]

When immigration from the Scandinavian countries was a trickle into places like California, Scandinavianism was an appropriate and functional cultural strategy, as it was in the Midwest and elsewhere. Moreover, nineteenth-century U.S. Scandinavianism was bulwarked by its transatlantic counterpart, a political and cultural movement that had developed during the latter half of the eighteenth century and persisted into the mid-nineteenth century. Arnold Barton points to "the failure of Sweden-Norway to come to Denmark's aid in its German war in 1864 . . . as the deathblow of political Scandinavianism" in the Nordic countries. Cultural Scandinavianism lingered, though, and Scandinavian religious congregations and secular societies were attempted throughout North America, with varying success. Scandinavianism was a strong trend in urban Norwegian and Swedish settlement but waned as those groups grew large enough to sustain national groups. However, it was also possible for at least a tentative cultural

Scandinavianism to develop among the immigrants to the smaller, more rural settlements of the inland West throughout the nineteenth century and well into the twentieth, if the conditions were right.[4]

In Montana, Norwegians and Swedes settled alongside each other in the greatest numbers in Cascade County, with its population center in Great Falls, and in Lewis and Clark County, with its center in Helena, counties on the eastern edge of the Rockies in the Missouri River drainage. This region offered Scandinavian men employment in railroad construction, silver and coal mining, and smelting and offered agricultural land for those with resources to start up farms and ranches. Substantial contiguous Norwegian and Swedish populations cropped up, too, in Custer and Dawson counties in the Yellowstone River drainage, eastern Montana.

Scandinavianism in Montana was developed, expressed, and supported in organizational life and popular media. Churches were important as meeting places among ethnic groups but functioned only tentatively as effective sites for Scandinavianism. Numbers of Norwegians and Swedes came into Montana only after the 1870 split between Swedish and Norwegian-Danish synods of the previously Scandinavian Augustana Synod; thus Lutheran churches tended to be established by Norwegian, Swedish, or German national groups—whichever was dominant in the particular region—even if attended by a mix of nationalities. Scandinavian newspapers and secular organizations also supported intragroup interactions.

The Swedish and Norwegian Lutherans were late in establishing churches in Montana; once established those churches experienced a slow growth. Scandinavian church groups like the Swedish Mission Covenant church and the Swedish Baptists were, in comparison to the Lutherans, even smaller and quite scattered. The Covenant minister in Butte, where a chapel had been established in 1899, despaired of ministering to the Swedes there, in "a nest of Satan filled with sin and shame." Norwegian Lutheran missionaries began work in Montana in 1885 with the visit of P. J. Reinertsen to Big Timber, where services included an afternoon session in English to accommodate the mixture of peoples who were interested in attending: Scots, French, and American Indians as well as a mix of Scandinavians. Traveling to Bozeman, Reinertsen encountered "a number of Scandinavian people in the city" but did not hold services. "They did not desire any religious service. They were too contaminated with Mormonism."[5]

Swedish-Lutheran missionaries visited Montana about ten years later than the Norwegians, and many Montana communities with Norwegian and Swedish residents eventually developed, throughout the 1890s and 1900s, Lutheran congregations affiliated with the Norwegian and Swedish Lutheran synods, alongside similar institutions affiliated with the German Lutherans. One observer writing in 1926 pronounced this an "economic and organic waste" that "cannot be justified." Even so, the presence of numerous nationally oriented churches also brought ministers to Montana whose interaction could promote bridges across doctrinal and language divisions as they cooperated locally, and some of the local church bodies, however clear their members may have been about their Swedish or Norwegian orientations, were ascribed as Scandinavian by outsiders. In Helena, which according to O. M. Grimsby became "the head station for mission work" in Montana, the 1891 Polk directory listed a "Scandinavian Lutheran Church," with pastor N. N. Boe, who was a Norwegian Synod missionary sent to nurture the organization of Lutheran congregations. This report was made just prior to the congregation's formal organization as the Trinity Evangelical Lutheran Church. The same directory listed a "First Evangelical Scandinavian Church" ministered to by Reverend J. F. Frederickson. This Swedish Mission Covenant church had been organized the previous year.[6]

Churches could be sites for Scandinavianism, but for the Lutherans there was a strong pull toward the synods related to each of the Swedish American, Norwegian American, and German American ethnicities and languages, with the attendant importance of liturgy in one's native language. Avis R. Anderson's examination of Lutheran congregations in Custer and Dawson counties provides a case study of how shaky the attempts at a Norwegian-Swedish combination could be in a religious context. Anderson documents the formation of the Glendive Lutheran congregation as an affiliate of the United Norwegian Lutheran Church of America. It was recorded in the church's Norwegian-language minute books as a "meeting of all interested Scandinavians," even though Norwegians have outnumbered the Swedes in Dawson County from settlement well into the twentieth century, as evidenced in the importance of Glendive's annual May 17 celebration. Nevertheless, the church was both perceived by the surrounding English-speaking community as Scandinavian and self-ascribed as a Scandinavian Lutheran church.[7]

According to Anderson, the Glendive church fostered First Lutheran in Miles City, Custer County, where a "more equal balance of Swedes to Norwegians" led to more Swedish influence in the religious practices, even though the official affiliation was Norwegian American and Norwegian was used in worship services. On the other hand, the Miles City church took its minutes in Swedish. The mixture produced tensions. According to one longtime resident interviewed by Anderson, "the Swedes and Norwegians had a misunderstanding in the early days so the Swedes threatened to leave and take their money along . . . They also did not like the idea that the pastors in Miles City were always Norwegians."[8]

Also indicative of the perceived affinity between language and religious practice was *Bergs-Väktaren*. The only purely Swedish-language newspaper that has been identified in Montana, *Bergs-Väktaren* was published by the Swedish Lutherans of Evangelical Lutheran church (St. John's) in Helena. It was begun as a monthly in 1898 and ran at least until 1899. In the first issue, the editors, Reverend C. E. Frisk of Helena and Reverend A. E. Gustafson of Missoula, couched their claim to be editing the first and only Swedish newspaper in Montana in terms of national loyalty, thus conflating religion and ethnicity: "we hope therefore that it will be highly valued by all of our patriotic Montana citizens," Frisk and Gustafson wrote, offering the first issue free of charge.[9]

Some of the churches explicitly reached out to Scandinavians. The Great Falls Swedish Baptist church's newspaper notices during 1915 ended with the statement, "Scandinavians are cordially welcome." The Scandinavian Methodist church in Butte, organized in 1892, apparently made a more intentional effort at Scandinavianism and received criticism for the attempt. In an 1893 opinion column, *Montana Posten* correspondent "Frederick" was skeptical of the feasibility of organizing Swedes and Norwegians "under the banner of Scandinavia." In his view, the idea was good in theory but had yielded little results. One should note that Frederick appears to have maintained a tone of skeptical cynicism in most of his columns. The small organization remained, though, in 1905 reporting twenty-five members. In 1915, Great Falls' active Scandinavian Methodist congregation held a Christmas tree celebration on Christmas evening, to which all Scandinavians were welcomed, with their children. Such a holiday tradition could unite Scandinavians across national lines. The following month this congregation invited all Scandinavians to a series of meetings, including an English-language speech by evangelist Lars Andersen.[10]

Secular organizations in Montana more freely subscribed to a pragmatic Scandinavianism. As had been the situation in California at midcentury, in turn-of-the-century Montana a Scandinavian benevolent society made sense. The main such organization documented in Montana was the Scandinavian Brotherhood of America and its auxiliary, the Scandinavian Sisterhood of America, which had lodges in Butte (two lodges organized in 1891 and 1912), Helena, Kalispell (a lodge disbanded in 1911 and then reestablished in 1924), and Great Falls.[11]

With the membership requirement that one be of Scandinavian "birth or descent," the Scandinavian Brother- and Sisterhood of America had an intentionally panethnic membership. Lodge programming was three pronged: members could progress through steps toward an Odin degree, beneficial members had death and illness benefits available to them, and social members planned and attended numerous events throughout the year. Explicit Scandinavianness seems to have been limited to the first of these, with the reference to Norse mythology. The many social events planned through the joint efforts of fraternity and sorority were not marked as Norwegian, Swedish, Danish, or even Scandinavian: summer picnics and outings with music and dancing, a leap year ball, evening card parties, progressive whist, a masque ball for Thanksgiving, and a barn dance on New Year's Eve; nothing specifically labeled as celebrations for

the Seventeenth of May, Midsommar, or Jul. Combined with the fact that minutes were taken in English, the panethnic content of this Scandinavianness seems
entirely empty unless, following Orm Øverland, one considers that the purpose
of the group included assimilation strategies to espouse that the Scandinavians
were especially American. Historian Jorgen Dahlie points out that among the
Scandinavian fraternal organizations, the Scandinavian Brother- and Sisterhood
had a "strong emphasis on Americanization."[12]

In addition to the Scandinavian Brotherhood and Sisterhood, Montana's
towns had, in the period 1890 through the 1920s, several scattered secular organizations with more expressly Scandinavian, Swedish, and Norwegian orientations
that selected and intensified particular, representative celebrations such as Midsommar. In Butte, in addition to the Scandinavian Brother- and Sisterhood were
a Svea Lodge of the International Order of Odd Fellows and a Sons of Norway branch. In 1916 the latter organization held an Ibsen Fest at the Norwegian
Lutheran church. Yet, the Scandinavians of Butte came together for their 1893
Midsommar celebration and for a summer outing with rail service to Columbian Garden. The summer outing was figured by both *Montana Posten* and the
English-language *Butte Miner* as a successful event drawing all Scandinavians:
"all Scandinavians were on their feet and taking part in the celebration"; the
Miner correspondent connected the event with the claim that "Norsemen" had
"no small amount of historic glory" in the discovery of the Americas. In contrast
to this reportedly successful Scandinavian event, the Midsommar celebration
was described as a "fiasco" by a newspaper correspondent who pointed specifically to the mixture of Swedish dialects and Nordic languages heard there, hence
questioning the viability of achieving a truly syncretic Scandinavian event. Yet,
the Scandinavian population of Butte was active enough as a body during the
mid-1890s to consider erecting its own assembly building.[13]

In Helena, Swedish, Norwegian, and Scandinavian groups included an Odin
singing group, Svea, and Scandia. In addition to their regular meetings, these
groups sponsored summer picnic outings, including the May 17, 1893, Scandia
celebration noted earlier, which was attended by Norwegians, Swedes, and
"other nationalities" and featured a performance by the brothers Berg, with festivities lasting until 3 AM. Helena's Svea organization also sponsored an expressly
Swedish Midsommar in 1893, inviting all Scandinavians—"no Scandinavian
should miss it"—to attend the event scheduled to correspond to Svenskarnas
Dag at the World's Fair in Chicago. Scandinavians in the Helena area were also
urged to come together at a series of picnics with musical entertainment planned
at Kranich's Grove.[14]

Great Falls, which received a slightly later wave of Norwegian and Swedish
immigration to agricultural developments, had Sons and Daughters of Norway
chapters as well as the Scandinavian Brotherhood and Sisterhood. May 17 was

celebrated there in 1916 and 1917 with Sons of Norway sponsorship, even though Scandinavian Montanans were well aware of the controversy over doing so as the United States entered the Great War in Europe, when displays of ethnicity were often seen as disloyal.[15]

Scandinavianism also appeared as a pragmatic strategy in the repeated and abortive attempts to establish Norwegian and Swedish newspapers in Montana. As noted above, the Lutheran *Bergs-Väktaren* was the only purely Swedish newspaper in Montana. Throughout the nineteenth and early twentieth centuries, Norwegian-language newspapers dominated the Scandinavian press in Montana. Although they were more strongly focused on Norwegian readers, these newspapers attempted to appeal to a broader readership by including news from other Scandinavian groups and publishing Swedish-language materials. Some of them labeled themselves as Scandinavian rather than Norwegian.

The Helena *Montana Posten* began in 1890 and ran through 1893 as a mostly Norwegian paper that included a Swedish page, claiming to be "the only paper in Montana published in both the Norwegian and Swedish languages." The paper's advertisers followed suit, identifying themselves as Scandinavian pharmacies, butcher shops, or dentists; political advertising also encouraged Scandinavians to vote for a particular ticket. The 1893 subscribers' premiums offered a choice among Norwegian, Swedish, or English editions of John Bunyan's *Pilgrim's Progress* or Henry Davenport Northrup's *Earth, Sea, and Sky*.

Another mainly Norwegian newspaper with a good claim that it served the Scandinavian population was Butte's *Montana Skandinav*. *Montana Skandinav* began publication in 1893 but soon merged with another 1893 Butte venture, *Montana Tidende,* to become *Montana Tidende og Skandinav,* published weekly until 1895. Rather than print a separate Swedish page, this paper intermingled Norwegian and Swedish articles and features. The editors' claim that the paper was "the only Scandinavian paper in Montana" was echoed twenty years later by the Great Falls paper *Indlandsposten* when it was begun in 1915. "The Only Scandinavian Paper in Montana" appeared in English on that newspaper's masthead, generating a correction from reader Hans C. Boe of Butte in the April 28, 1916, issue, in which the paper's publishers admitted to "a general belief here in the state that *Indlandsposten* is the first Norwegian newspaper in Montana" and devoted a front-page article to correcting their error. *Indlandsposten* was an entirely Norwegian newspaper that attempted to address the interests of Norwegian, Swedish, and Danish readers. Its pages contained features, advertisements, group announcements, and church announcements inviting Scandinavians, not just Norwegians, to take part in Scandinavian activities and commerce. Like its predecessors, *Indlandsposten* lasted but a few years, into 1917. A post–World War I paper with similar ambitions, but addressing a specifically Lutheran audience and using English rather than Norwegian, was the *Rocky*

Mountain Skandinavian, a weekly begun in 1920 and published in Helena. It lasted less than one year.

The Norwegians and Swedes of Montana maintained an uneasy Scandinavianism that served pragmatic purposes: where either nationality was too small to maintain effective organizations and events, their combined numbers sufficed. For the Utahans, the Nordic immigration was "Scandinavian" from its inception, a matter of Mormon ideology and programmatic planning rather than mere pragmatics. This much more deeply studied migration has received considerable attention from historians, linguists, and folklorists interested in the multiethnic communities that sprang up in the latter half of the nineteenth century as European LDS converts converged on Utah.

The LDS church attracted a scattering of Norwegian, Swedish, and Danish converts from among the ranks of converts in the United States during the 1840s. In 1849, when the Mormons instigated a major effort to convert Europeans through establishing on-site missions, the Scandinavian Mission was begun by seasoned American missionary Erastus Snow, Swedish American convert John E. Forsgren, and Danish American convert Peter O. Hansen. Partly as a result of the original structure of the mission, with Snow in Denmark overseeing the work farther north, and partly as a result of Forsgren's unsuccessful initial attempts at missionary work in Sweden, Copenhagen became the center of the Scandinavian Mission until 1905, when it was split between Swedish and Danish Norwegian missions coincident with Norwegian independence. Proximity, and the fact that Danish became the main language of translation for the mission's written materials, produced the greatest success in Denmark, followed by Sweden and then Norway. By 1905, the percentages of Scandinavian converts who had emigrated were 56 percent Danish, 32 percent Swedish, 11 percent Norwegian, and 1 percent Icelandic.[16]

With this mix of Scandinavians flowing into Utah throughout the second half of the century, those of Nordic heritage naturally tended to find common cause. They had converted to Mormonism as families, emigrated as families, and once in Utah, unless assigned to mixed communities, tended to settle together. The dominant mix was Swedish and Danish, with a significant Swedish and Danish settlement in two counties south of Salt Lake City: Sanpete and Sevier. The Swedes and Norwegians settled alongside each other in the largest numbers in the Salt Lake City area and in Cache County, its population center in Logan just eighty miles north of Salt Lake City. In Utah, Scandinavianism permeated several layers of culture. The vehicles for Scandinavianism included official structures, popular media, and cultural events. They included the LDS church's divisions, newspapers and other publications, social clubs, social patterns such as intermarriage, and folklore genres such as holiday celebrations.[17]

Even though the Danish converts outnumbered Swedes, Norwegians, and

Icelanders, the LDS church established Scandinavian meetings. These met separately from the English-language services held for the same membership and used a combination of Scandinavian languages. Local meetings were held weekly or monthly. Annual Scandinavian reunions or conference meetings with a combined religious and social purpose were held from 1890 through the 1920s. From the point of view of the LDS church, the Danes, Norwegians, Swedes, and Icelanders were *Scandinavian* immigrants.[18]

J. R. Christianson pointed out that English was important in facilitating inter-actions among Scandinavians in America. Certainly the use of English by orga-nizations like the Scandinavian Brother- and Sisterhood points to the important basis that English could provide as a leveler among Scandinavian immigrants. Because the Mormons saw English as, according to Mulder, "the Lord's favored language in which he had spoken his will in this last dispensation," the mixed Danish-Norwegian-Swedish language services of the LDS Scandinavian meet-ings were always seen as auxiliary to English-language services, and Scandinavian immigrants were members first of the English-speaking ward within which they lived and only secondarily of a Scandinavian meeting within that ward.[19]

Intermarriage was also affected by official structures within the LDS church. While the Scandinavian population in Montana was weighted toward single men, with the result that any single Scandinavian woman might pose a marriage interest even across nation-based ethnic lines, there was a decided preference for marrying within one's nationality if possible. By contrast, among the LDS Scandinavians, intermarriage patterns were complicated by polygamy, practiced by roughly one quarter of the Scandinavian Mormons. William Mulder credits polygamy as "[breaking] down ethnic barriers both among the Scandinavians themselves and between them and other nationalities," citing numerous exam-ples of Scandinavian intermarriage among Danes, Swedes, and Norwegians. These polygamous unions provided opportunities for strong bonds among women within the Scandinavian LDS community.[20]

Reinforcing these official structures that supported Scandinavianism was a secular Scandinavianism that was nurtured through social organizations and the Danish-Norwegian- and Swedish-language press. Kenneth O. Bjork sees the news-papers especially to have served as vehicles for "a persistent Scandinavianism . . . too potent to be wholly contained within the forms and routine functions of the [LDS] church" that included appeals to Scandinavians as a potential voting block and advertisements for Scandinavian events and merchants. The newspapers included the Danish, Swedish, and English *Utah Skandinav* (1875); the Danish-Norwegian *Utah Posten* (1873–74), *Bikuben* (1876–1935), *Familie Vennen* (1877), a second *Utah Posten* (1885), and *Utah Pioneeren* (1895); and the Swedish *Svenska Härolden* (1885–93), *Fyrbåken* (1895), *Utah Korrespondenten* (1890–1915), *Salt Lake Bladet* (1902–11), and *Utah Posten* (1900–1935). Bjork notes that *Bikuben* "came to be known as the paper of the Scandinavian Mormons." Its production was also representative of LDS Scandinavianism: written in Danish, it was edited and published by Swedish convert Anders W. Winberg. It was eventually officially underwritten by the LDS church, sponsorship also achieved by the initially very controversial *Utah Korrespondenten*. Like the Swedes and Norwegians of Montana, Utah's Scandinavians were made aware of the availability of expressly Scandinavian goods and services through advertising in these newspapers: Scandinavian doctors, mercantiles, apothecaries, lawyers, and so forth.[21]

The LDS church's support for Scandinavianism among its members was briefly a contentious issue in the newspapers when Otto Rydman, editor of *Utah Korrespondenten,* used his editorial position to espouse separate Swedish-language LDS meetings in Salt Lake City, especially a Swedish Julotta (Christmas service). Rydman was excommunicated for his staunch anti-Scandinavianist position; his support from some of the Swedish LDS in Salt Lake City prompted an official statement from the LDS church president that the immigrant converts should aim to "adopt the manners and customs of the American people." But while they assimilated, according to the church, the immigrants had the Scandinavian meeting available to them, where a careful balance of languages was maintained in a rotation of music and speakers that always included a fair share of Swedish language. It was the official position, too, to maintain this parity in church-organized social events labeled as Scandinavian.[22]

What Rydman's "Swedish uprising" served to do in Mormon Utah was make the programmatic intent of LDS Scandinavianism absolutely explicit, forcing the church and its members to acknowledge that their use of the panethnic label *Scandinavian* was ideological. The folklorist William A. Wilson suggests that the Scandinavian converts in Utah "did not become Yankees or English; they became Mormons—which is what the Yankees and English also became." The Scandinavian meeting was a vehicle for this transformation as much or more than it was a vehicle for panethnicity. The ethnic content, in fact, was limited to language—Mormon hymns and doctrine translated into Danish, Swedish, Norwegian, or Icelandic. Truly ethnic content would have also incorporated a religious custom such as Julotta. For Rydman, this was a cultural strategy too empty of ethnic content to be satisfying.[23]

Use of the explicit panethnic label *Scandinavian* was consistent even in secular events. Midsommar in 1891 was a "big Scandinavian outing" to Draper, to which all Scandinavians living in Salt Lake, Davis, and Utah counties were invited. A combined Salt Lake City and County committee with mixed-national membership organized the celebration. Performing were the Scandinavian Men's Quartet and the Norden Brass Band. The same year the Scandinavians of Ogden and of Pleasant Grove joined in Midsommar Day celebrations, selecting an event common enough in the Scandinavian countries that it could be perceived as panethnic.[24]

But it was not only Midsommar that brought the Scandinavians together. Events during the 1890s, some of them cooperatively planned by a Scandinavian Outings Committee and some planned by Scandinavian organizations, mainly Scandia and Norden, included—just in the spring-summer season—May Day, the Norwegian Constitution Day, Decoration Day, LDS leader Brigham Young's birthday on the first of June, the Danish Constitution Day on June 5, the anniversary of the founding of the LDS Scandinavian Mission (recognized on June 14), Midsommar, the Fourth of July, and Pioneer Day. Sprinkled throughout both seasons were other events celebrated in much the same way but not pinned to a particular holiday, outings especially for Scandinavian old-timers, for example. Perhaps resonating most with Scandinavianism are the invitations in a Swedish language newspaper to all Scandinavians to celebrate the Norwegian and Danish constitution days.[25]

These celebrations seem less empty of ethnic content than the Scandinavian meeting; rather, they attempt to select and intensify a sampling from all groups, and in one celebration, May Day, there was an attempt at syncretism outside of Scandinavia. In 1894 *Utah Korrespondenten* described a May Day celebration that included a Scandinavian choir, dancing, a May pole, a display entitled "Spring," and a Scandinavian national tableau with a representation of the Statue of Liberty. While this description departs considerably from what one might expect of Walpurgis Night and May Day in the Nordic countries, there may have been an influence upon the Scandinavians of Utah through their neighboring English immigrants.[26]

On both sides of the Atlantic, Scandinavianism had been an uneasy union. The turn-of-the-century attempts in the Rocky Mountain West reflect this larger pattern. In both Montana and LDS Utah, whether merely pragmatic or carefully programmatic, efforts at forming truly Scandinavian organizations, events, and even religious unions were not entirely without question. Some attempts existed more in name than practice, as in the claimed Scandinavianism of the Scandinavian meetings, their materials translated from English originals, and of the Scandinavian Brother- and Sisterhood, their social events lacking ethnic and panethnic content. Certainly, to critics like Rydman and the Montana correspondent "Frederick," the Scandinavianism attempted in the Rockies was sometimes merely symbolic and therefore unsatisfying. Other Scandinavian blendings achieved some success through careful selection of holidays or practices recognized throughout Scandinavia, intensifying Jul and Midsommar, for example, even when the results, such as Midsommar "picnics," were adaptations in an American environment.

Notes

1. *Montana Posten,* May 11 and 18, 1893. *Utah Korrespondenten,* May 11, 1892.

2. Herbert J. Gans, "Comment: Ethnic Invention and Acculturation, a Bumpy-Line Approach," *Journal of American Ethnic History* 12.1 (1992): 44. Barre Toelken, "Ethnic Selection and Intensification in the Native American Powwow," in *Creative Ethnicity: Symbols and Strategies of Contemporary Ethnic Life,* ed. Stephen Stern and John Allan Cicala (Logan: Utah State University Press, 1991), 155.

3. Ernst Ekman, "Wetterman and the Scandinavian Society of San Francisco," *Swedish Pioneer Historical Quarterly* 25 (1974): 91–92. Thomas I. Benson, "Gold, Salt Air, and Callouses," *Norwegian-American Studies* 24 (1970): 193–220, available: http://www.naha.stolaf.edu/pubs/nas/volume24/vol24_8.html. Kenneth Björk, "Scandinavian Experiment in California" Parts I, II, and III, *Swedish Pioneer Historical Quarterly* 5 (1954): 67–78.

4. H. Arnold Barton, *Essays on Scandinavian History* (Carbondale: Southern Illinois University Press, 2009), 138, 183; J. R. Christianson, "Cooperation in Scandinavian-American Studies," *Swedish-American Historical Quarterly* 35 (1984): 377. Ulf Beijbom, "The Societies—A Worldly Alternative in the Swedish Chicago Colony," *Swedish Pioneer Historical Quarterly* 23 (1972): 146–48. John R. Jenswold, "The Rise and Fall of Pan-Scandinavianism in Urban America," in *Scandinavians and Other Immigrants in Urban America,* ed. Odd S. Lovoll (Northfield, MN: St. Olaf College Press, 1985), 159–70.

5. Erik G. Westman, ed., *The Swedish Element in America* (Chicago: Swedish-American Biographical Society, 1931), 333–34; Karl A. Olsson, *By One Spirit* (Chicago: Covenant Press, 1962), 466–67. Grimsby, "The Contribution," 99.

6. Emeroy Johnson, "The Beginnings of Swedish Lutheran Church Work in Montana," *Swedish-American Historical Quarterly* 35 (1984): 151–61. Grimsby, "The Contribution," 107, 114, 115, 187. Westman, *The Swedish Element in America,* 334.

7. Anderson, "Scandinavians and Lutherans in Custer County and Dawson County, Montana," 34, 41, 45, 105, 185.

8. Anderson, "Scandinavians and Lutherans in Custer County and Dawson County, Montana," 142–43, 153–55, 165.

9. *Bergs-Väktaren,* Oct. 1898.

10. *Indlandsposten,* Nov. 26 and Dec. 17, 1915; Jan. 21, 1916. *Montana Posten,* Aug. 13, 1893. *R. L. Polk & Co.'s Butte City Directory* (Butte, MT: R.L. Polk, 1905), 70.

11. *Indlandsposten,* June 9, 1916; Butte Lodge No. 11, Scandinavian Fraternity of America, By-laws and minutes, Microfilm SC226 and 227; and Kallispell Lodge No. 233, Scandinavian Fraternity of America, Minutes, Microfilm 228 (both Rock Island, IL: Swenson Swedish Immigration Research Center, Augustana College).

12. Butte Lodge No. 11, By-laws and minutes; Kallispell Lodge No. 233, Minutes. Jorgen Dahlie, "A Social History of Scandinavian Immigration, Washington State, 1895–1910" (PhD diss., Washington State University, 1967), 161; Orm Øverland, *Immigrant Minds, American Identities: Making the United States Home, 1870–1930* (Urbana: University of Illinois Press, 2000).

13. *R. L. Polk,* Butte 1905; *Indlandsposten,* Nov. 26, 1915, Mar. 24, 1916. *Montana Posten,* June 22 and July 20, 1893. *Montana Tidende og Skandinav,* Feb. 9, 1894.

14. *Montana Posten,* May 18 and 25 and June 1 and 22, 1893.

15. *Indlandsposten,* Mar. 24, 1916, Apr. 11 and Mar. 14, 1917.

16. Andrew Jenson, *History of the Scandinavian Mission* (Salt Lake City, UT: Deseret News Press, 1927), 2–3, 411; William Mulder, "Norwegian Forerunners among the Early Mormons," *Norwegian-American Studies and Records* 19 (1956): 46–61; William Mulder, *Homeward to Zion: The Mormon Migration from Scandinavia* (1957; reprint, Minneapolis: University of Minnesota Press, 2000), 31–39, 107.

17. Mulder, *Homeward,* 107–8; Lynn Henrichsen, George Bailey, Timothy Wright, John Brumbaugh, Jacob Huckaby, and Ray LeBaron, "Building Community by Respecting Linguistic Diversity: Scandinavian Immigrants in Nineteenth Century Utah," *Utah Historical Quarterly* 78.1 (2010): 5–6.

18. Kenneth O. Bjork, "A Covenant Folk, with Scandinavian Colorings," *Norwegian-American Studies* 21 (1962): 214. Henrichsen et al., "Building Community by Respecting Linguistic Diversity," 8–12.

19. Christianson, "Cooperation in Scandinavian-American Studies," 376. William Mulder, "Mother Tongue, 'Skandinavisme,' and 'The Swedish Insurrection' in Utah," *Swedish Pioneer Historical Quarterly* 7 (1956): 11.

20. Janet E. Rasmussen, "'I met him at Normanna Hall': Ethnic Cohesion and Marital Patterns among Scandinavian Immigrant Women," *Norwegian-American Studies* 32.4 (1989): 71–89, available: http://www.naha.stolaf.edu/pubs/nas/volume32/vol32_04.htm. Mulder, *Homeward,* 238, 245.

21. Bjork, "A Covenant Folk," 215, 218; Lilly Setterdahl, "Swedish-American Newspapers" (Rock Island, IL: Augustana College Library, 1981), 30; Mulder, *Homeward* 258–66.

22. Mulder, "Mother Tongue," 18–19.

23. William A. Wilson, "Folklore of Utah's Little Scandinavia." *Utah Historical Quarterly* 47 (1979): 151.

24. *Utah Korrespondenten,* June 10, July 1, and July 8, 1891.

25. *Utah Korrespondenten,* July 1, 1891; May 11 and July 1, 1892; May 25 and June 1, 1893; July 12, 1894.

26. *Utah Korrespondenten,* May 3, 1894.

Notes on Contributors

PHILIP J. ANDERSON is professor of church history at North Park University in Chicago and since 1989 president of the Swedish-American Historical Society, also chairing its publications committee. His publications have included studies in British, American, and Swedish American religious history and culture.

JENNIFER EASTMAN ATTEBERY is professor of English at Idaho State University. She served as the 2011 Fulbright Distinguished Chair in American Studies at Uppsala University. Her research focuses on folk culture of the Rocky Mountain West in the nineteenth and early twentieth centuries, with an emphasis on Swedish Americans. Her current research project concerns sacralization and secularization of the Scandinavian American spring and summer holidays. *Up in the Rocky Mountains: Writing the Swedish Immigrant Experience* (University of Minnesota Press, 2007), a study of Swedish immigrant letters, is her most recent book.

H. ARNOLD BARTON is professor emeritus of history at Southern Illinois University–Carbondale. His research interests are Scandinavian, principally Swedish and Scandinavian history, with a particular focus on Swedes in North America. He has published widely in both fields and between 1974 and 1990 was editor of the *Swedish-American Historical Quarterly*.

ULF JONAS BJÖRK is a professor in the School of Journalism at Indiana University–Indianapolis. He has a long-standing interest in the immigrant press in general and in the Swedish American press in particular, having published several studies of editors, newspapers, and readers.

DAG BLANCK is director of the Swenson Swedish Immigration Research Center at Augustana College in Rock Island, Illinois, and associate professor of history at the Swedish Institute for North American Studies at Uppsala University. He has published a number of books and articles in his field of research, focusing on Swedish American history and cultural and social relations between Sweden and the United States.

JØRN BRØNDAL is associate professor of American history at the University of Southern Denmark. He specializes in ethnicity, race, and politics. His book *Ethnic Leadership and Midwestern Politics* (2004) received a Wisconsin Historical Society Book Award. Presently writing a history of black America, he is president of the Nordic Association for American Studies.

ANGELA FALK is a senior lecturer in English linguistics in the department of English at Uppsala University. Her sociolinguistic research interests focus on language contact between Swedish and English, especially in Swedish American communities in the American Midwest. Currently, she is analyzing life-history interviews that were recorded in Lindsborg, Kansas, her hometown.

DONNA R. GABACCIA is the Rudolph J. Vecoli chair in immigration history and director of the Immigration History Research Center at the University of Minnesota–Twin Cities. She has published extensively on immigrant life in the United States, interpreting it from global and comparative perspectives; on gender and migration; and on Italian migration around the world. Her next book, *Foreign Relations: American Immigration in Global Perspective,* will be published in 2012 by Princeton University Press.

MARK GRANQUIST is associate professor of church history at Luther Seminary in St. Paul, Minnesota. He specializes in Scandinavian American religious life. With Maria Erling he co-authored *The Augustana Story: Shaping Lutheran Identity in North America* (2008), a new history of the Augustana Synod.

PER-OLOF GRÖNBERG is a researcher with the Centre for Population Studies at Umeå University, Sweden. His research has focused on the return migration of Swedish immigrants, with particular emphasis on the role of engineers and technology transfer. Among his publications is the monograph *Learning and Returning: Return Migration of Swedish Engineers from the United States, 1880–1940* (2003).

INGEBORG KONGSLIEN is associate professor at the University of Oslo, Department of Linguistics and Scandinavian Studies. Her doctoral dissertation, published as *Draumen om fridom og jord. Ein studie i skandinaviaske emigrantromanar* (Oslo, 1989), focused on Scandinavian and Norwegian American emigrant literature. Her recent research interests and numerous publications are on contemporary Nordic writings by immigrants and multicultural writers, with special focus on identity formation and redefinition.

JAMES P. LEARY is professor of folklore and Scandinavian studies at the University of Wisconsin–Madison, where he also directs the Center for the Study of Upper Midwestern Cultures. His field and archival research into the folklore of the Upper Midwest's diverse peoples since the 1970s has resulted in numerous museum exhibits, media productions, and publications, including *Minnesota Polka, Wisconsin Folklore,* and *So Ole Says to Lena: Folk Humor of the Upper Midwest.*

JOY K. LINTELMAN is professor of history at Concordia College in Moorhead, Minnesota. Research interests include immigrant children, women, and food history. Her book *I Go to America: Swedish American Women and the Life of Mina Anderson* (Minnesota Historical Society Press, 2009) won a Minnesota Book Award.

ODD S. LOVOLL is professor emeritus of history at St. Olaf College and was the first King Olaf V Chair in Scandinavian-American Studies; until 2005 he held an adjunct appointment at the University of Oslo. Lovoll's major English-language publications include *The Promise of America: A History of the Norwegian-American People* (1984), *The Promise Fulfilled: A Portrait of Norwegian Americans Today* (1998), and *Norwegian Newspapers in America: Connecting Norway and the New Land* (2010).

DAVID C. MAUK specializes in U.S. social history, federal government and politics, and literature. He taught American history at New York University before moving to the University of Trondheim (now NTNU), where he led the program in American Studies. In 2005, he began his present position in North American Area Studies at the University of Oslo.

BYRON J. NORDSTROM is professor emeritus of history and Scandinavian studies at Gustavus Adolphus College in St. Peter, Minnesota. Since 1997 he has served as editor of the *Swedish-American Historical Quarterly*. His most recent book is *Culture and Customs of Sweden* (Greenwood Press, 2010).

KURT W. PETERSON is professor of history at North Park University in Chicago, where he also serves as division director and associate dean for the arts, humanities, and social sciences. His academic focus is on American religious history, culture, and multiethnicity. His current project, an edited volume entitled *American Evangelicalism: George Marsden and the Shape of American Religious History,* will be published in 2012 by the University of Notre Dame Press.

MARK SAFSTROM is lecturer in Swedish and Scandinavian studies at the University of Illinois–Urbana-Champaign. His research and writing is in the areas of Scandinavian history, immigration, and nineteenth-century social movements.

Index

Note: page numbers in *italics* refer to figures; those followed by t and n refer to tables and notes (with note number), respectively.

Teaching Evolution in Minnesota" (Szasz), 173
Willmar, Leon, 258
Willmar, Minnesota: American identity of ethnic residents, 264; celebrations and cultural events, 272; dilution of ethnic identity in second generation, 270, 271, 272–73; ethnic groups in, 258; ethnic residence distribution, 260, 260; as ethnic town, 272; Hispanic immigrants of modern era, 274n14; as melting pot, 273; Norwegian and Swedish employment and businesses in, 261, 262–63; Norwegian and Swedish families, profiles of, 269–72; peaceful ethnic coexistence in, 272–73; population, 258; resident profiles, early 20th century, 261–64, 264; women's employment and businesses in, 261, 262–63
Willmar Tribune (newspaper): as American paper, 269; characteristic contents of, 266; coverage of Union Crisis, 265–69; Scandinavian news in, 266, 268–69; staff of, 265
Wilson, William A., 304
Winberg, Anders W., 304
Windom, William, 287

Winrod, Gerald B., 172
Wisconsin, inter-Scandinavian political conflict, 125, 129–30
Witting, Albin, 213
women: employment, in Willmar, Minnesota, 261, 262–63; pan-Scandinavian organizations in Minneapolis–St. Paul, 290–91
Wood, A. DeLacy, 246
World's Christian Fundamentals Association (WCFA), 172
World War I: and Americanization of Scandinavians, 10, 300–301; Darwinian theories and, 175–76; and Swedish language instruction, 46
Worm-Müller, Jacob S., 40

Yorgesson, Yogi, 80
Yumpin' Yimminy: Scandinavian Dialect Selections (Springer), 74–76, 75, 77
Yust for Fun: Norwegian-American Dialect Monologues (Olson and Olson), 74
Yust Yokes bae Yansen (anon.), 74, 76

Zion Lutheran Church (Hovland, MN), 248

Image Credits